ALSO BY JONATHAN HAIDT

The Happiness Hypothesis: Finding Modern Truth in Ancient Wisdom

The Righteous Mind

The Righteous Mind

Why Good People Are Divided by
Politics and Religion

JONATHAN HAIDT

PANTHEON BOOKS, NEW YORK

All rights reserved. Published in the United States by Pantheon Books,
a division of Random House, Inc., New York, and in Canada
by Random House of Canada Limited, Toronto.
Pantheon Books and colophon are registered trademarks of Random House, Inc.

Library of Congress Cataloging-in-Publication Data
Haidt, Jonathan.
The righteous mind : why good people are divided
by politics and religion / Jonathan Haidt.
p. cm.
Includes bibliographical references and index.
ISBN 978-0-307-37790-6
1. Ethics. 2. Social psychology. 3. Political psychology. 4. Psychology, Religious.
I. Title.
BJ45.H25 2012   201'.615—dc23   2011032036

www.pantheonbooks.com
www.righteousmind.com

Jacket design by Sagmeister Inc.

Printed in the United States of America
First Edition

12 14 16 18 20 19 17 15 13 11

In memory of my father,
Harold Haidt

I have striven not to laugh at human actions, not to weep at them, not to hate them, but to understand them.

—Baruch Spinoza, *Tractatus Politicus*, 1676

Contents

Introduction

"Can we all get along?" That appeal was made famous on May 1, 1992, by Rodney King, a black man who had been beaten nearly to death by four Los Angeles police officers a year earlier. The entire nation had seen a videotape of the beating, so when a jury failed to convict the officers, their acquittal triggered widespread outrage and six days of rioting in Los Angeles. Fifty-three people were killed and more than seven thousand buildings were torched. Much of the mayhem was carried live; news cameras tracked the action from helicopters circling overhead. After a particularly horrific act of violence against a white truck driver, King was moved to make his appeal for peace.

King's appeal is now so overused that it has become cultural kitsch, a catchphrase[1] more often said for laughs than as a serious plea for mutual understanding. I therefore hesitated to use King's words as the opening line of this book, but I decided to go ahead, for two reasons. The first is because most Americans nowadays are asking King's question not about race relations but about political relations and the collapse of cooperation across party lines. Many Americans feel as though the nightly news from Washington is being sent to us from helicopters circling over the city, delivering dispatches from the war zone.

The second reason I decided to open this book with an overused phrase is because King followed it up with something lovely, something rarely quoted. As he stumbled through his television interview, fighting back tears and often repeating himself, he found these words: "Please, we can get along here. We all can get along. I mean, we're all stuck here for a while. Let's try to work it out."

This book is about why it's so hard for us to get along. We are indeed all stuck here for a while, so let's at least do what we can to understand why we are so easily divided into hostile groups, each one certain of its righteousness.

People who devote their lives to studying something often come to believe that the object of their fascination is the key to understanding everything. Books have been published in recent years on the transformative role in human history played by cooking, mothering, war . . . even salt. This is one of those books. I study moral psychology, and I'm going to make the case that morality is the extraordinary human capacity that made civilization possible. I don't mean to imply that cooking, mothering, war, and salt were not also necessary, but in this book I'm going to take you on a tour of human nature and history from the perspective of moral psychology.

By the end of the tour, I hope to have given you a new way to think about two of the most important, vexing, and divisive topics in human life: politics and religion. Etiquette books tell us not to discuss these topics in polite company, but I say go ahead. Politics and religion are both expressions of our underlying moral psychology, and an understanding of that psychology can help to bring people together. My goal in this book is to drain some of the heat, anger, and divisiveness out of these topics and replace them with awe, wonder, and curiosity. We are downright lucky that we evolved this complex moral psychology that allowed our species to burst out of the forests and savannas and into the delights, comforts, and extraordinary peacefulness of modern societies in just a few thousand years.[2] My hope is that this book will make conversations about morality, politics, and religion more common, more civil, and more fun, even in mixed company. My hope is that it will help us to get along.

BORN TO BE RIGHTEOUS

I could have titled this book *The Moral Mind* to convey the sense that the human mind is designed to "do" morality, just as it's designed to do language, sexuality, music, and many other things described in popular books reporting the latest scientific findings. But I chose the title *The Righteous Mind* to convey the sense that human nature is not just intrinsically moral, it's also intrinsically moralistic, critical, and judgmental.

The word *righteous* comes from the old Norse word *rettviss* and the old English word *rihtwis*, both of which mean "just, upright, virtuous."[3] This meaning has been carried into the modern English words *righteous* and *righteousness*, although nowadays those words have strong religious connotations because they are usually used to translate the Hebrew word *tzedek*. *Tzedek* is a common word in the Hebrew Bible, often used to describe people who act in accordance with God's wishes, but it is also an attribute of God and of God's judgment of people (which is often harsh but always thought to be just).

The linkage of righteousness and judgmentalism is captured in some modern definitions of *righteous*, such as "arising from an outraged sense of justice, morality, or fair play."[4] The link also appears in the term *self-righteous*, which means "convinced of one's own righteousness, especially in contrast with the actions and beliefs of others; narrowly moralistic and intolerant."[5] I want to show you that an obsession with righteousness (leading inevitably to self-righteousness) is the normal human condition. It is a feature of our evolutionary design, not a bug or error that crept into minds that would otherwise be objective and rational.[6]

Our righteous minds made it possible for human beings—but no other animals—to produce large cooperative groups, tribes, and nations without the glue of kinship. But at the same time, our righteous minds guarantee that our cooperative groups will always be cursed by moralistic strife. Some degree of conflict among groups may even be necessary for the health and development of any society. When I was a teenager I wished for world peace, but now I yearn for a world in which competing ideologies are kept in balance, systems of accountability keep us all from getting away with too much, and fewer people believe that righteous ends justify violent means. Not a very romantic wish, but one that we might actually achieve.

WHAT LIES AHEAD

This book has three parts, which you can think of as three separate books—except that each one depends on the one before it. Each part presents one major principle of moral psychology.

Part I is about the first principle: *Intuitions come first, strategic reasoning second.*[7] Moral intuitions arise automatically and almost instantaneously, long before moral reasoning has a chance to get started, and those first intuitions tend to drive our later reasoning. If you think that moral reasoning is something we do to figure out the truth, you'll be constantly frustrated by how foolish, biased, and illogical people become when they disagree with you. But if you think about moral reasoning as a skill we humans evolved to further our social agendas—to justify our own actions and to defend the teams we belong to—then things will make a lot more sense. Keep your eye on the intuitions, and don't take people's moral arguments at face value. They're mostly post hoc constructions made up on the fly, crafted to advance one or more strategic objectives.

The central metaphor of these four chapters is that *the mind is divided, like a rider on an elephant, and the rider's job is to serve the elephant.* The rider is our conscious reasoning—the stream of words and images of which we are fully aware. The elephant is the other 99 percent of mental processes—the ones that occur outside of awareness but that actually govern most of our behavior.[8] I developed this metaphor in my last book, *The Happiness Hypothesis*, where I described how the rider and elephant work together, sometimes poorly, as we stumble through life in search of meaning and connection. In this book I'll use the metaphor to solve puzzles such as why it seems like everyone (else) is a hypocrite[9] and why political partisans are so willing to believe outrageous lies and conspiracy theories. I'll also use the metaphor to show you how you can better persuade people who seem unresponsive to reason.

Part II is about the second principle of moral psychology, which is that *there's more to morality than harm and fairness.* The central metaphor of these four chapters is that *the righteous mind is like a tongue with six taste receptors*. Secular Western moralities are like cuisines that try to activate just one or two of these receptors—either concerns about harm and suffering, or concerns about fairness and injustice. But people have so many other powerful moral intuitions, such as those related to liberty, loyalty, authority, and sanctity. I'll explain where these six taste receptors come from, how they form the basis of the world's many moral cuisines, and why politicians on the right have a built-in advantage when it comes to cooking meals that voters like.

Part III is about the third principle: *Morality binds and blinds*. The central metaphor of these four chapters is that *human beings are 90 percent chimp and 10 percent bee*. Human nature was produced by natural selection working at two levels simultaneously. Individuals compete with individuals within every group, and we are the descendants of primates who excelled at that competition. This gives us the ugly side of our nature, the one that is usually featured in books about our evolutionary origins. We are indeed selfish hypocrites so skilled at putting on a show of virtue that we fool even ourselves.

But human nature was also shaped as groups competed with other groups. As Darwin said long ago, the most cohesive and cooperative groups generally beat the groups of selfish individualists. Darwin's ideas about group selection fell out of favor in the 1960s, but recent discoveries are putting his ideas back into play, and the implications are profound. We're not always selfish hypocrites. We also have the ability, under special circumstances, to shut down our petty selves and become like cells in a larger body, or like bees in a hive, working for the good of the group. These experiences are often among the most cherished of our lives, although our hivishness can blind us to other moral concerns. Our bee-like nature facilitates altruism, heroism, war, and genocide.

Once you see our righteous minds as primate minds with a hivish overlay, you get a whole new perspective on morality, politics, and religion. I'll show that our "higher nature" allows us to be profoundly altruistic, but that altruism is mostly aimed at members of our own groups. I'll show that religion is (probably) an evolutionary adaptation for binding groups together and helping them to create communities with a shared morality. It is not a virus or a parasite, as some scientists (the "New Atheists") have argued in recent years. And I'll use this perspective to explain why some people are conservative, others are liberal (or progressive), and still others become libertarians. People bind themselves into political teams that share moral narratives. Once they accept a particular narrative, they become blind to alternative moral worlds.

(A note on terminology: In the United States, the word *liberal* refers to progressive or left-wing politics, and I will use the word in this sense. But in Europe and elsewhere, the word *liberal* is truer to its original meaning—valuing liberty above all else, including in economic activities. When Europeans use the word *liberal,* they often mean something more like the American term *libertarian,* which cannot be placed easily on the left-right spectrum.[10] Readers from outside the United States may want to swap in the words *progressive* or *left-wing* whenever I say *liberal.*)

In the coming chapters I'll draw on the latest research in neuroscience, genetics, social psychology, and evolutionary modeling, but the take-home message of the book is ancient. It is the realization that we are all self-righteous hypocrites:

> Why do you see the speck in your neighbor's eye, but do not notice the log in your own eye? . . . You hypocrite, first take the log out of your own eye, and then you will see clearly to take the speck out of your neighbor's eye. (MATTHEW 7:3–5)

Enlightenment (or wisdom, if you prefer) requires us all to take the logs out of our own eyes and then escape from our ceaseless, petty, and divisive moralism. As the eighth-century Chinese Zen master Sen-ts'an wrote:

> The Perfect Way is only difficult
> for those who pick and choose;
> Do not like, do not dislike;

all will then be clear.
Make a hairbreadth difference,
and Heaven and Earth are set apart;
If you want the truth to stand clear before you,
never be for or against.
The struggle between "for" and "against"
is the mind's worst disease.[11]

I'm not saying we should live our lives like Sen-ts'an. In fact, I believe that a world without moralism, gossip, and judgment would quickly decay into chaos. But if we want to *understand* ourselves, our divisions, our limits, and our potentials, we need to step back, drop the moralism, apply some moral psychology, and analyze the game we're all playing.

Let us now examine the psychology of this struggle between "for" and "against." It is a struggle that plays out in each of our righteous minds, and among all of our righteous groups.

PART I

Intuitions Come First, Strategic Reasoning Second

Central Metaphor

The mind is divided, like a rider on an elephant, and the rider's job is to serve the elephant.

ONE

Where Does Morality Come From?

I'm going to tell you a brief story. Pause after you read it and decide whether the people in the story did anything morally wrong.

> A family's dog was killed by a car in front of their house. They had heard that dog meat was delicious, so they cut up the dog's body and cooked it and ate it for dinner. Nobody saw them do this.

If you are like most of the well-educated people in my studies, you felt an initial flash of disgust, but you hesitated before saying the family had done anything *morally* wrong. After all, the dog was dead already, so they didn't hurt it, right? And it was their dog, so they had a right to do what they wanted with the carcass, no? If I pushed you to make a judgment, odds are you'd give me a nuanced answer, something like "Well, I think it's disgusting, and I think they should have just buried the dog, but I wouldn't say it was *morally* wrong."

OK, here's a more challenging story:

> A man goes to the supermarket once a week and buys a chicken. But before cooking the chicken, he

has sexual intercourse with it. Then he cooks it and
eats it.

Once again, no harm, nobody else knows, and, like the dog-eating
family, it involves a kind of recycling that is—as some of my research
subjects pointed out—an efficient use of natural resources. But now
the disgust is so much stronger, and the action just seems so . . .
degrading. Does that make it wrong? If you're an educated and politically liberal Westerner, you'll probably give another nuanced answer,
one that acknowledges the man's right to do what he wants, as long
as he doesn't hurt anyone.

But if you are *not* a liberal or libertarian Westerner, you probably
think it's wrong—morally wrong—for someone to have sex with a
chicken carcass and then eat it. For you, as for most people on the
planet, morality is broad. Some actions are wrong even though they
don't hurt anyone. Understanding the simple fact that morality differs
around the world, and even within societies, is the first step toward
understanding your righteous mind. The next step is to understand
where these many moralities came from in the first place.

THE ORIGIN OF MORALITY (TAKE 1)

I studied philosophy in college, hoping to figure out the meaning of
life. After watching too many Woody Allen movies, I had the mistaken impression that philosophy would be of some help.[1] But I had
taken some psychology courses too, and I loved them, so I chose to
continue. In 1987 I was admitted to the graduate program in psychology at the University of Pennsylvania. I had a vague plan to conduct
experiments on the psychology of humor. I thought it might be fun
to do research that let me hang out in comedy clubs.

A week after arriving in Philadelphia, I sat down to talk with
Jonathan Baron, a professor who studies how people think and
make decisions. With my (minimal) background in philosophy, we
had a good discussion about ethics. Baron asked me point-blank: "Is
moral thinking any different from other kinds of thinking?" I said

that thinking about moral issues (such as whether abortion is wrong) seemed different from thinking about other kinds of questions (such as where to go to dinner tonight), because of the much greater need to provide reasons justifying your moral judgments to other people. Baron responded enthusiastically, and we talked about some ways one might compare moral thinking to other kinds of thinking in the lab. The next day, on the basis of little more than a feeling of encouragement, I asked him to be my advisor and I set off to study moral psychology.

In 1987, moral psychology was a part of developmental psychology. Researchers focused on questions such as how children develop in their thinking about rules, especially rules of fairness. The big question behind this research was: How do children come to know right from wrong? Where does morality come from?

There are two obvious answers to this question: nature or nurture. If you pick nature, then you're a *nativist*. You believe that moral knowledge is native in our minds. It comes preloaded, perhaps in our God-inscribed hearts (as the Bible says), or in our evolved moral emotions (as Darwin argued).[2]

But if you believe that moral knowledge comes from nurture, then you are an *empiricist*.[3] You believe that children are more or less blank slates at birth (as John Locke said).[4] If morality varies around the world and across the centuries, then how could it be innate? Whatever morals we have as adults must have been learned during childhood from our own experience, which includes adults telling us what's right and wrong. (*Empirical* means "from observation or experience.")

But this is a false choice, and in 1987 moral psychology was mostly focused on a third answer: *rationalism*, which says that kids figure out morality for themselves. Jean Piaget, the greatest developmental psychologist of all time, began his career as a zoologist studying mollusks and insects in his native Switzerland. He was fascinated by the stages that animals went through as they transformed themselves from, say, caterpillars to butterflies. Later, when his attention turned to children, he brought with him this interest in stages of development. Piaget wanted to know how the extraordinary sophistication of adult thinking (a cognitive butterfly) emerges from the limited abilities of young children (lowly caterpillars).

Piaget focused on the kinds of errors kids make. For example, he'd put water into two identical drinking glasses and ask kids to tell him if the glasses held the same amount of water. (Yes.) Then he'd pour the contents of one of the glasses into a tall skinny glass and ask the child to compare the new glass to the one that had not been touched. Kids younger than six or seven usually say that the tall skinny glass now holds more water, because the level is higher. They don't understand that the total volume of water is conserved when it moves from glass to glass. He also found that it's pointless for adults to explain the conservation of volume to kids. The kids won't get it until they reach an age (and cognitive stage) when their minds are ready for it. And when they are ready, they'll figure it out for themselves just by playing with cups of water.

In other words, the understanding of the conservation of volume wasn't innate, and it wasn't learned from adults. Kids *figure it out for themselves*, but only when their minds are ready *and* they are given the right kinds of experiences.

Piaget applied this cognitive-developmental approach to the study of children's moral thinking as well.[5] He got down on his hands and knees to play marbles with children, and sometimes he deliberately broke rules and played dumb. The children then responded to his mistakes, and in so doing, they revealed their growing ability to respect rules, change rules, take turns, and resolve disputes. This growing knowledge came in orderly stages, as children's cognitive abilities matured.

Piaget argued that children's understanding of morality is like their understanding of those water glasses: we can't say that it is innate, and we can't say that kids learn it directly from adults.[6] It is, rather, *self-constructed* as kids play with other kids. Taking turns in a game is like pouring water back and forth between glasses. No matter how often you do it with three-year-olds, they're just not ready to get the concept of fairness,[7] any more than they can understand the conservation of volume. But once they've reached the age of five or six, then playing games, having arguments, and working things out together will help them learn about fairness far more effectively than any sermon from adults.

This is the essence of psychological rationalism: We grow into our rationality as caterpillars grow into butterflies. If the caterpillar eats enough leaves, it will (eventually) grow wings. And if the child gets enough experiences of turn taking, sharing, and playground justice, it will (eventually) become a moral creature, able to use its rational capacities to solve ever harder problems. Rationality is our nature, and good moral reasoning is the end point of development.

Rationalism has a long and complex history in philosophy. In this book I'll use the word *rationalist* to describe anyone who believes that reasoning is the most important and reliable way to obtain moral knowledge.[8]

Piaget's insights were extended by Lawrence Kohlberg, who revolutionized the study of morality in the 1960s with two key innovations.[9] First, he developed a way to quantify Piaget's observation that children's moral reasoning changed over time. He created a set of moral dilemmas that he presented to children of various ages, and he recorded and coded their responses. For example, should a man named Heinz break into a drugstore to steal a drug that would save his dying wife? Should a girl named Louise reveal to her mother that her younger sister had lied to the mother? It didn't much matter whether the child said yes or no; what mattered were the *reasons* children gave when they tried to explain their answers.

Kohlberg found a six-stage progression in children's reasoning about the *social* world, and this progression matched up well with the stages Piaget had found in children's reasoning about the *physical* world. Young children judged right and wrong by very superficial features, such as whether a person was punished for an action. (If an adult punished the act, then the act must have been wrong.) Kohlberg called the first two stages the "pre-conventional" level of moral judgment, and they correspond to the Piagetian stage at which kids judge the physical world by superficial features (if a glass is taller, then it has more water in it).

But during elementary school, most children move on to the two "conventional" stages, becoming adept at understanding and even manipulating rules and social conventions. This is the age of petty legalism that most of us who grew up with siblings remember well ("I'm not hitting you. I'm using your hand to hit you. Stop hitting yourself!"). Kids at this stage generally care a lot about conformity, and they have great respect for authority—in word, if not always in deed. They rarely question the legitimacy of authority, even as they learn to maneuver within and around the constraints that adults impose on them.

After puberty, right when Piaget said that children become capable of abstract thought, Kohlberg found that some children begin to think for themselves about the nature of authority, the meaning of justice, and the reasons behind rules and laws. In the two "post-conventional" stages, adolescents still value honesty and respect rules and laws, but now they sometimes justify dishonesty or law-breaking in pursuit of still higher goods, particularly justice. Kohlberg painted an inspiring rationalist image of children as "moral philosophers" trying to work out coherent ethical systems for themselves.[10] In the post-conventional stages, they finally get good at it. Kohlberg's dilemmas were a tool for measuring these dramatic advances in moral reasoning.

THE LIBERAL CONSENSUS

Mark Twain once said that "to a man with a hammer, everything looks like a nail." Once Kohlberg developed his moral dilemmas and his scoring techniques, the psychological community had a new hammer, and a thousand graduate students used it to pound out dissertations on moral reasoning. But there's a deeper reason so many young psychologists began to study morality from a rationalist perspective, and this was Kohlberg's second great innovation: he used his research to build a scientific justification for a secular liberal moral order.

Kohlberg's most influential finding was that the most morally advanced kids (according to his scoring technique) were those who had frequent opportunities for role taking—for putting themselves into another person's shoes and looking at a problem from that person's perspective. Egalitarian relationships (such as with peers) invite role taking, but hierarchical relationships (such as with teachers and parents) do not. It's really hard for a child to see things from the teacher's point of view, because the child has never been a teacher. Piaget and Kohlberg both thought that parents and other authorities were *obstacles* to moral development. If you want your kids to learn about the physical world, let them play with cups and water; don't lecture them about the conservation of volume. And if you want your kids to learn about the social world, let them play with other kids and resolve disputes; don't lecture them about the Ten Commandments. And, for heaven's sake, don't force them to obey God or their teachers or you. That will only freeze them at the conventional level.

Kohlberg's timing was perfect. Just as the first wave of baby boomers was entering graduate school, he transformed moral psychology into a boomer-friendly ode to justice, and he gave them a tool to measure children's progress toward the liberal ideal. For the next twenty-five years, from the 1970s through the 1990s, moral psychologists mostly just interviewed young people about moral dilemmas and analyzed their justifications.[11] Most of this work was not politically motivated—it was careful and honest scientific research. But by using a framework that predefined morality as justice while denigrating authority, hierarchy, and tradition, it was inevitable that the research would support worldviews that were secular, questioning, and egalitarian.

AN EASIER TEST

If you force kids to explain complex notions, such as how to balance competing concerns about rights and justice, you're guaranteed to find age trends because kids get so much more articulate with each passing year. But if you are searching for the first appearance of a moral concept, then you'd better find a technique that doesn't require much verbal skill. Kohlberg's former student Elliot Turiel developed such a technique. His innovation was to tell children short stories about other kids who break rules and then give them a series of simple yes-or-no probe questions. For example, you tell a story about a child who goes to school wearing regular clothes, even though his school requires students to wear a uniform. You start by getting an overall judgment: "Is that OK, what the boy did?" Most kids say no. You ask if there's a rule about what to wear. ("Yes.") Then you probe to find out what kind of rule it is: "What if the teacher said it was OK for the boy to wear his regular clothes, then would it be OK?" and "What if this happened in another school, where they don't have any rules about uniforms, then would it be OK?"

Turiel discovered that children as young as five usually say that the boy was wrong to break the rule, but that it would be OK if the teacher gave permission or if it happened in another school where there was no such rule. Children recognize that rules about clothing, food, and many other aspects of life are *social conventions*, which are arbitrary and changeable to some extent.[12]

But if you ask kids about actions that hurt other people, such as a girl who pushes a boy off a swing because she wants to use it, you get a very different set of responses. Nearly all kids say that the girl was wrong and that she'd be wrong even if the teacher said it was OK, and even if this happened in another school where there were no rules about pushing kids off swings. Children recognize that rules that prevent harm are *moral rules*, which Turiel defined as rules related to "justice, rights, and welfare pertaining to how people ought to relate to each other."[13]

In other words, young children don't treat all rules the same, as Piaget and Kohlberg had supposed. Kids can't talk like moral philosophers, but they are busy sorting social information in a sophisticated way. They seem to grasp early on that rules that prevent harm are special, important, unalterable, and universal. And this realization, Turiel said, was the foundation of all moral development. Children construct their moral understanding on the bedrock of the absolute moral truth that *harm is wrong*. Specific rules may vary across cultures, but in all of the cultures Turiel examined, children still made a distinction between moral rules and conventional rules.[14]

Turiel's account of moral development differed in many ways from Kohlberg's, but the political implications were similar: morality is about *treating individuals well*. It's about harm and fairness (not loyalty, respect, duty, piety, patriotism, or tradition). Hierarchy and authority are generally bad things (so it's best to let kids figure things out for themselves). Schools and families should therefore embody progressive principles of equality and autonomy (not authoritarian principles that enable elders to train and constrain children).

MEANWHILE, IN THE REST OF THE WORLD . . .

Kohlberg and Turiel had pretty much defined the field of moral psychology by the time I sat in Jon Baron's office and decided to study morality.[15] The field I entered was vibrant and growing, yet something about it felt wrong to me. It wasn't the politics—I was very liberal back then, twenty-four years old and full of indignation at Ronald Reagan and conservative groups such as the righteously named Moral Majority. No, the problem was that the things I was reading were so . . . dry. I had grown up with two sisters, close in age to me. We fought every day, using every dirty rhetorical trick we could think of. Morality was such a passionate affair in my family, yet the articles I was reading were all about reasoning and cognitive structures and domains of knowledge. It just seemed too cerebral. There was hardly any mention of emotion.

As a first-year graduate student, I didn't have the confidence to trust my instincts, so I forced myself to continue reading. But then, in my second year, I took a course on cultural psychology and was captivated. The course was taught by a brilliant anthropologist, Alan Fiske, who had spent many years in West Africa studying the psychological foundations of social relationships.[16] Fiske asked us all to read several ethnographies (book-length reports of an anthropologist's fieldwork), each of which focused on a different topic, such as kinship, sexuality, or music. But no matter the topic, morality turned out to be a central theme.

I read a book on witchcraft among the Azande of Sudan.[17] It turns out that witchcraft beliefs arise in surprisingly similar forms in many parts of the world, which suggests either that there really are witches or (more likely) that there's something about human minds that often generates this cultural institution. The Azande believed that witches were just as likely to be men as women, and the fear of being called a witch made the Azande careful not to make their neighbors angry or envious. That was my first hint that groups create supernatural beings not to explain the universe but to order their societies.[18]

I read a book about the Ilongot, a tribe in the Philippines whose young men gained honor by cutting off people's heads.[19] Some of these beheadings were revenge killings, which offered Western readers a motive they could understand. But many of these murders were committed against strangers who were not involved in any kind of feud with the killer. The author explained these most puzzling killings as ways that small groups of men channeled resentments and frictions within the group into a group-strengthening "hunting party," capped off by a long night of communal celebratory singing. This was my first hint that morality often involves tension *within* the group linked to competition *between* different groups.

These ethnographies were fascinating, often beautifully written, and intuitively graspable despite the strangeness of their content. Reading each book was like spending a week in a new country: confusing at first, but gradually you tune up, finding yourself better able to guess what's going to happen next. And as with all foreign travel, you learn as much about where you're from as where you're visiting. I began to see the United States and Western Europe as extraordinary historical exceptions—new societies that had found a way to strip down and thin out the thick, all-encompassing moral orders that the anthropologists wrote about.

Nowhere was this thinning more apparent than in our lack of rules about what the anthropologists call "purity" and "pollution." Contrast us with the Hua of New Guinea, who have developed elaborate networks of food taboos that govern what men and women may eat. In order for their boys to become men, they have to avoid foods that in any way resemble vaginas, including anything that is red, wet, slimy, comes from a hole, or has hair. It sounds at first like arbitrary superstition mixed with the predictable sexism of a patriarchal society. Turiel would call these rules social conventions, because the Hua don't believe that men in other tribes have to follow these rules. But the Hua certainly seemed to think of their food rules as moral rules. They talked about them constantly, judged each other by their food habits, and governed their lives, duties, and relationships by what the anthropologist Anna Meigs called "a religion of the body."[20]

But it's not just hunter-gatherers in rain forests who believe that bodily practices can be moral practices. When I read the Hebrew Bible, I was shocked to discover how much of the book—one of the sources of Western morality—was taken up with rules about food, menstruation, sex, skin, and the handling of corpses. Some of these rules were clear attempts to avoid disease, such as the long sections of Leviticus on leprosy. But many of the rules seemed to follow a more emotional logic about avoiding disgust. For example, the Bible prohibits Jews from eating or even touching "the swarming things that swarm upon the earth" (and just think how much more disgusting a swarm of mice is than a single mouse).[21] Other rules seemed to follow a conceptual logic involving keeping categories pure or not mixing things together (such as clothing made from two different fibers).[22]

So what's going on here? If Turiel was right that morality is really about harm, then why do most non-Western cultures moralize so many practices that seem to have nothing to do with harm? Why do many Christians and Jews believe that "cleanliness is next to godliness"?[23] And why do so many Westerners, even secular ones, continue to see choices about food and sex as being heavily loaded with moral significance? Liberals sometimes say that religious conservatives are sexual prudes for whom anything other than missionary-position intercourse within marriage is a sin. But conservatives can just as well make fun of liberal struggles to choose a balanced breakfast— balanced among moral concerns about free-range eggs, fair-trade coffee, naturalness, and a variety of toxins, some of which (such as genetically modified corn and soybeans) pose a greater threat spiritually than biologically. Even if Turiel was right that children lock onto harmfulness as a method for identifying immoral actions, I couldn't see how kids in the West—let alone among the Azande, the Ilongot, and the Hua—could have come to all this purity and pollution stuff on their own. There must be more to moral development than kids constructing rules as they take the perspectives of other people and feel their pain. There must be something beyond rationalism.

THE GREAT DEBATE

When anthropologists wrote about morality, it was as though they spoke a different language from the psychologists I had been reading. The Rosetta stone that helped me translate between the two fields was a paper that had just been published by Fiske's former advisor, Richard Shweder, at the University of Chicago.[24] Shweder is a psychological anthropologist who had lived and worked in Orissa, a state on the east coast of India. He had found large differences in how Oriyans (residents of Orissa) and Americans thought about personality and individuality, and these differences led to corresponding differences in how they thought about morality. Shweder quoted the anthropologist Clifford Geertz on how unusual Westerners are in thinking about people as discrete individuals:

> The Western conception of the person as a bounded, unique, more or less integrated motivational and cognitive universe, a dynamic center of awareness, emotion, judgment, and action organized into a distinctive whole and set contrastively both against other such wholes and against its social and natural background, is, however incorrigible it may seem to us, a rather peculiar idea within the context of the world's cultures.[25]

Shweder offered a simple idea to explain why the self differs so much across cultures: all societies must resolve a small set of questions about how to order society, the most important being how to balance the needs of individuals and groups. There seem to be just two primary ways of answering this question. Most societies have chosen the *sociocentric* answer, placing the needs of groups and institutions first, and subordinating the needs of individuals. In contrast, the *individualistic* answer places individuals at the center and makes society a servant of the individual.[26] The sociocentric answer dominated most of the ancient world, but the individualistic answer became a powerful rival during the Enlightenment. The individualistic answer largely vanquished the sociocentric approach in the twentieth century as individual rights expanded rapidly, consumer culture spread, and the Western world reacted with horror to the evils perpetrated by the ultrasociocentric fascist and communist empires. (European nations with strong social safety nets are not sociocentric on this definition. They just do a very good job of protecting *individuals* from the vicissitudes of life.)

Shweder thought that the theories of Kohlberg and Turiel were produced by and for people from individualistic cultures. He doubted that those theories would apply in Orissa, where morality was sociocentric, selves were interdependent, and no bright line separated moral rules (preventing harm) from social conventions (regulating behaviors not linked directly to harm). To test his ideas, he and two collaborators came up with thirty-nine very short stories in which someone does something that would violate a rule either in the United States or in Orissa. The researchers then interviewed 180 children (ranging in age from five to thirteen) and 60 adults who lived in Hyde Park (the neighborhood surrounding the University of Chicago) about these stories. They also interviewed a matched sample of Brahmin children and adults in the town of Bhubaneswar (an ancient pilgrimage site in Orissa),[27] and 120 people from low ("untouchable") castes. Altogether it was an enormous undertaking—six hundred long interviews in two very different cities.

The interview used Turiel's method, more or less, but the scenarios covered many more behaviors than Turiel had ever asked about. As you can see in the top third of figure 1.1, people in some of the stories obviously hurt other people or treated them unfairly, and subjects (the people being interviewed) in both countries condemned these actions by saying that they were wrong, unalterably wrong, and universally wrong. But the Indians would not condemn other cases that seemed (to Americans) just as clearly to involve harm and unfairness (see middle third).

Most of the thirty-nine stories portrayed no harm or unfairness,

Actions that Indians and Americans agreed were wrong:

- While walking, a man saw a dog sleeping on the road. He walked up to it and kicked it.
- A father said to his son, "If you do well on the exam, I will buy you a pen." The son did well on the exam, but the father did not give him anything.

Actions that Americans said were wrong but Indians said were acceptable:

- A young married woman went alone to see a movie without informing her husband. When she returned home her husband said, "If you do it again, I will beat you black and blue." She did it again; he beat her black and blue. (Judge the husband.)
- A man had a married son and a married daughter. After his death his son claimed most of the property. His daughter got little. (Judge the son.)

Actions that Indians said were wrong but Americans said were acceptable:

- In a family, a twenty-five-year-old son addresses his father by his first name.
- A woman cooked rice and wanted to eat with her husband and his elder brother. Then she ate with them. (Judge the woman.)
- A widow in your community eats fish two or three times a week.
- After defecation a woman did not change her clothes before cooking.

FIGURE 1.1. *Some of the thirty-nine stories used in Shweder, Mahapatra, and Miller 1987.*

at least none that could have been obvious to a five-year-old child, and nearly all Americans said that these actions were permissible (see the bottom third of figure 1.1). If Indians said that these actions were wrong, then Turiel would predict that they were condemning the actions merely as violations of social conventions. Yet most of the Indian subjects—even the five-year-old children—said that these actions were wrong, universally wrong, and unalterably wrong. Indian practices related to food, sex, clothing, and gender relations were almost always judged to be moral issues, not social conventions, and there were few differences between the adults and children within each city. In other words, Shweder found almost no trace of social conventional thinking in the sociocentric culture of Orissa, where, as he put it, "the social order is a moral order." Morality was much broader and thicker in Orissa; almost any practice could be loaded up with moral force. And if that was true, then Turiel's theory became less plausible. Children were not figuring out morality for themselves, based on the bedrock certainty that harm is bad.

Even in Chicago, Shweder found relatively little evidence of social-conventional thinking. There were plenty of stories that contained no obvious harm or injustice, such as a widow eating fish, and Americans predictably said that those cases were fine. But more important, they didn't see these behaviors as social conventions that could be changed by popular consent. They believed that widows should be able to eat whatever they darn well please, and if there's some other country where people try to limit widows' freedoms, well, they're wrong to do so. Even in the United States the social order is a moral order, but it's an individualistic order built up around the protection of individuals and their freedom. The distinction between morals and mere conventions is not a tool that children everywhere use to self-construct their moral knowledge. Rather, the distinction turns out to be a cultural artifact, a necessary by-product of the individualistic answer to the question of how individuals and groups relate. When you put individuals first, before society, then any rule or social practice that limits personal freedom can be questioned. If it doesn't protect somebody from harm, then it can't be morally justified. It's just a social convention.

Shweder's study was a major attack on the whole rationalist approach, and Turiel didn't take it lying down. He wrote a long rebuttal essay pointing out that many of Shweder's thirty-nine stories were trick questions: they had very different meanings in India and America.[28] For example, Hindus in Orissa believe that fish is a "hot" food that will stimulate a person's sexual appetite. If a widow eats hot foods, she is more likely to have sex with someone, which would offend the spirit of her dead husband and prevent her from reincarnating at a higher level. Turiel argued that once you take into account Indian "informational assumptions" about the way the world works, you see that most of Shweder's thirty-nine stories really *were* moral violations, harming victims in ways that Americans could not see. So Shweder's study didn't contradict Turiel's claims; it might even support them, if we could find out for sure whether Shweder's Indian subjects saw harm in the stories.

DISGUST AND DISRESPECT

When I read the Shweder and Turiel essays, I had two strong reactions. The first was an intellectual agreement with Turiel's defense. Shweder had used "trick" questions not to be devious but to demonstrate that rules about food, clothing, ways of addressing people, and other seemingly conventional matters could all get woven into a thick moral web. Nonetheless, I agreed with Turiel that Shweder's study was missing an important experimental control: he didn't ask his subjects about harm. If Shweder wanted to show that morality extended beyond harm in Orissa, he had to show that people were willing to morally condemn actions that *they themselves* stated were harmless.

My second reaction was a gut feeling that Shweder was ultimately right. His explanation of sociocentric morality fit so perfectly with the ethnographies I had read in Fiske's class. His emphasis on the moral emotions was so satisfying after reading all that cerebral cognitive-developmental work. I thought that if somebody ran the right study—one that controlled for perceptions of harm—Shweder's claims about cultural differences would survive the test. I spent the next semester figuring out how to become that somebody.

I started writing very short stories about people who do offensive things, but do them in such a way that nobody is harmed. I called these stories "harmless taboo violations," and you read two of them at the start of this chapter (about dog-eating and chicken- . . . eating). I made up dozens of these stories but quickly found that the ones that worked best fell into two categories: disgust and disrespect. If you want to give people a quick flash of revulsion but deprive them of any victim they can use to justify moral condemnation, ask them about people who do disgusting or disrespectful things, but make sure the actions are done in private so that nobody else is offended. For example, one of my disrespect stories was: "A woman is cleaning out her closet, and she finds her old American flag. She doesn't want the flag anymore, so she cuts it up into pieces and uses the rags to clean her bathroom."

My idea was to give adults and children stories that pitted gut feelings about important cultural norms against reasoning about harmlessness, and then see which force was stronger. Turiel's rationalism predicted that reasoning about harm is the basis of moral judgment, so even though people might say it's wrong to eat your dog, they would have to treat the act as a violation of a social convention. (*We* don't eat our dogs, but hey, if people in another country want to eat their ex-pets rather than bury them, who are we to criticize?) Shweder's theory, on the other hand, said that Turiel's predictions should hold among members of individualistic secular societies but not elsewhere. I now had a study designed. I just had to find the elsewhere.

I spoke Spanish fairly well, so when I learned that a major conference of Latin American psychologists was to be held in Buenos Aires in July 1989, I bought a plane ticket. I had no contacts and no idea how to start an international research collaboration, so I just went to every talk that had anything to do with morality. I was chagrined to discover that psychology in Latin America was not very scientific. It was heavily theoretical, and much of that theory was Marxist, focused on oppression, colonialism, and power. I was beginning to despair when I chanced upon a session run by some Brazilian psychologists who were using Kohlbergian methods to study moral development. I spoke afterward to the chair of the session, Angela Biaggio, and her graduate student Silvia Koller. Even though they both liked Kohlberg's approach, they were interested in hearing about alternatives. Biaggio invited me to visit them after the conference at their university in Porto Alegre, the capital of the southernmost state in Brazil.

Southern Brazil is the most European part of the country, settled largely by Portuguese, German, and Italian immigrants in the nineteenth century. With its modern architecture and middle-class prosperity, Porto Alegre didn't look anything like the Latin America of my imagination, so at first I was disappointed. I wanted my cross-cultural study to involve someplace exotic, like Orissa. But Silvia Koller was a wonderful collaborator, and she had two great ideas about how to increase our cultural diversity. First, she suggested we run the study across social class. The divide between rich and poor is so vast in Brazil that it's as though people live in different countries. We decided to interview adults and children from the educated middle class, and also from the lower class—adults who worked as servants for wealthy people (and who rarely had more than an eighth-grade education) and children from a public school in the neighborhood where many of the servants lived. Second, Silvia had a friend who had just been hired as a professor in Recife, a city in the northeastern tip of the country, a region that is culturally very different from Porto Alegre. Silvia arranged for me to visit her friend, Graça Dias, the following month.

Silvia and I worked for two weeks with a team of undergraduate students, translating the harmless taboo stories into Portuguese, selecting the best ones, refining the probe questions, and testing our interview script to make sure that everything was understandable, even by the least educated subjects, some of whom were illiterate. Then I went off to Recife, where Graça and I trained a team of students to conduct interviews in exactly the way they were being done in Porto Alegre. In Recife I finally felt like I was working in an exotic tropical locale, with Brazilian music wafting through the streets and ripe mangoes falling from the trees. More important, the people of northeast Brazil are mostly of mixed ancestry (African and European), and the region is poorer and much less industrialized than Porto Alegre.

When I returned to Philadelphia, I trained my own team of interviewers and supervised the data collection for the four groups of subjects in Philadelphia. The design of the study was therefore what we call "three by two by two," meaning that we had three cities, and in each city we had two levels of social class (high and low), and within each social class we had two age groups: children (ages ten to twelve) and adults (ages eighteen to twenty-eight). That made for twelve groups in all, with thirty people in each group, for a total of 360 interviews. This large number of subjects allowed me to run statistical tests to examine the independent effects of city, social class, and age. I predicted that Philadelphia would be the most individualistic of the three cities (and therefore the most Turiel-like) and Recife would be the most sociocentric (and therefore more like Orissa in its judgments).

The results were as clear as could be in support of Shweder. First, all four of my Philadelphia groups confirmed Turiel's finding that Americans make a big distinction between moral and conventional violations. I used two stories taken directly from Turiel's research: a girl pushes a boy off a swing (that's a clear moral violation) and a boy refuses to wear a school uniform (that's a conventional violation). This validated my methods. It meant that any differences I found on the harmless taboo stories could not be attributed to some quirk about the way I phrased the probe questions or trained my interviewers. The upper-class Brazilians looked just like the Americans on these stories. But the working-class Brazilian kids usually thought that it was wrong, and universally wrong, to break the social convention and not wear the uniform. In Recife in particular, the working-class kids judged the uniform rebel in exactly the same way they judged the swing-pusher. This pattern supported Shweder: the size of the moral-conventional distinction varied across cultural groups.

The second thing I found was that people responded to the harmless taboo stories just as Shweder had predicted: the upper-class Philadelphians judged them to be violations of social conventions, and the lower-class Recifeans judged them to be moral violations. There were separate significant effects of city (Porto Alegreans moralized more than Philadelphians, and Recifeans moralized more than Porto Alegreans), of social class (lower-class groups moralized more than upper-class groups), and of age (children moralized more than adults). Unexpectedly, the effect of social class was much larger than the effect of city. In other words, well-educated people in all three cities were more similar to each other than they were to their lower-class neighbors. I had flown five thousand miles south to search for moral variation when in fact there was more to be found a few blocks west of campus, in the poor neighborhood surrounding my university.

My third finding was that all the differences I found held up when I controlled for perceptions of harm. I had included a probe question that directly asked, after each story: "Do you think anyone was harmed by what [the person in the story] did?" If Shweder's findings were caused by perceptions of hidden victims (as Turiel proposed), then my cross-cultural differences should have disappeared when I removed the subjects who said yes to this question. But when I filtered out these people, the cultural differences got *bigger*, not smaller. This was very strong support for Shweder's claim that the moral domain goes far beyond harm. Most of my subjects said that the harmless-taboo violations were universally wrong even though they harmed nobody.

In other words, Shweder won the debate. I had replicated Turiel's findings using Turiel's methods on people like me—educated Westerners raised in an individualistic culture—but had confirmed Shweder's claim that Turiel's theory didn't travel well. The moral domain varied across nations and social classes. For most of the people in my study, the moral domain extended well beyond issues of harm and fairness.

It was hard to see how a rationalist could explain these results. How could children self-construct their moral knowledge about disgust and disrespect from their private analyses of harmfulness? There must be other sources of moral knowledge, including cultural learning (as Shweder argued), or innate moral intuitions about disgust and disrespect (as I began to argue years later).

I once overheard a Kohlberg-style moral judgment interview being conducted in the bathroom of a McDonald's restaurant in northern Indiana. The person interviewed—the subject—was a Caucasian male roughly thirty years old. The interviewer was a Caucasian male approximately four years old. The interview began at adjacent urinals:

> INTERVIEWER: *Dad, what would happen if I pooped in here [the urinal]?*
> SUBJECT: *It would be yucky. Go ahead and flush. Come on, let's go wash our hands.*
> *[The pair then moved over to the sinks]*
> INTERVIEWER: *Dad, what would happen if I pooped in the sink?*
> SUBJECT: *The people who work here would get mad at you.*
> INTERVIEWER: *What would happen if I pooped in the sink at home?*
> SUBJECT: *I'd get mad at you.*
> INTERVIEWER: *What would happen if you pooped in the sink at home?*
> SUBJECT: *Mom would get mad at me.*
> INTERVIEWER: *Well, what would happen if we all pooped in the sink at home?*
> SUBJECT: *[pause] I guess we'd all get in trouble.*
> INTERVIEWER: *[laughing] Yeah, we'd all get in trouble!*
> SUBJECT: *Come on, let's dry our hands. We have to go.*

Note the skill and persistence of the interviewer, who probes for a deeper answer by changing the transgression to remove the punisher. Yet even when everyone cooperates in the rule violation so that nobody can play the role of punisher, the subject still clings to a notion of cosmic justice in which, somehow, the whole family would "get in trouble."

Of course, the father is not really trying to demonstrate his best moral reasoning. Moral reasoning is usually done to influence other people (see chapter 4), and what the father is trying to do is get his curious son to feel the right emotions—disgust and fear—to motivate appropriate bathroom behavior.

INVENTING VICTIMS

Even though the results came out just as Shweder had predicted, there were a number of surprises along the way. The biggest surprise was that so many subjects tried to invent victims. I had written the stories carefully to remove all conceivable harm to other people, yet in 38 percent of the 1,620 times that people heard a harmless-offensive story, they claimed that somebody was harmed. In the dog story, for example, many people said that the family itself would be harmed because they would get sick from eating dog meat. Was this an example of the "informational assumptions" that Turiel had talked about? Were people really condemning the actions *because* they foresaw these harms, or was it the reverse process—were people *inventing* these harms because they had already condemned the actions?

I conducted many of the Philadelphia interviews myself, and it was obvious that most of these supposed harms were post hoc fabrications. People usually condemned the actions very quickly—they didn't seem to need much time to decide what they thought. But it often took them a while to come up with a victim, and they usually offered those victims up halfheartedly and almost apologetically. As one subject said, "Well, I don't know, maybe the woman will feel guilty afterward about throwing out her flag?" Many of these victim claims were downright preposterous, such as the child who justified his condemnation of the flag shredder by saying that the rags might clog up the toilet and cause it to overflow.

But something even more interesting happened when I or the other interviewers challenged these invented-victim claims. I had trained my interviewers to correct people gently when they made claims that contradicted the text of the story. For example, if someone said, "It's wrong to cut up the flag because a neighbor might see her do it, and he might be offended," the interviewer replied, "Well, it says here in the story that nobody saw her do it. So would you still say it was wrong for her to cut up her flag?" Yet even when subjects recognized that their victim claims were bogus, they still refused to say that the act was OK. Instead, they kept searching for another victim. They said things like "I know it's wrong, but I just can't think of a reason why." They seemed to be *morally dumbfounded*—rendered speechless by their inability to explain verbally what they knew intuitively.[29]

These subjects were reasoning. They were working quite hard at reasoning. But it was not reasoning in search of truth; it was reasoning in support of their emotional reactions. It was reasoning as described by the philosopher David Hume, who wrote in 1739 that "reason is, and ought only to be the slave of the passions, and can never pretend to any other office than to serve and obey them."[30]

I had found evidence for Hume's claim. I had found that moral reasoning was often a servant of moral emotions, and this was a challenge to the rationalist approach that dominated moral psychology. I published these findings in one of the top psychology journals in October 1993[31] and then waited nervously for the response. I knew that the field of moral psychology was not going to change overnight just because one grad student produced some data that didn't fit into the prevailing paradigm. I knew that debates in moral psychology could be quite heated (though always civil). What I did not expect, however, was that there would be no response at all. Here I thought I had done the definitive study to settle a major debate in moral psychology, yet almost nobody cited my work—not even to attack it—in the first five years after I published it.

My dissertation landed with a silent thud in part because I published it in a social psychology journal. But in the early 1990s, the field of moral psychology was still a part of developmental psychology. If you called yourself a moral psychologist, it meant that you studied moral reasoning and how it changed with age, and you cited Kohlberg extensively whether you agreed with him or not.

But psychology itself was about to change and become a lot more emotional.

IN SUM

Where does morality come from? The two most common answers have long been that it is innate (the nativist answer) or that it comes from childhood learning (the empiricist answer). In this chapter I considered a third possibility, the rationalist answer, which dominated moral psychology when I entered the field: that morality is self-constructed by children on the basis of their experiences with harm. Kids know that harm is wrong because they hate to be harmed, and they gradually come to see that it is therefore wrong to harm others, which leads them to understand fairness and eventually justice. I explained why I came to reject this answer after conducting research in Brazil and the United States. I concluded instead that:

- The moral domain varies by culture. It is unusually narrow in Western, educated, and individualistic cultures. Sociocentric cultures broaden the moral domain to encompass and regulate more aspects of life.
- People sometimes have gut feelings—particularly about disgust and disrespect—that can drive their reasoning. Moral reasoning is sometimes a post hoc fabrication.
- Morality can't be entirely self-constructed by children based on their growing understanding of harm. Cultural learning or guidance must play a larger role than rationalist theories had given it.

If morality doesn't come primarily from reasoning, then that leaves some combination of innateness and social learning as the most likely candidates. In the rest of this book I'll try to explain how morality can be innate (as a set of evolved intuitions) and learned (as children learn to apply those intuitions within a particular culture). We're born to be righteous, but we have to learn what, exactly, people like us should be righteous about.

TWO

The Intuitive Dog and
Its Rational Tail

One of the greatest truths in psychology is that the mind is divided into parts that sometimes conflict.[1] To be human is to feel pulled in different directions, and to marvel—sometimes in horror—at your inability to control your own actions. The Roman poet Ovid lived at a time when people thought diseases were caused by imbalances of bile, but he knew enough psychology to have one of his characters lament: "I am dragged along by a strange new force. Desire and reason are pulling in different directions. I see the right way and approve it, but follow the wrong."[2]

Ancient thinkers gave us many metaphors to understand this conflict, but few are more colorful than the one in Plato's dialogue *Timaeus*. The narrator, Timaeus, explains how the gods created the universe, including us. Timaeus says that a creator god who was perfect and created only perfect things was filling his new universe with souls—and what could be more perfect in a soul than perfect rationality? So after making a large number of perfect, rational souls, the creator god decided to take a break, delegating the last bits of creation to some lesser deities, who did their best to design vessels for these souls.

The deities began by encasing the souls in that most perfect of shapes, the sphere, which explains why our heads are more or less round. But they quickly realized that these spherical heads would face difficulties and indignities as they rolled around the uneven surface of the Earth. So the gods created bodies to carry the heads, and they animated each body with a second soul—vastly inferior because it was neither rational nor immortal. This second soul contained

> those dreadful but necessary disturbances: pleasure, first of all, evil's most powerful lure; then pains, that make us run away from what is good; besides these, boldness also and fear, foolish counselors both; then also the spirit of anger hard to assuage, and expectation easily led astray. These they fused with unreasoning sense perception and all-venturing lust, and so, as was necessary, they constructed the mortal type of soul.[3]

Pleasures, emotions, senses . . . all were necessary evils. To give the divine head a bit of distance from the seething body and its "foolish counsel," the gods invented the neck.

Most creation myths situate a tribe or ancestor at the center of creation, so it seems odd to give the honor to a mental faculty—at least until you realize that this philosopher's myth makes philosophers look pretty darn good. It justifies their perpetual employment as the high priests of reason, or as dispassionate philosopher-kings. It's the ultimate rationalist fantasy—the passions are and ought only to be the servants of reason, to reverse Hume's formulation. And just in case there was any doubt about Plato's contempt for the passions, Timaeus adds that a man who masters his emotions will live a life of reason and justice, and will be reborn into a celestial heaven of eternal happiness. A man who is mastered by his passions, however, will be reincarnated as a woman.

Western philosophy has been worshipping reason and distrusting the passions for thousands of years.[4] There's a direct line running from Plato through Immanuel Kant to Lawrence Kohlberg. I'll refer to this worshipful attitude throughout this book as the *rationalist delusion*. I call it a delusion because when a group of people make something sacred, the members of the cult lose the ability to think clearly about it. Morality binds and blinds. The true believers produce pious fantasies that don't match reality, and at some point somebody comes along to knock the idol off its pedestal. That was Hume's project, with his philosophically sacrilegious claim that reason was nothing but the servant of the passions.[5]

Thomas Jefferson offered a more balanced model of the relationship between reason and emotion. In 1786, while serving as the American minister to France, Jefferson fell in love. Maria Cosway was a beautiful twenty-seven-year-old English artist who was introduced to Jefferson by a mutual friend. Jefferson and Cosway then spent the next few hours doing exactly what people should do to fall madly in love. They strolled around Paris on a perfect sunny day, two foreigners sharing each other's aesthetic appreciations of a grand city. Jefferson sent messengers bearing lies to cancel his evening meetings so that he could extend the day into night. Cosway was married, although the marriage seems to have been an open marriage of convenience, and historians do not know how far the romance progressed in the weeks that followed.[6] But Cosway's husband soon insisted on taking his wife back to England, leaving Jefferson in pain.

To ease that pain, Jefferson wrote Cosway a love letter using a literary trick to cloak the impropriety of writing about love to a married woman. Jefferson wrote the letter as a dialogue between his head and his heart debating the wisdom of having pursued a "friendship" even while he knew it would have to end. Jefferson's head is the Platonic ideal of reason, scolding the heart for having dragged them both into yet another fine mess. The heart asks the head for pity, but the head responds with a stern lecture:

> Everything in this world is a matter of calculation. Advance then with caution, the balance in your hand. Put into one scale the pleasures which any object may offer; but put fairly into the other the pains which are to follow, & see which preponderates.[7]

After taking round after round of abuse rather passively, the heart finally rises to defend itself, and to put the head in its proper place—which is to handle problems that don't involve people:

When nature assigned us the same habitation, she gave us over it a divided empire. To you she allotted the field of science; to me that of morals. When the circle is to be squared, or the orbit of a comet to be traced; when the arch of greatest strength, or the solid of least resistance is to be investigated, take up the problem; it is yours; nature has given me no cognizance of it. In like manner, in denying to you the feelings of sympathy, of benevolence, of gratitude, of justice, of love, of friendship, she has excluded you from their control. To these she has adapted the mechanism of the heart. Morals were too essential to the happiness of man to be risked on the incertain combinations of the head. She laid their foundation therefore in sentiment, not in science.[8]

So now we have three models of the mind. Plato said that reason *ought* to be the master, even if philosophers are the only ones who can reach a high level of mastery.[9] Hume said that reason is and ought to be the servant of the passions. And Jefferson gives us a third option, in which reason and sentiment are (and ought to be) independent co-rulers, like the emperors of Rome, who divided the empire into eastern and western halves. Who is right?

WILSON'S PROPHECY

Plato, Hume, and Jefferson tried to understand the design of the human mind without the help of the most powerful tool ever devised for understanding the design of living things: Darwin's theory of evolution. Darwin was fascinated by morality because any example of cooperation among living creatures had to be squared with his general emphasis on competition and the "survival of the fittest."[10] Darwin offered several explanations for how morality could have evolved, and many of them pointed to emotions such as sympathy, which he thought was the "foundation-stone" of the social instincts.[11] He also wrote about feelings of shame and pride, which were associated with the desire for a good reputation. Darwin was a nativist about morality: he thought that natural selection gave us minds that were preloaded with moral emotions.

But as the social sciences advanced in the twentieth century, their course was altered by two waves of moralism that turned nativism into a moral offense. The first was the horror among anthropologists and others at "social Darwinism"—the idea (raised but not endorsed by Darwin) that the richest and most successful nations, races, and individuals are the fittest. Therefore, giving charity to the poor interferes with the natural progress of evolution: it allows the poor to breed.[12] The claim that some races were innately superior to others was later championed by Hitler, and so if Hitler was a nativist, then all nativists were Nazis. (That conclusion is illogical, but it makes sense emotionally if you dislike nativism.)[13]

The second wave of moralism was the radical politics that washed over universities in America, Europe, and Latin America in the 1960s and 1970s. Radical reformers usually want to believe that human nature is a blank slate on which any utopian vision can be sketched. If evolution gave men and women different sets of desires and skills, for example, that would be an obstacle to achieving gender equality in many professions. If nativism could be used to justify existing power structures, then nativism must be wrong. (Again, this is a logical error, but this is the way righteous minds work.)

The cognitive scientist Steven Pinker was a graduate student at Harvard in the 1970s. In his 2002 book *The Blank Slate: The Modern Denial of Human Nature,* Pinker describes the ways scientists betrayed the values of science to maintain loyalty to the progressive movement. Scientists became "moral exhibitionists" in the lecture hall as they demonized fellow scientists and urged their students to evaluate ideas not for their truth but for their consistency with progressive ideals such as racial and gender equality.[14]

Nowhere was the betrayal of science more evident than in the attacks on Edward O. Wilson, a lifelong student of ants and ecosystems. In 1975 Wilson published *Sociobiology: The New Synthesis.* The book explored how natural selection, which indisputably shaped animal bodies, also shaped animal behavior. That wasn't controversial, but Wilson had the audacity to suggest in his final chapter that natural selection also influenced *human* behavior. Wilson believed that there is such a thing as human nature, and that human nature constrains the range of what we can achieve when raising our children or designing new social institutions.

Wilson used ethics to illustrate his point. He was a professor at Harvard, along with Lawrence Kohlberg and the philosopher John Rawls, so he was well acquainted with their brand of rationalist theorizing about rights and justice.[15] It seemed clear to Wilson that what the rationalists were *really* doing was generating clever justifications for moral intuitions that were best explained by evolution. Do people believe in human rights because such rights actually exist, like mathematical truths, sitting on a cosmic shelf next to the Pythagorean theorem just waiting to be discovered by Platonic reasoners? Or do people feel revulsion and sympathy when they read accounts of torture, and then invent a story about universal rights to help justify their feelings?

Wilson sided with Hume. He charged that what moral philosophers were really doing was fabricating justifications after "consulting the emotive centers" of their own brains.[16] He predicted that the study of ethics would soon be taken out of the hands of philosophers and "biologicized," or made to fit with the emerging science of human nature. Such a linkage of philosophy, biology, and evolution would be an example of the "new synthesis" that Wilson dreamed of, and that he later referred to as *consilience*—the "jumping together" of ideas to create a unified body of knowledge.[17]

Prophets challenge the status quo, often earning the hatred of those in power. Wilson therefore deserves to be called a prophet of moral psychology. He was harassed and excoriated in print and in public.[18] He was called a fascist, which justified (for some) the charge that he was a racist, which justified (for some) the attempt to stop him from speaking in public. Protesters who tried to disrupt one of his scientific talks rushed the stage and chanted, "Racist Wilson, you can't hide, we charge you with genocide."[19]

THE EMOTIONAL NINETIES

By the time I entered graduate school, in 1987, the shooting had stopped and sociobiology had been discredited—at least, that's the message I picked up from hearing scientists use the word as a pejorative term for the naive attempt to reduce psychology to evolution. Moral psychology was not about evolved emotions, it was about the development of reasoning and information processing.[20]

Yet when I looked outside of psychology, I found many wonderful books on the emotional basis of morality. I read Frans de Waal's *Good Natured: The Origins of Right and Wrong in Humans and Other Animals*.[21] De Waal did not claim that chimpanzees had morality; he argued only that chimps (and other apes) have most of the psychological building blocks that humans use to construct moral systems and communities. These building blocks are largely emotional, such as feelings of sympathy, fear, anger, and affection.

I also read *Descartes' Error*, by the neuroscientist Antonio Damasio.[22] Damasio had noticed an unusual pattern of symptoms in patients who had suffered brain damage to a specific part of the brain—the ventromedial (i.e., bottom-middle) prefrontal cortex (abbreviated vmPFC; it's the region just behind and above the bridge of the nose). Their emotionality dropped nearly to zero. They could look at the most joyous or gruesome photographs and feel nothing. They retained full knowledge of what was right and wrong, and they showed no deficits in IQ. They even scored well on Kohlberg's tests of moral reasoning. Yet when it came to making decisions in their personal lives and at work, they made foolish decisions or no decisions at all. They alienated their families and their employers, and their lives fell apart.

Damasio's interpretation was that gut feelings and bodily reactions were *necessary* to think rationally, and that one job of the vmPFC was to integrate those gut feelings into a person's conscious deliberations. When you weigh the advantages and disadvantages of murdering your parents . . . you can't even do it, because feelings of horror come rushing in through the vmPFC.

But Damasio's patients could think about anything, with no filtering or coloring from their emotions. With the vmPFC shut down, every option at every moment felt as good as every other. The only way to make a decision was to examine each option, weighing the pros and cons using conscious, verbal reasoning. If you've ever shopped for an appliance about which you have few feelings—say, a washing machine—you know how hard it can be once the number of options exceeds six or seven (which is the capacity of our short-term memory). Just imagine what your life would be like if at every moment, in every social situation, picking the right thing to do or say became like picking the best washing machine among ten options, minute after minute, day after day. You'd make foolish decisions too.

Damasio's findings were as anti-Platonic as could be. Here were people in whom brain damage had essentially shut down communication between the rational soul and the seething passions of the body (which, unbeknownst to Plato, were not based in the heart and stomach but in the emotion areas of the brain). No more of those "dreadful but necessary disturbances," those "foolish counselors" leading the rational soul astray. Yet the result of the separation was not the liberation of reason from the thrall of the passions. It was the shocking revelation that reasoning *requires* the passions. Jefferson's model fits better: when one co-emperor is knocked out and the other tries to rule the empire by himself, he's not up to the task.

If Jefferson's model were correct, however, then Damasio's patients should still have fared well in the half of life that was always ruled by the head. Yet the collapse of decision making, even in purely analytic and organizational tasks, was pervasive. The head can't even do head stuff without the heart. So Hume's model fit these cases best: when the master (passions) drops dead, the servant (reasoning) has neither the ability nor the desire to keep the estate running. Everything goes to ruin.

WHY ATHEISTS WON'T SELL THEIR SOULS

In 1995 I moved to the University of Virginia (UVA) to begin my first job as a professor. Moral psychology was still devoted to the study of moral reasoning. But if you looked beyond developmental psychology, Wilson's new synthesis was beginning. A few economists, philosophers, and neuroscientists were quietly constructing an alternative approach to morality, one whose foundation was the emotions, and the emotions were assumed to have been shaped by evolution.[23] These synthesizers were assisted by the rebirth of sociobiology in 1992 under a new name—evolutionary psychology.[24]

I read Jefferson's letter to Cosway during my first month in Charlottesville, as part of my initiation into his cult. (Jefferson founded UVA in 1819, and here at "Mr. Jefferson's University" we regard him as a deity.) But I had already arrived at a Jeffersonian view in which moral emotions and moral reasoning were separate processes.[25] Each process could make moral judgments on its own, and they sometimes fought it out for the right to do so (figure 2.1).

In my first few years at UVA I conducted several experiments to test this dual-process model by asking people to make judgments under conditions that strengthened or weakened one of the processes. For example, social psychologists often ask people to perform tasks while carrying a heavy cognitive load, such as holding the number 7250475 in mind, or while carrying a light cognitive load, such as remembering just the number 7. If performance suffers while people are carrying the heavy load, then we can conclude that "controlled" thinking (such as conscious reasoning) is necessary for that particular

FIGURE 2.1. *My early Jeffersonian dual-process model.* Emotion and reasoning are separate paths to moral judgment, although moral judgment can sometimes lead to post hoc reasoning as well.

task. But if people do fine on the task regardless of the load, then we can conclude that "automatic" processes (such as intuition and emotion) are sufficient for performing that task.

My question was simple: Can people make moral judgments just as well when carrying a heavy cognitive load as when carrying a light one? The answer turned out to be yes. I found no difference between conditions, no effect of cognitive load. I tried it again with different stories and got the same outcome. I tried another manipulation: I used a computer program to force some people to answer quickly, before they had time to think, and I forced other people to wait ten seconds before offering their judgment. Surely that manipulation would weaken or strengthen moral reasoning and shift the balance of power, I thought. But it didn't.[26]

When I came to UVA I was certain that a Jeffersonian dual-process model was right, but I kept failing in my efforts to prove it. My tenure clock was ticking, and I was getting nervous. I had to produce a string of publications in top journals within five years or I'd be turned down for tenure and forced to leave UVA.

In the meantime, I started running studies to follow up on the moral dumbfounding I had observed a few years earlier in my dissertation interviews. I worked with a talented undergraduate, Scott Murphy. Our plan was to increase the amount of dumbfounding by having Scott play devil's advocate rather than gentle interviewer. When Scott succeeded in stripping away arguments, would people change their judgments? Or would they become morally dumbfounded, clinging to their initial judgments while stammering and grasping for reasons?

Scott brought thirty UVA students into the lab, one at a time, for an extended interview. He explained that his job was to challenge their reasoning, no matter what they said. He then took them through five scenarios. One was Kohlberg's Heinz dilemma: Should Heinz steal a drug to save his wife's life? We predicted that this story would produce little dumbfounding. It pitted concerns about harm and life against concerns about law and property rights, and the story was well constructed to elicit cool, rational moral reasoning. Sure enough, Scott couldn't whip up any dumbfounding with the Heinz story. People offered good reasons for their answers, and Scott was not able to get them to abandon principles such as "Life is more important than property."

We also chose two scenarios that played more directly on gut feelings. In the "roach juice" scenario, Scott opened a small can of apple juice, poured it into a new plastic cup, and asked the subject to take a sip. Everyone did. Then Scott brought out a white plastic box and said:

> I have here in this container a sterilized cockroach. We bought some cockroaches from a laboratory supply company. The roaches were raised in a clean environment. But just to be certain, we sterilized the roaches again in an autoclave, which heats everything so hot that no germs can survive. I'm going to dip this cockroach into the juice, like this [using a tea strainer]. Now, would you take a sip?

In the second scenario, Scott offered subjects $2 if they would sign a piece of paper that said: *I, _____, hereby sell my soul, after my death, to Scott Murphy, for the sum of $2.* There was a line for a signature, and below the line was this note: *This form is part of a psychology experiment. It is* NOT *a legal or binding contract, in any way.*[27] Scott also told them they could rip up the paper as soon as they signed it, and they'd still get their $2.

Only 23 percent of subjects were willing to sign the paper without any goading from Scott. We were a bit surprised to find that 37 percent were willing to take a sip of the roach juice.[28] In these cases, Scott couldn't play devil's advocate.

For the majorities who said no, however, Scott asked them to explain their reasons and did his best to challenge those reasons. Scott convinced an extra 10 percent to sip the juice, and an extra 17 percent to sign the soul-selling paper. But most people in both scenarios clung to their initial refusal, even though many of them could not generate good reasons. A few people confessed that they were atheists, didn't believe in souls, and yet still felt uncomfortable about signing.

Here too there wasn't much dumbfounding. People felt that it was ultimately their own choice whether or not to drink the juice or sign the paper, so most subjects seemed comfortable saying, "I just don't want to do it, even though I can't give you a reason."

The main point of the study was to examine responses to two harmless taboo violations. We wanted to know if the moral judgment of disturbing but harmless events would look more like judgments in the Heinz task (closely linked to reasoning), or like those in the roach juice and soul-selling tasks (where people readily confessed that they were following gut feelings). Here's one story we used:

> Julie and Mark, who are sister and brother, are traveling together in France. They are both on summer vacation from college. One night they are staying alone in a cabin near the beach. They decide that it would be interesting and fun if they tried making love. At the very least it would be a new experience for each of them. Julie is already taking birth control pills, but Mark uses a condom too, just to be safe. They both enjoy it, but they decide not to do it again. They keep that night as a special secret between them, which makes them feel even closer to each other. So what do you think about this? Was it wrong for them to have sex?

In the other harmless-taboo story, Jennifer works in a hospital pathology lab. She's a vegetarian for moral reasons—she think it's wrong to kill animals. But one night she has to incinerate a fresh human cadaver, and she thinks it's a waste to throw away perfectly edible flesh. So she cuts off a piece of flesh and takes it home. Then she cooks it and eats it.

We knew these stories were disgusting, and we expected that they'd trigger immediate moral condemnation. Only 20 percent of subjects said it was OK for Julie and Mark to have sex, and only 13 percent said it was OK for Jennifer to eat part of a cadaver. But when Scott asked people to explain their judgments and then challenged those explanations, he found exactly the Humean pattern that we had predicted. In these harmless-taboo scenarios, people generated far more reasons and discarded far more reasons than in any of the other scenarios. They seemed to be flailing around, throwing out reason after reason, and rarely changing their minds when Scott proved that their latest reason was not relevant. Here is the transcript of one interview about the incest story:

EXPERIMENTER: So what do you think about this, was it wrong for Julie and Mark to have sex?

SUBJECT: Yeah, I think it's totally wrong to have sex. You know, because I'm pretty religious and I just think incest is wrong anyway. But, I don't know.

EXPERIMENTER: What's wrong with incest, would you say?

SUBJECT: Um, the whole idea of, well, I've heard— I don't even know if this is true, but in the case, if the girl did get pregnant, the kids become deformed, most of the time, in cases like that.

EXPERIMENTER: But they used a condom and birth control pills—

SUBJECT: Oh, OK. Yeah, you did say that.

EXPERIMENTER: —so there's no way they're going to have a kid.

SUBJECT: Well, I guess the safest sex is abstinence, but, um, uh . . . um, I don't know, I just think that's wrong. I don't know, what did you ask me?

EXPERIMENTER: Was it wrong for them to have sex?

SUBJECT: Yeah, I think it's wrong.

EXPERIMENTER: And I'm trying to find out why, what you think is wrong with it.

SUBJECT: OK, um . . . well . . . let's see, let me think about this. Um—how old were they?

EXPERIMENTER: They were college age, around 20 or so.

SUBJECT: Oh, oh [looks disappointed]. I don't know,

I just . . . it's just not something you're brought up
to do. It's just not—well, I mean I wasn't. I assume
most people aren't [laughs]. I just think that you
shouldn't—I don't—I guess my reason is, um . . . just
that, um . . . you're not brought up to it. You don't
see it. It's not, um—I don't think it's accepted. That's
pretty much it.

EXPERIMENTER: You wouldn't say anything you're not
brought up to see is wrong, would you? For example,
if you're not brought up to see women working outside the home, would you say that makes it wrong for
women to work?

SUBJECT: Um . . . well . . . oh, gosh. This is hard. I
really—um, I mean, there's just no way I could
change my mind but I just don't know how to—how
to show what I'm feeling, what I feel about it. It's
crazy![29]

In this transcript and in many others, it's obvious that people
were making a moral judgment immediately and emotionally. Reasoning was merely the servant of the passions, and when the servant
failed to find any good arguments, the master did not change his
mind. We quantified some of the behaviors that seemed most indica-
tive of being morally dumbfounded, and these analyses showed big
differences between the way people responded to the harmless-taboo
scenarios compared to the Heinz dilemma.[30]

These results supported Hume, not Jefferson or Plato. People
made moral judgments quickly and emotionally. Moral reasoning
was mostly just a post hoc search for reasons to justify the judgments
people had already made. But were these judgments representative
of moral judgment in general? I had to write some bizarre stories to
give people these flashes of moral intuition that they could not easily
explain. That can't be how most of our thinking works, can it?

"SEEING-THAT" VERSUS "REASONING-WHY"

Two years before Scott and I ran the dumbfounding studies I read an extraordinary book that psychologists rarely mention: *Patterns, Thinking, and Cognition*, by Howard Margolis, a professor of public policy at the University of Chicago. Margolis was trying to understand why people's beliefs about political issues are often so poorly connected to objective facts, and he hoped that cognitive science could solve the puzzle. Yet Margolis was turned off by the approaches to thinking that were prevalent in the 1980s, most of which used the metaphor of the mind as a computer.

Margolis thought that a better model for studying higher cognition, such as political thinking, was lower cognition, such as vision, which works largely by rapid unconscious pattern matching. He began his book with an investigation of perceptual illusions, such as the well-known Muller-Lyer illusion (figure 2.2), in which one line continues to look longer than the other even after you know that the two lines are the same length. He then moved on to logic problems such as the Wason 4-card task, in which you are shown four cards on a table.[31] You know that each card comes from a deck in which all cards have a letter on one side and a number on the other. Your task is to choose the smallest number of cards in figure 2.3 that you must turn over to decide whether this rule is true: "If there is a vowel on one side, then there is an even number on the other side."

Everyone immediately sees that you have to turn over the E, but many people also say you need to turn over the 4. They seem

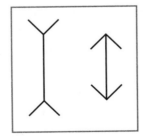

FIGURE 2.2. *The Muller-Lyer illusion.*

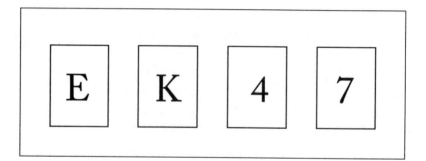

FIGURE 2.3. *The Wason 4-card task.* Which card(s) must you turn over to verify the rule that if a card shows a vowel on one face, then it has an even number on the other?

to be doing simple-minded pattern matching: *There was a vowel and an even number in the question, so let's turn over the vowel and the even number.* Many people resist the explanation of the simple logic behind the task: turning over the 4 and finding a B on the other side would *not* invalidate the rule, whereas turning over the 7 and finding a U would do it, so you need to turn over the E and the 7.

When people are told up front what the answer is and asked to explain why that answer is correct, they can do it. But amazingly, they are just as able to offer an explanation, and just as confident in their reasoning, whether they are told the right answer (E and 7) or the popular but wrong answer (E and 4).[32] Findings such as these led Wason to the conclusion that *judgment and justification are separate processes.* Margolis shared Wason's view, summarizing the state of affairs like this:

> Given the judgments (themselves produced by the non-conscious cognitive machinery in the brain, sometimes correctly, sometimes not so), human beings produce rationales they believe account for their judgments. But the rationales (on this argument) are only ex post rationalizations.[33]

Margolis proposed that there are two very different kinds of cognitive processes at work when we make judgments and solve problems: "seeing-that" and "reasoning-why." "Seeing-that" is the pattern matching that brains have been doing for hundreds of millions of years. Even the simplest animals are wired to respond to certain patterns of input (such as light, or sugar) with specific behaviors (such as turning away from the light, or stopping and eating the sugary food). Animals easily learn new patterns and connect them up to their existing behaviors, which can be reconfigured into new patterns as well (as when an animal trainer teaches an elephant a new trick).

As brains get larger and more complex, animals begin to show more cognitive sophistication—making choices (such as where to forage today, or when to fly south) and judgments (such as whether a subordinate chimpanzee showed properly deferential behavior). But in all cases, the basic psychology is pattern matching. It's the sort of rapid, automatic, and effortless processing that drives our perceptions in the Muller-Lyer illusion. You can't choose whether or not to see the illusion; you're just "seeing-that" one line is longer than the other. Margolis also called this kind of thinking "intuitive."

"Reasoning-why," in contrast, is the process "by which we describe how we think we reached a judgment, or how we think another person could reach that judgment."[34] "Reasoning-why" can occur only for creatures that have language and a need to explain themselves to other creatures. "Reasoning-why" is not automatic; it's conscious, it sometimes *feels* like work, and it's easily disrupted by cognitive load. Kohlberg had convinced moral psychologists to study "reasoning-why" and to neglect "seeing-that."[35]

Margolis's ideas were a perfect fit with everything I had seen in my studies: rapid intuitive judgment ("That's just wrong!") followed by slow and sometimes tortuous justifications ("Well, their two methods of birth control might fail, and the kids they produce might be deformed"). The intuition launched the reasoning, but the intuition did not depend on the success or failure of the reasoning. My harmless-taboo stories were like Muller-Lyer illusions: they still felt wrong, even after you had measured the amount of harm involved and agreed that the stories were harmless.

Margolis's theory worked just as well for the easier dilemmas. In the Heinz scenario, most people intuitively "see that" Heinz should steal the drug (his wife's life is at stake), but in this case it's easy to find reasons. Kohlberg had constructed the dilemma to make good reasons available on both sides, so nobody gets dumbfounded.

The roach juice and soul-selling dilemmas instantly make people "see that" they want to refuse, but they don't feel much conversational pressure to offer reasons. Not wanting to drink roach-tainted juice isn't a moral judgment, it's a personal preference. Saying "Because I don't want to" is a perfectly acceptable justification for one's subjective preferences. Yet moral judgments are *not* subjective statements; they are claims that somebody did something wrong. I can't call for the community to punish you simply because I don't like what you're doing. I have to point to something outside of my own preferences, and that pointing is our moral reasoning. We do moral reasoning not to reconstruct the actual reasons why *we ourselves* came to a judgment; we reason to find the best possible reasons why *somebody else ought to join us* in our judgment.[36]

THE RIDER AND THE ELEPHANT

It took me years to appreciate fully the implications of Margolis's ideas. Part of the problem was that my thinking was entrenched in a prevalent but useless dichotomy between cognition and emotion. After failing repeatedly to get cognition to act independently of emotion, I began to realize that the dichotomy made no sense. Cognition just refers to information processing, which includes higher cognition (such as conscious reasoning) as well as lower cognition (such as visual perception and memory retrieval).[37]

Emotion is a bit harder to define. Emotions were long thought to be dumb and visceral, but beginning in the 1980s, scientists increasingly recognized that emotions were filled with cognition. Emotions occur in steps, the first of which is to appraise something that just happened based on whether it advanced or hindered your goals.[38] These appraisals are a kind of information processing; they are cognitions. When an appraisal program detects particular input patterns, it launches a set of changes in your brain that prepare you to respond appropriately. For example, if you hear someone running up behind you on a dark street, your fear system detects a threat and triggers your sympathetic nervous system, firing up the fight-or-flight response, cranking up your heart rate, and widening your pupils to help you take in more information.

Emotions are not dumb. Damasio's patients made terrible decisions because they were deprived of emotional input into their decision making. *Emotions are a kind of information processing.*[39] Contrasting emotion with cognition is therefore as pointless as contrasting rain with weather, or cars with vehicles.

Margolis helped me ditch the emotion-cognition contrast. His work helped me see that *moral judgment is a cognitive process,* as are all forms of judgment. The crucial distinction is really between *two different kinds of cognition:* intuition and reasoning. Moral emotions are one type of moral intuition, but most moral intuitions are more subtle; they don't rise to the level of emotions.[40] The next time you read a newspaper or drive a car, notice the many tiny flashes of condemnation that flit through your consciousness. Is each such flash an emotion? Or ask yourself whether it is better to save the lives of five strangers or one (assuming all else is equal). Do you need an emotion to tell you to go for the five? Do you need reasoning? No, you just see, instantly, that five is better than one. *Intuition* is the best word to describe the dozens or hundreds of rapid, effortless moral judgments and decisions that we all make every day. Only a few of these intuitions come to us embedded in full-blown emotions.

In *The Happiness Hypothesis,* I called these two kinds of cognition the rider (controlled processes, including "reasoning-why") and the elephant (automatic processes, including emotion, intuition, and all forms of "seeing-that").[41] I chose an elephant rather than a horse because elephants are so much bigger—and smarter—than horses. Automatic processes run the human mind, just as they have been running animal minds for 500 million years, so they're very good at what they do, like software that has been improved through thousands of product cycles. When human beings evolved the capacity for language and reasoning at some point in the last million years, the brain did not rewire itself to hand over the reins to a new and inexperienced charioteer. Rather, the rider (language-based reasoning) evolved because it did something useful for the elephant.

The rider can do several useful things. It can see further into the future (because we can examine alternative scenarios in our heads) and therefore it can help the elephant make better decisions in the present. It can learn new skills and master new technologies, which can be deployed to help the elephant reach its goals and sidestep disasters. And, most important, the rider acts as the spokesman for the elephant, even though it doesn't necessarily know what the elephant is really thinking. The rider is skilled at fabricating post hoc explanations for whatever the elephant has just done, and it is good at finding reasons to justify whatever the elephant wants to do next. Once human beings developed language and began to use it to gossip about each other, it became extremely valuable for elephants to carry around on their backs a full-time public relations firm.[42]

I didn't have the rider and elephant metaphor back in the 1990s, but once I stopped thinking about emotion versus cognition and started thinking about intuition versus reasoning, everything fell into place. I took my old Jeffersonian dual-process model (figure 2.1) and made two big changes. First, I weakened the arrow from reasoning to judgment, demoting it to a dotted line (link 5 in figure 2.4). The dots mean that independently reasoned judgment is possible in theory but rare in practice. This simple change converted the model into a Humean model in which intuition (rather than passion) is the main cause of moral judgment (link 1), and then reasoning typically follows that judgment (link 2) to construct post hoc justifications. Reason is the servant of the intuitions. The rider was put there in the first place to serve the elephant.

I also wanted to capture the *social* nature of moral judgment. Moral talk serves a variety of strategic purposes such as managing your reputation, building alliances, and recruiting bystanders to support your side in the disputes that are so common in daily life. I wanted to go beyond the first judgments people make when they hear some juicy gossip or witness some surprising event. I wanted my model to capture the give-and-take, the round after round of discussion and argumentation that sometimes leads people to change their minds.

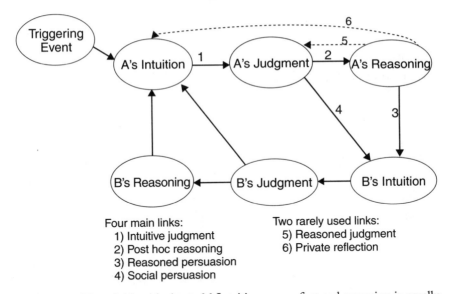

Four main links:
1) Intuitive judgment
2) Post hoc reasoning
3) Reasoned persuasion
4) Social persuasion

Two rarely used links:
5) Reasoned judgment
6) Private reflection

FIGURE 2.4. *The social intuitionist model.* Intuitions come first and reasoning is usually produced after a judgment is made, in order to influence other people. But as a discussion progresses, the reasons given by other people sometimes change our intuitions and judgments. (From Haidt 2001, p. 815. Published by the American Psychological Association. Adapted with permission.)

We make our first judgments rapidly, and we are dreadful at seeking out evidence that might disconfirm those initial judgments.[43] Yet friends can do for us what we cannot do for ourselves: they can challenge us, giving us reasons and arguments (link 3) that sometimes trigger new intuitions, thereby making it possible for us to change our minds. We occasionally do this when mulling a problem by ourselves, suddenly seeing things in a new light or from a new perspective (to use two visual metaphors). Link 6 in the model represents this process of private reflection. The line is dotted because this process doesn't seem to happen very often.[44] For most of us, it's not every day or even every month that we change our mind about a moral issue without any prompting from anyone else.

Far more common than such private mind changing is social influence. Other people influence us constantly just by revealing that they like or dislike somebody. That form of influence is link 4, the social persuasion link. Many of us believe that we follow an inner moral compass, but the history of social psychology richly demonstrates that other people exert a powerful force, able to make cruelty seem acceptable[45] and altruism seem embarrassing,[46] without giving us any reasons or arguments.

Because of these two changes I called my theory the "social intuitionist model of moral judgment," and I published it in 2001 in an article titled "The Emotional Dog and Its Rational Tail."[47] In hindsight I wish I'd called the dog "intuitive" because psychologists who are still entrenched in the emotion-versus-cognition dichotomy often assume from the title that I'm saying that morality is always driven by emotion. Then they prove that cognition matters, and think they have found evidence against intuitionism.[48] But intuitions (including emotional responses) are a kind of cognition. They're just not a kind of reasoning.

HOW TO WIN AN ARGUMENT

The social intuitionist model offers an explanation of why moral and political arguments are so frustrating: *because moral reasons are the tail wagged by the intuitive dog.* A dog's tail wags to communicate. You can't make a dog happy by forcibly wagging its tail. And you can't change people's minds by utterly refuting their arguments. Hume diagnosed the problem long ago:

> And as reasoning is not the source, whence either disputant derives his tenets; it is in vain to expect, that any logic, which speaks not to the affections, will ever engage him to embrace sounder principles.[49]

If you want to change people's minds, you've got to talk to their elephants. You've got to use links 3 and 4 of the social intuitionist model to elicit new intuitions, not new rationales.

Dale Carnegie was one of the greatest elephant-whisperers of all time. In his classic book *How to Win Friends and Influence People,* Carnegie repeatedly urged readers to avoid direct confrontations. Instead he advised people to "begin in a friendly way," to "smile," to "be a good listener," and to "never say 'you're wrong.' " The persuader's goal should be to convey respect, warmth, and an openness to dialogue before stating one's own case. Carnegie was urging readers to use link 4, the social persuasion link, to prepare the ground before attempting to use link 3, the reasoned persuasion link.

From my description of Carnegie so far, you might think his techniques are superficial and manipulative, appropriate only for salespeople. But Carnegie was in fact a brilliant moral psychologist who grasped one of the deepest truths about conflict. He used a quotation from Henry Ford to express it: "If there is any one secret of success it lies in the ability to get the other person's point of view and see things from their angle as well as your own."[50]

It's such an obvious point, yet few of us apply it in moral and political arguments because our righteous minds so readily shift into combat mode. The rider and the elephant work together smoothly to fend off attacks and lob rhetorical grenades of our own. The performance may impress our friends and show allies that we are committed members of the team, but no matter how good our logic, it's not going to change the minds of our opponents if they are in combat mode too. If you really want to change someone's mind on a moral or political matter, you'll need to see things from that person's angle as well as your own. And if you do truly see it the other person's way—deeply and intuitively—you might even find your own mind opening in response. Empathy is an antidote to righteousness, although it's very difficult to empathize across a moral divide.

IN SUM

People reason and people have moral intuitions (including moral emotions), but what is the relationship among these processes? Plato believed that reason could and should be the master; Jefferson believed that the two processes were equal partners (head and heart) ruling a divided empire; Hume believed that reason was (and was only fit to be) the servant of the passions. In this chapter I tried to show that Hume was right:

- The mind is divided into parts, like a rider (controlled processes) on an elephant (automatic processes). The rider evolved to serve the elephant.

- You can see the rider serving the elephant when people are morally dumbfounded. They have strong gut feelings about what is right and wrong, and they struggle to construct post hoc justifications for those feelings. Even when the servant (reasoning) comes back empty-handed, the master (intuition) doesn't change his judgment.
- The social intuitionist model starts with Hume's model and makes it more social. Moral reasoning is part of our lifelong struggle to win friends and influence people. That's why I say that "intuitions come first, strategic reasoning second." You'll misunderstand moral reasoning if you think about it as something people do by themselves in order to figure out the truth.
- Therefore, if you want to change someone's mind about a moral or political issue, *talk to the elephant first.* If you ask people to believe something that violates their intuitions, they will devote their efforts to finding an escape hatch—a reason to doubt your argument or conclusion. They will almost always succeed.

I have tried to use intuitionism while writing this book. My goal is to change the way a diverse group of readers—liberal and conservative, secular and religious—think about morality, politics, religion, and each other. I knew that I had to take things slowly and address myself more to elephants than to riders. I couldn't just lay out the theory in chapter 1 and then ask readers to reserve judgment until I had presented all of the supporting evidence. Rather, I decided to weave together the history of moral psychology and my own personal story to create a sense of movement from rationalism to intuitionism. I threw in historical anecdotes, quotations from the ancients, and praise of a few visionaries. I set up metaphors (such as the rider and the elephant) that will recur throughout the book. I did these things in order to "tune up" your intuitions about moral psychology. If I have failed and you have a visceral dislike of intuitionism or of me, then no amount of evidence I could present will convince you that intuitionism is correct. But if you now feel an intuitive sense that intuitionism *might* be true, then let's keep going. In the next two chapters I'll address myself more to riders than to elephants.

THREE

Elephants Rule

On February 3, 2007, shortly before lunch, I discovered that I was a chronic liar. I was at home, writing a review article on moral psychology, when my wife, Jayne, walked by my desk. In passing, she asked me not to leave dirty dishes on the counter where she prepared our baby's food. Her request was polite but its tone added a postscript: "As I have asked you a hundred times before."

My mouth started moving before hers had stopped. Words came out. Those words linked themselves up to say something about the baby having woken up at the same time that our elderly dog barked to ask for a walk and I'm sorry but I just put my breakfast dishes down wherever I could. In my family, caring for a hungry baby and an incontinent dog is a surefire excuse, so I was acquitted.

Jayne left the room and I continued working. I was writing about the three basic principles of moral psychology.[1] The first principle is *Intuitions come first, strategic reasoning second.* That's a six-word summary of the social intuitionist model.[2] To illustrate the principle, I described a study I did with Thalia Wheatley, who is now a professor at Dartmouth College.[3] Back when Thalia was a grad student at UVA, she had learned how to hypnotize people, and she came up with a clever way to test the social intuitionist model. Thalia hypnotized people to feel a flash of disgust whenever they saw a certain word (*take* for half of the subjects; *often* for the others).[4] While they were still in a trance Thalia instructed them that they would not be able to remember anything she had told them, and then she brought them out of the trance.

Once they were fully awake, we asked them to fill out a questionnaire packet in which they had to judge six short stories about moral violations. For each story, half of the subjects read a version that had their hypnotic code word embedded in it. For example, one story was about a congressman who claims to fight corruption, yet "takes bribes from the tobacco lobby." The other subjects read a version that was identical except for a few words (the congressman is "often bribed by the tobacco lobby"). On average, subjects judged each of the six stories to be more disgusting and morally wrong when their code word was embedded in the story. That supported the social intuitionist model. By giving people a little artificial flash of negativity while they were reading the story, without giving them any new information, we made their moral judgments more severe.

The real surprise, though, came with a seventh story we tacked on almost as an afterthought, a story that contained no moral violation of any kind. It was about a student council president named Dan who is in charge of scheduling discussions between students and faculty. Half of our subjects read that Dan "tries to take topics that appeal to both professors and students in order to stimulate discussion." The other half read the same story except that Dan "often picks topics" that appeal to professors and students. We added this story to demonstrate that there is a limit to the power of intuition. We predicted that subjects who felt a flash of disgust while reading this story would *have* to overrule their gut feelings. To condemn Dan would be bizarre.

Most of our subjects did indeed say that Dan's actions were fine. But a third of the subjects who had found their code word in the story still followed their gut feelings and condemned Dan. They said that what he did was wrong, sometimes very wrong. Fortunately, we had asked everyone to write a sentence or two explaining their judgments, and we found gems such as "Dan is a popularity-seeking snob" and "I don't know, it just seems like he's up to something." These subjects made up absurd reasons to justify judgments that they had made on the basis of gut feelings—feelings Thalia had implanted with hypnosis.

So there I was at my desk, writing about how people automatically fabricate justifications of their gut feelings, when suddenly I realized that I had just done the same thing with my wife. I disliked being criticized, and I had felt a flash of negativity by the time Jayne had gotten to her third word ("*Can you not . . .*"). Even before I knew why she was criticizing me, I knew I disagreed with her (because intuitions come first). The instant I knew the content of the criticism ("*. . . leave dirty dishes on the . . .*"), my inner lawyer went to work searching for an excuse (strategic reasoning second). It's true that I had eaten breakfast, given Max his first bottle, and let Andy out for his first walk, but these events had all happened at separate times. Only when my wife criticized me did I merge them into a composite image of a harried father with too few hands, and I created this fabrication by the time she had completed her one-sentence criticism ("*. . . counter where I make baby food?*"). I then lied so quickly and convincingly that my wife and I both believed me.

I had long teased my wife for altering stories to make them more dramatic when she told them to friends, but it took twenty years of studying moral psychology to see that I altered my stories too. I finally understood—not just cerebrally but intuitively and with an open heart—the admonitions of sages from so many eras and cultures warning us about self-righteousness. I've already quoted Jesus (on seeing "the speck in your neighbor's eye"). Here's the same idea from Buddha:

> It is easy to see the faults of others, but difficult to see one's own faults. One shows the faults of others like chaff winnowed in the wind, but one conceals one's own faults as a cunning gambler conceals his dice.[5]

Jesus and Buddha were right, and in this chapter and the next one I'll show you how our automatic self-righteousness works. It begins with rapid and compelling intuitions (that's link 1 in the social intu-itionist model), and it continues on with post hoc reasoning, done for socially strategic purposes (links 2 and 3). Here are six major research findings that collectively illustrate the first half of the first principle: *Intuitions Come First*. (In the next chapter I'll give evidence for the second half—*Strategic Reasoning Second*). Elephants rule, although they are sometimes open to persuasion by riders.

1. BRAINS EVALUATE INSTANTLY AND CONSTANTLY

Brains evaluate everything in terms of potential threat or benefit to the self, and then adjust behavior to get more of the good stuff and less of the bad.[6] Animal brains make such appraisals thousands of times a day with no need for conscious reasoning, all in order to opti-mize the brain's answer to the fundamental question of animal life: Approach or avoid?

In the 1890s Wilhelm Wundt, the founder of experimental psy-chology, formulated the doctrine of "affective primacy."[7] *Affect* refers to small flashes of positive or negative feeling that prepare us to approach or avoid something. Every emotion (such as happiness or disgust) includes an affective reaction, but most of our affective reac-tions are too fleeting to be called emotions (for example, the subtle feelings you get just from reading the words *happiness* and *disgust*).

Wundt said that affective reactions are so tightly integrated with perception that we find ourselves liking or disliking something the instant we notice it, sometimes even before we know what it is.[8] These flashes occur so rapidly that they precede all other thoughts about the thing we're looking at. You can feel affective primacy in action the next time you run into someone you haven't seen in many years. You'll usually know within a second or two whether you liked or disliked the person, but it can take much longer to remember who the person is or how you know each other.

In 1980 social psychologist Robert Zajonc (the name rhymes with "science") revived Wundt's long-forgotten notion of affective pri-macy. Zajonc was fed up with the common view among psychologists at the time that people are cool, rational information processors who first perceive and categorize objects and then react to them. He did a number of ingenious experiments that asked people to rate arbitrary things such as Japanese pictograms, words in a made-up language, and geometric shapes. It may seem odd to ask people to rate how much they like foreign words and meaningless squiggles, but people can do it because almost *everything* we look at triggers a tiny flash of affect. More important, Zajonc was able to make people like any word or image more just by showing it to them several times.[9] The brain tags familiar things as good things. Zajonc called this the "mere exposure effect," and it is a basic principle of advertising.

In a landmark article, Zajonc urged psychologists to use a dual-process model in which affect or "feeling" is the first process.[10] It has primacy both because it happens first (it is part of perception and is therefore extremely fast) and because it is more powerful (it is closely linked to motivation, and therefore it strongly influences behavior). The second process—thinking—is an evolutionarily newer ability, rooted in language and not closely related to motivation. In other words, thinking is the rider; affect is the elephant. The thinking system is not equipped to lead—it simply doesn't have the power to make things happen—but it can be a useful advisor.

Zajonc said that thinking could work independently of feeling in theory, but in practice affective reactions are so fast and compelling that they act like blinders on a horse: they "reduce the universe of alternatives" available to later thinking.[11] The rider is an attentive servant, always trying to anticipate the elephant's next move. If the elephant leans even slightly to the left, as though preparing to take a step, the rider looks to the left and starts preparing to assist the elephant on its imminent leftward journey. The rider loses interest in everything off to the right.

2. SOCIAL AND POLITICAL JUDGMENTS ARE PARTICULARLY INTUITIVE

Here are four pairs of words. Your job is to look only at the second word in each pair and then categorize it as good or bad:

flower–happiness
hate–sunshine
love–cancer
cockroach–lonely

It's absurdly easy, but imagine if I asked you to do it on a computer, where I can flash the first word in each pair for 250 milliseconds (a quarter of a second, just long enough to read it) and then I immediately display the second word. In that case we'd find that it takes you longer to make your value judgment for *sunshine* and *cancer* than for *happiness* and *lonely*.

This effect is called "affective priming" because the first word triggers a flash of affect that primes the mind to go one way or the other.[12] It's like getting the elephant to lean slightly to the right or the left, in anticipation of walking to the right or the left. The flash kicks in within 200 milliseconds, and it lasts for about a second beyond that if there's no other jolt to back it up.[13] If you see the second word within that brief window of time, and if the second word has the same valence, then you'll be able to respond extra quickly because your mind is already leaning that way. But if the first word primes your mind for a negative evaluation (*hate*) and I then show you a positive word (*sunshine*), it'll take you about 250 milliseconds longer to respond because you have to undo the lean toward negativity.

So far this is just a confirmation of Zajonc's theory about the speed and ubiquity of affect, but a big payoff came when social psychologists began using *social groups* as primes. Would it affect your response speed if I used photographs of black people and white people as the primes? As long as you're not prejudiced, it won't affect your reaction times. But if you do prejudge people implicitly (i.e., automatically and unconsciously), then those prejudgments include affective flashes, and those flashes will change your reaction times.

The most widely used measure of these implicit attitudes is the Implicit Association Test (IAT), developed by Tony Greenwald, Mahzarin Banaji, and my UVA colleague Brian Nosek.[14] You can take the IAT yourself at ProjectImplicit.org. But be forewarned: it can be disturbing. You can actually feel yourself moving more slowly when you are asked to associate good things with the faces of one race rather than another. You can watch as your implicit attitude contradicts your explicit values. Most people turn out to have negative implicit associations with many social groups, such as black people, immigrants, obese people, and the elderly.

And if the elephant tends to lean away from groups such as the elderly (whom few would condemn morally), then we should certainly expect some leaning (prejudging) when people think about their political enemies. To look for such effects, my UVA colleague Jamie Morris measured the brain waves of liberals and conservatives as they read politically loaded words.[15] He replaced the words *flower* and *hate* in the above example with words such as *Clinton, Bush, flag, taxes, welfare,* and *pro-life*. When partisans read these words, followed immediately by words that everyone agrees are good (*sunshine*) or bad (*cancer*), their brains sometimes revealed a conflict. *Pro-life* and *sunshine* were affectively incongruous for liberals, just as *Clinton* and *sunshine* were for conservatives. The words *pro* and *life* are both positive on their own, but part of what it means to be a partisan is that you have acquired the right set of intuitive reactions to hundreds of words and phrases. Your elephant knows which way to lean in response to terms such as *pro-life*, and as your elephant sways back and forth throughout the day, you find yourself liking and trusting the people around you who sway in sync with you.

The intuitive nature of political judgments is even more striking in the work of Alex Todorov, at Princeton. Todorov studies how we form impressions of people. When he began his work, there was already a lot of research showing that we judge attractive people to be smarter and more virtuous, and we are more likely to give a pretty face the benefit of any doubt.[16] Juries are more likely to acquit attractive defendants, and when beautiful people are convicted, judges give them lighter sentences, on average.[17] That's normal affective primacy making everyone lean toward the defendant, which tips off their riders to interpret the evidence in a way that will support the elephant's desire to acquit.

But Todorov found that there was more going on than just attractiveness. He collected photographs of the winners and runners-up in hundreds of elections for the U.S. Senate and the House of Representatives. He showed people the pairs of photographs from each contest with no information about political party, and he asked them to pick which person seemed more competent. He found that the candidate that people judged more competent was the one who actually won the race about two-thirds of the time.[18] People's snap judgments of the candidates' physical attractiveness and overall likability were not as good predictors of victory, so these competence judgments were not just based on an overall feeling of positivity. We can have multiple intuitions arising simultaneously, each one processing a different kind of information.

And strangely, when Todorov forced people to make their competence judgments after flashing the pair of pictures on the screen for just *a tenth of a second*—not long enough to let their eyes fixate on each image—their snap judgments of competence predicted the real outcomes just as well.[19] Whatever the brain is doing, it's doing it instantly, just like when you look at the Muller-Lyer illusion.

The bottom line is that human minds, like animal minds, are constantly reacting intuitively to everything they perceive, and basing their responses on those reactions. Within the first second of seeing, hearing, or meeting another person, the elephant has already begun to lean toward or away, and that lean influences what you think and do next. Intuitions come first.[20]

3. OUR BODIES GUIDE OUR JUDGMENTS

One way to reach the elephant is through its trunk. The olfactory nerve carries signals about odors to the insular cortex (the insula), a region along the bottom surface of the frontal part of the brain. This part of the brain used to be known as the "gustatory cortex" because in all mammals it processes information from the nose and the tongue. It helps guide the animal toward the right foods and away from the wrong ones. But in humans, this ancient food-processing center has taken on new duties, and it now guides our taste in people. It gets more active when we see something morally fishy, particularly something disgusting, as well as garden-variety unfairness.[21] If we had some sort of tiny electrode that could be threaded up through people's noses and into their insulas, we could then control their elephants, making them steer away from whatever they were viewing at the moment when we pressed the button. We've got such an electrode. It's called fart spray.

Alex Jordan, a grad student at Stanford, came up with the idea of asking people to make moral judgments while he secretly tripped their disgust alarms. He stood at a pedestrian intersection on the Stanford campus and asked passersby to fill out a short survey. It asked people to make judgments about four controversial issues, such as marriage between first cousins, or a film studio's decision to release a documentary with a director who had tricked some people into being interviewed.

Alex stood right next to a trash can he had emptied. Before he recruited each subject, he put a new plastic liner into the metal can. Before half of the people walked up (and before they could see him), he sprayed the fart spray twice into the bag, which "perfumed" the whole intersection for a few minutes. Before other recruitments, he left the empty bag unsprayed.

Sure enough, people made harsher judgments when they were breathing in foul air.[22] Other researchers have found the same effect by asking subjects to fill out questionnaires after drinking bitter versus sweet drinks.[23] As my UVA colleague Jerry Clore puts it, we use "affect as information."[24] When we're trying to decide what we think about something, we look inward, at how we're feeling. If I'm feeling good, I must like it, and if I'm feeling anything unpleasant, that must mean I don't like it.

You don't even need to trigger feelings of disgust to get these effects. Simply washing your hands will do it. Chenbo Zhong at the University of Toronto has shown that subjects who are asked to wash their hands with soap before filling out questionnaires become more moralistic about issues related to moral purity (such as pornography and drug use).[25] Once you're clean, you want to keep dirty things far away.

Zhong has also shown the reverse process: immorality makes people want to get clean. People who are asked to recall their own moral transgressions, or merely to copy by hand an account of someone else's moral transgression, find themselves thinking about cleanliness more often, and wanting more strongly to cleanse themselves.[26] They are more likely to select hand wipes and other cleaning products when given a choice of consumer products to take home with them after the experiment. Zhong calls this the Macbeth effect, named for Lady Macbeth's obsession with water and cleansing after she goads her husband into murdering King Duncan. (She goes from "A little water clears us of this deed" to "Out, damn'd spot! out, I say!")

In other words, there's a two-way street between our bodies and our righteous minds. Immorality makes us feel physically dirty, and cleansing ourselves can sometimes make us more concerned about guarding our moral purity. In one of the most bizarre demonstrations of this effect, Eric Helzer and David Pizarro asked students at Cornell University to fill out surveys about their political attitudes while standing near (or far from) a hand sanitizer dispenser. Those told to stand near the sanitizer became temporarily more conservative.[27]

Moral judgment is not a purely cerebral affair in which we weigh concerns about harm, rights, and justice. It's a kind of rapid, automatic process more akin to the judgments animals make as they move through the world, feeling themselves drawn toward or away from various things. Moral judgment is mostly done by the elephant.

4. PSYCHOPATHS REASON BUT DON'T FEEL

Roughly one in a hundred men (and many fewer women) are psychopaths. Most are not violent, but the ones who are commit nearly half of the most serious crimes, such as serial murder, serial rape, and the killing of police officers.[28] Robert Hare, a leading researcher, defines psychopathy by two sets of features. There's the unusual stuff that psychopaths *do*—impulsive antisocial behavior, beginning in child-hood—and there are the moral emotions that psychopaths *lack*. They feel no compassion, guilt, shame, or even embarrassment, which makes it easy for them to lie, and to hurt family, friends, and animals.

Psychopaths do have *some* emotions. When Hare asked one man if he ever felt his heart pound or stomach churn, he responded: "Of course! I'm not a robot. I really get pumped up when I have sex or when I get into a fight."[29] But psychopaths don't show emotions that indicate that they care about other people. Psychopaths seem to live in a world of objects, some of which happen to walk around on two legs. One psychopath told Hare about a murder he committed while burglarizing an elderly man's home:

> I was rummaging around when this old geezer comes down stairs and ... uh ... he starts yelling and hav-ing a fucking fit ... so I pop him one in the, uh, head and he still doesn't shut up. So I give him a chop to the throat and he ... like ... staggers back and falls on the floor. He's gurgling and making sounds like a stuck pig! [laughs] and he's really getting on my fucking nerves so I ... uh ... boot him a few times in the head. That shut him up ... I'm pretty tired by now so I grab a few beers from the fridge and turn on the TV and fall asleep. The cops woke me up [laughs].[30]

The ability to reason combined with a lack of moral emotions is dangerous. Psychopaths learn to say whatever gets them what they want. The serial killer Ted Bundy, for example, was a psychology major in college, where he volunteered on a crisis hotline. On those phone calls he learned how to speak to women and gain their trust. Then he raped, mutilated, and murdered at least thirty young women before being captured in 1978.

Psychopathy does not appear to be caused by poor mothering or early trauma, or to have any other nurture-based explanation. It's a genetically heritable condition[31] that creates brains that are unmoved by the needs, suffering, or dignity of others.[32] The elephant doesn't respond with the slightest lean to the gravest injustice. The rider is perfectly normal—he does strategic reasoning quite well. But the rider's job is to serve the elephant, not to act as a moral compass.

5. BABIES FEEL BUT DON'T REASON

Psychologists used to assume that infant minds were blank slates. The world babies enter is "one great blooming, buzzing confusion," as William James put it,[33] and they spend the next few years trying to make sense of it all. But when developmental psychologists invented ways to look into infant minds, they found a great deal of writing already on that slate.

The trick was to see what surprises babies. Infants as young as two months old will look longer at an event that surprises them than at an event they were expecting. If everything is a buzzing confusion, then everything should be equally surprising. But if the infant's mind comes already wired to interpret events in certain ways, then infants can be surprised when the world violates their expectations.

Using this trick, psychologists discovered that infants are born with some knowledge of physics and mechanics: they expect that objects will move according to Newton's laws of motion, and they get startled when psychologists show them scenes that should be physically impossible (such as a toy car seeming to pass through a solid object). Psychologists know this because infants stare longer at impossible scenes than at similar but less magical scenes (seeing the toy car pass *just behind* the solid object).[34] Babies seem to have some innate ability to process events in their physical world—the world of objects.

But when psychologists dug deeper, they found that infants come equipped with innate abilities to understand their *social* world as well. They understand things like harming and helping.[35] Yale psychologists Kiley Hamlin, Karen Wynn, and Paul Bloom put on puppet shows for six- and ten-month-old infants in which a "climber" (a wooden shape with eyes glued to it) struggled to climb up a hill. Sometimes a second puppet came along and helped the climber from below. Other times, a different puppet appeared at the top of the hill and repeatedly bashed the climber down the slope.

A few minutes later, the infants saw a new puppet show. This time the climber looked back and forth between the helper puppet and the hinderer puppet, and then it decided to cozy up to the hinderer. To the infants, that was the social equivalent of seeing a car pass through a solid box; it made no sense, and the infants stared longer than when the climber decided to cozy up to the helper.[36]

At the end of the experiment, the helper and hinderer puppets were placed on a tray in front of the infants. The infants were much more likely to reach out for the helper. If the infants weren't parsing their social world, they wouldn't have cared which puppet they picked up. But they clearly wanted the nice puppet. The researchers concluded that "the capacity to evaluate individuals on the basis of their social interactions is universal and unlearned."[37]

It makes sense that infants can easily learn who is nice to *them*. Puppies can do that too. But these findings suggest that by six months of age, infants are watching how people behave toward *other people*, and they are developing a preference for those who are nice rather than those who are mean. In other words, the elephant begins making something like moral judgments during infancy, long before language and reasoning arrive.

Looking at the discoveries from infants and psychopaths at the same time, it's clear that moral intuitions emerge very early and are necessary for moral development.[38] The ability to reason emerges much later, and when moral reasoning is not accompanied by moral intuition, the results are ugly.

6. AFFECTIVE REACTIONS ARE IN THE RIGHT PLACE AT THE RIGHT TIME IN THE BRAIN

Damasio's studies of brain-damaged patients show that the emotional areas of the brain are the right *places* to be looking for the foundations of morality, because losing them interferes with moral competence. The case would be even stronger if these areas were active at the right *times*. Do they become more active just before someone makes a moral judgment or decision?

In 1999, Joshua Greene, who was then a graduate student in philosophy at Princeton, teamed up with leading neuroscientist Jonathan Cohen to see what actually happens in the brain as people make moral judgments. He studied moral dilemmas in which two major ethical principles seem to push against each other. For example, you've probably heard of the famous "trolley dilemma,"[39] in which the only way you can stop a runaway trolley from killing five people is by pushing one person off a bridge onto the track below.

Philosophers have long disagreed about whether it's acceptable to harm one person in order to help or save several people. Utilitarianism is the philosophical school that says you should always aim to bring about the greatest total good, even if a few people get hurt along the way, so if there's really no other way to save those five lives, go ahead and push. Other philosophers believe that we have duties to respect the rights of individuals, and we must not harm people in our pursuit of other goals, even moral goals such as saving lives. This view is known as deontology (from the Greek root that gives us our word *duty*). Deontologists talk about high moral principles derived and justified by careful reasoning; they would never agree that these principles are merely post hoc rationalizations of gut feelings. But Greene had a hunch that gut feelings were what often drove people to make deontological judgments, whereas utilitarian judgments were more cool and calculating.

To test his hunch, Greene wrote twenty stories that, like the trolley story, involved direct personal harm, usually done for a good reason. For example, should you throw an injured person out of a lifeboat to keep the boat from sinking and drowning the other passengers? All of these stories were written to produce a strong negative affective flash.

Greene also wrote twenty stories involving *impersonal* harm, such as a version of the trolley dilemma in which you save the five people by flipping a switch that diverts the trolley onto a side track, where it will kill just one person. It's the same objective trade-off of one life for five, so some philosophers say that the two cases are morally equivalent, but from an intuitionist perspective, there's a world of difference.[40] Without that initial flash of horror (that bare-handed push), the subject is free to examine both options and choose the one that saves the most lives.

Greene brought eighteen subjects into an fMRI scanner and presented each of his stories on the screen, one at a time. Each person had to press one of two buttons to indicate whether or not it was appropriate for a person to take the course of action described—for example, to push the man or throw the switch.

The results were clear and compelling. When people read stories involving personal harm, they showed greater activity in several regions of the brain related to emotional processing. Across many stories, the relative strength of these emotional reactions predicted the average moral judgment.

Greene published this now famous study in 2001 in the journal *Science*.[41] Since then, many other labs have put people into fMRI scanners and asked them to look at photographs about moral violations, make charitable donations, assign punishments for crimes, or play games with cheaters and cooperators.[42] With few exceptions, the results tell a consistent story: the areas of the brain involved in emotional processing activate almost immediately, and high activity in these areas correlates with the kinds of moral judgments or decisions that people ultimately make.[43]

In an article titled "The Secret Joke of Kant's Soul," Greene summed up what he and many others had found.[44] Greene did not know what E. O. Wilson had said about philosophers consulting their "emotive centers" when he wrote the article, but his conclusion was the same as Wilson's:

> We have strong feelings that tell us in clear and certain
> terms that some things simply cannot be done and that
> other things simply must be done. But it's not obvious
> how to make sense of these feelings, and so we, with the
> help of some especially creative philosophers, make up a
> rationally appealing story [about rights].

This is a stunning example of consilience. Wilson had prophesied
in 1975 that ethics would soon be "biologicized" and refounded as the
interpretation of the activity of the "emotive centers" of the brain.
When he made that prophecy he was going against the dominant
views of his time. Psychologists such as Kohlberg said that the action
in ethics was in reasoning, not emotion. And the political climate was
harsh for people such as Wilson who dared to suggest that evolutionary thinking was a valid way to examine human behavior.

Yet in the thirty-three years between the Wilson and Greene
quotes, everything changed. Scientists in many fields began recognizing the power and intelligence of automatic processes, including
emotion.[45] Evolutionary psychology became respectable, not in all
academic departments but at least among the interdisciplinary community of scholars that now studies morality.[46] In the last few years,
the "new synthesis" that Wilson predicted back in 1975 has arrived.

ELEPHANTS ARE SOMETIMES OPEN TO REASON

I have argued that the Humean model (reason is a servant) fits the
facts better than the Platonic model (reason could and should rule) or
the Jeffersonian model (head and heart are co-emperors). But when
Hume said that reason is the "slave" of the passions, I think he went
too far.

A slave is never supposed to question his master, but most of us
can think of times when we questioned and revised our first intuitive judgment. The rider-and-elephant metaphor works well here.
The rider evolved to serve the elephant, but it's a dignified partnership, more like a lawyer serving a client than a slave serving a master.

Good lawyers do what they can to help their clients, but they some-times refuse to go along with requests. Perhaps the request is impos-sible (such as finding a reason to condemn Dan, the student council president—at least for most of the people in my hypnosis experi-ment). Perhaps the request is self-destructive (as when the elephant wants a third piece of cake, and the rider refuses to go along and find an excuse). The elephant is far more powerful than the rider, but it is not an absolute dictator.

When does the elephant listen to reason? The main way that we change our minds on moral issues is by interacting with other people. We are terrible at seeking evidence that challenges our own beliefs, but other people do us this favor, just as we are quite good at finding errors in other people's beliefs. When discussions are hostile, the odds of change are slight. The elephant leans away from the opponent, and the rider works frantically to rebut the opponent's charges.

But if there is affection, admiration, or a desire to please the other person, then the elephant leans *toward* that person and the rider tries to find the truth in the other person's arguments. The elephant may not often change its direction in response to objections from its *own* rider, but it is easily steered by the mere presence of friendly elephants (that's the social persuasion link in the social intuitionist model) or by good arguments given to it by the riders of those friendly elephants (that's the reasoned persuasion link).

There are even times when we change our minds on our own, with no help from other people. Sometimes we have conflicting intu-

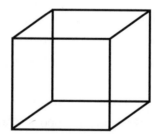

FIGURE 3.1. *A Necker cube, which your visual system can read in two conflicting ways, although not at the same time.* Similarly, some moral dilemmas can be read by your righteous mind in two conflicting ways, but it's hard to feel both intuitions at the same time.

itions about something, as many people do about abortion and other controversial issues. Depending on which victim, which argument, or which friend you are thinking about at a given moment, your judgment may flip back and forth as if you were looking at a Necker cube (figure 3.1).

And finally, it is possible for people simply to reason their way to a moral conclusion that contradicts their initial intuitive judgment, although I believe this process is rare. I know of only one study that has demonstrated this overruling experimentally, and its findings are revealing.

Joe Paxton and Josh Greene asked Harvard students to judge the story about Julie and Mark that I told you in chapter 2.[47] They supplied half of the subjects with a really bad argument to justify consensual incest ("If Julie and Mark make love, then there is more love in the world"). They gave the other half a stronger supporting argument (about how the aversion to incest is really caused by an ancient evolutionary adaptation for avoiding birth defects in a world without contraception, but because Julie and Mark use contraception, that concern is not relevant). You'd think that Harvard students would be more persuaded by a good reason than a bad reason, but it made no difference. The elephant leaned as soon as subjects heard the story. The rider then found a way to rebut the argument (good or bad), and subjects condemned the story equally in both cases.

But Paxton and Greene added a twist to the experiment: some subjects were not allowed to respond right away. The computer forced them to wait for two minutes before they could declare their judgment about Julie and Mark. For these subjects the elephant leaned, but quick affective flashes don't last for two minutes. While the subject was sitting there staring at the screen, the lean diminished and the rider had the time and freedom to think about the supporting argument. People who were forced to reflect on the weak argument still ended up condemning Julie and Mark—slightly more than people who got to answer immediately. But people who were forced to reflect on the good argument for two minutes actually did become substantially more tolerant toward Julie and Mark's decision to have sex. The delay allowed the rider to think for himself and to decide upon a judgment that for many subjects was contrary to the elephant's initial inclination.

In other words, under normal circumstances the rider takes its cue from the elephant, just as a lawyer takes instructions from a client. But if you force the two to sit around and chat for a few minutes, the elephant actually opens up to advice from the rider and arguments from outside sources. Intuitions come first, and under normal circumstances they cause us to engage in socially strategic reasoning, but there are ways to make the relationship more of a two-way street.

IN SUM

The first principle of moral psychology is *Intuitions come first, strategic reasoning second.* In support of this principle, I reviewed six areas of experimental research demonstrating that:

- Brains evaluate instantly and constantly (as Wundt and Zajonc said).
- Social and political judgments depend heavily on quick intuitive flashes (as Todorov and work with the IAT have shown).
- Our bodily states sometimes influence our moral judgments. Bad smells and tastes can make people more judgmental (as can anything that makes people think about purity and cleanliness).
- Psychopaths reason but don't feel (and are severely deficient morally).
- Babies feel but don't reason (and have the beginnings of morality).
- Affective reactions are in the right place at the right time in the brain (as shown by Damasio, Greene, and a wave of more recent studies).

Putting all six together gives us a pretty clear portrait of the rider and the elephant, and the roles they play in our righteous minds.

The elephant (automatic processes) is where most of the action is in moral psychology. Reasoning matters, of course, particularly between people, and particularly when reasons trigger new intuitions. Elephants rule, but they are neither dumb nor despotic. Intuitions can be shaped by reasoning, especially when reasons are embedded in a friendly conversation or an emotionally compelling novel, movie, or news story.[48]

But the bottom line is that when we see or hear about the things other people do, the elephant begins to lean immediately. The rider, who is always trying to anticipate the elephant's next move, begins looking around for a way to support such a move. When my wife reprimanded me for leaving dirty dishes on the counter, I honestly believed that I was innocent. I sent my reasoning forth to defend me and it came back with an effective legal brief in just three seconds. It's only because I happened—at that very moment—to be writing about the nature of moral reasoning that I bothered to look closely at my lawyer's arguments and found them to be historical fictions, based only loosely on real events.

Why do we have this weird mental architecture? As hominid brains tripled in size over the last 5 million years, developing language and a vastly improved ability to reason, why did we evolve an inner lawyer, rather than an inner judge or scientist? Wouldn't it have been most adaptive for our ancestors to figure out the *truth*, the real truth about who did what and why, rather than using all that brainpower just to find evidence in support of what they wanted to believe? That depends on which you think was more important for our ancestors' survival: truth or reputation.

FOUR

Vote for Me (Here's Why)

Suppose the gods were to flip a coin on the day of your birth. Heads, you will be a supremely honest and fair person throughout your life, yet everyone around you will believe you're a scoundrel. Tails, you will cheat and lie whenever it suits your needs, yet everyone around you will believe you're a paragon of virtue. Which outcome would you prefer? Plato's *Republic*—one of the most influential works in the Western canon—is an extended argument that you should pick heads, for your own good. It is better to *be* than to *seem* virtuous.

Early in *The Republic*, Glaucon (Plato's brother) challenges Socrates to prove that justice itself—and not merely the reputation for justice—leads to happiness. Glaucon asks Socrates to imagine what would happen to a man who had the mythical ring of Gyges, a gold ring that makes its wearer invisible at will:

> Now, no one, it seems, would be so incorruptible that he would stay on the path of justice or stay away from other people's property, when he could take whatever he wanted from the marketplace with impunity, go into people's houses and have sex with anyone he wished, kill or release from prison anyone he wished, and do all

the other things that would make him like a god among humans. Rather his actions would be in no way different from those of an unjust person, and both would follow the same path.[1]

Glaucon's thought experiment implies that people are only virtuous because they fear the consequences of getting caught—especially the damage to their reputations. Glaucon says he will not be satisfied until Socrates can prove that a just man with a bad reputation is happier than an unjust man who is widely thought to be good.[2]

It's quite a challenge, and Socrates approaches it with an analogy: Justice in a man is like justice in a city (a *polis*, or city-state). He then argues that a just city is one in which there is harmony, cooperation, and a division of labor between all the castes.[3] Farmers farm, carpenters build, and rulers rule. All contribute to the common good, and all lament when misfortune happens to any of them.

But in an unjust city, one group's gain is another's loss, faction schemes against faction, the powerful exploit the weak, and the city is divided against itself. To make sure the *polis* doesn't descend into the chaos of ruthless self-interest, Socrates says that philosophers must rule, for only they will pursue what is truly good, not just what is good for themselves.[4]

Having gotten his listeners to agree to this picture of a just, harmonious, and happy city, Socrates then argues that exactly these sorts of relationships apply within a just, harmonious, and happy *person*. If philosophers must rule the happy city, then reason must rule the happy person. And if reason rules, then it cares about what is truly good, not just about the appearance of virtue.

Plato (who had been a student of Socrates) had a coherent set of beliefs about human nature, and at the core of these beliefs was his faith in the perfectibility of reason. Reason is our original nature, he thought; it was given to us by the gods and installed in our spherical heads. Passions often corrupt reason, but if we can learn to control those passions, our God-given rationality will shine forth and guide us to do the right thing, not the popular thing.

As is often the case in moral philosophy, arguments about what we *ought* to do depend upon assumptions—often unstated—about human nature and human psychology.[5] And for Plato, the assumed psychology is just plain wrong. In this chapter I'll show that reason is not fit to rule; it was designed to seek justification, not truth. I'll show that Glaucon was right: people care a great deal more about appearance and reputation than about reality. In fact, I'll praise Glaucon for the rest of the book as the guy who got it right—the guy who realized that the most important principle for designing an ethical society is to *make sure that everyone's reputation is on the line all the time*, so that bad behavior will always bring bad consequences.

William James, one of the founders of American psychology, urged psychologists to take a "functionalist" approach to the mind. That means examining things in terms of what they *do*, within a larger system. The function of the heart is to pump blood within the circulatory system, and you can't understand the heart unless you keep that in mind. James applied the same logic to psychology: if you want to understand any mental mechanism or process, you have to know its function within some larger system. Thinking is for doing, he said.[6]

What, then, is the function of moral reasoning? Does it seem to have been shaped, tuned, and crafted (by natural selection) to help us find the truth, so that we can know the right way to behave and condemn those who behave wrongly? If you believe that, then you are a rationalist, like Plato, Socrates, and Kohlberg.[7] Or does moral reasoning seem to have been shaped, tuned, and crafted to help us pursue socially strategic goals, such as guarding our reputations and convincing other people to support us, or our team, in disputes? If you believe that, then you are a Glauconian.

WE ARE ALL INTUITIVE POLITICIANS

If you see one hundred insects working together toward a common goal, it's a sure bet they're siblings. But when you see one hundred people working on a construction site or marching off to war, you'd be astonished if they all turned out to be members of one large family. Human beings are the world champions of cooperation beyond kinship, and we do it in large part by creating systems of formal and informal accountability. We're really good at holding others accountable for their actions, and we're really skilled at navigating through a world in which others hold us accountable for our own.

Phil Tetlock, a leading researcher in the study of accountability, defines accountability as the "explicit expectation that one will be called upon to justify one's beliefs, feelings, or actions to others," coupled with an expectation that people will reward or punish us based on how well we justify ourselves.[8] When nobody is answerable to anybody, when slackers and cheaters go unpunished, everything falls apart. (How zealously people punish slackers and cheaters will emerge in later chapters as an important difference between liberals and conservatives.)

Tetlock suggests a useful metaphor for understanding how people behave within the webs of accountability that constitute human societies: we act like *intuitive politicians* striving to maintain appealing moral identities in front of our multiple constituencies. Rationalists such as Kohlberg and Turiel portrayed children as little scientists who use logic and experimentation to figure out the truth for themselves. When we look at children's efforts to understand the physical world, the scientist metaphor is apt; kids really are formulating and testing hypotheses, and they really do converge, gradually, on the truth.[9] But in the social world, things are different, according to Tetlock. The social world is Glauconian.[10] Appearance is usually far more important than reality.

In Tetlock's research, subjects are asked to solve problems and make decisions.[11] For example, they're given information about a legal case and then asked to infer guilt or innocence. Some subjects are told that they'll have to explain their decisions to someone else. Other subjects know that they won't be held accountable by anyone. Tetlock found that when left to their own devices, people show the usual catalogue of errors, laziness, and reliance on gut feelings that has been documented in so much decision-making research.[12] But when people know in advance that they'll have to explain themselves, they think more systematically and self-critically. They are less likely to jump to premature conclusions and more likely to revise their beliefs in response to evidence.

That might be good news for rationalists—maybe we can think carefully whenever we believe it matters? Not quite. Tetlock found two very different kinds of careful reasoning. *Exploratory thought* is an "evenhanded consideration of alternative points of view." *Confirmatory thought* is "a one-sided attempt to rationalize a particular point of view."[13] Accountability increases exploratory thought only when three conditions apply: (1) decision makers learn before forming any opinion that they will be accountable to an audience, (2) the audience's views are unknown, and (3) they believe the audience is well informed and interested in accuracy.

When all three conditions apply, people do their darnedest to figure out the truth, because that's what the audience wants to hear. But the rest of the time—which is almost all of the time—accountability pressures simply increase confirmatory thought. People are trying harder to *look* right than to *be* right. Tetlock summarizes it like this:

> A central function of thought is making sure that one acts in ways *that can be persuasively justified or excused to others*. Indeed, the process of considering the justifiability of one's choices may be so prevalent that decision makers not only search for convincing reasons to make a choice when they must explain that choice to others, *they search for reasons to convince themselves* that they have made the "right" choice.[14]

Tetlock concludes that conscious reasoning is carried out largely for the purpose of persuasion, rather than discovery. But Tetlock adds that we are also trying to persuade ourselves. We want to believe the things we are about to say to others. In the rest of this chapter I'll review five bodies of experimental research supporting Tetlock and Glaucon. Our moral thinking is much more like a politician searching for votes than a scientist searching for truth.

1. WE ARE OBSESSED WITH POLLS

Ed Koch, the brash mayor of New York City in the 1980s, was famous for greeting constituents with the question "How'm I doin'?" It was a humorous reversal of the usual New York "How you doin'?" but it conveyed the chronic concern of elected officials. Few of us will ever run for office, yet most of the people we meet belong to one or more constituencies that we want to win over. Research on self-esteem suggests that we are all unconsciously asking Koch's question every day, in almost every encounter.

For a hundred years, psychologists have written about the need to think well of oneself. But Mark Leary, a leading researcher on self-consciousness, thought that it made no evolutionary sense for there to be a deep need for *self*-esteem.[15] For millions of years, our ancestors' survival depended upon their ability to get small groups to include them and trust them, so if there is any innate drive here, it should be a drive to get *others* to think well of us. Based on his review of the research, Leary suggested that self-esteem is more like an internal gauge, a "sociometer" that continuously measures your value as a relationship partner. Whenever the sociometer needle drops, it triggers an alarm and changes our behavior.

As Leary was developing the sociometer theory in the 1990s, he kept meeting people who denied that they were affected by what others thought of them. Do some people truly steer by their own compass?

Leary decided to put these self-proclaimed mavericks to the test. First, he had a large group of students rate their self-esteem and how much it depended on what other people think. Then he picked out the few people who—question after question—said they were completely unaffected by the opinions of others, and he invited them to the lab a few weeks later. As a comparison, he also invited people who had consistently said that they *were* strongly affected by what other people think of them. The test was on.

Everyone had to sit alone in a room and talk about themselves for five minutes, speaking into a microphone. At the end of each minute they saw a number flash on a screen in front of them. That number indicated how much another person listening in from another room wanted to interact with them in the next part of the study. With ratings from 1 to 7 (where 7 is best), you can imagine how it would feel to see the numbers drop while you're talking: 4 . . . 3 . . . 2 . . . 3 . . . 2.

In truth, Leary had rigged it. He gave some people declining ratings while other people got rising ratings: 4 . . . 5 . . . 6 . . . 5 . . . 6. Obviously it's more pleasant to see your numbers rise, but would seeing either set of numbers (ostensibly from a complete stranger) change what you believe to be true about yourself, your merits, your self-worth?

Not surprisingly, people who admitted that they cared about other people's opinions had big reactions to the numbers. Their self-esteem sank. But the self-proclaimed mavericks suffered shocks almost as big. They might indeed have steered by their own compass, but they didn't realize that their compass tracked public opinion, not true north. It was just as Glaucon said.

Leary's conclusion was that "the sociometer operates at a nonconscious and preattentive level to scan the social environment for any and all indications that one's relational value is low or declining."[16] The sociometer is part of the elephant. Because appearing concerned about other people's opinions makes us look weak, we (like politicians) often deny that we care about public opinion polls. But the fact is that we care a lot about what others think of us. The only people known to have no sociometer are psychopaths.[17]

2. OUR IN-HOUSE PRESS SECRETARY AUTOMATICALLY JUSTIFIES EVERYTHING

If you want to see post hoc reasoning in action, just watch the press secretary of a president or prime minister take questions from reporters. No matter how bad the policy, the secretary will find some way to praise or defend it. Reporters then challenge assertions and bring up contradictory quotes from the politician, or even quotes straight from the press secretary on previous days. Sometimes you'll hear an awkward pause as the secretary searches for the right words, but what you'll never hear is: "Hey, that's a great point! Maybe we should rethink this policy."

Press secretaries can't say that because they have no power to make or revise policy. They're told what the policy is, and their job is to find evidence and arguments that will justify the policy to the public. And that's one of the rider's main jobs: to be the full-time in-house press secretary for the elephant.

In 1960, Peter Wason (creator of the 4-card task from chapter 2) published his report on the "2–4–6 problem."[18] He showed people a series of three numbers and told them that the triplet conforms to a rule. They had to guess the rule by generating other triplets and then asking the experimenter whether the new triplet conformed to the rule. When they were confident they had guessed the rule, they were supposed to tell the experimenter their guess.

Suppose a subject first sees 2–4–6. The subject then generates a triplet in response: "4–6–8?"

"Yes," says the experimenter.

"How about 120–122–124?"

"Yes."

It seemed obvious to most people that the rule was consecutive even numbers. But the experimenter told them this was wrong, so they tested out other rules: "3–5–7?"

"Yes."

"What about 35–37–39?"

"Yes."

"OK, so the rule must be any series of numbers that rises by two?"

"No."

People had little trouble generating new hypotheses about the rule, sometimes quite complex ones. But what they hardly ever did was to test their hypotheses by offering triplets that *did not conform to their hypothesis*. For example, proposing 2–4–5 (yes) and 2–4–3 (no) would have helped people zero in on the actual rule: any series of ascending numbers.

Wason called this phenomenon the *confirmation bias*, the tendency to seek out and interpret new evidence in ways that confirm what you already think. People are quite good at challenging statements made by *other* people, but if it's *your* belief, then it's your possession—your child, almost—and you want to protect it, not challenge it and risk losing it.[19]

Deanna Kuhn, a leading researcher of everyday reasoning, found evidence of the confirmation bias even when people solve a problem that is important for survival: knowing what foods make us sick. To bring this question into the lab she created sets of eight index cards, each of which showed a cartoon image of a child eating something— chocolate cake versus carrot cake, for example—and then showed what happened to the child afterward: the child is smiling, or else is frowning and looking sick. She showed the cards one at a time, to children and to adults, and asked them to say whether the "evidence" (the 8 cards) suggested that either kind of food makes kids sick.

The kids as well as the adults usually started off with a hunch—in this case, that chocolate cake is the more likely culprit. They usually concluded that the evidence proved them right. Even when the cards showed a stronger association between carrot cake and sickness, people still pointed to the one or two cards with sick chocolate cake eaters as evidence for their theory, and they ignored the larger number of cards that incriminated carrot cake. As Kuhn puts it, people seemed to say to themselves: "Here is some evidence I can point to as supporting my theory, and therefore the theory is right."[20]

This is the sort of bad thinking that a good education should correct, right? Well, consider the findings of another eminent reasoning researcher, David Perkins.[21] Perkins brought people of various ages and education levels into the lab and asked them to think about social issues, such as whether giving schools more money would improve the quality of teaching and learning. He first asked subjects to write down their initial judgment. Then he asked them to think about the issue and write down all the reasons they could think of—on either side—that were relevant to reaching a final answer. After they were done, Perkins scored each reason subjects wrote as either a "my-side" argument or an "other-side" argument.

Not surprisingly, people came up with many more "my-side" arguments than "other-side" arguments. Also not surprisingly, the more education subjects had, the more reasons they came up with. But when Perkins compared fourth-year students in high school, college, or graduate school to first-year students in those same schools, he found barely any improvement within each school. Rather, the high school students who generate a lot of arguments are the ones who are more likely to go on to college, and the college students who generate a lot of arguments are the ones who are more likely to go on to graduate school. Schools don't *teach* people to reason thoroughly; they *select* the applicants with higher IQs, and people with higher IQs are able to generate more reasons.

The findings get more disturbing. Perkins found that IQ was by far the biggest predictor of how well people argued, but it predicted *only the number of my-side arguments*. Smart people make really good lawyers and press secretaries, but they are no better than others at finding reasons on the other side. Perkins concluded that "people invest their IQ in buttressing their own case rather than in exploring the entire issue more fully and evenhandedly."[22]

Research on everyday reasoning offers little hope for moral rationalists. In the studies I've described, there is no self-interest at stake. When you ask people about strings of digits, cakes and illnesses, and school funding, people have rapid, automatic intuitive reactions. One side looks a bit more attractive than the other. The elephant leans, ever so slightly, and the rider gets right to work looking for supporting evidence—and invariably succeeds.

This is how the press secretary works on trivial issues where there is no motivation to support one side or the other. If thinking is confirmatory rather than exploratory in these dry and easy cases, then what chance is there that people will think in an open-minded, exploratory way when self-interest, social identity, and strong emotions make them want or even *need* to reach a preordained conclusion?

LIE, CHEAT, AND JUSTIFY SO WELL THAT WE HONESTLY
BELIEVE WE ARE HONEST

In the United Kingdom, members of Parliament (MPs) have long been allowed to bill taxpayers for the reasonable expense of maintaining a second home, given that they're required to spend time in London and in their home districts. But because the office responsible for deciding what was reasonable approved nearly every request, members of Parliament treated it like a big blank check. And because their expenses were hidden from the public, MPs thought they were wearing the ring of Gyges—until a newspaper printed a leaked copy of those expense claims in 2009.[23]

Just as Glaucon predicted, they had behaved abominably. Many MPs declared their second home to be whichever one was due for major and lavish renovations (including dredging the moats). When the renovations were completed, they simply redesignated their primary home as their secondary home and renovated that one too, sometimes selling the newly renovated home for a huge profit.

Late-night comedians are grateful for the never-ending stream of scandals coming out of London, Washington, and other centers of power. But are the rest of us any better than our leaders? Or should we first look for logs in our own eyes?

Many psychologists have studied the effects of having "plausible deniability." In one such study, subjects performed a task and were then given a slip of paper and a verbal confirmation of how much they were to be paid. But when they took the slip to another room to get their money, the cashier misread one digit and handed them too much money. Only 20 percent spoke up and corrected the mistake.[24]

But the story changed when the cashier asked them if the payment was correct. In that case, 60 percent said no and returned the extra money. Being asked directly removes plausible deniability; it would take a direct lie to keep the money. As a result, people are three times more likely to be honest.

You can't predict who will return the money based on how people rate their own honesty, or how well they are able to give the high-minded answer on a moral dilemma of the sort used by Kohl-berg.[25] If the rider were in charge of ethical behavior, then there would be a big correlation between people's moral reasoning and their moral behavior. But he's not, so there isn't.

In his book *Predictably Irrational*, Dan Ariely describes a brilliant series of studies in which participants had the opportunity to earn more money by claiming to have solved more math problems than they really did. Ariely summarizes his findings from many variations of the paradigm like this:

> When given the opportunity, many honest people will cheat. In fact, rather than finding that a few bad apples weighted the averages, we discovered that *the majority of people cheated*, and that they cheated just a little bit.[26]

People didn't try to get away with as much as they could. Rather, when Ariely gave them anything like the invisibility of the ring of Gyges, they cheated only up to the point where they themselves could no longer find a justification that would preserve their belief in their own honesty.

The bottom line is that in lab experiments that give people invis-ibility combined with plausible deniability, *most people cheat*. The press secretary (also known as the *inner lawyer*)[27] is so good at finding justifications that most of these cheaters leave the experiment as con-vinced of their own virtue as they were when they walked in.

4. REASONING (AND GOOGLE) CAN TAKE YOU WHEREVER YOU WANT TO GO

When my son, Max, was three years old, I discovered that he's aller-gic to *must*. When I would tell him that he *must* get dressed so that we can go to school (and he loved to go to school), he'd scowl and whine. The word *must* is a little verbal handcuff that triggered in him the desire to squirm free.

The word *can* is so much nicer: "Can you get dressed, so that we can go to school?" To be certain that these two words were really night and day, I tried a little experiment. After dinner one night, I said "Max, you *must* eat ice cream now."

"But I don't want to!"

Four seconds later: "Max, you can have ice cream if you want."

"I want some!"

The difference between *can* and *must* is the key to understanding the profound effects of self-interest on reasoning. It's also the key to understanding many of the strangest beliefs—in UFO abductions, quack medical treatments, and conspiracy theories.

The social psychologist Tom Gilovich studies the cognitive mechanisms of strange beliefs. His simple formulation is that when we *want* to believe something, we ask ourselves, "*Can* I believe it?"[28] Then (as Kuhn and Perkins found), we search for supporting evidence, and if we find even a single piece of pseudo-evidence, we can stop thinking. We now have permission to believe. We have a justification, in case anyone asks.

In contrast, when we *don't* want to believe something, we ask ourselves, "*Must* I believe it?" Then we search for contrary evidence, and if we find a single reason to doubt the claim, we can dismiss it. You only need one key to unlock the handcuffs of *must*.

Psychologists now have file cabinets full of findings on "motivated reasoning,"[29] showing the many tricks people use to reach the conclusions they want to reach. When subjects are told that an intelligence test gave them a low score, they choose to read articles criticizing (rather than supporting) the validity of IQ tests.[30] When people read a (fictitious) scientific study that reports a link between caffeine consumption and breast cancer, women who are heavy coffee drinkers find more flaws in the study than do men and less caffeinated women.[31] Pete Ditto, at the University of California at Irvine, asked subjects to lick a strip of paper to determine whether they have a serious enzyme deficiency. He found that people wait longer for the paper to change color (which it never does) when a color change is desirable than when it indicates a deficiency, and those who get the undesirable prognosis find more reasons why the test might not be accurate (for example, "My mouth was unusually dry today").[32]

The difference between a mind asking "Must I believe it?" versus "Can I believe it?" is so profound that it even influences visual perception. Subjects who thought that they'd get something good if a computer flashed up a letter rather than a number were more likely to see the ambiguous figure **13** as the letter *B*, rather than as the number 13.[33]

If people can literally see what they want to see—given a bit of ambiguity—is it any wonder that scientific studies often fail to persuade the general public? Scientists are really good at finding flaws in studies that contradict their own views, but it sometimes happens that evidence accumulates across many studies to the point where scientists *must* change their minds. I've seen this happen in my colleagues (and myself) many times,[34] and it's part of the accountability system of science—you'd look foolish clinging to discredited theories. But for nonscientists, there is no such thing as a study you must believe. It's *always* possible to question the methods, find an alternative interpretation of the data, or, if all else fails, question the honesty or ideology of the researchers.

And now that we all have access to search engines on our cell phones, we can call up a team of supportive scientists for almost any conclusion twenty-four hours a day. Whatever you want to believe about the causes of global warming or whether a fetus can feel pain, just Google your belief. You'll find partisan websites summarizing and sometimes distorting relevant scientific studies. Science is a smorgasbord, and Google will guide you to the study that's right for you.

5. WE CAN BELIEVE ALMOST ANYTHING THAT SUPPORTS OUR TEAM

Many political scientists used to assume that people vote selfishly, choosing the candidate or policy that will benefit them the most. But decades of research on public opinion have led to the conclusion that self-interest is a weak predictor of policy preferences. Parents of children in public school are not more supportive of government aid to schools than other citizens; young men subject to the draft are not more opposed to military escalation than men too old to be drafted; and people who lack health insurance are not more likely to support government-issued health insurance than people covered by insurance.[35]

Rather, people care about their *groups*, whether those be racial, regional, religious, or political. The political scientist Don Kinder summarizes the findings like this: "In matters of public opinion, citizens seem to be asking themselves not 'What's in it for me?' but rather 'What's in it for my group?' "[36] Political opinions function as "badges of social membership."[37] They're like the array of bumper stickers people put on their cars showing the political causes, universities, and sports teams they support. Our politics is groupish, not selfish.

If people can see what they want to see in the figure **B**, just imagine how much room there is for partisans to see different facts in the social world.[38] Several studies have documented the "attitude polarization" effect that happens when you give a single body of information to people with differing partisan leanings. Liberals and conservatives actually move further apart when they read about research on whether the death penalty deters crime, or when they rate the quality of arguments made by candidates in a presidential debate, or when they evaluate arguments about affirmative action or gun control.[39]

In 2004, in the heat of the U.S. presidential election, Drew Westen used fMRI to catch partisan brains in action.[40] He recruited fifteen highly partisan Democrats and fifteen highly partisan Republicans and brought them into the scanner one at a time to watch eighteen sets of slides. The first slide in each set showed either a statement from President George W. Bush or one from his Democratic challenger, John Kerry. For example, people saw a quote from Bush in 2000 praising Ken Lay, the CEO of Enron, which later collapsed when its massive frauds came to light:

> I love the man. . . . When I'm president, I plan to run the government like a CEO runs a country. Ken Lay and Enron are a model of how I'll do that.

Then they saw a slide describing an action taken later that seemed to contradict the earlier statement:

> Mr. Bush now avoids any mention of Ken Lay, and is critical of Enron when asked.

At this point, Republicans were squirming. But right then, Westen showed them another slide that gave more context, resolving the contradiction:

> People who know the President report that he feels betrayed by Ken Lay, and was genuinely shocked to find that Enron's leadership had been corrupt.

There was an equivalent set of slides showing Kerry caught in a contradiction and then released. In other words, Westen engineered situations in which partisans would temporarily feel threatened by their candidates' apparent hypocrisy. At the same time, they'd feel no threat—and perhaps even pleasure—when it was the other party's guy who seemed to have been caught.

Westen was actually pitting two models of the mind against each other. Would subjects reveal Jefferson's dual-process model, in which the head (the reasoning parts of the brain) processes information about contradictions equally for all targets, but then gets overruled by a stronger response from the heart (the emotion areas)? Or does the partisan brain work as Hume says, with emotional and intuitive processes running the show and only putting in a call to reasoning when its services are needed to justify a desired conclusion?

The data came out strongly supporting Hume. The threatening information (their own candidate's hypocrisy) immediately activated a network of emotion-related brain areas—areas associated with negative emotion and responses to punishment.[41] The handcuffs (of "Must I believe it?") hurt.

Some of these areas are known to play a role in reasoning, but there was no increase in activity in the dorso-lateral prefrontal cortex (dlPFC). The dlPFC is the main area for cool reasoning tasks.[42]

Whatever thinking partisans were doing, it was not the kind of objective weighing or calculating that the dlPFC is known for.[43]

Once Westen released them from the threat, the ventral striatum started humming—that's one of the brain's major reward centers. All animal brains are designed to create flashes of pleasure when the animal does something important for its survival, and small pulses of the neurotransmitter dopamine in the ventral striatum (and a few other places) are where these good feelings are manufactured. Heroin and cocaine are addictive because they artificially trigger this dopamine response. Rats who can press a button to deliver electrical stimulation to their reward centers will continue pressing until they collapse from starvation.[44]

Westen found that partisans escaping from handcuffs (by thinking about the final slide, which restored their confidence in their candidate) got a little hit of that dopamine. And if this is true, then it would explain why extreme partisans are so stubborn, closed-minded, and committed to beliefs that often seem bizarre or paranoid. Like rats that cannot stop pressing a button, partisans may be simply unable to stop believing weird things. The partisan brain has been reinforced so many times for performing mental contortions that free it from unwanted beliefs. Extreme partisanship may be literally addictive.

THE RATIONALIST DELUSION

Webster's Third New International Dictionary defines *delusion* as "a false conception and persistent belief unconquerable by reason in something that has no existence in fact."[45] As an intuitionist, I'd say that the worship of reason is itself an illustration of one of the most long-lived delusions in Western history: the rationalist delusion. It's the idea that reasoning is our most noble attribute, one that makes us like the gods (for Plato) or that brings us beyond the "delusion" of believing in gods (for the New Atheists).[46] The rationalist delusion is not just a claim about human nature. It's also a claim that the rational caste (philosophers or scientists) should have more power, and it usually comes along with a utopian program for raising more rational children.[47]

From Plato through Kant and Kohlberg, many rationalists have asserted that the ability to reason well about ethical issues *causes* good behavior. They believe that reasoning is the royal road to moral truth, and they believe that people who reason well are more likely to act morally.

But if that were the case, then moral philosophers—who reason about ethical principles all day long—should be more virtuous than other people. Are they? The philosopher Eric Schwitzgebel tried to find out. He used surveys and more surreptitious methods to measure how often moral philosophers give to charity, vote, call their mothers, donate blood, donate organs, clean up after themselves at philosophy conferences, and respond to emails purportedly from students.[48] And in none of these ways are moral philosophers better than other philosophers or professors in other fields.

Schwitzgebel even scrounged up the missing-book lists from dozens of libraries and found that academic books on ethics, which are presumably borrowed mostly by ethicists, are more likely to be stolen or just never returned than books in other areas of philosophy.[49] In other words, expertise in moral reasoning does not seem to improve moral behavior, and it might even make it worse (perhaps by making the rider more skilled at post hoc justification). Schwitzgebel still has yet to find a single measure on which moral philosophers behave better than other philosophers.

Anyone who values truth should stop worshipping reason. We all need to take a cold hard look at the evidence and see reasoning for what it is. The French cognitive scientists Hugo Mercier and Dan Sperber recently reviewed the vast research literature on motivated reasoning (in social psychology) and on the biases and errors of reasoning (in cognitive psychology). They concluded that most of the bizarre and depressing research findings make perfect sense once you see reasoning as having evolved not to help us find truth but to help us engage in arguments, persuasion, and manipulation in the context of discussions with other people. As they put it, "skilled arguers . . . are not after the truth but after arguments supporting their views."[50] This explains why the confirmation bias is so powerful, and so ineradicable. How hard could it be to teach students to look on the other side, to look for evidence against their favored view? Yet, in fact, it's very hard, and nobody has yet found a way to do it.[51] It's hard because the confirmation bias is a built-in feature (of an argumentative mind), not a bug that can be removed (from a platonic mind).

I'm not saying we should all stop reasoning and go with our gut feelings. Gut feelings are sometimes better guides than reasoning for making consumer choices and interpersonal judgments,[52] but they are often disastrous as a basis for public policy, science, and law.[53] Rather, what I'm saying is that we must be wary of any *individual's* ability to reason. We should see each individual as being limited, like a neuron. A neuron is really good at one thing: summing up the stimulation coming into its dendrites to "decide" whether to fire a pulse along its axon. A neuron by itself isn't very smart. But if you put neurons together in the right way you get a brain; you get an emergent system that is much smarter and more flexible than a single neuron.

In the same way, each individual reasoner is really good at one thing: finding evidence to support the position he or she already holds, usually for intuitive reasons. We should not expect individuals to produce good, open-minded, truth-seeking reasoning, particularly when self-interest or reputational concerns are in play. But if you put individuals together in the right way, such that some individuals can use their reasoning powers to disconfirm the claims of others, and all individuals feel some common bond or shared fate that allows them to interact civilly, you can create a group that ends up producing good reasoning as an emergent property of the social system. This is why it's so important to have intellectual and ideological diversity within any group or institution whose goal is to find truth (such as an intelligence agency or a community of scientists) or to produce good public policy (such as a legislature or advisory board).

And if our goal is to produce good *behavior*, not just good thinking, then it's even more important to reject rationalism and embrace intuitionism. Nobody is ever going to invent an ethics class that makes people behave ethically after they step out of the classroom. Classes are for riders, and riders are just going to use their new knowledge to serve their elephants more effectively. If you want to make people behave more ethically, there are two ways you can go. You can change the elephant, which takes a long time and is hard to do. Or, to borrow an idea from the book *Switch*, by Chip Heath and Dan Heath,[54] you can change the path that the elephant and rider find themselves traveling on. You can make minor and inexpensive tweaks to the environment, which can produce big increases in ethical behavior.[55] You can hire Glaucon as a consultant and ask him how to design institutions in which real human beings, always concerned about their reputations, will behave more ethically.

IN SUM

The first principle of moral psychology is *Intuitions come first, strategic reasoning second.* To demonstrate the strategic functions of moral reasoning, I reviewed five areas of research showing that moral thinking is more like a politician searching for votes than a scientist searching for truth:

- We are obsessively concerned about what others think of us, although much of the concern is unconscious and invisible to us.
- Conscious reasoning functions like a press secretary who automatically justifies any position taken by the president.
- With the help of our press secretary, we are able to lie and cheat often, and then cover it up so effectively that we convince even ourselves.
- Reasoning can take us to almost any conclusion we want to reach, because we ask "Can I believe it?" when we want to believe something, but "Must I believe it?" when we don't want to believe. The answer is almost always yes to the first question and no to the second.
- In moral and political matters we are often groupish, rather than selfish. We deploy our reasoning skills to support our team, and to demonstrate commitment to our team.

I concluded by warning that the worship of reason, which is sometimes found in philosophical and scientific circles, is a delusion.

It is an example of faith in something that does not exist. I urged instead a more intuitionist approach to morality and moral education, one that is more humble about the abilities of individuals, and more attuned to the contexts and social systems that enable people to think and act well.

I have tried to make a reasoned case that our moral capacities are best described from an intuitionist perspective. I do not claim to have examined the question from all sides, nor to have offered irrefutable proof. Because of the insurmountable power of the confirmation bias, counterarguments will have to be produced by those who disagree with me. Eventually, if the scientific community works as it is supposed to, the truth will emerge as a large number of flawed and limited minds battle it out.

This concludes Part I of this book, which was about the first principle of moral psychology: *Intuitions come first, strategic reasoning second.* To explain this principle I used the metaphor of the mind as a rider (reasoning) on an elephant (intuition), and I said that the rider's function is to serve the elephant. Reasoning matters, particularly because reasons do sometimes influence other people, but most of the action in moral psychology is in the intuitions. In Part II I'll get much more specific about what those intuitions are and where they came from. I'll draw a map of moral space, and I'll show why that map is usually more favorable to conservative politicians than to liberals.

There's More to Morality than Harm and Fairness

Central Metaphor

*The righteous mind is like a tongue
with six taste receptors.*

FIVE

Beyond WEIRD Morality

I got my Ph.D. at McDonald's. Part of it, anyway, given the hours I spent standing outside of a McDonald's restaurant in West Philadelphia trying to recruit working-class adults to talk with me for my dissertation research. When someone agreed, we'd sit down together at the restaurant's outdoor seating area, and I'd ask them what they thought about the family that ate its dog, the woman who used her flag as a rag, and all the rest. I got some odd looks as the interviews progressed, and also plenty of laughter—particularly when I told people about the guy and the chicken. I was expecting that, because I had written the stories to surprise and even shock people.

But what I didn't expect was that these working-class subjects would sometimes find my request for justifications so perplexing. Each time someone said that the people in a story had done something wrong, I asked, "Can you tell me why that was wrong?" When I had interviewed college students on the Penn campus a month earlier, this question brought forth their moral justifications quite smoothly. But a few blocks west, this same question often led to long pauses and disbelieving stares. Those pauses and stares seemed to say, *You mean you don't* know *why it's wrong to do that to a chicken? I have to explain this to you? What planet are you from?*

These subjects were right to wonder about me because I really was weird. I came from a strange and different moral world—the University of Pennsylvania. Penn students were the most unusual of all twelve groups in my study. They were unique in their unwavering devotion to the "harm principle," which John Stuart Mill had put forth in 1859: "The only purpose for which power can be rightfully exercised over any member of a civilized community, against his will, is to prevent harm to others."[1] As one Penn student said: "It's his chicken, he's eating it, nobody is getting hurt."

The Penn students were just as likely as people in the other eleven groups to say that it would bother them to witness the taboo violations, but they were the *only* group that frequently ignored their own feelings of disgust and said that an action that bothered them was nonetheless morally permissible. And they were the only group in which a majority (73 percent) were able to tolerate the chicken story. As one Penn student said, "It's perverted, but if it's done in private, it's his right."

I and my fellow Penn students were weird in a second way too. In 2010, the cultural psychologists Joe Henrich, Steve Heine, and Ara Norenzayan published a profoundly important article titled "The Weirdest People in the World?"[2] The authors pointed out that nearly all research in psychology is conducted on a very small subset of the human population: people from cultures that are Western, educated, industrialized, rich, and democratic (forming the acronym WEIRD). They then reviewed dozens of studies showing that WEIRD people are statistical outliers; they are the least typical, least representative people you could study if you want to make generalizations about human nature. Even within the West, Americans are more extreme outliers than Europeans, and within the United States, the educated upper middle class (like my Penn sample) is the most unusual of all.

Several of the peculiarities of WEIRD culture can be captured in this simple generalization: *The WEIRDer you are, the more you see a world full of separate objects, rather than relationships.* It has long been reported that Westerners have a more independent and autonomous concept of the self than do East Asians.[3] For example, when asked to write twenty statements beginning with the words "I am . . . ,"

Americans are likely to list their own internal psychological charac-
teristics (happy, outgoing, interested in jazz), whereas East Asians are
more likely to list their roles and relationships (a son, a husband, an
employee of Fujitsu).

The differences run deep; even visual perception is affected. In
what's known as the framed-line task, you are shown a square with a
line drawn inside it. You then turn the page and see an empty square
that is larger or smaller than the original square. Your task is to draw a
line that is the same as the line you saw on the previous page, either in
absolute terms (same number of centimeters; ignore the new frame)
or in relative terms (same proportion relative to the frame). Westerners, and particularly Americans, excel at the absolute task, because
they saw the line as an independent object in the first place and stored
it separately in memory. East Asians, in contrast, outperform Americans at the relative task, because they automatically perceived and
remembered the relationship among the parts.[4]

Related to this difference in perception is a difference in thinking style. Most people think holistically (seeing the whole context
and the relationships among parts), but WEIRD people think more
analytically (detaching the focal object from its context, assigning it
to a category, and then assuming that what's true about the category
is true about the object).[5] Putting this all together, it makes sense
that WEIRD philosophers since Kant and Mill have mostly generated moral systems that are individualistic, rule-based, and universalist. That's the morality you need to govern a society of autonomous
individuals.

But when holistic thinkers in a non-WEIRD culture write about
morality, we get something more like the Analects of Confucius,
a collection of aphorisms and anecdotes that can't be reduced to a
single rule.[6] Confucius talks about a variety of relationship-specific
duties and virtues (such as filial piety and the proper treatment of
one's subordinates).

If WEIRD and non-WEIRD people think differently and see
the world differently, then it stands to reason that they'd have different moral concerns. If you see a world full of individuals, then you'll
want the morality of Kohlberg and Turiel—a morality that protects

those individuals and their individual rights. You'll emphasize concerns about harm and fairness.

But if you live in a non-WEIRD society in which people are more likely to see relationships, contexts, groups, and institutions, then you won't be so focused on protecting individuals. You'll have a more *sociocentric* morality, which means (as Shweder described it back in chapter 1) that you place the needs of groups and institutions first, often ahead of the needs of individuals. If you do that, then a morality based on concerns about harm and fairness won't be sufficient. You'll have additional concerns, and you'll need additional virtues to bind people together.

Part II of this book is about those additional concerns and virtues. It's about the second principle of moral psychology: *There's more to morality than harm and fairness.* I'm going to try to convince you that this principle is true *descriptively*—that is, as a portrait of the moralities we see when we look around the world. I'll set aside the question of whether any of these alternative moralities are *really* good, true, or justifiable. As an intuitionist, I believe it is a mistake to even *raise* that emotionally powerful question until we've calmed our elephants and cultivated some understanding of what such moralities are trying to accomplish. It's just too easy for our riders to build a case against every morality, political party, and religion that we don't like.[7] So let's try to understand moral diversity first, before we judge other moralities.

THREE ETHICS ARE MORE DESCRIPTIVE THAN ONE

The University of Chicago is proud of its ranking by *Playboy* magazine as the "worst party school" in the United States. Winters are long and brutal, bookstores outnumber bars, and students wear T-shirts showing the university crest above phrases such as "Where Fun Goes to Die" and "Hell Does Freeze Over." I arrived at the university on a September evening in 1992, unpacked my rental truck, and went out for a beer. At the table next to mine, there was a heated argument. A bearded man slammed his hands on the table and shouted, "Damn it, I'm talking about Marx!"

This was Richard Shweder's culture. I had been granted a fellow-ship to work with Shweder for two years after I finished my Ph.D. at Penn. Shweder was the leading thinker in cultural psychology—a new discipline that combined the anthropologist's love of context and variability with the psychologist's interest in mental processes.[8] A dictum of cultural psychology is that "culture and psyche make each other up."[9] In other words, you can't study the mind while ignoring culture, as psychologists usually do, because minds function only once they've been filled out by a particular culture. And you can't study culture while ignoring psychology, as anthropologists usually do, because social practices and institutions (such as initiation rites, witchcraft, and religion) are to some extent shaped by concepts and desires rooted deep within the human mind, which explains why they often take similar forms on different continents.

I was particularly drawn to a new theory of morality Shweder had developed based on his research in Orissa (which I described in chapter 1). After he published that study, he and his colleagues continued to analyze the six hundred interview transcripts they had collected. They found three major clusters of moral themes, which they called the ethics of autonomy, community, and divinity.[10] Each one is based on a different idea about what a person really is.

The ethic of *autonomy* is based on the idea that people are, first and foremost, autonomous individuals with wants, needs, and prefer-ences. People should be free to satisfy these wants, needs, and preferences as they see fit, and so societies develop moral concepts such as rights, liberty, and justice, which allow people to coexist peacefully without interfering too much in each other's projects. This is the dominant ethic in individualistic societies. You find it in the writings of utilitar-ians such as John Stuart Mill and Peter Singer[11] (who value justice and rights only to the extent that they increase human welfare), and you find it in the writings of deontologists such as Kant and Kohlberg (who prize justice and rights even in cases where doing so may reduce overall welfare).

But as soon as you step outside of Western secular society, you hear people talking in two additional moral languages. The ethic of *community* is based on the idea that people are, first and foremost, members of larger entities such as families, teams, armies, companies, tribes, and nations. These larger entities are more than the sum of the people who compose them; they are real, they matter, and they must be protected. People have an obligation to play their assigned roles in these entities. Many societies therefore develop moral concepts such as duty, hierarchy, respect, reputation, and patriotism. In such societies, the Western insistence that people should design their own lives and pursue their own goals seems selfish and dangerous—a sure way to weaken the social fabric and destroy the institutions and collective entities upon which everyone depends.

The ethic of *divinity* is based on the idea that people are, first and foremost, temporary vessels within which a divine soul has been implanted.[12] People are not just animals with an extra serving of consciousness; they are children of God and should behave accordingly. The body is a temple, not a playground. Even if it does no harm and violates nobody's rights when a man has sex with a chicken carcass, he still shouldn't do it because it degrades him, dishonors his creator, and violates the sacred order of the universe. Many societies therefore develop moral concepts such as sanctity and sin, purity and pollution, elevation and degradation. In such societies, the personal liberty of secular Western nations looks like libertinism, hedonism, and a celebration of humanity's baser instincts.[13]

I first read about Shweder's three ethics in 1991, after I had collected my data in Brazil but before I had written my dissertation. I realized that all of my best stories—the ones that got people to react emotionally without being able to find a victim—involved either disrespect, which violated the ethics of community (for example, using a flag as a rag), or disgust and carnality, which violated the ethics of divinity (for example, the thing with the chicken).

I used Shweder's theory to analyze the justifications people gave (when I asked them "Can you tell me why?"), and it worked like magic. The Penn students spoke almost exclusively in the language of the ethic of autonomy, whereas the other groups (particularly the working-class groups) made much more use of the ethic of community, and a bit more use of the ethic of divinity.[14]

Soon after I arrived in Chicago, I applied for a Fulbright fellow-ship to spend three months in India, where I hoped to get a closer look at the ethic of divinity. (It had been the rarest of the three ethics in my dissertation data.) Because I was able to draw on Shweder's extensive network of friends and colleagues in Bhubaneswar, the capital city of Orissa, it was easy for me to put together a detailed research proposal, which was funded. After spending a year in Chicago reading cultural psychology and learning from Shweder and his students, I flew off to India in September 1993.

HOW I BECAME A PLURALIST

I was extraordinarily well hosted and well treated. I was given the use of a lovely apartment, which came with its own full-time cook and servant.[15] For $5 a day I rented a car and driver. I was welcomed at the local university by Professor Biranchi Puhan, an old friend of Shweder's, who gave me an office and introduced me to the rest of the psychology department, from which I recruited a research team of eager students. Within a week I was ready to begin my work, which was supposed to be a series of experiments on moral judgment, particularly violations of the ethics of divinity. But these experiments taught me little in comparison to what I learned just from stumbling around the complex social web of a small Indian city and then talking with my hosts and advisors about my confusion.

One cause of confusion was that I had brought with me two incompatible identities. On one hand, I was a twenty-nine-year-old liberal atheist with very definite views about right and wrong. On the other hand, I wanted to be like those open-minded anthropologists I had read so much about and had studied with, such as Alan Fiske and Richard Shweder. My first few weeks in Bhubaneswar were therefore filled with feelings of shock and dissonance. I dined with men whose wives silently served us and then retreated to the kitchen, not speaking to me the entire evening. I was told to be stricter with my servants, and to stop thanking them for serving me. I watched people bathe in and cook with visibly polluted water that was held to be sacred. In short, I was immersed in a sex-segregated, hierarchically stratified, devoutly religious society, and I was committed to understanding it on its own terms, not on mine.

It only took a few weeks for my dissonance to disappear, not because I was a natural anthropologist but because the normal human capacity for empathy kicked in. I *liked* these people who were hosting me, helping me, and teaching me. Wherever I went, people were kind to me. And when you're grateful to people, it's easier to adopt their perspective. My elephant leaned toward them, which made my rider search for moral arguments in their defense. Rather than automatically rejecting the men as sexist oppressors and pitying the women, children, and servants as helpless victims, I began to see a moral world in which families, not individuals, are the basic unit of society, and the members of each extended family (including its servants) are intensely interdependent. In this world, equality and personal autonomy were not sacred values. Honoring elders, gods, and guests, protecting subordinates, and fulfilling one's role-based duties were more important.

I had read about Shweder's ethic of community and had understood it intellectually. But now, for the first time in my life, I began to feel it. I could see beauty in a moral code that emphasizes duty, respect for one's elders, service to the group, and negation of the self's desires. I could still see its ugly side: I could see that power sometimes leads to pomposity and abuse. And I could see that subordinates—particularly women—were often blocked from doing what they wanted to do by the whims of their elders (male and female). But for the first time in my life, I was able to step outside of my home morality, the ethic of autonomy. I had a place to stand, and from the vantage point of the ethic of community, the ethic of autonomy now seemed overly individualistic and self-focused. In my three months in India I met very few Americans. But when I boarded the plane to fly back to Chicago I heard a loud voice with an unmistakably American accent saying, "Look, you tell him that this is the compartment over *my* seat, and I have a *right* to use it." I cringed.

The same thing happened with the ethic of divinity. I understood intellectually what it meant to treat the body as a temple rather than as a playground, but that was an analytical concept I used to make sense of people who were radically different from me. I personally was quite fond of pleasure and could see little reason to choose less of it rather than more. And I was quite devoted to efficiency, so I could see little reason to spend an hour or two each day saying prayers and performing rituals. But there I was in Bhubaneswar, interviewing Hindu priests, monks, and laypeople about their concepts of purity and pollution and trying to understand why Hindus place so much emphasis on bathing, food choices, and concerns about what or whom a person has touched. Why do Hindu gods care about the state of their devotees' bodies? (And it's not just Hindu gods; the Koran and the Hebrew Bible reveal similar concerns, and many Christians believe that "cleanliness is next to godliness.")[16]

In graduate school I had done some research on moral disgust, and that prepared me to think about these questions. I had teamed up with Paul Rozin (one of the leading experts on the psychology of food and eating) and Clark McCauley (a social psychologist at nearby Bryn Mawr College). We wanted to know why the emotion of disgust—which clearly originated as an emotion that keeps us away from dirty and contaminating things—can now be triggered by some moral violations (such as betrayal or child abuse) but not by others (such as robbing a bank or cheating on one's taxes).[17]

Our theory, in brief, was that the human mind automatically perceives a kind of vertical dimension of social space, running from God or moral perfection at the top down through angels, humans, other animals, monsters, demons, and then the devil, or perfect evil, at the bottom.[18] The list of supernatural beings varies from culture to culture, and you don't find this vertical dimension elaborated in every culture. But you do find the idea that high = good = pure = God whereas low = bad = dirty = animal quite widely. So widely, in fact, that it seems to be a kind of archetype (if you like Jungian terminology) or innately prepared idea (if you prefer the language of evolutionary psychology).

Our idea was that moral disgust is felt whenever we see or hear about people whose behavior shows them to be low on this vertical dimension. People feel degraded when they think about such things, just as they feel elevated by hearing about virtuous actions.[19] A man who robs a bank does a bad thing, and we want to see him punished.

But a man who betrays his own parents or who enslaves children for the sex trade seems monstrous—lacking in some basic human sentiment. Such actions revolt us and seem to trigger some of the same physiology of disgust as would seeing rats scampering out of a trash can.[20]

That was our theory, and it was rather easy to find evidence for it in India. Hindu notions of reincarnation could not be more explicit: Our souls reincarnate into higher or lower creatures in the next life, based on the virtue of our conduct during this life. But as with the ethic of community, the big surprise for me was that after a few months I began to *feel* the ethic of divinity in subtle ways.

Some of these feelings were related to the physical facts of dirt and cleanliness in Bhubaneswar. Cows and dogs roamed freely around town, so you had to step carefully around their droppings; you sometimes saw people defecating by the roadside; and garbage was often heaped into fly-swarmed piles. It therefore began to feel natural to me to adopt the Indian practice of removing my shoes when I entered any private home, creating a sharp boundary between dirty and clean spaces. As I visited temples I became attuned to their spiritual topography: the courtyard is higher (more pure) than the street; the antechamber of the temple higher still, and the inner sanctum, where the god was housed, could be entered only by the Brahmin priest, who had followed all the necessary rules of personal purity. Private homes had a similar topography, and I had to be sure never to enter the kitchen or the room where offerings were made to deities. The topography of purity even applies to your own body: you eat with your right hand (after washing it), and you use your left hand to clean yourself (with water) after defecation, so you develop an intuitive sense that left = dirty and right = clean. It becomes second nature that you don't give things to others using your left hand.

If these new feelings were just a new ability to detect invisible dirt rays emanating from objects, they would have helped me to understand obsessive-compulsive disorder, but not morality. These feelings were more than that. In the ethic of divinity, there is an order to the universe, and things (as well as people) should be treated with the reverence or disgust that they deserve. When I returned to Chicago,

I began to feel positive essences emanating from some objects. It felt right to me to treat certain books with reverence—not leaving them on the floor or taking them into the bathroom. Funeral services and even burial (which had previously seemed to me to be such a waste of money and space) began to make more emotional sense. The human body does not suddenly become an object, like that of any other animal corpse, at the moment of death. There are right ways and wrong ways of treating bodies, even when there is no conscious being inside the body to experience mistreatment.

I also began to understand why the American culture wars involved so many battles over sacrilege. Is a flag just a piece of cloth, which can be burned as a form of protest? Or does each flag contain within it something nonmaterial such that when protesters burn it, they have done something bad (even if nobody were to see them do it)? When an artist submerges a crucifix in a jar of his own urine, or smears elephant dung on an image of the Virgin Mary, do these works belong in art museums?[21] Can the artist simply tell religious Christians, "If you don't want to see it, don't go to the museum"? Or does the mere existence of such works make the world dirtier, more profane, and more degraded?

If you can't see anything wrong here, try reversing the politics. Imagine that a conservative artist had created these works using images of Martin Luther King Jr. and Nelson Mandela instead of Jesus and Mary. Imagine that his intent was to mock the quasi-deification by the left of so many black leaders. Could such works be displayed in museums in New York or Paris without triggering angry demonstrations? Might some on the left feel that the museum itself had been polluted by racism, even after the paintings were removed?[22]

As with the ethic of community, I had read about the ethic of divinity before going to India, and had understood it intellectually. But in India, and in the years after I returned, I felt it. I could see beauty in a moral code that emphasized self-control, resistance to temptation, cultivation of one's higher, nobler self, and negation of the self's desires. I could see the dark side of this ethic too: once you allow visceral feelings of disgust to guide your conception of what God wants, then minorities who trigger even a hint of disgust in the majority (such as homosexuals or obese people) can be ostracized and treated cruelly. The ethic of divinity is sometimes incompatible with compassion, egalitarianism, and basic human rights.[23]

But at the same time, it offers a valuable perspective from which we can understand and critique some of the ugly parts of secular societies. For example, why are many of us bothered by rampant materialism? If some people want to work hard in order to earn money in order to buy luxury goods in order to impress others, how can we criticize them using the ethic of autonomy?

To offer another example, I was recently eating lunch at a UVA dining hall. At the table next to me two young women were talking. One of them was very grateful for something the other had agreed to do for her. To express her gratitude she exclaimed, "Oh my God! If you were a guy, I'd be so on your dick right now!" I felt a mixture of amusement and revulsion, but how could I criticize her from within the ethic of autonomy?

The ethic of divinity lets us give voice to inchoate feelings of elevation and degradation—our sense of "higher" and "lower." It gives us a way to condemn crass consumerism and mindless or trivialized sexuality. We can understand long-standing laments about the spiritual emptiness of a consumer society in which everyone's mission is to satisfy their personal desires.[24]

STEPPING OUT OF THE MATRIX

Among the most profound ideas that have arisen around the world and across eras is that the world we experience is an illusion, akin to a dream. Enlightenment is a form of waking up. You find this idea in many religions and philosophies,[25] and it's also a staple of science fiction, particularly since William Gibson's 1984 novel *Neuromancer*. Gibson coined the term *cyberspace* and described it as a "matrix" that emerges when a billion computers are connected and people get enmeshed in "a consensual hallucination."

The creators of the movie *The Matrix* developed Gibson's idea into a gorgeous and frightening visual experience. In one of its most famous scenes, the protagonist, Neo, is given a choice. He can take a red pill, which will disconnect him from the matrix, dissolve the hallucination, and give him command of his actual, physical body (which is lying in a vat of goo). Or he can take a blue pill, forget he was ever given this choice, and his consciousness will return to the rather pleasant hallucination in which nearly all human beings spend their conscious existence. Neo swallows the red pill, and the matrix dissolves around him.

It wasn't quite as dramatic for me, but Shweder's writings were my red pill. I began to see that many moral matrices coexist within each nation. Each matrix provides a complete, unified, and emotionally compelling worldview, easily justified by observable evidence and nearly impregnable to attack by arguments from outsiders.

I grew up Jewish in the suburbs of New York City. My grandparents had fled czarist Russia and found work in New York's garment industry. For their generation, socialism and labor unions were effective responses to the exploitation and terrible working conditions they faced. Franklin Roosevelt was the heroic leader who protected workers and defeated Hitler. Jews ever since have been among the most reliable voters for the Democratic Party.[26]

My morality wasn't just shaped by my family and ethnicity. I attended Yale University, which was ranked at the time as the second most liberal of the Ivy League schools. It was not uncommon during class discussions for teachers and students to make jokes and critical comments about Ronald Reagan, the Republican Party, or the conservative position on controversial current events. Being liberal was cool; being liberal was righteous. Yale students in the 1980s strongly supported the victims of apartheid, the people of El Salvador, the government of Nicaragua, the environment, and Yale's own striking labor unions, which deprived us all of dining halls for much of my senior year.

Liberalism seemed so obviously ethical. Liberals marched for peace, workers' rights, civil rights, and secularism. The Republican Party was (as we saw it) the party of war, big business, racism, and evangelical Christianity. I could not understand how any thinking person would voluntarily embrace the party of evil, and so I and my fellow liberals looked for psychological explanations of conservatism, but not liberalism. *We* supported liberal policies because we saw the world clearly and wanted to help people, but *they* supported conservative policies out of pure self-interest (lower my taxes!) or thinly veiled racism (stop funding welfare programs for minorities!). We never considered the possibility that there were alternative moral worlds in which reducing harm (by helping victims) and increasing fairness (by pursuing group-based equality) were not the main goals.[27] And if we could not imagine other moralities, then we could not believe that conservatives were as sincere in their moral beliefs as we were in ours.

When I moved from Yale to Penn, and then from Penn to the University of Chicago, the matrix stayed pretty much the same. It was only in India that I had to stand alone. Had I been there as a tourist it would have been easy to maintain my matrix membership for three months; I'd have met up now and then with other Western tourists, and we would have swapped stories about the sexism, poverty, and oppression we had seen. But because I was there to study cultural psychology I did everything I could to fit into another matrix, one woven mostly from the ethics of community and divinity.

When I returned to America, social conservatives no longer seemed so crazy. I could listen to leaders of the "religious right" such as Jerry Falwell and Pat Robertson with a kind of clinical detachment. They want more prayer and spanking in schools, and less sex education and access to abortion? I didn't think those steps would reduce AIDS and teen pregnancy, but I could see why Christian conservatives wanted to "thicken up" the moral climate of schools and discourage the view that children should be as free as possible to act on their desires. Social conservatives think that welfare programs and feminism increase rates of single motherhood and weaken the traditional social structures that compel men to support their own children? Well, now that I was no longer on the defensive, I could see that those arguments made sense, even if there are also many good effects of liberating women from dependence on men. I had escaped from my prior partisan mind-set (reject first, ask rhetorical questions later) and began to think about liberal and conservative policies as manifestations of deeply conflicting but equally heartfelt visions of the good society.[28]

It felt good to be released from partisan anger. And once I was no longer angry, I was no longer committed to reaching the conclusion that righteous anger demands: we are right, they are wrong. I was able to explore new moral matrices, each one supported by its own intellectual traditions. It felt like a kind of awakening.

In 1991, Shweder wrote about the power of cultural psychology to cause such awakenings:

> Yet the conceptions held by others are available to us, in the sense that when we truly understand their conception of things we come to recognize *possibilities latent within our own rationality* . . . and those ways of conceiving of things become salient for us for the first time, or once again. In other words, there is no homogeneous "backcloth" to our world. We are multiple from the start.[29]

I cannot overstate the importance of this quotation for moral and political psychology. We are multiple from the start. Our minds have the potential to become righteous about many different concerns, and only a few of these concerns are activated during childhood. Other potential concerns are left undeveloped and unconnected to the web of shared meanings and values that become our adult moral matrix. If you grow up in a WEIRD society, you become so well educated in the ethic of autonomy that you can detect oppression and inequality even where the apparent victims see nothing wrong. But years later, when you travel, or become a parent, or perhaps just read a good novel about a traditional society, you might find some other moral intuitions latent within yourself. You might find yourself responding to dilemmas involving authority, sexuality, or the human body in ways that are hard to explain.

Conversely, if you are raised in a more traditional society, or within an evangelical Christian household in the United States, you become so well educated in the ethics of community and divinity that you can detect disrespect and degradation even where the apparent victims see nothing wrong. But if you then face discrimination yourself (as conservatives and Christians sometimes do in the academic world),[30] or if you simply listen to Martin Luther King Jr.'s "I Have a Dream" speech, you may find a new resonance in moral arguments about oppression and equality.

IN SUM

The second principle of moral psychology is: *There's more to morality than harm and fairness.* In support of this claim I described research showing that people who grow up in Western, educated, industrial, rich, and democratic (WEIRD) societies are statistical outliers on many psychological measures, including measures of moral psychology. I also showed that:

- The WEIRDer you are, the more you perceive a world full of separate objects, rather than relationships.
- Moral pluralism is true *descriptively*. As a simple matter of anthropological fact, the moral domain varies across cultures.
- The moral domain is unusually narrow in WEIRD cultures, where it is largely limited to the ethic of autonomy (i.e., moral concerns about individuals harming, oppressing, or cheating other individuals). It is broader—including the ethics of community and divinity—in most other societies, and within religious and conservative moral matrices within WEIRD societies.
- Moral matrices bind people together and blind them to the coherence, or even existence, of other matrices. This makes it very difficult for people to consider the possibility that there might really be more than one form of moral truth, or more than one valid framework for judging people or running a society.

In the next three chapters I'll catalogue the moral intuitions, showing exactly what else there is beyond harm and fairness. I'll show how a small set of innate and universal moral foundations can be used to construct a great variety of moral matrices. I'll offer tools you can use to understand moral arguments emanating from matrices that are not your own.

SIX

Taste Buds of the Righteous Mind

A few years ago I tried a restaurant called The True Taste. The interior was entirely white. Each table was set only with spoons—five small spoons at each place setting. I sat down at a table and looked at the menu. It was divided into sections labeled "Sugars," "Honeys," "Tree Saps," and "Artificials." I called the waiter over and asked him to explain. Did they not serve food?

The waiter, it turned out, was also the owner and sole employee of the restaurant. He told me that the restaurant was the first of its kind in the world: it was a tasting bar for sweeteners. I could sample sweeteners from thirty-two countries. He explained that he was a biologist who specialized in the sense of taste. He described to me the five kinds of taste receptor found in each taste bud on the tongue—sweet, sour, salty, bitter, and savory (also called umami). He said that in his research he had discovered that activation of the sweet receptor produced the strongest surge of dopamine in the brain, which indicated to him that humans are hard-wired to seek sweetness above the other four tastes. He therefore reasoned that it was most efficient, in terms of units of pleasure per calorie, to consume sweeteners, and he conceived the idea of opening a restaurant aimed entirely at stimulating this one taste receptor. I asked him how business was going. "Terrible," he said, "but at least I'm doing better than the chemist down the street who opened a salt-tasting bar."

OK, this didn't really happen to me, but it's a metaphor for how I feel sometimes when I read books about moral philosophy and psychology. Morality is so rich and complex, so multifaceted and internally contradictory. Pluralists such as Shweder rise to the challenge, offering theories that can explain moral diversity within and across cultures. Yet many authors reduce morality to a single principle, usually some variant of welfare maximization (basically, help people, don't hurt them).[1] Or sometimes it's justice or related notions of fairness, rights, or respect for individuals and their autonomy.[2] There's The Utilitarian Grill, serving only sweeteners (welfare), and The Deontological Diner, serving only salts (rights). Those are your options.

Neither Shweder nor I am saying that "anything goes," or that all societies or all cuisines are equally good. But we believe that moral monism—the attempt to ground all of morality on a single principle—leads to societies that are unsatisfying to most people and at high risk of becoming inhumane because they ignore so many other moral principles.[3]

We humans all have the same five taste receptors, but we don't all like the same foods. To understand where these differences come from, we can start with an evolutionary story about sugary fruits and fatty animals, which were good food for our common ancestors. But we'll also have to examine the history of each culture, and we'll have to look at the childhood eating habits of each individual. Just knowing that everyone has sweetness receptors can't tell you why one person prefers Thai food to Mexican, or why hardly anyone stirs sugar into beer. It takes a lot of additional work to connect the universal taste receptors to the specific things that a particular person eats and drinks.

It's the same for moral judgments. To understand why people are so divided by moral issues, we can start with an exploration of our common evolutionary heritage, but we'll also have to examine the history of each culture and the childhood socialization of each individual within that culture. Just knowing that we all care about harm can't tell you why one person prefers hunting to badminton or why hardly anyone devotes their waking hours primarily to serving the poor. It will take a lot of additional work for us to connect the universal moral taste receptors to the specific moral judgments that a particular person makes.

The Chinese sage Mencius made the analogy between morality and food 2,300 years ago when he wrote that "moral principles please our minds as beef and mutton and pork please our mouths."[4] In this chapter and the next two, I'll develop the analogy that *the righteous mind is like a tongue with six taste receptors*. In this analogy, morality is like cuisine: it's a cultural construction, influenced by accidents of environment and history, but it's not so flexible that anything goes. You can't have a cuisine based on tree bark, nor can you have one based primarily on bitter tastes. Cuisines vary, but they all must please tongues equipped with the same five taste receptors.[5] Moral matrices vary, but they all must please righteous minds equipped with the same six social receptors.

THE BIRTH OF MORAL SCIENCE

Nowadays, secular people often see the Enlightenment as a battle between two mortal enemies: on one side was science, with its principal weapon, reason, and on the other was religion, with its ancient shield of superstition. Reason defeated superstition, light replaced darkness. But when David Hume was alive, he was fighting a three-way battle. Enlightenment thinkers were united in rejecting divine revelation as the source of moral knowledge, but they were divided as to whether morality *transcended* human nature—that is, it emerged from the very nature of rationality and could therefore be deduced by reasoning, as Plato believed—or whether morality was a *part* of human nature, like language or taste, which had to be studied by observation.[6] Given Hume's concerns about the limits of reasoning, he believed that philosophers who tried to reason their way to moral truth without looking at human nature were no better than theologians who thought they could find moral truth revealed in sacred texts. Both were transcendentalists.[7]

Hume's work on morality was the quintessential Enlightenment project: an exploration of an area previously owned by religion, using the methods and attitudes of the new natural sciences. His first great work, *A Treatise of Human Nature,* had this subtitle: *Being an Attempt to Introduce the Experimental Method of Reasoning into Moral Subjects.* Hume believed that "moral science" had to begin with careful inquiry into what humans are really like. And when he examined human nature—in history, in political affairs, and among his fellow philosophers—he saw that "sentiment" (intuition) is the driving force of our moral lives, whereas reasoning is biased and impotent, fit primarily to be a servant of the passions.[8] He also saw a diversity of virtues, and he rejected attempts by some of his contemporaries to reduce all of morality to a single virtue such as kindness, or to do away with virtues and replace them with a few moral laws.

Because he thought that morality was based in a variety of sentiments, which give us pleasure when we encounter virtue and displeasure when we encounter vice, Hume often relied upon sensory analogies, and particularly the taste analogy:

> Morality is nothing in the abstract Nature of Things, but is entirely relative to the Sentiment or mental Taste of each particular Being; in the same Manner as the Distinctions of sweet and bitter, hot and cold, arise from the particular feeling of each Sense or Organ. Moral Perceptions therefore, ought not to be class'd with the Operations of the Understanding, but with the Tastes or Sentiments.[9]

Moral judgment is a kind of perception, and moral science should begin with a careful study of the moral taste receptors. You can't possibly deduce the list of five taste receptors by pure reasoning, nor should you search for it in scripture. There's nothing transcendental about them. You've got to examine tongues.

Hume got it right. When he died in 1776, he and other sentimen-talists[10] had laid a superb foundation for "moral science," one that has, in my view, been largely vindicated by modern research.[11] You would think, then, that in the decades after his death, the moral sciences progressed rapidly. But you would be wrong. In the decades after Hume's death the rationalists claimed victory over religion and took the moral sciences off on a two-hundred-year tangent.

ATTACK OF THE SYSTEMIZERS

Autism has bedeviled psychiatric classifiers for decades because it is not a single, discrete disease. It's usually described as a "spectrum" disorder because people can be more or less autistic, and it's not clear where to draw the line between those who have a serious mental ill-ness and those who are just not very good at reading other people. At the extreme end of the spectrum, autistic people are "mind-blind."[12] They are missing the social-cognitive software that the rest of us use to guess the intentions and desires of other people.

According to one of the leading autism researchers, Simon Baron-Cohen, there are in fact two spectra, two dimensions on which we can place each person: empathizing and systemizing. Empathiz-ing is "the drive to identify another person's emotions and thoughts, and to respond to these with an appropriate emotion."[13] If you prefer fiction to nonfiction, or if you often enjoy conversations about people you don't know, you are probably above average on empathizing. Sys-temizing is "the drive to analyse the variables in a system, to derive the underlying rules that govern the behaviour of the system."[14] If you are good at reading maps and instruction manuals, or if you enjoy figuring out how machines work, you are probably above average on systemizing.

If we cross these two traits, we get a two-dimensional space (see figure 6.1), and each person can be placed at a particular spot in that space. Baron-Cohen has shown that autism is what you get when genes and prenatal factors combine to produce a brain that is excep-tionally low on empathizing and exceptionally high on systemizing.

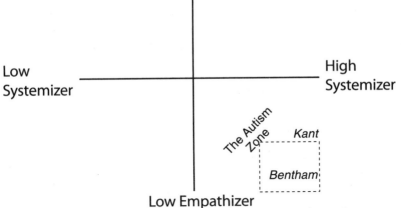

FIGURE 6.1. *Two dimensions of cognitive style.* People with autism are very high on systemizing and very low on empathizing. So were some important moral philosophers. (Adapted from Baron-Cohen 2009.)

Autism, including Asperger's syndrome (a subtype of high-functioning autism), is better thought of as a region of personality-space—the lower right corner of the lower right quadrant—than as a discrete disease.[15] The two leading ethical theories in Western philosophy were founded by men who were as high as could be on systemizing, and were rather low on empathizing.

BENTHAM AND THE UTILITARIAN GRILL

Jeremy Bentham was born in England in 1748. He went to Oxford at the age of twelve, trained as a lawyer, and devoted his career to reforming the mess of contradictory and often pointless rules and punishments that had accreted over many centuries to constitute English law. His most important work was titled *Introduction to the Principles of Morals and Legislation.* In it he proposed that a single principle should govern all reforms, all laws, and even all human actions: the *principle of utility,* which he defined as "the principle which approves or disapproves of every action whatsoever, according to the tendency which it appears to have to augment or diminish the happiness of the party whose interest is in question."[16] Each law should aim to maximize the utility of the community, which is defined as the simple arithmetic sum of the expected utilities of each member. Bentham then systematized the parameters needed to calculate utility, including the intensity, duration, and certainty of "hedons" (pleasures) and "dolors" (pains). He offered an algorithm, the "felicific calculus," for summing the hedons and dolors to reach a moral verdict on any action, for any person, in any country.

Bentham's philosophy showed an extraordinary degree of systemizing, and as Baron-Cohen says, systemizing is a strength. Problems arise, however, when systemizing occurs in the absence of empathizing. In an article titled "Asperger's Syndrome and the Eccentricity and Genius of Jeremy Bentham," Philip Lucas and Anne Sheeran collect accounts of Bentham's personal life and compare them to the diagnostic criteria for Asperger's syndrome.[17] They find a close match on the main diagnostic criteria, including those involving low empathy and poor social relationships. Bentham had few friends as a child, and he left a string of angry ex-friends as an adult. He never married, referred to himself as a hermit, and seemed to care little about other people. One contemporary said of him: "He regards the people about him no more than the flies of a summer."[18]

A related criterion is an impaired imaginative capacity, particularly with respect to the inner lives of other people. In his philosophy as in his personal behavior, Bentham offended many of his contemporaries by his inability to perceive variety and subtlety in human motives. John Stuart Mill—a decidedly non-autistic utilitarian—came to despise Bentham. He wrote that Bentham's personality disqualified him as a philosopher because of the "incompleteness" of his mind:

> In many of the most natural and strongest feelings of
> human nature he had no sympathy; from many of its
> graver experiences he was altogether cut off; and the
> faculty by which one mind understands a mind dif-

ferent from itself, and throws itself into the feelings of that other mind, was denied him by his deficiency of Imagination.[19]

Lucas and Sheeran conclude that had Bentham been alive today, "it is likely he would have received the diagnosis of Asperger's syndrome."[20]

KANT AND THE DEONTOLOGICAL DINER

Immanuel Kant was born in Prussia in 1724. He was well acquainted with Hume's work and was favorably disposed toward sentimentalist theories early in his career, particularly when he wrote about aesthetics and the sublime. But although he granted that sentiments such as sympathy are crucial for a description of why people *in fact* behave morally, he was disturbed by the subjectivity that such an account implied for ethics. If one person has different moral sentiments from another, does she have different moral obligations? And what if people in one culture have different sentiments from people in another?

Kant, like Plato, wanted to discover the timeless, changeless form of the Good. He believed that morality had to be the same for all rational creatures, regardless of their cultural or individual proclivities. To discover this timeless form, it simply would not do to use observational methods—to look around the world and see what virtues people happened to pursue. Rather, he said that moral law could only be established by the process of a priori (prior to experience) philosophizing. It had to consist of principles that are inherent in and revealed through the operation of reason.[21] And Kant found such a principle: noncontradiction. Rather than offering a concrete rule with some specific content, such as "help the poor" or "honor your parents," Kant provided an abstract rule from which (he claimed) all other valid moral rules could be derived. He called it the categorical (or unconditional) imperative: "Act only according to that maxim whereby you can at the same time will that it should become a universal law."[22]

Bentham told us to use arithmetic to figure out the right course of action, but Kant told us to use logic. Both men accomplished miracles of systemization, boiling all of morality down to a single sentence, a single formula. Did Kant also have Asperger's syndrome?

Like Bentham, Kant was a loner who never married and whose inner life seems cold. He was famous for his love of routine (he set out for his afternoon walk at precisely three-thirty every day, regardless of the weather), and some experts have speculated that he too had Asperger's syndrome.[23] After reading accounts of Kant's personal life, however, I think the case is not as clear as it is for Bentham. Kant was widely liked, and he did seem to enjoy company, although some of his socializing had a calculated feel to it (he valued laughter and companionship because they were good for his health).[24] The safest thing to do is to take advantage of Baron-Cohen's two dimensions and say that Kant was one of the most extraordinary systemizers in human history while being rather low on empathizing, without joining Bentham at the bottom right corner of figure 6.1.

GETTING BACK ON TRACK

I do not want to suggest that utilitarianism and Kantian deontology are incorrect as moral theories just because they were founded by men who may have had Asperger's syndrome. That would be an ad hominem argument, a logical error, and a mean thing to say. Besides, both utilitarianism and Kantian deontology have been enormously generative in philosophy and public policy.

But in psychology our goal is descriptive. We want to discover how the moral mind *actually* works, not how it *ought* to work, and that can't be done by reasoning, math, or logic. It can be done only by observation, and observation is usually keener when informed by empathy.[25] However, philosophy began retreating from observation and empathy in the nineteenth century, placing ever more emphasis on reasoning and systematic thought. As Western societies became more educated, industrialized, rich, and democratic, the minds of its intellectuals changed. They became more analytic and less holistic.[26]

Utilitarianism and deontology became far more appealing to ethicists than Hume's messy, pluralist, sentimentalist approach.

This trend explains why I found moral psychology so dull when I first studied it in graduate school. Kohlberg had embraced Kant's rationalism. He created a theory in which moral development had one and only one end point: a full understanding of justice. This whole approach felt wrong to me. It was oversystemized and underempathized. It was The True Taste restaurant, serving up a one-receptor morality.[27]

BROADENING THE PALATE

So what else is there beyond harm and fairness? Shweder's three ethics offered a useful starting point, but like most cultural anthropologists Shweder was wary of evolutionary explanations of human behavior. The prevailing view among anthropologists had long been that evolution got our species to the point of becoming bipedal, tool-using, large-brained creatures, but once we developed the capacity for culture, biological evolution stopped, or at least became irrelevant. Culture is so powerful that it can cause humans to behave in ways that override whatever ancient instincts we share with other primates.

I was convinced that the prevailing view in anthropology was wrong, and that it would never be possible to understand morality without evolution. But Shweder had taught me to be careful about evolutionary explanations, which are sometimes reductionist (because they ignore the shared meanings that are the focus of cultural anthropology) and naively functionalist (because they are too quick to assume that every behavior evolved to serve a function). Could I formulate an evolutionary account of moral intuition that was not reductionist, and that was cautious in its claims about the "purpose" or "function" of evolved psychological mechanisms? I couldn't just point to features of morality that seemed universal—such as compassion and reciprocity—and assert that they were innate merely because they were found everywhere. I had to have a careful evolutionary story for each one, and I had to be able to say how these innate intuitions interacted with cultural evolution to produce the variety of moral matrices that now cover the Earth.

I began by analyzing lists of virtues from around the world. Virtues are social constructions. The virtues taught to children in a warrior culture are different from those taught in a farming culture or a modern industrialized culture. There's always some overlap among lists, but even then there are different shades of meaning. Buddha, Christ, and Muhammad all talked about compassion, but in rather different ways.[28] Nonetheless, when you see that some version of kindness, fairness, and loyalty is valued in most cultures, you start wondering if there might be some low-level pan-human social receptors (analogous to taste receptors) that make it particularly easy for people to notice some kinds of social events rather than others.

To put it in terms of the taste analogy: Most cultures have one or more sweet beverages that are widely consumed—usually derived from a local fruit, or, in industrialized nations, just from sugar and a few flavorings. It would be silly to posit the existence of separate receptors for mango juice, apple juice, Coca-Cola, and Fanta. There's one main receptor at work here—the sweetness receptor—and each culture has invented various ways to trigger it.[29] If an anthropologist tells us that an Eskimo tribe has no such beverage, it would not mean that they lack the sweetness receptor; it would just show that Eskimo cuisine makes little use of it, for the obvious reason that Eskimos, until recently, had little access to fruit. And when primatologists tell us that chimpanzees and bonobos love fruit and will work hard in a laboratory task to obtain a sip of Coca-Cola, the case for an innate sweet receptor becomes even stronger.

My goal was to find links between virtues and well-established evolutionary theories. I didn't want to make the classic mistake of amateur evolutionary theorists, which is to pick a trait and then ask: "Can I think of a story about how this trait might once have been adaptive?" The answer to that question is almost always yes because reasoning can take you wherever you want to go. Anyone with access to an armchair can sit down and generate what Rudyard Kipling called "just-so stories"—fantastical accounts of how the camel got a hump and the elephant got a trunk. My goal, in contrast, was to identify the most obvious links between two fields I deeply respected: anthropology and evolutionary psychology.

MORAL FOUNDATIONS THEORY

I teamed up with a friend from my years at the University of Chicago, Craig Joseph, who had also worked with Shweder. Craig's research examined virtue concepts among Muslims in Egypt and the United States.

We borrowed the idea of "modularity" from the cognitive anthropologists Dan Sperber and Lawrence Hirschfeld.[30] Modules are like little switches in the brains of all animals. They are switched on by patterns that were important for survival in a particular ecological niche, and when they detect that pattern, they send out a signal that (eventually) changes the animal's behavior in a way that is (usually) adaptive. For example, many animals react with fear the very first time they see a snake because their brains include neural circuits that function as snake detectors.[31] As Sperber and Hirschfeld put it:

> An evolved cognitive module—for instance a snake detector, a face-recognition device . . . is an adaptation to a range of phenomena that presented problems or opportunities in the ancestral environment of the species. Its function is to process a given type of stimuli or inputs—for instance snakes [or] human faces.

This was a perfect description of what universal moral "taste receptors" would look like. They would be adaptations to long-standing threats and opportunities in social life. They would draw people's attention to certain kinds of events (such as cruelty or disrespect), and trigger instant intuitive reactions, perhaps even specific emotions (such as sympathy or anger).

This approach was just what we needed to account for cultural learning and variation. Sperber and Hirschfeld distinguished between the *original* triggers of a module and its *current* triggers.[32] The original triggers are the set of objects for which the module was designed[33] (that is, the set of all snakes is the original trigger for a snake-detector module). The current triggers are all the things in the world that happen to trigger it (including real snakes, as well as toy snakes, curved sticks, and thick ropes, any of which might give you a scare if you see them in the grass). Modules make mistakes, and many animals have evolved tricks to exploit the mistakes of other animals. For example, the hover fly has evolved yellow and black stripes, making it look like a wasp, which triggers the wasp-avoidance module in some birds that would otherwise enjoy eating hover flies.

Cultural variation in morality can be explained in part by noting that cultures can shrink or expand the current triggers of any module. For example, in the past fifty years people in many Western societies have come to feel compassion in response to many more kinds of animal suffering, and they've come to feel disgust in response to many fewer kinds of sexual activity. The current triggers can change in a single generation, even though it would take many generations for genetic evolution to alter the design of the module and its original triggers.

Furthermore, within any given culture, many moral controversies turn out to involve competing ways to link a behavior to a moral module. Should parents and teachers be allowed to spank children for disobedience? On the left side of the political spectrum, spanking typically triggers judgments of cruelty and oppression. On the right, it is sometimes linked to judgments about proper enforcement of rules, particularly rules about respect for parents and teachers. So even if we all share the same small set of cognitive modules, we can hook actions up to modules in so many ways that we can build conflicting moral matrices on the same small set of foundations.

Craig and I tried to identify the best candidates for being the universal cognitive modules upon which cultures construct moral matrices. We therefore called our approach Moral Foundations Theory.[34] We created it by identifying the adaptive challenges of social life that evolutionary psychologists frequently wrote about and then connecting those challenges to virtues that are found in some form in many cultures.[35]

	Care/ harm	Fairness/ cheating	Loyalty/ betrayal	Authority/ subversion	Sanctity/ degradation
Adaptive challenge	Protect and care for children	Reap benefits of two-way partnerships	Form cohesive coalitions	Forge beneficial relationships within hierarchies	Avoid contaminants
Original triggers	Suffering, distress, or neediness expressed by one's child	Cheating, cooperation, deception	Threat or challenge to group	Signs of dominance and submission	Waste products, diseased people
Current triggers	Baby seals, cute cartoon characters	Marital fidelity, broken vending machines	Sports teams, nations	Bosses, respected professionals	Taboo ideas (communism, racism)
Characteristic emotions	Compassion	Anger, gratitude, guilt	Group pride, rage at traitors	Respect, fear	Disgust
Relevant virtues	Caring, kindness	Fairness, justice, trustworthiness	Loyalty, patriotism, self-sacrifice	Obedience, deference	Temperance, chastity, piety, cleanliness

FIGURE 6.2. *The five foundations of morality (first draft).*

Five adaptive challenges stood out most clearly: caring for vulnerable children, forming partnerships with non-kin to reap the benefits of reciprocity, forming coalitions to compete with other coalitions, negotiating status hierarchies, and keeping oneself and one's kin free from parasites and pathogens, which spread quickly when people live in close proximity to each other. (I'll present the sixth foundation—Liberty/oppression—in chapter 8.)

In figure 6.2 I have drawn a column for each of the five foundations we initially proposed.[36] The first row gives the adaptive challenges. If our ancestors faced these challenges for hundreds of thousands of years, then natural selection would favor those whose cognitive modules helped them to get things right—rapidly and intuitively—compared to those who had to rely upon their general intelligence (the rider) to solve recurrent problems. The second row gives the original triggers—that is, the sorts of social patterns that such a module should detect. (Note that the foundations are really *sets* of modules that work together to meet the adaptive challenge.)[37] The third row lists examples of the current triggers—the sorts of things that do in fact trigger the relevant modules (sometimes by mistake) for people in a modern Western society. The fourth row lists some emotions that are part of the output of each foundation, at least when the foundation is activated very strongly. The fifth row lists some of the virtue words that we use to talk about people who trigger a particular moral "taste" in our minds.

I'll talk about each foundation in more detail in the next chapter. For now, I just want to demonstrate the theory using the Care/harm foundation. Imagine that your four-year-old son is taken to the hospital to have his appendix removed. You are allowed to watch the procedure from behind a glass window. Your son is given a general anesthetic and you see him lying, unconscious, on the operating table. Next, you see the surgeon's knife puncture his abdomen. Would you feel a wave of relief, knowing that he is finally getting an operation that will save his life? Or would you feel pain so strongly that you'd have to look away? If your "dolors" (pains) outweigh your "hedons" (pleasures), then your reaction is irrational, from a utilitarian point of view, but it makes perfect sense as the output of a module. We respond emotionally to signs of violence or suffering, particularly when a child is involved, particularly our own child. We respond even when we know consciously that it's not really violence and he's not really suffering. It's like the Muller-Lyer illusion: we can't help but see one line as longer, even when we know consciously that they are the same length.

As you watch the surgery, you notice two nurses assisting in the operation—one older, one younger. Both are fully attentive to the procedure, but the older nurse occasionally strokes your son's head, as though trying to comfort him. The younger nurse is all business. Suppose, for the sake of argument, that there was conclusive proof that patients under deep anesthetic don't hear or feel anything. If that were the case, then what should be your reaction to the two nurses? If you are a utilitarian, you should have no preference. The older nurse's actions did nothing to reduce suffering or improve the surgical outcome. If you are a Kantian, you'd also give the older nurse no extra credit. She seems to have acted absentmindedly, or (even worse, for Kant) she acted on her feelings. She did not act out of commitment to a universalizable principle. But if you are a Humean, then it is perfectly proper for you to like and praise the older nurse. She has so fully acquired the virtue of caring that she does it automatically and effortlessly, even when it has no effect. She is a virtuoso of caring, which is a fine and beautiful thing in a nurse. It tastes good.

IN SUM

The second principle of moral psychology is: *There's more to morality than harm and fairness.* In this chapter I began to say exactly what more there is:

- Morality is like taste in many ways—an analogy made long ago by Hume and Mencius.
- Deontology and utilitarianism are "one-receptor" moralities that are likely to appeal most strongly to people who are high on systemizing and low on empathizing.
- Hume's pluralist, sentimentalist, and naturalist approach to ethics is more promising than utilitarianism or deontology for modern moral psychology. As a first step in resuming Hume's project, we should try to identify the taste receptors of the righteous mind.
- Modularity can help us think about innate receptors, and how they produce a variety of initial perceptions that get developed in culturally variable ways.
- Five good candidates for being taste receptors of the righteous mind are care, fairness, loyalty, authority, and sanctity.

In psychology, theories are cheap. Anyone can invent one. Progress happens when theories are tested, supported, and corrected by empirical evidence, especially when a theory proves to be useful—for example, if it helps people to understand why half of the people in their country seem to live in a different moral universe. That's what happened next.

SEVEN

The Moral Foundations of Politics

Behind every act of altruism, heroism, and human decency you'll find either selfishness or stupidity. That, at least, is the view long held by many social scientists who accepted the idea that *Homo sapiens* is really *Homo economicus*.[1] "Economic man" is a simple creature who makes all of life's choices like a shopper in a supermarket with plenty of time to compare jars of applesauce. If that's your view of human nature, then it's easy to create mathematical models of behavior because there's really just one principle at work: self-interest. People do whatever gets them the most benefit for the lowest cost.

To see how wrong this view is, answer the ten questions in figure 7.1. *Homo economicus* would put a price on sticking a needle into his own arm, and a lower price—perhaps zero—on the other nine actions, none of which hurts him directly or costs him anything.

More important than the numbers you wrote are the comparisons between columns. *Homo economicus* would find the actions in column B no more aversive than those in column A. If you found any of the actions in column B worse than their counterparts in column A, then congratulations, you are a human being, not an economist's fantasy. You have concerns beyond narrow self-interest. You have a working set of moral foundations.

How much would someone have to pay you to perform each of these actions? Assume that you'd be paid secretly and that there would be no social, legal, or other harmful consequences to you afterward. Answer by writing a number from 0 to 4 after each action, where:

0 = $0, I'd do it for free
1 = $100
2 = $10,000
3 = $1,000,000
4 = I would not do this for any amount of money

Column A	Column B
1a. Stick a sterile hypodermic needle into your arm. _____	1b. Stick a sterile hypodermic needle into the arm of a child you don't know. _____
2a. Accept a plasma-screen television that a friend of yours wants to give you. You know that the friend got the TV a year ago when the company that made it sent it to your friend, by mistake and at no charge. _____	2b. Accept a plasma-screen television that a friend of yours wants to give you. You know that your friend bought the TV a year ago from a thief who had stolen it from a wealthy family. _____
3a. Say something critical about your nation (which you believe to be true) while calling in, anonymously, to a talk-radio show in your nation. _____	3b. Say something critical about your nation (which you believe to be true) while calling in, anonymously, to a talk-radio show in a foreign nation. _____
4a. Slap a male friend in the face (with his permission) as part of a comedy skit. _____	4b. Slap your father in the face (with his permission) as part of a comedy skit. _____
5a. Attend a short avant-garde play in which the actors act like fools for thirty minutes, including failing to solve simple problems and falling down repeatedly onstage. _____	5b. Attend a short avant-garde play in which the actors act like animals for 30 minutes, including crawling around naked and grunting like chimpanzees. _____
Total for Column A: _____	Total for Column B: _____

FIGURE 7.1. *What's your price?*

I wrote these five pairs of actions so that the B column would give you an intuitive flash from each foundation, like putting a grain of salt or sugar on your tongue. The five rows illustrate violations of Care (hurting a child), Fairness (profiting from someone else's undeserved loss), Loyalty (criticizing your nation to outsiders), Authority (disrespecting your father), and Sanctity (acting in a degrading or disgusting way).

In the rest of this chapter I'll describe these foundations and how they became part of human nature. I'll show that these foundations are used differently, and to different degrees, to support moral matrices on the political left and right.

A NOTE ON INNATENESS

It used to be risky for a scientist to assert that anything about human behavior was innate. To back up such claims, you had to show that the trait was hardwired, unchangeable by experience, and found in all cultures. With that definition, not much is innate, aside from a few infant reflexes such as that cute thing they do when you put one finger into their little hands. If you proposed that anything more complex than that was innate—particularly a sex difference—you'd be told that there was a tribe somewhere on Earth that didn't show the trait, so therefore it's not innate.

We've advanced a lot since the 1970s in our understanding of the brain, and now we know that traits can be innate without being either hardwired or universal. As the neuroscientist Gary Marcus explains, "Nature bestows upon the newborn a considerably complex brain, but one that is best seen as *prewired*—flexible and subject to change—rather than *hardwired*, fixed, and immutable."[2]

To replace wiring diagrams, Marcus suggests a better analogy: The brain is like a book, the first draft of which is written by the genes during fetal development. No chapters are complete at birth, and some are just rough outlines waiting to be filled in during childhood. But not a single chapter—be it on sexuality, language, food preferences, or morality—consists of blank pages on which a society can inscribe any conceivable set of words. Marcus's analogy leads to the best definition of innateness I have ever seen:

> Nature provides a first draft, which experience then revises. . . . "Built-in" does not mean unmalleable; it means "*organized in advance of experience.*"[3]

The list of five moral foundations was my first attempt to specify how the righteous mind was "organized in advance of experience." But Moral Foundations Theory also tries to explain how that first draft gets revised during childhood to produce the diversity of moralities that we find across cultures—and across the political spectrum.

1. THE CARE/HARM FOUNDATION

Reptiles get a bad rap for being cold—not just cold-blooded but coldhearted. Some reptile mothers do hang around after their babies hatch, to provide some protection, but in many species they don't. So when the first mammals began suckling their young, they raised the cost of motherhood. No longer would females turn out dozens of babies and bet that a few would survive on their own.

Mammals make fewer bets and invest a lot more in each one, so mammals face the challenge of caring for and nurturing their children for a long time. Primate moms place even fewer bets and invest still more in each one. And human babies, whose brains are so enormous that a child must be pushed out through the birth canal a year before he or she can walk, are bets so huge that a woman can't even put her chips on the table by herself. She needs help in the last months of pregnancy, help to deliver the baby, and help to feed and care for the child for years after the birth. Given this big wager, there is an enormous adaptive challenge: to care for the vulnerable and expensive child, keep it safe, keep it alive, keep it from harm.

It is just not conceivable that the chapter on mothering in the book of human nature is entirely blank, leaving it for mothers to learn everything by cultural instruction or trial and error. Mothers who

FIGURE 7.2. *Baby Gogo, Max, and Gogo.*

were innately sensitive to signs of suffering, distress, or neediness improved their odds, relative to their less sensitive sisters.

And it's not only mothers who need innate knowledge. Given the number of people who pool their resources to bet on each child, evolution favored women and (to a lesser extent) men who had an automatic reaction to signs of need or suffering, such as crying, from children in their midst (who, in ancient times, were likely to be kin).[4] The suffering of your own children is the original trigger of one of the key modules of the Care foundation. (I'll often refer to foundations using only the first of their two names—Care rather than Care/ harm.) This module works with other related modules[5] to meet the adaptive challenge of protecting and caring for children.

This is not a just-so story. It is my retelling of the beginning of attachment theory, a well-supported theory that describes the system by which mothers and children regulate each other's behavior so that the child gets a good mix of protection and opportunities for independent exploration.[6]

The set of current triggers for any module is often much larger than the set of original triggers. The photo in figure 7.2 illustrates this expansion in four ways. First, you might find it cute. If you do, it's because your mind is automatically responsive to certain proportions

FIGURE 7.3. *A current trigger for the Care/harm foundation.*

and patterns that distinguish human children from adults. Cuteness primes us to care, nurture, protect, and interact.[7] It gets the elephant leaning. Second, although this is not your child, you might still have an instant emotional response because the Care foundation can be triggered by any child. Third, you might find my son's companions (Gogo and Baby Gogo) cute, even though they are not real children, because they were designed by a toy company to trigger your Care foundation. Fourth, Max loves Gogo; he screams when I accidentally sit on Gogo, and he often says, "I am Gogo's mommy," because his attachment system and Care foundation are developing normally.

If your buttons can get pushed by a photo of a child sleeping with two stuffed monkeys, just imagine how you'd feel if you saw a child or a cute animal facing the threat of violence, as in figure 7.3.

It makes no evolutionary sense for you to care about what happens to my son Max, or a hungry child in a faraway country, or a baby seal. But Darwin doesn't have to explain why you shed any *particular* tear. He just has to explain why you have tear ducts in the first place, and why those ducts can sometimes be activated by suffering that is not your own.[8] Darwin must explain the original triggers of each module. The current triggers can change rapidly. We care about violence toward many more classes of victims today than our grandparents did in their time.[9]

Political parties and interest groups strive to make their concerns become current triggers of your moral modules. To get your vote, your money, or your time, they must activate at least one of your moral foundations.[10] For example, figure 7.4 shows two cars I photographed in Charlottesville. What can you guess about the drivers' politics?

Bumper stickers are often tribal badges; they advertise the teams we support, including sports teams, universities, and rock bands. The driver of the "Save Darfur" car is announcing that he or she is on the liberal team. You know that intuitively, but I can give a more formal reason: The moral matrix of liberals, in America and elsewhere, rests more heavily on the Care foundation than do the matrices of conservatives, and this driver has selected three bumper stickers urging people to protect innocent victims.[11] The driver has no relationship to these victims. The driver is trying to get you to connect your thinking about Darfur and meat-eating to the intuitions generated by your Care foundation.

It was harder to find bumper stickers related to compassion for conservatives, but the "wounded warrior" car is an example. This driver is also trying to get you to care, but conservative caring is somewhat different—it is aimed not at animals or at people in other countries but at those who've sacrificed for the group.[12] It is not universalist; it is more local, and blended with loyalty.

2. THE FAIRNESS/CHEATING FOUNDATION

Suppose a coworker offers to take on your workload for five days so that you can add a second week to your Caribbean vacation. How would you feel? *Homo economicus* would feel unalloyed pleasure, as though he had just been given a free bag of groceries. But the rest

FIGURE 7.4. *Liberal and conservative caring.*

of us know that the bag isn't free. It's a big favor, and you can't repay your coworker by bringing back a bottle of rum. If you accept her offer, you're likely to do so while gushing forth expressions of gratitude, praise for her kindness, and a promise to do the same for her whenever she goes on vacation.

Evolutionary theorists often speak of genes as being "selfish," meaning that they can only influence an animal to do things that will spread copies of that gene. But one of the most important insights into the origins of morality is that "selfish" genes can give rise to generous creatures, as long as those creatures are selective in their generosity. Altruism toward kin is not a puzzle at all. Altruism toward non-kin, on the other hand, has presented one of the longest-running puzzles in the history of evolutionary thinking.[13] A big step toward its solution came in 1971 when Robert Trivers published his theory of reciprocal altruism.[14]

Trivers noted that evolution could create altruists in a species where individuals could remember their prior interactions with other individuals and then limit their current niceness to those who were likely to repay the favor. We humans are obviously just such a species. Trivers proposed that we evolved a set of moral emotions that make us play "tit for tat." We're usually nice to people when we first meet them. But after that we're selective: we cooperate with those who have been nice to us, and we shun those who took advantage of us.

Human life is a series of opportunities for mutually beneficial cooperation. If we play our cards right, we can work with others to enlarge the pie that we ultimately share. Hunters work together to bring down large prey that nobody could catch alone. Neighbors watch each other's houses and loan each other tools. Coworkers cover each other's shifts. For millions of years, our ancestors faced the adaptive challenge of reaping these benefits without getting suckered. Those whose moral emotions compelled them to play "tit for tat" reaped more of these benefits than those who played any other strategy, such as "help anyone who needs it" (which invites exploitation), or "take but don't give" (which can work just once with each person; pretty soon nobody's willing to share pie with you).[15] The original triggers of the Fairness modules are acts of cooperation or selfishness that people show toward us. We feel pleasure, liking, and friendship when people show signs that they can be trusted to reciprocate. We feel anger, contempt, and even sometimes disgust when people try to cheat us or take advantage of us.[16]

The current triggers of the Fairness modules include a great

FIGURE 7.5. *Fairness left and right.* Top: Sign at Occupy Wall Street, Zuccotti Park, New York City. Bottom: Sign at Tea Party rally, Washington, DC (photo by Emily Ekins). Everyone believes that taxes should be "fair."

many things that have gotten linked, culturally and politically, to the dynamics of reciprocity and cheating. On the left, concerns about equality and social justice are based in part on the Fairness foundation—wealthy and powerful groups are accused of gaining by exploiting those at the bottom while not paying their "fair share" of the tax burden. This is a major theme of the Occupy Wall Street movement, which I visited in October 2011 (see figure 7.5).[17] On the right, the Tea Party movement is also very concerned about fairness. They see Democrats as "socialists" who take money from hardworking Americans and give it to lazy people (including those who receive welfare or unemployment benefits) and to illegal immigrants (in the form of free health care and education).[18]

Everyone cares about fairness, but there are two major kinds. On the left, fairness often implies equality, but on the right it means proportionality—people should be rewarded in proportion to what they contribute, even if that guarantees unequal outcomes.

3. THE LOYALTY/BETRAYAL FOUNDATION

In the summer of 1954, Muzafar Sherif convinced twenty-two sets of working-class parents to let him take their twelve-year-old boys off their hands for three weeks. He brought the boys to a summer camp he had rented in Robbers Cave State Park, Oklahoma. There he conducted one of the most famous studies in social psychology, and one of the richest for understanding the foundations of morality. Sherif brought the boys to the camp in two groups of eleven, on two consecutive days, and housed them in different parts of the park. For the first five days, each group thought it was alone. Even still, they set about marking territory and creating tribal identities.

One group called themselves the "Rattlers," and the other group took the name "Eagles." The Rattlers discovered a good swimming hole upstream from the main camp and, after an initial swim, they made a few improvements to the site, such as laying a rock path down to the water. They then claimed the site as their own, as their special hideout, which they visited each day. The Rattlers were disturbed one day to discover paper cups at the site (which in fact they themselves had left behind); they were angry that "outsiders" had used their swimming hole.

A leader emerged in each group by consensus. When the boys were deciding what to do, they all suggested ideas. But when it came time to choose one of those ideas, the leader usually made the choice. Norms, songs, rituals, and distinctive identities began to form in each group (Rattlers are tough and never cry; Eagles never curse). Even though they were there to have fun, and even though they believed they were alone in the woods, each group ended up doing the sorts of things that would have been quite useful if they were about to face a rival group that claimed the same territory. Which they were.

On day 6 of the study, Sherif let the Rattlers get close enough to the baseball field to hear that other boys—the Eagles—were using it, even though the Rattlers had claimed it as their field. The Rattlers begged the camp counselors to let them challenge the Eagles to a baseball game. As he had planned to do from the start, Sherif then arranged a weeklong tournament of sports competitions and camping skills. From that point forward, Sherif says, "performance in all activities which might now become competitive (tent pitching, baseball, etc.) was entered into with more zest and also with more efficiency."[19] Tribal behavior increased dramatically. Both sides created flags and hung them in contested territory. They destroyed each other's flags, raided and vandalized each other's bunks, called each other nasty names, made weapons (socks filled with rocks), and would often have come to blows had the counselors not intervened.

We all recognize this portrait of boyhood. The male mind appears to be innately tribal—that is, structured in advance of experience so that boys and men *enjoy* doing the sorts of things that lead to group cohesion and success in conflicts between groups (including warfare).[20] The virtue of loyalty matters a great deal to both sexes, though the objects of loyalty tend to be teams and coalitions for boys, in contrast to two-person relationships for girls.[21]

Despite some claims by anthropologists in the 1970s, human beings are not the only species that engages in war or kills its own kind. It now appears that chimpanzees guard their territory, raid the territory of rivals, and, if they can pull it off, kill the males of the neighboring group and take their territory and their females.[22] And it now appears that warfare has been a constant feature of human life since long before agriculture and private property.[23] For millions of years, therefore, our ancestors faced the adaptive challenge of form-ing and maintaining coalitions that could fend off challenges and attacks from rival groups. We are the descendants of successful tribal-ists, not their more individualistic cousins.

Many psychological systems contribute to effective tribalism and success in inter-group competition. The Loyalty/betrayal founda-tion is just a part of our innate preparation for meeting the adaptive challenge of forming cohesive coalitions. The original trigger for the Loyalty foundation is anything that tells you who is a team player and who is a traitor, particularly when your team is fighting with other teams. But because we love tribalism so much, we seek out ways to form groups and teams that can compete just for the fun of compet-ing. Much of the psychology of sports is about expanding the current triggers of the Loyalty foundation so that people can have the plea-sures of binding themselves together to pursue harmless trophies. (A trophy is evidence of victory. The urge to take trophies—including body parts from slain foes—is widespread in warfare, occurring even during modern times.)[24]

I can't be certain that the owner of the car in figure 7.6 is a man, but I'm fairly confident that the owner is a Republican based on his or her choice to decorate the car using only the Loyalty foundation. The *V* with crossed swords is the symbol of the UVA sports teams (the Cavaliers) and the owner chose to pay an extra $20 every year to have a customized license plate honoring the American flag ("Old Glory") and American unity ("United We Stand").

The love of loyal teammates is matched by a corresponding hatred of traitors, who are usually considered to be far worse than enemies. The Koran, for example, is full of warnings about the duplicity of out-group members, particularly Jews, yet the Koran does not com-mand Muslims to kill Jews. Far worse than a Jew is an apostate— a Muslim who has betrayed or simply abandoned the faith. The Koran commands Muslims to kill apostates, and Allah himself promises that he "shall certainly roast them at a Fire; as often as their skins are wholly burned, We shall give them in exchange other skins, that they may taste the chastisement. Surely God is All-mighty,

FIGURE 7.6. *A car decorated with emblems of loyalty, and a sign modified to reject one kind of loyalty.*

All-wise."[25] Similarly, in *The Inferno,* Dante reserves the innermost circle of hell—and the most excruciating suffering—for the crime of treachery. Far worse than lust, gluttony, violence, or even heresy is the betrayal of one's family, team, or nation.

Given such strong links to love and hate, is it any wonder that the Loyalty foundation plays an important role in politics? The left tends toward universalism and away from nationalism,[26] so it often has trouble connecting to voters who rely on the Loyalty foundation. Indeed, because of its strong reliance upon the Care foundation, American liberals are often hostile to American foreign policy. For example, during the last year of George W. Bush's presidency, somebody vandalized a stop sign near my home (figure 7.6). I can't be certain that the vandal rejects teams and groups of all sorts, but I can be confident that he or she is far to the left of the owner of "OGLORY." The two photographs show opposing statements about the need for Americans to be team players at a time when America was fighting wars in Iraq and Afghanistan. Liberal activists often make it easy for conservatives to connect liberalism to the Loyalty foundation—and not in a good way. The title of Ann Coulter's 2003 book says it all: *Treason: Liberal Treachery from the Cold War to the War on Terrorism.*[27]

4. THE AUTHORITY/SUBVERSION FOUNDATION

Soon after I returned from India I was talking with a taxi driver who told me that he had just become a father. I asked him if he planned on staying in the United States or returning to his native Jordan. I'll never forget his response: "We will return to Jordan because I never want to hear my son say 'fuck you' to me." Now, most American children will never say such an awful thing to their parents, but some will, and many more will say it indirectly. Cultures vary enormously in the degree to which they demand that respect be shown to parents, teachers, and others in positions of authority.

The urge to respect hierarchical relationships is so deep that many languages encode it directly. In French, as in other romance languages, speakers are forced to choose whether they'll address someone using the respectful form (*vous*) or the familiar form (*tu*). Even English, which doesn't embed status into verb conjugations, embeds it elsewhere. Until recently, Americans addressed strangers and superiors using title plus last name (Mrs. Smith, Dr. Jones), whereas intimates and subordinates were called by first name. If you've ever felt a flash of distaste when a salesperson called you by first name without being invited to do so, or if you felt a pang of awkwardness when an older person you have long revered asked you to call him by first name, then you have experienced the activation of some of the modules that comprise the Authority/subversion foundation.

The obvious way to begin thinking about the evolution of the Authority foundation is to consider the pecking orders and dominance hierarchies of chickens, dogs, chimpanzees, and so many other species that live in groups. The displays made by low-ranking individuals are often similar across species because their function is always the same—to appear submissive, which means small and nonthreatening. The failure to detect signs of dominance and then to respond accordingly often results in a beating.

So far this doesn't sound like a promising origin story for a "moral" foundation; it sounds like the origin of oppression of the weak by the powerful. But authority should not be confused with power.[28] Even among chimpanzees, where dominance hierarchies are indeed about raw power and the ability to inflict violence, the alpha male performs some socially beneficial functions, such as taking on the "control role."[29] He resolves some disputes and suppresses much of the violent conflict that erupts when there is no clear alpha male. As the primatologist Frans de Waal puts it: "Without agreement on rank and a certain respect for authority there can be no great sensitivity to social rules, as anyone who has tried to teach simple house rules to a cat will agree."[30]

This control role is quite visible in human tribes and early civilizations. Many of the earliest legal texts begin by grounding the king's rule in divine choice, and then they dedicate the king's authority to providing order and justice. The very first sentence of the Code of Hammurabi (eighteenth century BCE) includes this clause: "Then Anu and Bel [two gods] called by name me, Hammurabi, the exalted prince, who feared God, to bring about the rule of righteousness in the land, to destroy the wicked and the evil-doers; so that the strong should not harm the weak."[31]

Human authority, then, is not just raw power backed by the threat of force. Human authorities take on responsibility for maintaining order and justice. Of course, authorities often exploit their subordinates for their own benefit while believing they are perfectly just. But if we want to understand how human civilizations burst forth and covered the Earth in just a few thousand years, we'll have to look closely at the role of authority in creating moral order.

When I began graduate school I subscribed to the common liberal belief that hierarchy = power = exploitation = evil. But when I began to work with Alan Fiske, I discovered that I was wrong. Fiske's theory of the four basic kinds of social relationships includes one called "Authority Ranking." Drawing on his own fieldwork in Africa, Fiske showed that people who relate to each other in this way have mutual expectations that are more like those of a parent and child than those of a dictator and fearful underlings:

> In Authority Ranking, people have asymmetric positions
> in a linear hierarchy in which subordinates defer, respect,

and (perhaps) obey, while superiors take precedence and take pastoral responsibility for subordinates. Examples are military hierarchies . . . ancestor worship ([includ-ing] offerings of filial piety and expectations of protec-tion and enforcement of norms), [and] monotheistic religious moralities . . . Authority Ranking relationships are based on perceptions of legitimate asymmetries, not coercive power; they are not inherently exploitative.[32]

The Authority foundation, as I describe it, is borrowed directly from Fiske. It is more complex than the other foundations because its modules must look in two directions—up toward superiors and down toward subordinates. These modules work together to help individu-als meet the adaptive challenge of forging beneficial relationships within hierarchies. We are the descendants of the individuals who were best able to play the game—to rise in status while cultivating the protection of superiors and the allegiance of subordinates.[33]

The original triggers of some of these modules include patterns of appearance and behavior that indicate higher versus lower rank. Like chimpanzees, people track and remember who is above whom.[34] When people within a hierarchical order act in ways that negate or subvert that order, we feel it instantly, even if we ourselves have not been directly harmed. If authority is in part about protecting order and fending off chaos, then everyone has a stake in supporting the existing order and in holding people accountable for fulfilling the obligations of their station.[35]

The current triggers of the Authority/subversion foundation, therefore, include anything that is construed as an act of obedience, disobedience, respect, disrespect, submission, or rebellion, with regard to authorities perceived to be legitimate. Current triggers also include acts that are seen to subvert the traditions, institutions, or values that are perceived to provide stability. As with the Loyalty foundation, it is much easier for the political right to build on this foundation than it is for the left, which often defines itself in part by its opposition to hierarchy, inequality, and power. It should not be difficult for you to guess the politics of the magazine advertised in figure 7.7. Conversely,

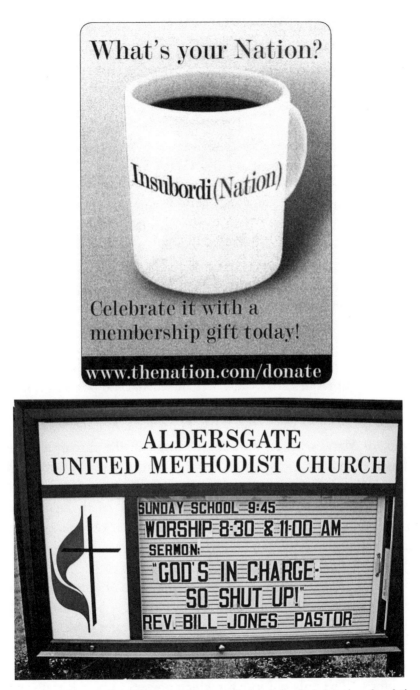

FIGURE 7.7. *Two rather different valuations of the Authority/subversion foundation.* Advertisement for the liberal magazine *The Nation* (top); church in Charlottesville, Virginia (bottom; photo by Sarah Estes Graham).

while Methodists are not necessarily conservative, the sign in front of their church tells you they ain't no Unitarians.

5. THE SANCTITY/DEGRADATION FOUNDATION

In early 2001, Armin Meiwes, a German computer technician, posted an unusual advertisement on the Web: "Looking for a well-built 21-to-30-year-old to be slaughtered and then consumed." Hundreds of men responded by email, and Meiwes interviewed a few of them at his farmhouse. Bernd Brandes, a forty-three-year-old computer engineer, was the first respondent who didn't change his mind when he realized that Meiwes was not engaging in mere fantasy. (Warning: Squeamish readers should skip the entire next paragraph.)

On the evening of March 9, the two men made a video to prove that Brandes fully consented to what was about to happen. Brandes then took some sleeping pills and alcohol, but he was still alert when Meiwes cut off Brandes's penis, after being unable to bite it off (as Brandes had requested). Meiwes then sautéed the penis in a frying pan with wine and garlic. Brandes took a bite of it, then went off to a bathtub to bleed to death. A few hours later Brandes was not yet dead, so Meiwes kissed him, stabbed him in the throat, and then hung the body on a meat hook to strip off the flesh. Meiwes stored the flesh in his freezer and ate it gradually over the next ten months. Meiwes was ultimately caught, arrested, and tried, but because Brandes's participation was fully voluntary, Meiwes was convicted only of manslaughter, not murder, the first time the case went to trial.[36]

If your moral matrix is limited to the ethic of autonomy, you're at high risk of being dumbfounded by this case. You surely find it disturbing, and the violence of it probably activates your Care/harm foundation. But any attempt to condemn Meiwes or Brandes runs smack into John Stuart Mill's harm principle, which I introduced in chapter 5: "The only purpose for which power can be rightfully exercised over any member of a civilized community, against his will, is to prevent harm to others." The next line of the original quote is: "His own good, either physical or moral, is not sufficient warrant." From within the ethic of autonomy, people have a right to live their lives as they please (as long as they harm nobody), and they have a right to end their lives how and when they please (as long as they leave no dependents unsupported). Brandes chose an extraordinarily revolting means of death, but as the Penn students in my dissertation research often said, just because something is disgusting, that doesn't make it wrong. Yet most people feel that there *was* something terribly wrong here, and that it should be against the law for adults to engage in consensual activities such as this. Why?

Imagine that Meiwes served his prison sentence and then returned to his home. (Assume that a team of psychiatrists established that he posed no threat to anyone who did not explicitly ask to be eaten.) Imagine that his home was one block away from your home. Would you find his return unsettling? If Meiwes was then forced by social pressure to move out of your town, might you feel some relief? And what about the house where this atrocity happened? How much would someone have to pay you to live in it for a week? Might you feel that the stain would be expunged only if the house was burned to the ground?

These feelings—of stain, pollution, and purification—are irrational from a utilitarian point of view, but they make perfect sense in Shweder's ethic of divinity. Meiwes and Brandes colluded to treat Brandes's body as a piece of meat, to which they added the extra horror of a splash of sexuality. They behaved monstrously—as low as any humans can go on the vertical dimension of divinity that I discussed in chapter 5. Only worms and demons eat human flesh. But why do we care so much what other people choose to do with their bodies?

Most animals are born knowing what to eat. A koala bear's sensory systems are "structured in advance of experience" to guide it to eucalyptus leaves. Humans, however, must learn what to eat. Like rats and cockroaches, we're omnivores.

Being an omnivore has the enormous advantage of flexibility: You can wander into a new continent and be quite confident that you'll find something to eat. But it also has the disadvantage that new foods can be toxic, infected with microbes, or riddled with parasitic worms. The "omnivore's dilemma" (a term coined by Paul Rozin)[37] is that omnivores must seek out and explore new potential foods while remaining wary of them until they are proven safe.

Omnivores therefore go through life with two competing motives: neophilia (an attraction to new things) and neophobia (a fear of new things). People vary in terms of which motive is stronger, and this variation will come back to help us in later chapters: Liberals score higher on measures of neophilia (also known as "openness to experience"), not just for new foods but also for new people, music, and ideas. Conservatives are higher on neophobia; they prefer to stick with what's tried and true, and they care a lot more about guarding borders, boundaries, and traditions.[38]

The emotion of disgust evolved initially to optimize responses to the omnivore's dilemma.[39] Individuals who had a properly calibrated sense of disgust were able to consume more calories than their overly disgustable cousins while consuming fewer dangerous microbes than their insufficiently disgustable cousins. But it's not just food that posed a threat: when early hominids came down from the trees and began living in larger groups on the ground, they greatly increased their risk of infection from each other, and from each other's waste products. The psychologist Mark Schaller has shown that disgust is part of what he calls the "behavioral immune system"—a set of cognitive modules that are triggered by signs of infection or disease in other people and that make you want to get away from those people.[40] It's a lot more effective to prevent infection by washing your food, casting out lepers, or simply avoiding dirty people than it is to let the microbes into your body and then hope that your biological immune system can kill every last one of them.

The original adaptive challenge that drove the evolution of the Sanctity foundation, therefore, was the need to avoid pathogens, parasites, and other threats that spread by physical touch or proximity. The original triggers of the key modules that compose this foundation include smells, sights, or other sensory patterns that predict the presence of dangerous pathogens in objects or people. (Examples include human corpses, excrement, scavengers such as vultures, and people with visible lesions or sores.)

The current triggers of the Sanctity foundation, however, are extraordinarily variable and expandable across cultures and eras. A common and direct expansion is to out-group members. Cultures differ in their attitudes toward immigrants, and there is some evidence that liberal and welcoming attitudes are more common in times and places where disease risks are lower.[41] Plagues, epidemics, and new diseases are usually brought in by foreigners—as are many new ideas, goods, and technologies—so societies face an analogue of the omnivore's dilemma, balancing xenophobia and xenophilia.

As with the Authority foundation, Sanctity seems to be off to a poor start as a foundation of morality. Isn't it just a primitive response to pathogens? And doesn't this response lead to prejudice and discrimination? Now that we have antibiotics, we should reject this foundation entirely, right?

Not so fast. The Sanctity foundation makes it easy for us to regard some things as "untouchable," both in a bad way (because something is so dirty or polluted we want to stay away) and in a good way (because something is so hallowed, so sacred, that we want to protect it from desecration). If we had no sense of disgust, I believe we would also have no sense of the sacred. And if you think, as I do, that one of the greatest unsolved mysteries is how people ever came together to form large cooperative societies, then you might take a special interest in the psychology of sacredness. Why do people so readily treat objects (flags, crosses), places (Mecca, a battlefield related to the birth of your nation), people (saints, heroes), and principles (liberty, fraternity, equality) as though they were of infinite value? Whatever its origins, the psychology of sacredness helps bind individuals into moral communities.[42] When someone in a moral community desecrates one of the sacred pillars supporting the community, the reaction is sure to be swift, emotional, collective, and punitive.

To return, finally, to Meiwes and Brandes: They caused no harm to anyone in a direct, material, or utilitarian way.[43] But they desecrated several of the bedrock moral principles of Western society, such as our shared beliefs that human life is supremely valuable, and that the human body is more than just a walking slab of meat. They trampled on these principles not out of necessity, and not in service to a higher goal, but out of carnal desire. If Mill's harm principle prevents us from outlawing their actions, then Mill's harm principle seems inadequate as the basis for a moral community. Whether or not God exists, people feel that some things, actions, and people are noble, pure, and elevated; others are base, polluted, and degraded.

Does the Meiwes case tell us anything about politics? It's too revolting a case to use in research; I'm confident that liberals and conservatives would all condemn Meiwes (although I'm not so sure about libertarians).[44] But if we turn down the disgust a few notches, we see a vast difference between left and right over the use of concepts such as sanctity and purity. American conservatives are more likely to talk about "the sanctity of life" and "the sanctity of marriage." Conservatives—particularly religious conservatives—are more likely to view the body as a temple, housing a soul within, rather than as a machine to be optimized, or as a playground to be used for fun.

The two images in figure 7.8 show exactly the contrast that Shweder had described in his ethic of divinity. The image on top is from a fifteenth-century painting, *The Allegory of Chastity*.[45] It shows the Virgin Mary raised and protected by an amethyst rock formation. From beneath her flows a stream (symbolizing her purity) guarded by two lions. The painting portrays chastity as a virtue, a treasure to be guarded.

This idea is not just ancient history; it inspired a virginity pledge movement in the United States as recently as the 1990s. The group Silver Ring Thing asks its members to vow to remain celibate and pure until marriage. Those who make the vow are given a silver ring, to wear like a wedding ring, inscribed with the name of Bible verses such as "1 Thessalonians 4:3–4." Those verses state: "For this is the will of God, your sanctification: that you abstain from fornication; that each one of you know how to control your own body in holiness and honor."[46]

On the left, however, the virtue of chastity is usually dismissed as outdated and sexist. Jeremy Bentham urged us to maximize our "hedons" (pleasures) and minimize our "dolors" (pains). If your morality focuses on individuals and their conscious experiences, then why on earth should anyone *not* use their body as a playground? Devout Christians are often lampooned by secular liberals as uptight, pleasure-fearing prudes.

FIGURE 7.8. *Two different views of the Sanctity/degradation foundation. The Allegory of Chastity*, by Hans Memling (1475), and a bumper sticker on a car in Charlottesville, Virginia. Another sticker on the car (supporting Democratic Senator Jim Webb) confirmed that the owner leaned left.

The Sanctity foundation is used most heavily by the religious right, but it is also used on the spiritual left. You can see the foundation's original impurity-avoidance function in New Age grocery stores, where you'll find a variety of products that promise to cleanse you of "toxins." And you'll find the Sanctity foundation underlying some of the moral passions of the environmental movement. Many environmentalists revile industrialism, capitalism, and automobiles not just for the physical pollution they create but also for a more symbolic kind of pollution—a degradation of nature, and of humanity's original nature, before it was corrupted by industrial capitalism.[47]

The Sanctity foundation is crucial for understanding the American culture wars, particularly over biomedical issues. If you dismiss the Sanctity foundation entirely, then it's hard to understand the fuss over most of today's biomedical controversies. The only ethical question about abortion becomes: At what point can a fetus feel pain? Doctor-assisted suicide becomes an obviously good thing: People who are suffering should be allowed to end their lives, and should be given medical help to do it painlessly. Same for stem cell research: Why not take tissue from all those embryos living in suspended animation in fertility clinics? They can't feel pain, but their tissues could help researchers develop cures that would spare sentient people from pain.

The philosopher Leon Kass is among the foremost spokesmen for Shweder's ethic of divinity, and for the Sanctity foundation on which it is based. Writing in 1997, the year after Dolly the sheep became the first cloned mammal, Kass lamented the way that technology often erases moral boundaries and brings people ever closer to the dangerous belief that they can do anything they want to do. In an essay titled "The Wisdom of Repugnance," Kass argued that our feelings of disgust can sometimes provide us with a valuable warning that we are going too far, even when we are morally dumbfounded and can't justify those feelings by pointing to victims:

> Repugnance, here as elsewhere, revolts against the excesses of human willfulness, warning us not to transgress what is unspeakably profound. Indeed, in this age

in which everything is held to be permissible so long as it is freely done, in which our given human nature no longer commands respect, in which our bodies are regarded as mere instruments of our autonomous rational wills, repugnance may be the only voice left that speaks up to defend the central core of our humanity. Shallow are the souls that have forgotten how to shudder.[48]

IN SUM

I began this chapter by trying to trigger your intuitions about the five moral foundations that I introduced in chapter 6. I then defined innateness as "organized in advance of experience," like the first draft of a book that gets revised as individuals grow up within diverse cultures. This definition allowed me to propose that the moral foundations are innate. Particular rules and virtues vary across cultures, so you'll get fooled if you look for universality in the finished books. You won't find a single paragraph that exists in identical form in every human culture. But if you look for links between evolutionary theory and anthropological observations, you can take some educated guesses about what was in the universal first draft of human nature. I tried to make (and justify) five such guesses:

- The Care/harm foundation evolved in response to the adaptive challenge of caring for vulnerable children. It makes us sensitive to signs of suffering and need; it makes us despise cruelty and want to care for those who are suffering.
- The Fairness/cheating foundation evolved in response to the adaptive challenge of reaping the rewards of cooperation without getting exploited. It makes us sensitive to indications that another person is likely to be a good (or bad) partner for collaboration and reciprocal altruism. It makes us want to shun or punish cheaters.

- The Loyalty/betrayal foundation evolved in response to the adaptive challenge of forming and maintaining coalitions. It makes us sensitive to signs that another person is (or is not) a team player. It makes us trust and reward such people, and it makes us want to hurt, ostracize, or even kill those who betray us or our group.
- The Authority/subversion foundation evolved in response to the adaptive challenge of forging relationships that will benefit us within social hierarchies. It makes us sensitive to signs of rank or status, and to signs that other people are (or are not) behaving properly, given their position.
- The Sanctity/degradation foundation evolved initially in response to the adaptive challenge of the omnivore's dilemma, and then to the broader challenge of living in a world of pathogens and parasites. It includes the behavioral immune system, which can make us wary of a diverse array of symbolic objects and threats. It makes it possible for people to invest objects with irrational and extreme values—both positive and negative—which are important for binding groups together.

I showed how the two ends of the political spectrum rely upon each foundation in different ways, or to different degrees. It appears that the left relies primarily on the Care and Fairness foundations, whereas the right uses all five. If this is true, then is the morality of the left like the food served in The True Taste restaurant? Does left-wing morality activate just one or two taste receptors, whereas right-wing morality engages a broader palate, including loyalty, authority, and sanctity? And if so, does that give conservative politicians a broader variety of ways to connect with voters?

EIGHT

The Conservative Advantage

In January 2005, I was invited to speak to the Charlottesville Democratic Party about moral psychology. I welcomed the chance because I had spent much of 2004 as a speechwriter for John Kerry's presidential campaign. Not a paid speechwriter—just a guy who, while walking his dog every evening, mentally rewrote some of Kerry's ineffectual appeals. For example, in Kerry's acceptance speech at the Democratic National Convention, he listed a variety of failures of the Bush administration and after each one he proclaimed, "America can do better" and "Help is on the way." The first slogan connected to no moral foundation at all. The second one connected weakly to the Care/harm foundation, but only if you think of America as a nation of helpless citizens who need a Democratic president to care for them.

In my rewrite, Kerry listed a variety of Bush's campaign promises and after each one he asked, "You gonna pay for that, George?" That simple slogan would have made Bush's many new programs, coming on top of his tax cuts and vast expenditures on two wars, look like shoplifting rather than generosity. Kerry could have activated the cheater detection modules of the Fairness/cheating foundation.

The message of my talk to the Charlottesville Democrats was

simple: *Republicans understand moral psychology. Democrats don't.* Republicans have long understood that the elephant is in charge of political behavior, not the rider, and they know how elephants work.[1] Their slogans, political commercials, and speeches go straight for the gut, as in the infamous 1988 ad showing a mug shot of a black man, Willie Horton, who committed a brutal murder after being released from prison on a weekend furlough by the "soft-on-crime" Democratic candidate, Governor Michael Dukakis. Democrats have often aimed their appeals more squarely at the rider, emphasizing specific policies and the benefits they'll bring to you, the voter.

Neither George W. Bush nor his father, George H. W. Bush, had the ability to move audiences to tears, but both had the great fortune to run against cerebral and emotionally cool Democrats (Michael Dukakis, Al Gore, and John Kerry). It is no coincidence that the only Democrat since Franklin Roosevelt to win election and then reelection combined gregariousness and oratorical skill with an almost musical emotionality. Bill Clinton knew how to charm elephants.

Republicans don't just aim to cause fear, as some Democrats charge. They trigger the full range of intuitions described by Moral Foundations Theory. Like Democrats, they can talk about innocent victims (of harmful Democratic policies) and about fairness (particularly the unfairness of taking tax money from hardworking and prudent people to support cheaters, slackers, and irresponsible fools). But Republicans since Nixon have had a near-monopoly on appeals to loyalty (particularly patriotism and military virtues) and authority (including respect for parents, teachers, elders, and the police, as well as for traditions). And after they embraced Christian conservatives during Ronald Reagan's 1980 campaign and became the party of "family values," Republicans inherited a powerful network of Christian ideas about sanctity and sexuality that allowed them to portray Democrats as the party of Sodom and Gomorrah. Set against the rising crime and chaos of the 1960s and 1970s, this five-foundation morality had wide appeal, even to many Democrats (the so-called Reagan Democrats). The moral vision offered by the Democrats since the 1960s, in contrast, seemed narrow, too focused on helping victims and fighting for the rights of the oppressed. The Democrats offered just sugar (Care) and salt (Fairness as equality), whereas Republican morality appealed to all five taste receptors.

That was the story I told to the Charlottesville Democrats. I didn't blame the Republicans for trickery. I blamed the Democrats for psychological naiveté. I expected an angry reaction, but after two consecutive losses to George W. Bush, Democrats were so hungry for an explanation that the audience seemed willing to consider mine. Back then, however, my explanation was just speculation. I had not yet collected any data to support my claim that conservatives responded to a broader set of moral tastes than did liberals.[2]

MEASURING MORALS

Fortunately, a graduate student arrived at UVA that year who made an honest man out of me. If Match.com had offered a way to pair up advisors and grad students, I couldn't have found a better partner than Jesse Graham. He had graduated from the University of Chicago (scholarly breadth), earned a master's degree at the Harvard Divinity School (an appreciation of religion), and then spent a year teaching English in Japan (cross-cultural experience). For Jesse's first-year research project, he created a questionnaire to measure people's scores on the five moral foundations.

We worked with my colleague Brian Nosek to create the first version of the Moral Foundations Questionnaire (MFQ), which began with these instructions: "When you decide whether something is right or wrong, to what extent are the following considerations relevant to your thinking?" We then explained the response scale, from 0 ("not at all relevant—this has nothing to do with my judgments of right and wrong") to 5 ("extremely relevant—this is one of the most important factors when I judge right and wrong"). We then listed fifteen statements—three for each of the five foundations—such as "whether or not someone was cruel" (for the Care foundation) or "whether or not someone showed a lack of respect for authority" (for the Authority foundation).

Brian was the director of ProjectImplicit.org, one of the largest

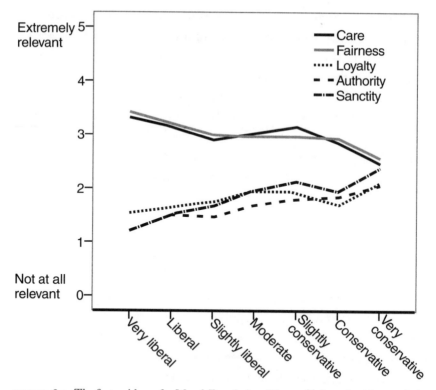

FIGURE 8.1. *The first evidence for Moral Foundations Theory.* (Adapted with permission from Graham, Haidt, and Nosek 2009, p. 1033; published by the American Psychological Association.)

research sites on the Internet, so we were able recruit 1,600 subjects to fill out the MFQ within a week. When Jesse graphed the data, he found exactly the differences we had predicted. I've reprinted Jesse's graph in figure 8.1, which shows responses from people who said they were "very liberal" on the far left, and then moves along the political spectrum through moderates (in the middle) to people who self-identified as "very conservative" (on the far right).[3]

As you can see, the lines for Care and Fairness (the two top lines) are moderately high across the board. Everyone—left, right, and center—says that concerns about compassion, cruelty, fairness, and injustice are relevant to their judgments about right and wrong. Yet still, the lines slope downward. Liberals say that these issues are a bit more relevant to morality than do conservatives.

But when we look at the Loyalty, Authority, and Sanctity foundations, the story is quite different. Liberals largely reject these considerations. They show such a large gap between these foundations versus the Care and Fairness foundations that we might say, as shorthand, that liberals have a two-foundation morality.[4] As we move to the right, however, the lines slope upward. By the time we reach people who are "very conservative," all five lines have converged. We can say, as shorthand, that conservatives have a five-foundation morality. But can it really be true that conservatives care about a broader range of moral values and issues than do liberals? Or did this pattern only arise because of the particular questions that we happened to ask?

Over the next year, Jesse, Brian, and I refined the MFQ. We added questions that asked people to rate their agreement with statements we wrote to trigger intuitions related to each foundation. For example, do you agree with this Care item: "One of the worst things a person can do is to hurt a defenseless animal"? How about this Loyalty item: "It is more important to be a team player than to express oneself"? Jesse's original findings replicated beautifully. We found the same pattern as in figure 8.1, and we found it in subjects from many countries besides the United States.[5]

I began to show our graphs whenever I gave lectures about moral psychology. Ravi Iyer, a graduate student at the University of Southern California, heard me speak in the fall of 2006 and emailed me to ask if he could use the MFQ in his research on attitudes about immigration. Ravi was a skilled Web programmer, and he offered to help Jesse and me create a website for our own research. At around the same time, Sena Koleva, a graduate student at the University of California at Irvine, asked me if she could use the MFQ. Sena was studying political psychology with her advisor, Pete Ditto (whose work on "motivated reasoning" I described in chapter 4). I said yes to both requests.

Every January, social psychologists from all over the world flock to a single conference to learn about each other's work—and to gossip, network, and drink. In 2007, that conference was held in Memphis, Tennessee. Ravi, Sena, Pete, Jesse, and I met late one evening at the hotel bar, to share our findings and get to know one another.

All five of us were politically liberal, yet we shared the same concern about the way our liberal field approached political psychology. The goal of so much research was to explain what was wrong with conservatives. (Why don't conservatives embrace equality, diversity, and change, like normal people?) Just that day, in a session on political psychology, several of the speakers had made jokes about conservatives, or about the cognitive limitations of President Bush. All five of us felt this was wrong, not just morally (because it creates a hostile climate for the few conservatives who might have been in the audience) but also scientifically (because it reveals a motivation to reach certain conclusions, and we all knew how easy it is for people to reach their desired conclusions).[6] The five of us also shared a deep concern about the polarization and incivility of American political life, and we wanted to use moral psychology to help political partisans understand and respect each other.

We talked about several ideas for future studies, and for each one Ravi said, "You know, we could do that online." He proposed that we create a website where people could register when they first visit, and then take part in dozens of studies on moral and political psychology. We could then link all of their responses together and develop a comprehensive moral profile for each (anonymous) visitor. In return, we'd give visitors detailed feedback, showing them how they compared to others. If we made the feedback interesting enough, people would tell their friends about the site.

Over the next few months, Ravi designed the website—www .YourMorals.org—and the five of us worked together to improve it. On May 9 we got approval from the UVA human subjects committee to conduct the research, and the site went live the next day. Within a few weeks we were getting ten or more visitors a day. Then, in August, the science writer Nicholas Wade interviewed me for an article in the *New York Times* on the roots of morality.[7] He included the name of our website. The article ran on September 18, and by the end of that week, 26,000 new visitors had completed one or more of our surveys.

Figure 8.2 shows our data on the MFQ as it stood in 2011, with more than 130,000 subjects. We've made many improvements since

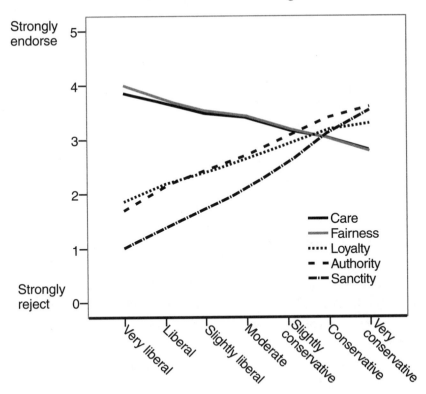

FIGURE 8.2. *Scores on the MFQ, from 132,000 subjects, in 2011.* Data from YourMorals.org.

Jesse's first simple survey, but we always find the same basic pattern that he found in 2006. The lines for Care and Fairness slant downward; the lines for Loyalty, Authority, and Sanctity slant upward. Liberals value Care and Fairness far more than the other three foundations; conservatives endorse all five foundations more or less equally.[8]

We've found this basic difference no matter how we ask the questions. For example, in one study we asked people which traits would make them more or less likely to choose a particular breed of dog as a pet. On which side of the political spectrum do you suppose these traits would be most appealing?

- The breed is extremely gentle.
- The breed is very independent-minded and relates to its owner as a friend and equal.

- The breed is extremely loyal to its home and family and it doesn't warm up quickly to strangers.
- The breed is very obedient and is easily trained to take orders.
- The breed is very clean and, like a cat, takes great care with its personal hygiene.

We found that people want dogs that fit their own moral matrices. Liberals want dogs that are gentle (i.e., that fit with the values of the Care foundation) and relate to their owners as equals (Fairness as equality). Conservatives, on the other hand, want dogs that are loyal (Loyalty) and obedient (Authority). (The Sanctity item showed no partisan tilt; both sides prefer clean dogs.)

The converging pattern shown in figure 8.2 is not just something we find in Internet surveys. We found it in church too. Jesse obtained the text of dozens of sermons that were delivered in Unitarian (liberal) churches, and dozens more that were delivered in Southern Baptist (conservative) churches. Before reading the sermons, Jesse identified hundreds of words that were conceptually related to each foundation (for example, *peace*, *care*, and *compassion* on the positive side of Care, and *suffer*, *cruel*, and *brutal* on the negative side; *obey*, *duty*, and *honor* on the positive side of Authority, and *defy*, *disrespect*, and *rebel* on the negative side). Jesse then used a computer program called LIWC to count the number of times that each word was used in the two sets of texts.[9] This simple-minded method confirmed our findings from the MFQ: Unitarian preachers made greater use of Care and Fairness words, while Baptist preachers made greater use of Loyalty, Authority, and Sanctity words.[10]

We find this pattern in brain waves too. We teamed up with Jamie Morris, a social neuroscientist at UVA, to present liberal and conservative students with sixty sentences that came in two versions. One version endorsed an idea consistent with a particular foundation, and the other version rejected the idea. For example, half of our subjects read "Total equality in the workplace is necessary." The other half read "Total equality in the workplace is unrealistic." Subjects wore a special cap to measure their brain waves as the words in each sentence were flashed up on a screen, one word at a time. We later looked at the encephalogram (EEG) to determine whose brains showed evidence of surprise or shock at the moment that the key word was presented (e.g., *necessary* versus *unrealistic*).[11]

Liberal brains showed more surprise, compared to conservative brains, in response to sentences that rejected Care and Fairness concerns. They also showed more surprise in response to sentences that endorsed Loyalty, Authority, and Sanctity concerns (for example, "In the teenage years, parental advice should be heeded" versus " . . . should be questioned"). In other words, when people choose the labels "liberal" or "conservative," they are not just choosing to endorse different values on questionnaires. Within the first half second after hearing a statement, partisan brains are already reacting differently. These initial flashes of neural activity *are* the elephant, leaning slightly, which then causes their riders to reason differently, search for different kinds of evidence, and reach different conclusions. Intuitions come first, strategic reasoning second.

WHAT MAKES PEOPLE VOTE REPUBLICAN?

When Barack Obama clinched the Democratic nomination for the presidential race, I was thrilled. At long last, it seemed, the Democrats had chosen a candidate with a broader moral palate, someone able to speak about all five foundations. In his book *The Audacity of Hope,* Obama showed himself to be a liberal who understood conservative arguments about the need for order and the value of tradition. When he gave a speech on Father's Day at a black church, he praised marriage and the traditional two-parent family, and he called on black men to take more responsibility for their children.[12] When he gave a speech on patriotism, he criticized the liberal counterculture of the 1960s for burning American flags and for failing to honor veterans returning from Vietnam.[13]

But as the summer of 2008 went on, I began to worry. His speech to a major civil rights organization was all about social justice and corporate greed.[14] It used only the Care and Fairness foundations, and fairness often meant equality of outcomes. In his famous speech in Berlin, he introduced himself as "a fellow citizen of the world" and he spoke of "global citizenship."[15] He had created a controversy earlier in the summer by refusing to wear an American flag pin on the lapel of his jacket, as American politicians typically do. The controversy seemed absurd to liberals, but the Berlin speech reinforced the emerging conservative narrative that Obama was a liberal universalist, someone who could not be trusted to put the interests of his nation above the interests of the rest of the world. His opponent, John McCain, took advantage of Obama's failure to build on the Loyalty foundation with his own campaign motto: "Country First."

Anxious that Obama would go the way of Gore and Kerry, I wrote an essay applying Moral Foundations Theory to the presidential race. I wanted to show Democrats how they could talk about policy issues in ways that would activate more than two foundations. John Brockman, who runs an online scientific salon at Edge.org, invited me to publish the essay at Edge,[16] as long as I stripped out most of the advice and focused on the moral psychology.

I titled the essay "What Makes People Vote Republican?" I began by summarizing the standard explanations that psychologists had offered for decades: Conservatives are conservative because they were raised by overly strict parents, or because they are inordinately afraid of change, novelty, and complexity, or because they suffer from existential fears and therefore cling to a simple worldview with no shades of gray.[17] These approaches all had one feature in common: they used psychology to explain away conservatism. They made it unnecessary for liberals to take conservative ideas seriously because these ideas are caused by bad childhoods or ugly personality traits. I suggested a very different approach: start by assuming that conservatives are just as sincere as liberals, and then use Moral Foundations Theory to understand the moral matrices of both sides.

The key idea in the essay was that there are two radically different approaches to the challenge of creating a society in which unrelated people can live together peacefully. One approach was exemplified by John Stuart Mill, the other by the great French sociologist Emile Durkheim. I described Mill's vision like this:

First, imagine society as a social contract invented for our mutual benefit. All individuals are equal, and all should be left as free as possible to move, develop talents, and form relationships as they please. The patron saint of a contractual society is John Stuart Mill, who wrote (in *On Liberty*) that "the only purpose for which power can be rightfully exercised over any member of a civilized community, against his will, is to prevent harm to others." Mill's vision appeals to many liberals and libertarians; a Millian society at its best would be a peaceful, open, and creative place where diverse individuals respect each other's rights and band together voluntarily (as in Obama's calls for "unity") to help those in need or to change the laws for the common good.

I showed how this vision of society rests exclusively on the Care and Fairness foundations. If you assume that everyone relies on those two foundations, you can assume that people will be bothered by cruelty and injustice and will be motivated to respect each other's rights. I then contrasted Mill's vision with Durkheim's:

Now imagine society not as an agreement among individuals but as something that emerged organically over time as people found ways of living together, binding themselves to each other, suppressing each other's selfishness, and punishing the deviants and free riders who eternally threaten to undermine cooperative groups. The basic social unit is not the individual, it is the hierarchically structured family, which serves as a model for other institutions. Individuals in such societies are born into strong and constraining relationships that profoundly limit their autonomy. The patron saint of this more binding moral system is the sociologist Emile Durkheim, who warned of the dangers of anomie (normlessness) and wrote, in 1897, that "man cannot become attached to higher aims and submit to a rule if he sees nothing above him to which he belongs. To free himself from all social pressure is to abandon himself and demoralize him." A Durkheimian society at its best would be a stable network composed of many nested and overlapping groups that socialize, reshape, and care for individuals who, if left to their own devices, would pursue shallow, carnal, and selfish pleasures. A Durkheimian society would value self-control over self-expression, duty over rights, and loyalty to one's groups over concerns for out-groups.

I showed that a Durkheimian society cannot be supported by the Care and Fairness foundations alone.[18] You have to build on the Loyalty, Authority, and Sanctity foundations as well. I then showed how the American left fails to understand social conservatives and the religious right because it cannot see a Durkheimian world as anything other than a moral abomination.[19] A Durkheimian world is usually hierarchical, punitive, and religious. It places limits on people's autonomy and it endorses traditions, often including traditional gender roles. For liberals, such a vision must be combated, not respected.

If your moral matrix rests entirely on the Care and Fairness foundations, then it's hard to hear the sacred overtones in America's unofficial motto: *E pluribus unum* (from many, one). By "sacred" I mean the concept I introduced with the Sanctity foundation in the last chapter. It's the ability to endow ideas, objects, and events with infinite value, particularly those ideas, objects, and events that bind a group together into a single entity. The process of converting *pluribus* (diverse people) into *unum* (a nation) is a miracle that occurs in every successful nation on Earth.[20] Nations decline or divide when they stop performing this miracle.

In the 1960s, the Democrats became the party of *pluribus*. Democrats generally celebrate diversity, support immigration without assimilation, oppose making English the national language, don't like to wear flag pins, and refer to themselves as citizens of the world. Is it any wonder that they have done so poorly in presidential elections since 1968?[21] The president is the high priest of what sociologist Robert Bellah calls the "American civil religion."[22] The president must invoke the name of God (though not Jesus), glorify America's heroes and history, quote its sacred texts (the Declaration of Independence and the Constitution), and perform the transubstantiation of *pluribus* into *unum*. Would Catholics ever choose a priest who refuses to speak Latin, or who considers himself a devotee of all gods?

In the remainder of the essay I advised Democrats to stop dismissing conservatism as a pathology and start thinking about morality beyond care and fairness. I urged them to close the sacredness gap between the two parties by making greater use of the Loyalty, Authority, and Sanctity foundations, not just in their "messaging," but in how they think about public policy and the best interests of the nation.[23]

WHAT I HAD MISSED

The essay provoked strong reactions from readers, which they sometimes shared with me by email. On the left, many readers stayed locked inside their Care-based moral matrices and refused to believe that conservatism was an alternative moral vision. For example, one reader said that he agreed with my diagnosis but thought that narcissism was an additional factor that I had not mentioned: "Lack of compassion fits them [Republicans], and narcissists are also lacking this important human trait." He thought it was "sad" that Republican narcissism would prevent them from understanding my perspective on their "illness."

Reactions from the right were generally more positive. Many readers with military or religious backgrounds found my portrayal of their morality accurate and useful, as in this email:

> I recently retired from the U.S. Coast Guard after 22 years of service.... After I retired, I took a job with [a government science agency]. The [new office's] culture tends more towards the liberal independent model.... What I am finding here is an organization

rife with individualism and infighting, at the expense of larger goals. In the military, I was always impressed with the great deeds that could be accomplished by a small number of dedicated people with limited resources. In my new group, I am impressed when we can accomplish anything at all.[24]

I also received quite a few angry responses, particularly from economic conservatives who believed I had misunderstood their morality. One such reader sent me an email with the subject line "Head up ass," which he explained in this way:

> I vote republican because I'm against other people (authority figures) taking my money (that I work hard for) and giving it to a non-producing, welfare collecting, single mother, crack baby producing future democrat. Simple . . . You're an over educated "philosopher" with soft hands who gets paid to ask stupid questions and come up with "reasonable" answers. . . . Go drop some acid and read some Jung.

Another angry reader posted to a blog discussion his own list of the "top fifteen reasons that people vote Democrat." His number one reason was "Low IQ," but the rest of his list revealed a lot about his moral matrix and its central value. It included the following:

- Laziness.
- You want something for nothing.
- You need someone to blame for your problems.
- You're afraid of personal responsibility or simply not willing to accept any.
- You despise people who work hard for their money, live their own lives, and don't rely on the government for help cradle to grave.
- You've had 5 kids from 3 different men and you need the welfare check.

These emails were overflowing with moral content, yet I had a hard time categorizing that content using Moral Foundations Theory. Much of it was related to fairness, but this kind of fairness had nothing to do with equality. It was the fairness of the Protestant work ethic and the Hindu law of karma: People should reap what they sow. People who work hard should get to keep the fruits of their labor. People who are lazy and irresponsible should suffer the consequences.

This email and other responses from economic conservatives made me realize that I and my colleagues at YourMorals.org had done a poor job of capturing conservative notions of fairness, which focused on proportionality, not equality. People should get what they deserve, based on what they have done. We had assumed that equality and proportionality were both part of the Fairness foundation, but the questions we used to measure this foundation were mostly about equality and equal rights. We therefore found that liberals cared more about fairness, and that's what had made these economic conservatives so angry at me. They believed that liberals don't give a damn about fairness (as proportionality).

Are proportionality and equality two different expressions of the same underlying cognitive module, as we had been assuming? Are they both related to reciprocal altruism, as Robert Trivers had described it? It's easy to explain why people care about proportionality and are so keen to catch cheaters. That follows directly from Trivers's analysis of how we gain by exchanging favors with reliable partners. But what about equality? Are liberal concerns about political and economic equality really related to reciprocal altruism? Is the passionate anger people feel toward bullies and oppressors the same as the anger they feel toward cheaters?

I looked into what was known about the egalitarianism of hunter-gatherers, and found a strong argument for splitting apart these two kinds of fairness. The desire for equality seems to be more closely related to the psychology of liberty and oppression than to the psychology of reciprocity and exchange. After talking about these issues with my colleagues at YourMorals.org, and after we ran some new studies on various kinds of fairness and liberty, we added a provisional sixth foundation—Liberty/oppression.[25] We also decided to revise our thinking about fairness to place more emphasis on proportionality. Let me explain.

THE LIBERTY/OPPRESSION FOUNDATION

In the last chapter I suggested that humans are, like our primate ancestors, innately equipped to live in dominance hierarchies that can be quite brutal. But if that's true, then how come nomadic hunter-gatherers are always egalitarian? There's no hierarchy (at least among the adult males), there's no chief, and the norms of the group actively encourage sharing resources, particularly meat.[26] The archaeological evidence supports this view, indicating that our ancestors lived for hundreds of thousands of years in egalitarian bands of mobile hunter-gatherers.[27] Hierarchy only becomes widespread around the time that groups take up agriculture or domesticate animals and become more sedentary. These changes create much more private property and much larger group sizes. They also put an end to equality. The best land and a share of everything people produce typically get dominated by a chief, leader, or elite class (who take some of their wealth with them to the grave for easy interpretation by later archaeologists). So were our minds "structured in advance of experience" for hierarchy or for equality?

For hierarchy, according to the anthropologist Christopher Boehm. Boehm studied tribal cultures early in his career, but had also studied chimpanzees with Jane Goodall. He recognized the extraordinary similarities in the ways that humans and chimpanzees display dominance and submission. In his book *Hierarchy in the Forest*, Boehm concluded that human beings are innately hierarchical, but that at some point during the last million years our ancestors underwent a "political transition" that allowed them to live as egalitarians by banding together to rein in, punish, or kill any would-be alpha males who tried to dominate the group.

Alpha male chimps are not truly *leaders* of their groups. They perform some public services, such as mediating conflicts.[28] But most of the time, they are better described as *bullies* who take what they want. Yet even among chimpanzees, it sometimes happens that subordinates gang up to take down alphas, occasionally going as far as to kill them.[29] Alpha male chimps must therefore know their limits and have enough political skill to cultivate a few allies and stave off rebellion.

Imagine early hominid life as a tense balance of power between the alpha (and an ally or two) and the larger set of males who are shut out of power. Then arm everyone with spears. The balance of power is likely to shift when physical strength no longer decides the outcome of every fight. That's essentially what happened, Boehm suggests, as our ancestors developed better weapons for hunting and butchering beginning around five hundred thousand years ago, when the archaeological record begins to show a flowering of tool and weapon types.[30] Once early humans had developed spears, anyone could kill a bullying alpha male. And if you add the ability to communicate with language, and note that every human society uses language to gossip about moral violations,[31] then it becomes easy to see how early humans developed the ability to unite in order to shame, ostracize, or kill anyone whose behavior threatened or simply annoyed the rest of the group.

Boehm's claim is that at some point during the last half-million years, well after the advent of language, our ancestors created the first true moral communities.[32] In these communities, people used gossip to identify behavior they didn't like, particularly the aggressive, dominating behaviors of would-be alpha males. On the rare occasions when gossip wasn't enough to bring them into line, they had the ability to use weapons to take them down. Boehm quotes a dramatic account of such a community in action among the !Kung people of the Kalahari Desert:

> A man named Twi had killed three other people, when the community, in a rare move of unanimity, ambushed and fatally wounded him in full daylight. As he lay dying, all of the men fired at him with poisoned arrows until, in the words of one informant, "he looked like a porcupine." Then, after he was dead, all the women as

well as the men approached his body and stabbed him with spears, symbolically sharing the responsibility for his death.[33]

It's not that human nature suddenly changed and became egalitarian; men still tried to dominate others when they could get away with it. Rather, people armed with weapons and gossip created what Boehm calls "reverse dominance hierarchies" in which the rank and file band together to dominate and restrain would-be alpha males. (It's uncannily similar to Marx's dream of the "dictatorship of the proletariat.")[34] The result is a fragile state of political egalitarianism achieved by cooperation among creatures who are innately predisposed to hierarchical arrangements. It's a great example of how "innate" refers to the first draft of the mind. The final edition can look quite different, so it's a mistake to look at today's hunter-gatherers and say, "See, that's what human nature *really* looks like!"

For groups that made this political transition to egalitarianism, there was a quantum leap in the development of moral matrices. People now lived in much denser webs of norms, informal sanctions, and occasionally violent punishments. Those who could navigate this new world skillfully and maintain good reputations were rewarded by gaining the trust, cooperation, and political support of others. Those who could not respect group norms, or who acted like bullies, were removed from the gene pool by being shunned, expelled, or killed. Genes and cultural practices (such as the collective killing of deviants) coevolved.

The end result, says Boehm, was a process sometimes called "self-domestication." Just as animal breeders can create tamer, gentler creatures by selectively breeding for those traits, our ancestors began to selectively breed themselves (unintentionally) for the ability to construct shared moral matrices and then live cooperatively within them.

The Liberty/oppression foundation, I propose, evolved in response to the adaptive challenge of living in small groups with individuals who would, if given the chance, dominate, bully, and constrain others. The original triggers therefore include signs of attempted domination. Anything that suggests the aggressive, controlling behavior of an alpha male (or female) can trigger this form of righteous anger, which is sometimes called *reactance*. (That's the feeling you get when an authority tells you you can't do something and you feel yourself wanting to do it even more strongly.)[35] But people don't suffer oppression in private; the rise of a would-be dominator triggers a motivation to unite as equals with other oppressed individuals to resist, restrain, and in extreme cases kill the oppressor. Individuals who failed to detect signs of domination and respond to them with righteous and group-unifying anger faced the prospect of reduced access to food, mates, and all the other things that make individuals (and their genes) successful in the Darwinian sense.[36]

The Liberty foundation obviously operates in tension with the Authority foundation. We all recognize some kinds of authority as legitimate in some contexts, but we are also wary of those who claim to be leaders unless they have first earned our trust. We're vigilant for signs that they've crossed the line into self-aggrandizement and tyranny.[37]

The Liberty foundation supports the moral matrix of revolutionaries and "freedom fighters" everywhere. The American Declaration of Independence is a long enumeration of "repeated injuries and usurpations, all having in direct object the establishment of absolute Tyranny over these states." The document begins with the claim that "all men are created equal" and ends with a stirring pledge of unity: "We mutually pledge to each other our Lives, our Fortunes and our sacred Honor." The French revolutionaries, similarly, had to call for *fraternité* and *égalité* if they were going to entice commoners to join them in their regicidal quest for *liberté*.

The flag of my state, Virginia, celebrates assassination (see figure 8.3). It's a bizarre flag, unless you understand the Liberty/oppression foundation. The flag shows virtue (embodied as a woman) standing on the chest of a dead king, with the motto *Sic semper tyrannis* ("Thus always to tyrants"). That was the rallying cry said to have been shouted by Marcus Brutus as he and his co-conspirators murdered Julius Caesar for acting like an alpha male. John Wilkes Booth shouted it from center stage at Ford's Theatre moments after shooting Abraham Lincoln (whom Southerners perceived to be a tyrant who prevented them from declaring independence).

FIGURE 8.3. *The flag of Virginia, illustrating the Liberty/oppression foundation.*

Murder often seems virtuous to revolutionaries. It just somehow *feels* like the right thing to do, and these feelings seem far removed from Trivers's reciprocal altruism and tit for tat. This is not fairness. This is Boehm's political transition and reverse dominance.

If the original triggers of this foundation include bullies and tyrants, the current triggers include almost anything that is perceived as imposing illegitimate restraints on one's liberty, including government (from the perspective of the American right). In 1993, when Timothy McVeigh was arrested a few hours after he blew up a federal office building in Oklahoma City, killing 168 people, he was wearing a T-shirt that said *Sic semper tyrannis*. Less ominously, the populist anger of the Tea Party relies on this foundation, as shown in their unofficial flag, which says "Don't tread on me" (see figure 7.4).

But despite these manifestations on the right, the urge to band together to oppose oppression and replace it with political equality seems to be at least as prevalent on the left. For example, one liberal reader of my "Republicans" essay stated Boehm's thesis precisely:

> The enemy of society to a Liberal is someone who abuses their power (Authority) and still demands, and in some cases forces, others to "respect" them anyway. . . . A Lib-

eral authority is someone or something that earns society's respect through making things happen *that unify society and suppress its enemy*. [Emphasis added.][38]

It's not just the accumulation and abuse of political power that activates the anger of the Liberty/oppression foundation; the current triggers can expand to encompass the accumulation of wealth, which helps to explain the pervasive dislike of capitalism on the far left. For example, one liberal reader explained to me, "Capitalism is, in the end, predatory—a moral society will be socialist, i.e., people will help each other."

You can hear the heavy reliance on the Liberty/oppression foundation whenever people talk about social justice. The owners of a progressive coffee shop and "cultural collective" in New Paltz, New York, used this foundation, along with the Care foundation, to guide their decorating choices, as you can see in figure 8.4.

The hatred of oppression is found on both sides of the political spectrum. The difference seems to be that for liberals—who are more universalistic and who rely more heavily upon the Care/harm foundation—the Liberty/oppression foundation is employed in the service of underdogs, victims, and powerless groups everywhere. It leads liberals (but not others) to sacralize equality, which is then pursued by fighting for civil rights and human rights. Liberals sometimes go beyond equality of *rights* to pursue equality of *outcomes*, which cannot be obtained in a capitalist system. This may be why the left usually favors higher taxes on the rich, high levels of services provided to the poor, and sometimes a guaranteed minimum income for everyone.

Conservatives, in contrast, are more parochial—concerned about their groups, rather than all of humanity. For them, the Liberty/oppression foundation and the hatred of tyranny supports many of the tenets of economic conservatism: don't tread on me (with your liberal nanny state and its high taxes), don't tread on my business (with your oppressive regulations), and don't tread on my nation (with your United Nations and your sovereignty-reducing international treaties).

FIGURE 8.4. *Liberal liberty: Interior of a coffee shop in New Paltz, New York.* The sign on the left says, "No one is free when others are oppressed." The flag on the right shows corporate logos replacing stars on the American flag. The sign in the middle says, "How to end violence against women and children."

American conservatives, therefore, sacralize the word *liberty*, not the word *equality*. This unites them politically with libertarians. The evangelical preacher Jerry Falwell chose the name Liberty University when he founded his ultraconservative school in 1971. Figure 8.5 shows the car of a Liberty student. Liberty students are generally pro-authority. They favor traditional patriarchal families. But they oppose domination and control by a secular government, particularly a liberal government that will (they fear) use its power to redistribute wealth (as "comrade Obama" was thought likely to do).

FAIRNESS AS PROPORTIONALITY

The Tea Party emerged as if from nowhere in the early months of the Obama presidency to reshape the American political landscape and realign the American culture war. The movement began in earnest on February 19, 2009, when Rick Santelli, a correspondent for a business news network, launched a tirade against a new $75 billion program to help homeowners who had borrowed more money than they could now repay. Santelli, who was broadcasting live from the floor of the Chicago Mercantile Exchange, said, "The government is promoting bad behavior." He then urged President Obama to put up a website to hold a national referendum

FIGURE 8.5. *Conservative liberty: car at a dormitory at Liberty University, Lynchburg, Virginia.* The lower sticker says, "Libertarian: More Freedom, Less Government."

to see if we really want to *subsidize the losers' mortgages*, or would we like to at least buy cars and buy houses in foreclosure and give them to people that might have a chance to actually prosper down the road and *reward people that could carry the water instead of drink the water.* [At this point, cheers erupted behind him] . . . This is America. How many of you people want *to pay for your neighbors' mortgage that has an extra bathroom and can't pay their bills?* President Obama, are you listening? [Emphasis added.]

Santelli then announced that he was thinking of hosting a "Chicago Tea Party" in July.[39] Commentators on the left mocked Santelli, and many thought he was endorsing an ugly dog-eat-dog morality in which the "losers" (many of whom had been tricked by unscrupulous lenders) should be left to die. But in fact Santelli was arguing for the law of karma.

It took me a long time to understand fairness because, like many people who study morality, I had thought of fairness as a form of enlightened self-interest, based on Trivers's theory of reciprocal altruism. Genes for fairness evolved, said Trivers, because people who had those genes outcompeted people who didn't. We don't have to abandon the idea of *Homo economicus*; we just have to give him emotional reactions that compel him to play tit for tat.

In the last ten years, however, evolutionary theorists have realized that reciprocal altruism is not so easy to find among nonhuman species.[40] The widely reported claim that vampire bats share blood meals with other bats who had previously shared with them turned out to be a case of kin selection (relatives sharing blood), not reciprocal altruism.[41] The evidence for reciprocity in chimpanzees and capuchins is better but still ambiguous.[42] It seems to take more than just a high level of social intelligence to get reciprocal altruism going. It takes the sort of gossiping, punitive, moralistic community that emerged only when language and weaponry made it possible for early humans to take down bullies and then keep them down with a shared moral matrix.[43]

Reciprocal altruism also fails to explain why people cooperate in group activities. Reciprocity works great for pairs of people, who can play tit for tat, but in groups it's usually not in an individual's self-interest to be the enforcer—the one who punishes slackers. Yet punish we do, and our propensity to punish turns out to be one of the keys to large-scale cooperation.[44] In one classic experiment, economists Ernst Fehr and Simon Gächter asked Swiss students to play twelve rounds of a "public goods" game.[45] The game goes like this: You and your three partners each get 20 tokens on each round (each worth about ten American cents). You can keep your tokens, or you can "invest" some or all of them in the group's common pot. At the end of each round, the experimenters multiply the tokens in the pot by 1.6 and then divide the pot among the four players, so if everyone puts in all 20 tokens, the pot grows from 80 to 128, and everyone gets to keep 32 tokens (which get turned into real money at the end of the experiment). But each individual does best by holding back: If you put in nothing while your partners put in 20 each, you get to keep your 20 tokens plus a quarter of the pot provided by your trusting partners (a quarter of 96), so you end the round with 44 tokens.

Each person sat at a computer in a cubicle, so nobody knew who their partners were on any particular round, although they saw a feedback screen after each round revealing exactly how much each of the four players had contributed. Also, after each round, Fehr and Gächter scrambled the groups so that each person played with three new partners—there was no chance to develop norms of trust, and no chance for anyone to use tit for tat (by holding back on the next round if anyone "cheated" on the current round).

Under these circumstances, the right choice for *Homo economicus* is clear: contribute nothing, ever. Yet in fact the students did contribute to the common pot—about ten tokens on the first round. As the game went on, however, people felt burned by the low contributions of some of their partners, and contributions dropped steadily, down to about six tokens on the sixth round.

That pattern—partial but declining cooperation—has been reported before. But here's the reason this is such a brilliant study: After the sixth round, the experimenters told subjects that there was a new rule: After learning how much each of your partners contributed on each round, you now would have the option of paying, with your own tokens, to *punish* specific other players. Every token you paid to punish would take three tokens away from the player you punished.

For *Homo economicus,* the right course of action is once again perfectly clear: never pay to punish, because you will never again play with those three partners, so there is no chance to benefit from reciprocity or from gaining a tough reputation. Yet remarkably, *84 percent of subjects paid to punish*, at least once. And even more remarkably, *cooperation skyrocketed* on the very first round where punishment was allowed, and it kept on climbing. By the twelfth round, the average contribution was fifteen tokens.[46] Punishing bad behavior promotes virtue and benefits the group. And just as Glaucon argued in his ring of Gyges example, when the threat of punishment is removed, people behave selfishly.

Why did most players pay to punish? In part, because it felt good to do so.[47] We hate to see people take without giving. We want to see cheaters and slackers "get what's coming to them." We want the law of karma to run its course, and we're willing to help enforce it.

When people trade favors, both parties end up equal, more or less, and so it is easy to think (as I had) that reciprocal altruism was the source of moral intuitions about equality. But egalitarianism seems to be rooted more in the hatred of domination than in the love of equality per se.[48] The feeling of being dominated or oppressed by a bully is very different from the feeling of being cheated in an exchange of goods or favors.

Once my team at YourMorals.org had identified Liberty/oppression as a (provisionally) separate sixth foundation, we began to notice that in our data, concerns about political equality were related to a dislike of oppression and a concern for victims, not a desire for reciprocity.[49] And if the love of political equality rests on the Liberty/oppression and Care/harm foundations rather than the Fairness/cheating foundation, then the Fairness foundation no longer has a split personality; it's no longer about equality *and* proportionality. It is primarily about proportionality.

When people work together on a task, they generally want to see the hardest workers get the largest gains.[50] People often want equality of outcomes, but that is because it is so often the case that people's inputs were equal. When people divide up money, or any other kind of reward, equality is just a special case of the broader principle of proportionality. When a few members of a group contributed far more than the others—or, even more powerfully, when a few contributed nothing—most adults do *not* want to see the benefits distributed equally.[51]

We can therefore refine the description of the Fairness foundation that I gave in the last chapter. It's still a set of modules that evolved in response to the adaptive challenge of reaping the rewards of cooperation without getting exploited by free riders.[52] But now that we've begun to talk about moral communities within which cooperation is maintained by gossip and punishment, we can look beyond *individuals* trying to choose partners (which I talked about in the last chapter). We can look more closely at people's strong desires to protect their *communities* from cheaters, slackers, and free riders, who, if allowed to continue their ways without harassment, would cause others to stop cooperating, which would cause society to unravel. The Fairness foundation supports righteous anger when anyone cheats you directly (for example, a car dealer who knowingly sells you a lemon). But it also supports a more generalized concern with cheaters, leeches, and anyone else who "drinks the water" rather than carries it for the group.

The current triggers of the Fairness foundation vary depending on a group's size and on many historical and economic circumstances. In a large industrial society with a social safety net, the current triggers are likely to include people who rely upon the safety net for more than an occasional lifesaving bounce. Concerns about the abuse of the safety net explain the angry emails I received from economic conservatives, such as the man who did not want his tax dollars going to "a non-producing, welfare collecting, single mother, crack baby producing future democrat." It explains the conservative's list of reasons why people vote Democratic, such as "laziness" and "You despise people who work hard for their money, live their own lives, and don't rely on the government for help cradle to grave." It explains Santelli's rant about bailing out homeowners, many of whom had lied on their mortgage applications to qualify for large loans they did not deserve. And it explains the campaign poster in figure 8.6, from David Cameron's Conservative Party in the United Kingdom.

THREE VERSUS SIX

To put this all together: Moral Foundations Theory says that there are (at least) six psychological systems that comprise the universal foundations of the world's many moral matrices.[53] The various moralities found on the political left tend to rest most strongly on the Care/harm and Liberty/oppression foundations. These two foundations support ideals of social justice, which emphasize compassion for the poor and a struggle for political equality among the subgroups that comprise society. Social justice movements emphasize solidarity—

FIGURE 8.6. *Fairness as proportionality.* The right is usually more concerned about catching and punishing free riders than is the left. (Campaign poster for the Conservative Party in the UK parliamentary elections of 2010.)

they call for people to come together to fight the oppression of bullying, domineering elites. (This is why there is no separate equality foundation. People don't crave equality for its own sake; they fight for equality when they perceive that they are being bullied or dominated, as during the American and French revolutions, and the cultural revolutions of the 1960s.)[54]

Everyone—left, right, and center—cares about Care/harm, but liberals care more. Across many scales, surveys, and political controversies, liberals turn out to be more disturbed by signs of violence and suffering, compared to conservatives and especially to libertarians.[55]

Everyone—left, right, and center—cares about Liberty/oppression, but each political faction cares in a different way. In the contemporary United States, liberals are most concerned about the rights of certain vulnerable groups (e.g., racial minorities, children, animals), and they look to government to defend the weak against oppression by the strong. Conservatives, in contrast, hold more traditional ideas of liberty as the right to be left alone, and they often resent liberal programs that use government to infringe on their liberties in order to protect the groups that liberals care most about.[56] For example, small business owners overwhelmingly support the Republican Party[57] in part because they resent the government telling them how to run their businesses under its banner of protecting workers, minorities, consumers, and the environment. This helps explain why libertarians have sided with the Republican Party in recent decades. Libertarians care about liberty almost to the exclusion of all other concerns,[58] and their conception of liberty is the same as that of the Republicans: it is the right to be left alone, free from government interference.

The Fairness/cheating foundation is about proportionality and the law of karma. It is about making sure that people get what they deserve, and do not get things they do not deserve. Everyone—left, right, and center—cares about proportionality; everyone gets angry when people take more than they deserve. But conservatives care more, and they rely on the Fairness foundation more heavily—once fairness is restricted to proportionality. For example, how relevant is it to your morality whether "everyone is pulling their own weight"? Do you agree that "employees who work the hardest should be paid the most"? Liberals don't reject these items, but they are ambivalent. Conservatives, in contrast, endorse items such as these enthusiastically.[59]

Liberals may think that they own the concept of karma because of its New Age associations, but a morality based on compassion and concerns about oppression forces you to violate karma (proportionality) in many ways. Conservatives, for example, think it's self-evident that responses to crime should be based on proportionality, as shown in slogans such as "Do the crime, do the time," and "Three strikes and you're out." Yet liberals are often uncomfortable with the negative side of karma—retribution—as shown on the bumper sticker in figure 8.7. After all, retribution causes harm, and harm activates the Care/harm foundation. A recent study even found that liberal professors give out a narrower range of grades than do conservative professors. Conservative professors are more willing to reward the best students and punish the worst.[60]

The remaining three foundations—Loyalty/betrayal, Authority/subversion, and Sanctity/degradation—show the biggest and most consistent partisan differences. Liberals are ambivalent about these foundations at best, whereas social conservatives embrace them. (Libertarians have little use for them, which is why they tend to support

FIGURE 8.7. *A car in Charlottesville, Virginia, whose owner prefers compassion to proportionality.*

liberal positions on social issues such as gay marriage, drug use, and laws to "protect" the American flag.)

I began this chapter by telling you our original finding: Liberals have a two-foundation morality, based on the Care and Fairness foundations, whereas conservatives have a five-foundation morality. But on the basis of what we've learned in the last few years, I need to revise that statement. Liberals have a three-foundation morality, whereas conservatives use all six. Liberal moral matrices rest on the Care/harm, Liberty/oppression, and Fairness/cheating foundations, although liberals are often willing to trade away fairness (as proportionality) when it conflicts with compassion or with their desire to fight oppression. Conservative morality rests on all six foundations, although conservatives are more willing than liberals to sacrifice Care and let some people get hurt in order to achieve their many other moral objectives.

IN SUM

Moral psychology can help to explain why the Democratic Party has had so much difficulty connecting with voters since 1980. Republicans understand the social intuitionist model better than do Democrats. Republicans speak more directly to the elephant. They also have a better grasp of Moral Foundations Theory; they trigger every single taste receptor.

I presented the Durkheimian vision of society, favored by social conservatives, in which the basic social unit is the family, rather than the individual, and in which order, hierarchy, and tradition are highly valued. I contrasted this vision with the liberal Millian vision, which is more open and individualistic. I noted that a Millian society has difficulty binding *pluribus* into *unum*. Democrats often pursue policies that promote *pluribus* at the expense of *unum*, policies that leave them open to charges of treason, subversion, and sacrilege.

I then described how my colleagues and I revised Moral Foundations Theory to do a better job of explaining intuitions about liberty and fairness:

- We added the Liberty/oppression foundation, which makes people notice and resent any sign of attempted domination. It triggers an urge to band together to resist or overthrow bullies and tyrants. This foundation supports the egalitarianism and antiauthoritarianism of the left, as well as the don't-tread-on-me and give-me-liberty antigovernment anger of libertarians and some conservatives.
- We modified the Fairness foundation to make it focus more strongly on proportionality. The Fairness foundation begins with the psychology of reciprocal altruism, but its duties expanded once humans created gossiping and punitive moral communities. Most people have a deep intuitive concern for the law of karma—they want to see cheaters punished and good citizens rewarded in proportion to their deeds.

With these revisions, Moral Foundations Theory can now explain one of the great puzzles that has preoccupied Democrats in recent years: Why do rural and working-class Americans generally vote Republican when it is the Democratic Party that wants to redistribute money more evenly?

Democrats often say that Republicans have duped these people into voting against their economic self-interest. (That was the thesis of the popular 2004 book *What's the Matter with Kansas?*.)[61] But from the perspective of Moral Foundations Theory, rural and working-class voters were in fact voting for their *moral* interests. They don't want to eat at The True Taste restaurant, and they don't want their nation to devote itself primarily to the care of victims and the pursuit of social justice. Until Democrats understand the Durkheimian vision of society and the difference between a six-foundation morality and a three-foundation morality, they will not understand what makes people vote Republican.

In Part I of this book I presented the first principle of moral psychology: *Intuitions come first, strategic reasoning second.* In Part II, I described those intuitions in detail while presenting the second principle: *There's more to morality than harm and fairness.* Now we're ready to examine how moral diversity can so easily divide good people into hostile groups that do not want to understand each other. We're ready to move on to the third principle: *Morality binds and blinds.*

PART III

Morality Binds and Blinds

Central Metaphor

We Are 90 Percent Chimp and 10 Percent Bee.

NINE

Why Are We So Groupish?

In the terrible days after the terrorist attacks of September 11, 2001, I felt an urge so primitive I was embarrassed to admit it to my friends: I wanted to put an American flag decal on my car.

The urge seemed to come out of nowhere, with no connection to anything I'd ever done. It was as if there was an ancient alarm box in the back of my brain with a sign on it that said, "In case of foreign attack, break glass and push button." I hadn't known the alarm box was there, but when those four planes broke the glass and pushed the button I had an overwhelming sense of being an American. I wanted to do something, anything, to support my team. Like so many others, I gave blood and donated money to the Red Cross. I was more open and helpful to strangers. And I wanted to display my team membership by showing the flag in some way.

But I was a professor, and professors don't do such things. Flag waving and nationalism are for conservatives. Professors are liberal globetrotting universalists, reflexively wary of saying that their nation is better than other nations.[1] When you see an American flag on a car in a UVA staff parking lot, you can bet that the car belongs to a secretary or a blue-collar worker.

After three days and a welter of feelings I'd never felt before, I found a solution to my dilemma. I put an American flag in one corner of my rear windshield, and I put the United Nations flag in the opposite corner. That way I could announce that I loved my country, but don't worry, folks, I don't place it above other countries, and this was, after all, an attack on the whole world, sort of, right?

So far in this book I've painted a portrait of human nature that is somewhat cynical. I've argued that Glaucon was right and that we care more about *looking* good than about truly *being* good.[2] Intuitions come first, *strategic* reasoning second. We lie, cheat, and cut ethical corners quite often when we think we can get away with it, and then we use our moral thinking to manage our reputations and justify ourselves to others. We believe our own post hoc reasoning so thoroughly that we end up self-righteously convinced of our own virtue.

I do believe that you can understand most of moral psychology by viewing it as a form of enlightened self-interest, and if it's self-interest, then it's easily explained by Darwinian natural selection working at the level of the individual. Genes are selfish,[3] selfish genes create people with various mental modules, and some of these mental modules make us strategically altruistic, not reliably or universally altruistic. Our righteous minds were shaped by kin selection plus reciprocal altruism augmented by gossip and reputation management. That's the message of nearly every book on the evolutionary origins of morality, and nothing I've said so far contradicts that message.

But in Part III of this book I'm going to show why that portrait is incomplete. Yes, people are often selfish, and a great deal of our moral, political, and religious behavior can be understood as thinly veiled ways of pursuing self-interest. (Just look at the awful hypocrisy of so many politicians and religious leaders.) But it's also true that people are *groupish*. We love to join teams, clubs, leagues, and fraternities. We take on group identities and work shoulder to shoulder with strangers toward common goals so enthusiastically that it seems as if our minds were designed for teamwork. I don't think we can understand morality, politics, or religion until we have a good picture

of human groupishness and its origins. We cannot understand conservative morality and the Durkheimian societies I described in the
last chapter. Neither can we understand socialism, communism, and
the communalism of the left.

Let me be more precise. When I say that human nature is *selfish*,
I mean that our minds contain a variety of mental mechanisms that
make us adept at promoting our own interests, in competition with
our peers. When I say that human nature is also *groupish*, I mean
that our minds contain a variety of mental mechanisms that make us
adept at promoting our *group's* interests, in competition with other
groups.[4] We are not saints, but we are sometimes good team players.

Stated in this way, the origin of these groupish mechanisms
becomes a puzzle. Do we have groupish minds today because groupish
individuals long ago outcompeted less groupish individuals *within the
same group*? If so, then this is just standard, bread-and-butter natural
selection operating at the level of the individual. And if that's the
case, then this is Glauconian groupishness—we should expect to find
that people care about the *appearance* of loyalty, not the reality.[5] Or
do we have groupish mechanisms (such as the rally-round-the-flag
reflex) because groups that succeeded in coalescing and cooperating outcompeted groups that couldn't get it together? If so, then I'm
invoking a process known as "group selection," and group selection
was banished as a heresy from scientific circles in the 1970s.[6]

In this chapter I'll argue that group selection was falsely convicted and unfairly banished. I'll present four pieces of new evidence
that I believe exonerate group selection (in some but not all forms).
This new evidence demonstrates the value of thinking about groups
as real entities that compete with each other. This new evidence
leads us directly to the third and final principle of moral psychology: *Morality binds and blinds*. I will suggest that human nature is
mostly selfish, but with a groupish overlay that resulted from the fact
that natural selection works at multiple levels simultaneously. Individuals compete with individuals, and that competition rewards selfishness—which includes some forms of strategic cooperation (even
criminals can work together to further their own interests).[7] But at
the same time, groups compete with groups, and that competition

favors groups composed of true team players—those who are willing to cooperate and work for the good of the group, even when they could do better by slacking, cheating, or leaving the group.[8] These two processes pushed human nature in different directions and gave us the strange mix of selfishness and selflessness that we know today.

VICTORIOUS TRIBES?

Here's an example of one kind of group selection. In a few remarkable pages of *The Descent of Man*, Darwin made the case for group selection, raised the principal objection to it, and then proposed a way around the objection:

> When two tribes of primeval man, living in the same country, came into competition, if (other circumstances being equal) the one tribe included a great number of courageous, sympathetic and faithful members, who were always ready to warn each other of danger, to aid and defend each other, *this tribe would succeed better and conquer the other.* . . . The advantage which disciplined soldiers have over undisciplined hordes follows chiefly from the confidence which each man feels in his comrades. . . . *Selfish and contentious people will not cohere, and without coherence nothing can be effected. A tribe rich in the above qualities would spread and be victorious over other tribes.*[9]

Cohesive tribes began to function like individual organisms, competing with other organisms. The tribes that were more cohesive generally won. Natural selection therefore worked on tribes the same way it works on every other organism.

But in the very next paragraph, Darwin raised the free rider problem, which is still the main objection raised against group selection:

> But it may be asked, how within the limits of the same tribe did a large number of members first become en-

dowed with these social and moral qualities, and how was the standard of excellence raised? *It is extremely doubtful whether the offspring of the more sympathetic and benevolent parents, or of those who were the most faithful to their comrades, would be reared in greater numbers than the children of selfish and treacherous parents belonging to the same tribe.* He who was ready to sacrifice his life, as many a savage has been, rather than betray his comrades, would often leave no offspring to inherit his noble nature.[10]

Darwin grasped the basic logic of what is now known as *multilevel selection*.[11] Life is a hierarchy of nested levels, like Russian dolls: genes within chromosomes within cells within individual organisms within hives, societies, and other groups. There can be competition at any level of the hierarchy, but for our purposes (studying morality) the only two levels that matter are those of the individual organism and the group. When groups compete, the cohesive, cooperative group usually wins. But within each group, selfish individuals (free riders) come out ahead. They share in the group's gains while contributing little to its efforts. The bravest army wins, but within the bravest army, the few cowards who hang back are the most likely of all to survive the fight, go home alive, and become fathers.

Multilevel selection refers to a way of quantifying how strong the selection pressure is at each level, which means how strongly the competition of life favors genes for particular traits.[12] A gene for suicidal self-sacrifice would be favored by group-level selection (it would help the team win), but it would be so strongly opposed by selection at the individual level that such a trait could evolve only in species such as bees, where competition within the hive has been nearly eliminated and almost all selection is group selection.[13] Bees (and ants and termites) are the ultimate team players: one for all, all for one, all the time, even if that means dying to protect the hive from invaders.[14] (Humans can be turned into suicide bombers, but it takes a great deal of training, pressure, and psychological manipulation. It doesn't come naturally to us.)[15]

Once human groups had some minimal ability to band together

and compete with other groups, then group-level selection came into play and the most groupish groups had an advantage over groups of selfish individualists. But how did early humans get those groupish abilities in the first place? Darwin proposed a series of "probable steps" by which humans evolved to the point where there could be groups of team players in the first place.

The first step was the "social instincts." In ancient times, loners were more likely to get picked off by predators than were their more gregarious siblings, who felt a strong need to stay close to the group. The second step was reciprocity. People who helped others were more likely to get help when they needed it most.

But the most important "stimulus to the development of the social virtues" was the fact that people are passionately concerned with "the praise and blame of our fellow-men."[16] Darwin, writing in Victorian England, shared Glaucon's view (from aristocratic Athens) that people are obsessed with their reputations. Darwin believed that the emotions that drive this obsession were acquired by natural selection acting at the individual level: those who lacked a sense of shame or a love of glory were less likely to attract friends and mates. Darwin also added a final step: the capacity to treat duties and principles as sacred, which he saw as part of our religious nature.

When you put these steps together, they take you along an evolutionary path from earlier primates to humans, among whom free riding is no longer so attractive. In a real army, which sacralizes honor, loyalty, and country, the coward is not the most likely to make it home and father children. He's the most likely to get beaten up, left behind, or shot in the back for committing sacrilege. And if he does make it home alive, his reputation will repel women and potential employers.[17] Real armies, like most effective groups, have many ways of suppressing selfishness. And anytime a group finds a way to suppress selfishness, it changes the balance of forces in a multi-level analysis: individual-level selection becomes less important, and group-level selection becomes more powerful. For example, if there is a genetic basis for feelings of loyalty and sanctity (i.e., the Loyalty and Sanctity foundations), then intense intergroup competition will make these genes become more common in the next generation. The reason is that groups in which these traits are common will replace groups in which they are rare, even if these genes impose a small cost on their bearers (relative to those that lack them within each group).

In what might be the pithiest and most prescient statement in the history of moral psychology, Darwin summarized the evolutionary origin of morality in this way:

> Ultimately our moral sense or conscience becomes a highly complex sentiment—originating in the social instincts, largely guided by the approbation of our fellow-men, ruled by reason, self-interest, and in later times by deep religious feelings, and confirmed by instruction and habit.[18]

Darwin's response to the free rider problem satisfied readers for nearly a hundred years, and group selection became a standard part of evolutionary thinking. Unfortunately, most writers did not bother to work out exactly how each particular species solved the free rider problem, as Darwin had done for human beings. Claims about animals behaving "for the good of the group" proliferated—for example, the claim that individual animals restrain their grazing or their breeding so as not to put the group at risk of overexploiting its food supply. Even more lofty claims were made about animals acting for the good of the species, or even of the ecosystem.[19] These claims were naive because individuals that followed the selfless strategy would leave fewer surviving offspring and would soon be replaced in the population by the descendants of free riders.

In 1966, this loose thinking was brought to a halt, along with almost all thinking about group selection.

A FAST HERD OF DEER?

In 1955, a young biologist named George Williams attended a lecture at the University of Chicago by a termite specialist. The speaker claimed that many animals are cooperative and helpful, just like termites. He said that old age and death are the way that nature makes room for the younger and fitter members of each species. But Williams was well versed in genetics and evolution, and he was repulsed by the speaker's Panglossian mushiness. He saw that animals are not going to die to benefit others, except in very special circumstances such as those that prevail in a termite nest (where all are sisters). He set out to write a book that would "purge biology" of such sloppy thinking once and for all.[20]

In *Adaptation and Natural Selection* (published in 1966), Williams told biologists how to think clearly about adaptation. He saw natural selection as a design process. There's no conscious or intelligent designer, but Williams found the language of design useful nonetheless.[21] For example, wings can only be understood as biological mechanisms designed to produce flight. Williams noted that adaptation at a given level always implies a selection (design) process operating at that level, and he warned readers not to look to higher levels (such as groups) when selection effects at lower levels (such as individuals) can fully explain the trait.

He worked through the example of running speed in deer. When deer run in a herd, we observe a fast herd of deer, moving as a unit and sometimes changing course as a unit. We might be tempted to explain the herd's behavior by appealing to group selection: for millions of years, faster herds have escaped predators better than slower herds, and so over time fast herds replaced slower herds. But Williams pointed out that deer have been exquisitely well designed as *individuals* to flee from predators. The selection process operated at the level of individuals: slower deer got eaten, while their faster cousins *in the same herd* escaped. There is no need to bring in selection at the level of the herd. A fast herd of deer is nothing more than a herd of fast deer.[22]

Williams gave an example of what it would take to force us up to a group-level analysis: behavioral mechanisms whose goal or function was clearly the protection of the *group*, rather than the individual. If deer with particularly keen senses served as sentinels, while the fastest runners in the herd tried to lure predators away from the herd, we'd have evidence of group-related adaptations, and, as Williams put it, "only by a theory of between-group selection could we achieve a scientific explanation of group-related adaptations."[23]

Williams said that group selection was possible in theory. But then he devoted most of the book to proving his thesis that "group-related adaptations do not in fact exist."[24] He gave examples from across the animal kingdom, showing in every case that what looks like altruism or self-sacrifice to a naive biologist (such as that termite specialist) turns out to be either individual selfishness or kin selection (whereby costly actions make sense because they benefit other copies of the same genes in closely related individuals, as happens with termites). Richard Dawkins did the same thing in his 1976 best seller *The Selfish Gene,* granting that group selection is possible but then debunking apparent cases of group-related adaptations. By the late 1970s there was a strong consensus that anyone who said that a behavior occurred "for the good of the group" was a fool who could be safely ignored.

We sometimes look back on the 1970s as the "me decade." That term was first applied to the growing individualism of American society, but it describes a broad set of changes in the social sciences as well. The idea of people as *Homo economicus* spread far and wide. In social psychology, for example, the leading explanation of fairness (known as "equity theory") was based on four axioms, the first of which was "Individuals will try to maximize their outcomes." The authors then noted that "even the most contentious scientist would find it difficult to challenge our first proposition. Theories in a wide variety of disciplines rest on the assumption that 'man is selfish.' "[25] All acts of apparent altruism, cooperation, and even simple fairness had to be explained, ultimately, as covert forms of self-interest.[26]

Of course, real life is full of cases that violate the axiom. People leave tips in restaurants they'll never return to; they donate anonymously to charities; they sometimes drown after jumping into rivers to save children who are not their own. No problem, said the cynics; these are just misfirings of ancient systems designed for life in the small groups of the Pleistocene, where most people were close kin.[27] Now that we live in large anonymous societies, our ancient selfish circuits erroneously lead us to help strangers who will not help us in return. Our "moral qualities" are not adaptations, as Darwin had believed. They are by-products; they are mistakes. Morality, said Williams, is "an accidental capability produced, in its boundless stupidity, by a biological process that is normally opposed to the expression of such a capability."[28] Dawkins shared this cynicism: "Let us try to teach generosity and altruism because we are born selfish."[29]

I disagree. Human beings are the giraffes of altruism. We're one-of-a-kind freaks of nature who occasionally—even if rarely—can be as selfless and team-spirited as bees.[30] If your moral ideal is the person who devotes her life to helping strangers, well then, OK—such people are so rare that we send film crews out to record them for the evening news. But if you focus, as Darwin did, on behavior in *groups* of people who know each other and share goals and values, then our ability to work together, divide labor, help each other, and function as a team is so all-pervasive that we don't even notice it. You'll never see the headline "Forty-five Unrelated College Students Work Together Cooperatively, and for No Pay, to Prepare for Opening Night of *Romeo and Juliet*."

When Williams proposed his fanciful example of deer dividing labor and working together to protect the herd, was it not obvious that human groups do exactly that? By his own criterion, if people in every society readily organize themselves into cooperative groups with a clear division of labor, then this ability is an excellent candidate for being a group-related adaptation. As Williams himself put it: "Only by a theory of between-group selection could we achieve a scientific explanation of group-related adaptations."

The 9/11 attacks activated several of these group-related adaptations in my mind. The attacks turned me into a team player, with a powerful and unexpected urge to display my team's flag and then do things to support the team, such as giving blood, donating money, and, yes, supporting the leader.[31] And my response was tepid compared to the hundreds of Americans who got in their cars that afternoon and drove great distances to New York in the vain hope that they could help to dig survivors out of the wreckage, or the thousands of young people who volunteered for military service in the following weeks. Were these people acting on selfish motives, or groupish motives?

The rally-round-the-flag reflex is just one example of a groupish mechanism.[32] It is exactly the sort of mental mechanism you'd expect to find if we humans were shaped by group selection in the way that Darwin described. I can't be certain, however, that this reflex really *did* evolve by group-level selection. Group selection is controversial among evolutionary theorists, most of whom still agree with Williams that group selection never actually happened among humans. They think that anything that looks like a group-related adaptation will—if you look closely enough—turn out to be an adaptation for helping individuals outcompete their neighbors within the same group, not an adaptation for helping groups outcompete other groups.

Before we can move on with our exploration of morality, politics, and religion, we've got to address this problem. If the experts are divided, then why should we side with those who believe that morality is (in part) a group-related adaptation?[33]

In the following sections I'll give you four reasons. I'll show you four "exhibits" in my defense of multilevel selection (which includes group selection). But my goal here is not just to build a legal case in an academic battle that you might care nothing about. My goal is to show you that morality is the key to understanding humanity. I'll take you on a brief tour of humanity's origins in which we'll see how groupishness helped us transcend selfishness. I'll show that our groupishness—despite all of the ugly and tribal things it makes us do—is one of the magic ingredients that made it possible for civilizations to burst forth, cover the Earth, and live ever more peacefully in just a few thousand years.[34]

EXHIBIT A: MAJOR TRANSITIONS IN EVOLUTION

Suppose you entered a boat race. One hundred rowers, each in a separate rowboat, set out on a ten-mile race along a wide and slow-moving river. The first to cross the finish line will win $10,000. Halfway into the race, you're in the lead. But then, from out of nowhere, you're passed by a boat with two rowers, each pulling just one oar. No fair! Two rowers joined together into one boat! And then, stranger still, you watch as that rowboat is overtaken by a train of three such rowboats, all tied together to form a single long boat. The rowers are identical septuplets. Six of them row in perfect synchrony while the seventh is the coxswain, steering the boat and calling out the beat for the rowers. But those cheaters are deprived of victory just before they cross the finish line, for they in turn are passed by an enterprising group of twenty-four sisters who rented a motorboat. It turns out that there are no rules in this race about what kinds of vehicles are allowed.

That was a metaphorical history of life on Earth. For the first billion years or so of life, the only organisms were prokaryotic cells (such as bacteria). Each was a solo operation, competing with others and reproducing copies of itself.

But then, around 2 billion years ago, two bacteria somehow joined together inside a single membrane, which explains why mitochondria have their own DNA, unrelated to the DNA in the nucleus.[35] These are the two-person rowboats in my example. Cells that had internal organelles could reap the benefits of cooperation and the division of labor (see Adam Smith). There was no longer any competition between these organelles, for they could reproduce only when the entire cell reproduced, so it was "one for all, all for one." Life on Earth underwent what biologists call a "major transition."[36] Natural selection went on as it always had, but now there was a radically new kind of creature to be selected. There was a new kind of *vehicle* by which selfish genes could replicate themselves. Single-celled eukaryotes were wildly successful and spread throughout the oceans.

A few hundred million years later, some of these eukaryotes developed a novel adaptation: they stayed together after cell division to form multicellular organisms in which every cell had exactly the same genes. These are the three-boat septuplets in my example. Once again, competition is suppressed (because each cell can only reproduce if the organism reproduces, via its sperm or egg cells). A group of cells becomes an individual, able to divide labor among the cells (which specialize into limbs and organs). A powerful new kind of vehicle appears, and in a short span of time the world is covered with plants, animals, and fungi.[37] It's another major transition.

Major transitions are rare. The biologists John Maynard Smith and Eörs Szathmáry count just eight clear examples over the last 4 billion years (the last of which is human societies).[38] But these transitions are among the most important events in biological history, and they are examples of multilevel selection at work. It's the same story over and over again: Whenever a way is found to suppress free riding so that individual units can cooperate, work as a team, and divide labor, selection at the lower level becomes less important, selection at the higher level becomes more powerful, and that higher-level selection favors the most cohesive superorganisms.[39] (A superorganism is an organism made out of smaller organisms.) As these superorganisms proliferate, they begin to compete with each other, and to evolve for greater success in that competition. This competition among superorganisms is one form of group selection.[40] There is variation among the groups, and the fittest groups pass on their traits to future generations of groups.

Major transitions may be rare, but when they happen, the Earth often changes.[41] Just look at what happened more than 100 million years ago when some wasps developed the trick of dividing labor between a queen (who lays all the eggs) and several kinds of workers who maintain the nest and bring back food to share. This trick was discovered by the early hymenoptera (members of the order that includes wasps, which gave rise to bees and ants) and it was discovered independently several dozen other times (by the ancestors of termites, naked mole rats, and some species of shrimp, aphids, beetles, and spiders).[42] In each case, the free rider problem was surmounted and selfish genes began to craft relatively selfless group members who together constituted a supremely selfish group.

These groups were a new kind of vehicle: a hive or colony of close genetic relatives, which functioned as a unit (e.g., in foraging and fighting) and reproduced as a unit. These are the motorboating sisters in my example, taking advantage of technological innovations and mechanical engineering that had never before existed. It was another transition. Another kind of group began to function as though it were a single organism, and the genes that got to ride around in colonies crushed the genes that couldn't "get it together" and rode around in the bodies of more selfish and solitary insects. The colonial insects represent just 2 percent of all insect species, but in a short period of time they claimed the best feeding and breeding sites for themselves, pushed their competitors to marginal grounds, and changed most of the Earth's terrestrial ecosystems (for example, by enabling the evolution of flowering plants, which need pollinators).[43] Now they're the majority, by weight, of all insects on Earth.

What about human beings? Since ancient times, people have likened human societies to beehives. But is this just a loose analogy? If you map the queen of the hive onto the queen or king of a city-state, then yes, it's loose. A hive or colony has no ruler, no boss. The queen is just the ovary. But if we simply ask whether humans went through the same evolutionary process as bees—a major transition from selfish individualism to groupish hives that prosper when they find a way to suppress free riding—then the analogy gets much tighter.

Many animals are social: they live in groups, flocks, or herds. But only a few animals have crossed the threshold and become *ultrasocial*, which means that they live in very large groups that have some internal structure, enabling them to reap the benefits of the division of labor.[44] Beehives and ant nests, with their separate castes of soldiers, scouts, and nursery attendants, are examples of ultrasociality, and so are human societies.

One of the key features that has helped all the nonhuman ultrasocials to cross over appears to be the *need to defend a shared nest.* The biologists Bert Hölldobler and E. O. Wilson summarize the recent finding that ultrasociality (also called "eusociality")[45] is found among a few species of shrimp, aphids, thrips, and beetles, as well as among wasps, bees, ants, and termites:

> In all the known [species that] display the earliest stages of eusociality, their behavior protects a *persistent, defensible resource* from predators, parasites, or competitors.

The resource is *invariably a nest plus dependable food* within foraging range of the nest inhabitants.[46]

Hölldobler and Wilson give supporting roles to two other factors: the need to feed offspring over an extended period (which gives an advantage to species that can recruit siblings or males to help out Mom) and intergroup conflict. All three of these factors applied to those first early wasps camped out together in defensible naturally occurring nests (such as holes in trees). From that point on, the most cooperative groups got to keep the best nesting sites, which they then modified in increasingly elaborate ways to make themselves even more productive and more protected. Their descendants include the honeybees we know today, whose hives have been described as "a factory inside a fortress."[47]

Those same three factors applied to human beings. Like bees, our ancestors were (1) territorial creatures with a fondness for defensible nests (such as caves) who (2) gave birth to needy offspring that required enormous amounts of care, which had to be given while (3) the group was under threat from neighboring groups. For hundreds of thousands of years, therefore, conditions were in place that pulled for the evolution of ultrasociality, and as a result, we are the only ultrasocial primate. The human lineage may have started off acting very much like chimps,[48] but by the time our ancestors started walking out of Africa, they had become at least a little bit like bees.

And much later, when some groups began planting crops and orchards, and then building granaries, storage sheds, fenced pastures, and permanent homes, they had an even steadier food supply that had to be defended even more vigorously. Like bees, humans began building ever more elaborate nests, and in just a few thousand years, a new kind of vehicle appeared on Earth—the city-state, able to raise walls and armies.[49] City-states and, later, empires spread rapidly across Eurasia, North Africa, and Mesoamerica, changing many of the Earth's ecosystems and allowing the total tonnage of human beings to shoot up from insignificance at the start of the Holocene (around twelve thousand years ago) to world domination today.[50] As the colonial insects did to the other insects, we have pushed all other mammals to the margins, to extinction, or to servitude. The analogy to bees is not shallow or loose. Despite their many differences, human civilizations and beehives are both products of major transitions in evolutionary history. They are motorboats.

The discovery of major transitions is Exhibit A in the retrial of group selection. Group selection may or may not be common among other animals, but it happens whenever individuals find ways to suppress selfishness and work as a team, in competition with other teams.[51] Group selection creates group-related adaptations. It is not far-fetched, and it should not be a heresy to suggest that this is how we got the groupish overlay that makes up a crucial part of our righteous minds.

EXHIBIT B: SHARED INTENTIONALITY

In 49 BCE, Gaius Julius made the momentous decision to cross the Rubicon, a shallow river in northern Italy. He broke Roman law (which forbade generals to approach Rome with their armies), started a civil war, and became Julius Caesar, the absolute ruler of Rome. He also gave us a metaphor for any small action that sets in motion an unstoppable train of events with momentous consequences.

It's great fun to look back at history and identify Rubicon crossings. I used to believe that there were too many small steps in the evolution of morality to identify one as the Rubicon, but I changed my mind when I heard Michael Tomasello, one of the world's foremost experts on chimpanzee cognition, utter this sentence: "It is inconceivable that you would ever see two chimpanzees carrying a log together."[52]

I was stunned. Chimps are arguably the second-smartest species on the planet, able to make tools, learn sign language, predict the intentions of other chimps, and deceive each other to get what they want. As individuals, they're brilliant. So why can't they work together? What are they missing?

Tomasello's great innovation was to create a set of simple tasks that could be given to chimps and to human toddlers in nearly identical form.[53] Solving the task earned the chimp or child a treat (usually a piece of food for the chimp, a small toy for the child). Some of the tasks required thinking only about physical objects in physical space—for example, using a stick to pull in a treat that was out of reach, or choosing the dish that had the larger number of treats in it rather than the smaller number. Across all ten tasks, the chimps and the two-year-olds did equally well, solving the problems correctly about 68 percent of the time.

But other tasks required collaborating with the experimenter, or at least recognizing that she intended to share information. For example, in one task, the experimenter demonstrated how to remove a treat from a clear tube by poking a hole in the paper that covered one end, and then she gave an identical tube to the chimp or child. Would the subjects understand that the experimenter was trying to teach them what to do? In another task, the experimenter hid the treat under one of two cups and then tried to show the chimp or child the correct cup (by looking at it or pointing to it). The kids aced these social challenges, solving them correctly 74 percent of the time. The chimps bombed, solving them just 35 percent of the time (no better than chance on many of the tasks).

According to Tomasello, human cognition veered away from that of other primates when our ancestors developed *shared intentionality*.[54] At some point in the last million years, a small group of our ancestors developed the ability to share mental representations of tasks that two or more of them were pursuing together. For example, while foraging, one person pulls down a branch while the other plucks the fruit, and they both share the meal. Chimps never do this. Or while hunting, the pair splits up to approach an animal from both sides. Chimps sometimes appear to do this, as in the widely reported cases of chimps hunting colobus monkeys,[55] but Tomasello argues that the chimps are not really working together. Rather, each chimp is surveying the scene and then taking the action that seems best to him at that moment.[56] Tomasello notes that these monkey hunts are the *only* time that chimps seem to be working together, yet even in these rare cases they fail to show the signs of real cooperation. They make no effort to communicate with each other, for example, and they are terrible at sharing the spoils among the hunters, each of whom must use force to obtain a share of meat at the end. They all chase the monkey at the same time, yet they don't all seem to be on the same page about the hunt.

In contrast, when early humans began to share intentions, their ability to hunt, gather, raise children, and raid their neighbors increased exponentially. Everyone on the team now had a mental representation of the task, knew that his or her partners shared the same representation, knew when a partner had acted in a way that impeded success or that hogged the spoils, and reacted negatively to such violations. When everyone in a group began to share a common understanding of how things were supposed to be done, and then felt a flash of negativity when any individual violated those expectations, the first moral matrix was born.[57] (Remember that a matrix is a *consensual* hallucination.) That, I believe, was our Rubicon crossing.

Tomasello believes that human ultrasociality arose in two steps. The first was the ability to share intentions in groups of two or three people who were actively hunting or foraging together. (That was the Rubicon.) Then, after several hundred thousand years of evolution for better sharing and collaboration as nomadic hunter-gatherers, more collaborative groups began to get larger, perhaps in response to the threat of other groups. Victory went to the most cohesive groups—the ones that could scale up their ability to share intentions from three people to three hundred or three thousand people. This was the second step: Natural selection favored increasing levels of what Tomasello calls "group-mindedness"—the ability to learn and conform to social norms, feel and share group-related emotions, and, ultimately, to create and obey social institutions, including religion. A new set of selection pressures operated *within* groups (e.g., nonconformists were punished, or at very least were less likely to be chosen as partners for joint ventures)[58] as well as *between* groups (cohesive groups took territory and other resources from less cohesive groups).

Shared intentionality is Exhibit B in the retrial of group selection. Once you grasp Tomasello's deep insight, you begin to see the vast webs of shared intentionality out of which human groups are constructed. Many people assume that language was our Rubicon, but language became possible only *after* our ancestors got shared intentionality. Tomasello notes that a word is not a relationship between a sound and an object. It is an agreement *among people* who share a joint representation of the things in their world, and who share a set of conventions for communicating with each other about those things. If the key to group selection is a shared defensible nest, then shared intentionality allowed humans to construct nests that were vast and ornate yet weightless and portable. Bees construct hives out of wax and wood fibers, which they then fight, kill, and die to defend. Humans construct moral communities out of shared norms, institutions, and gods that, even in the twenty-first century, they fight, kill, and die to defend.

EXHIBIT C: GENES AND CULTURES COEVOLVE

When did our ancestors cross the Rubicon? We'll never know when the first pair of foragers worked as a team to pluck figs from a tree, but when we begin to see signs in the fossil record of cultural innovations accumulating and building on earlier innovations, we can guess that the innovators had crossed over. When culture accumulates, it means that people are learning from each other, adding their own innovations, and then passing their ideas on to later generations.[59]

Our ancestors first began to diverge from the common ancestor we share with chimps and bonobos between 5 million and 7 million years ago. For the next few million years, there were many species of hominids walking around on two legs in Africa. But judging from their brain size and their limited use of tools, these creatures (including australopithecines such as "Lucy") are better thought of as bipedal apes than as early humans.[60]

Then, beginning around 2.4 million years ago, hominids with larger brains begin to appear in the fossil record. These were the first members of the genus *Homo*, including *Homo habilis*, so named because these creatures were "handy men" compared to their ancestors. They left behind a profusion of simple stone tools known as the Oldowan tool kit. These tools, mostly just sharp flakes they had

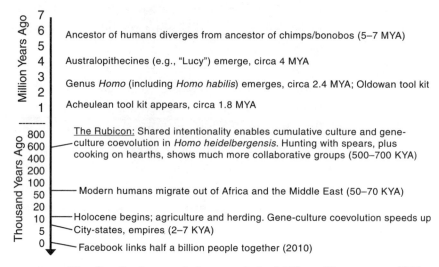

FIGURE 9.1. *Time line of major events in human evolution.* MYA = million years ago; KYA = thousand years ago. Dates drawn from Potts and Sloan 2010; Richerson and Boyd 2005; and Tattersall 2009.

knocked off larger stones, helped *Homo habilis* to cut and scrape meat off carcasses killed by other animals. *Homo habilis* was not much of a hunter.

Then, beginning around 1.8 million years ago, some hominids in East Africa began making new and more finely crafted tools, known as the Acheulean tool kit.[61] The main tool was a teardrop-shaped hand axe, and its symmetry and careful crafting jump out at us as something new under the sun, something made by minds like ours (see figure 9.2). This seems like a promising place to start talking about cumulative culture. But here's the weird thing: Acheulean tools are nearly identical everywhere, from Africa to Europe to Asia, for more than a million years. *There's hardly any variation,* which suggests that the knowledge of how to make these tools may not have been passed on culturally. Rather, the knowledge of how to make these tools may have become innate, just as the "knowledge" of how to build a dam is innate in beavers.[62]

It's only around 600,000 or 700,000 years ago that we begin to see creatures who may have crossed over. The first hominids with brains as large as ours begin appearing in Africa and then Europe.

FIGURE 9.2. *Acheulean hand axe.*

They are known collectively as *Homo heidelbergensis,* and they were the ancestors of Neanderthals as well as of us. At their campsites we find the first clear evidence of hearths, and of spears. The oldest known spears were just sharpened sticks, but later they became sharp stone points attached to wooden shafts and balanced for accurate throwing. These people made complex weapons and then worked together to hunt and kill large animals, which they brought back to a central campsite to be butchered, cooked, and shared.[63]

Homo heidelbergensis is therefore our best candidate for Rubicon crosser.[64] These people had cumulative culture, teamwork, and a division of labor. They must have had shared intentionality, including at least some rudimentary moral matrix that helped them work together and then share the fruits of their labor. By crossing over, they transformed not just the course of human evolution but the very nature of the evolutionary process. From that point onward, people lived in an environment that was increasingly of their own making.

The anthropologists Pete Richerson and Rob Boyd have argued that cultural innovations (such as spears, cooking techniques, and religions) evolve in much the same way that biological innovations evolve, and the two streams of evolution are so intertwined that you can't study one without studying both.[65] For example, one of the best-understood cases of gene-culture coevolution occurred among the first people who domesticated cattle. In humans, as in all other mammals, the ability to digest lactose (the sugar in milk) is lost during childhood. The gene that makes lactase (the enzyme that breaks down lactose) shuts off after a few years of service, because mammals don't drink milk after they are weaned. But those first cattle keepers, in northern Europe and in a few parts of Africa, had a vast new supply of fresh milk, which could be given to their children but not to adults. Any individual whose mutated genes delayed the shutdown of lactase production had an advantage. Over time, such people left more milk-drinking descendants than did their lactose-intolerant cousins. (The gene itself has been identified.)[66] Genetic changes then drove cultural innovations as well: groups with the new lactase gene then kept even larger herds, and found more ways to use and process milk, such as turning it into cheese. These cultural innovations then drove further genetic changes, and on and on it went.

If cultural innovations (such as keeping cattle) can lead to genetic responses (such as adult lactose tolerance), then might cultural innovations related to morality have led to genetic responses as well? Yes. Richerson and Boyd argue that gene-culture coevolution helped to move humanity up from the small-group sociability of other primates to the tribal ultrasociality that is found today in all human societies.[67]

According to their "tribal instincts hypothesis," human groups have always been in competition to some degree with neighboring groups. The groups that figured out (or stumbled upon) cultural innovations that helped them cooperate and cohere in groups larger than the family tended to win these competitions (just as Darwin said).

Among the most important such innovations is the human love of using symbolic markers to show our group memberships. From the tattoos and face piercings used among Amazonian tribes through the male circumcision required of Jews to the tattoos and facial piercings used by punks in the United Kingdom, human beings take extraordinary, costly, and sometimes painful steps to make their bodies advertise their group memberships. This practice surely started modestly, perhaps just with colored powders for body painting.[68] But however it began, groups that built on it and invented more permanent markers found a way to forge a sense of "we" that extended beyond kinship. We trust and cooperate more readily with people who look and sound like us.[69] We expect them to share our values and norms.

And once some groups developed the *cultural* innovation of pro-
totribalism, they changed the environment within which *genetic* evolution took place. As Richerson and Boyd explain:

> Such environments favored the evolution of a suite of
> new social instincts suited to life in such groups, includ-
> ing a psychology which "expects" life to be structured
> by moral norms and is designed to learn and internal-
> ize such norms; new emotions such as shame and guilt,
> which increase the chance that the norms are followed,
> and a psychology which "expects" the social world to be
> divided into symbolically marked groups.[70]

In such prototribal societies, individuals who found it harder to
play along, to restrain their antisocial impulses, and to conform to the
most important collective norms would not have been anyone's top
choice when it came time to choose partners for hunting, foraging,
or mating. In particular, people who were violent would have been
shunned, punished, or in extreme cases killed.

This process has been described as "self-domestication."[71] The
ancestors of dogs, cats, and pigs got less aggressive as they were
domesticated and shaped for partnership with human beings. Only
the friendliest ones approached human settlements in the first place;
they volunteered to become the ancestors of today's pets and farm
animals.

In a similar way, early humans domesticated themselves when
they began to select friends and partners based on their ability to live
within the tribe's moral matrix. In fact, our brains, bodies, and behavior show many of the same signs of domestication that are found in
our domestic animals: smaller teeth, smaller body, reduced aggression, and greater playfulness, carried on even into adulthood.[72] The
reason is that domestication generally takes traits that disappear at
the end of childhood and keeps them turned on for life. Domesticated animals (including humans) are more childlike, sociable, and
gentle than their wild ancestors.

These tribal instincts are a kind of overlay, a set of groupish emotions and mental mechanisms laid down over our older and more selfish primate nature.[73] It may sound depressing to think that our righteous minds are basically tribal minds, but consider the alternative. Our tribal minds make it easy to divide us, but without our long period of tribal living there'd be nothing to divide in the first place. There'd be only small families of foragers—not nearly as sociable as today's hunter-gatherers—eking out a living and losing most of their members to starvation during every prolonged drought. The coevolution of tribal minds and tribal cultures didn't just prepare us for war; it also prepared us for far more peaceful coexistence within our groups, and, in modern times, for cooperation on a vast scale as well.

Gene-culture coevolution is Exhibit C in the retrial of group selection. Once our ancestors crossed the Rubicon and became cumulatively cultural creatures, their genes began to coevolve with their cultural innovations. At least some of these innovations were directed at marking members of a moral community, fostering group cohesion, suppressing aggression and free riding within the group, and defending the territory shared by that moral community. These are precisely the sorts of changes that make major transitions happen.[74] Even if group selection played no role in the evolution of any other mammal,[75] human evolution has been so different since the arrival of shared intentionality and gene-culture coevolution that humans may well be a special case. The wholesale dismissal of group selection in the 1960s and 1970s, based mostly on arguments and examples from other species, was premature.

EXHIBIT D: EVOLUTION CAN BE FAST

When exactly did we become ultrasocial? Humans everywhere are so groupish that most of the genetic changes must have been in place before our ancestors spread out from Africa and the Middle East around 50,000 years ago.[76] (I suspect it was the development of cooperative groupishness that enabled these ancestors to conquer the world and take over Neanderthal territory so quickly.) But did gene-culture coevolution stop at that point? Did our genes freeze in place, leaving all later adaptation to be handled by cultural innovation? For decades, many anthropologists and evolutionary theorists said yes. In an interview in 2000, the paleontologist Stephen Jay Gould said that "natural selection has almost become irrelevant in human evolution" because cultural change works "orders of magnitude" faster than genetic change. He next asserted that "there's been *no biological change* in humans in 40,000 or 50,000 years. Everything we call culture and civilization we've built *with the same body and brain.*"[77]

If you believe Gould's assertion that there's been no biological evolution in the last 50,000 years, then you'll be most interested in the Pleistocene era (the roughly 2 million years prior to the rise of agriculture), and you'll dismiss the Holocene (the last 12,000 years) as irrelevant for understanding human evolution. But is 12,000 years really just an eye blink in evolutionary time? Darwin didn't think so; he wrote frequently about the effects obtained by animal and plant breeders in just a few generations.

The speed at which genetic evolution can occur is best illustrated by an extraordinary study by Dmitri Belyaev, a Soviet scientist who had been demoted in 1948 for his belief in Mendelian genetics. (Soviet morality required the belief that traits acquired during one's lifetime could be passed on to one's children.)[78] Belyaev moved to a Siberian research institute, where he decided to test his ideas by conducting a simple breeding experiment with foxes. Rather than selecting foxes based on the quality of their pelts, as fox breeders would normally do, he selected them for tameness. Whichever fox pups were least fearful of humans were bred to create the next generation. Within just a few generations the foxes became tamer. But more important, after nine generations, novel traits began to appear in a few of the pups, and they were largely the same ones that distinguish dogs from wolves. For example, patches of white fur appeared on the head and chest; jaws and teeth shrank; and tails formerly straight began to curl. After just thirty generations the foxes had become so tame that they could be kept as pets. Lyudmila Trut, a geneticist who had worked with Belyaev on the project and who ran it after his death, described the foxes as "docile, eager to please, and unmistakably domesticated."[79]

It's not just individual-level selection that is fast. A second study

FIGURE 9.3. *Lyudmila Trut with Pavlik, a forty-second generation decendant of Belyaev's original study.*

done with chickens shows that group selection can produce equally dramatic results. If you want to increase egg output, common sense tells you to breed only the hens that lay the most eggs. But the reality of the egg industry is that hens live crammed together into cages, and the best laying hens tend to be the more aggressive, dominant hens. Therefore, if you use individual selection (breeding only the most productive hens), total productivity actually goes down because aggressive behavior—including killing and cannibalism—goes up.

In the 1980s the geneticist William Muir used group selection to get around this problem.[80] He worked with cages containing twelve hens each, and he simply picked the *cages* that produced the most eggs in each generation. Then he bred *all* of the hens in those cages to produce the next generation. Within just three generations, aggression levels plummeted. By the sixth generation, the death rate fell from the horrific baseline of 67 percent to a mere 8 percent. Total eggs produced per hen jumped from 91 to 237, mostly because the hens started living longer, but also because they laid more eggs per day. The group-selected hens were more productive than were those subjected to individual-level selection. They also actually looked like the pictures of chickens you see in children's books—plump and well-feathered, in contrast to the battered, beaten-up, and partially defeathered hens that resulted from individual-level selection.

Humans were probably never subjected to such a strong and consistent selection pressure as were those foxes and hens, so it would take more than six or ten generations to produce novel traits. But how much longer? Can the human genome respond to new selection pressures in, say, thirty generations (six hundred years)? Or would it take more than five hundred generations (ten thousand years) for a new selection pressure to produce any genetic adaptation?

The actual speed of genetic evolution is a question that can be answered with data, and thanks to the Human Genome Project, we now have that data. Several teams have sequenced the genomes of thousands of people from every continent. Genes mutate and drift through populations, but it is possible to distinguish such random drift from cases in which genes are being "pulled" by natural selection.[81] The results are astonishing, and they are exactly the opposite of Gould's claim: genetic evolution *greatly accelerated* during the last 50,000 years. The rate at which genes changed in response to selection pressures began rising around 40,000 years ago, and the curve got steeper and steeper after 20,000 years ago. Genetic change reached a crescendo during the Holocene era, in Africa as well as in Eurasia.

It makes perfect sense. In the last ten years, geneticists have discovered just how active genes are. Genes are constantly turning on and off in response to conditions such as stress, starvation, or sickness. Now imagine these dynamic genes building vehicles (people) who are hell-bent on exposing themselves to new climates, predators, parasites, food options, social structures, and forms of warfare. Imagine population densities skyrocketing during the Holocene, so that there are more people putting more genetic mutations into play. If genes and cultural adaptations coevolve in a "swirling waltz" (as Richerson and Boyd put it), and if the cultural partner suddenly starts dancing the jitterbug, the genes are going to pick up the pace too.[82] This is why genetic evolution kicked into overdrive in the Holocene era, pulling along mutations such as the lactose tolerance gene, or a gene that changed the blood of Tibetans so that they could live at high altitudes.[83] Genes for these recent traits and dozens of others have already been identified.[84] If genetic evolution was able to fine-tune our bones, teeth, skin, and metabolism in just a few thousand years as our diets and climates changed, how could genetic evolution not have tinkered with our brains and behaviors as our social environments underwent the most radical transformation in primate history?

I don't think evolution can create a new mental module from scratch in just 12,000 years, but I can see no reason why existing features—such as the six foundations I described in chapters 7 and 8, or the tendency to feel shame—would not be tweaked if conditions changed and then stayed stable for a thousand years. For example, when a society becomes more hierarchical or entrepreneurial, or when a group takes up rice farming, herding, or trade, these changes alter human relationships in many ways, and reward very different sets of virtues.[85] Cultural change would happen very rapidly—the moral matrix constructed upon the six foundations can change radically within a few generations. But if that new moral matrix then stays somewhat steady for a few dozen generations, new selection pressures will apply and there could be some additional gene-culture coevolution.[86]

Fast evolution is Exhibit D in the retrial of group selection. If genetic evolution can be fast, and if the human genome coevolves with cultural innovations, then it becomes quite possible that human nature was altered in just a few thousand years, somewhere in Africa, by group selection during particularly harsh periods.

For example, the climate in Africa fluctuated wildly between 70,000 and 140,000 years ago.[87] With each swing from warmer to cooler, or from wetter to drier, food sources changed and widespread starvation was probably common. A catastrophic volcanic eruption 74,000 years ago from the Toba volcano in Indonesia may have dramatically changed the Earth's climate within a single year.[88] Whatever the cause, we know that almost all humans were killed off at some point during this time period. Every person alive today is descended from just a few thousand people who made it through one or more population bottlenecks.[89]

What was their secret? We'll probably never know, but let's imagine that 95 percent of the food on Earth magically disappears tonight, guaranteeing that almost all of us will starve to death within two months. Law and order collapse. Chaos and mayhem ensue. Who among us will still be alive a year from now? Will it be the biggest, strongest, and most violent individuals in each town? Or will it be the people who manage to work together in groups to monopolize, hide, and share the remaining food supplies among themselves?

Now imagine starvations like that occurring every few centuries, and think about what a few such events would do to the human gene pool. Even if group selection was confined to just a few thousand years, or to the longer period between 70,000 and 140,000 years ago, it could have given us the group-related adaptations that allowed us to burst forth from Africa soon after the bottleneck to conquer and populate the globe.[90]

IT'S NOT ALL ABOUT WAR

I've presented group selection so far in its simplest possible form: groups compete with each other as if they were individual organisms, and the most cohesive groups wipe out and replace the less cohesive ones during intertribal warfare. That's the way that Darwin first imagined it. But when the evolutionary psychologist Lesley Newson read an early draft of this chapter, she sent me this note:

> I think it is important not to give readers the impression that groups competing necessarily meant groups being at war or fighting with one another. They were competing to be the most efficient at turning resources into offspring. Don't forget that women and children were also very important members of these groups.

Of course she's right. Group selection does not require war or violence. Whatever traits make a group more efficient at procuring food and turning it into children makes that group more fit than its neighbors. Group selection pulls for cooperation, for the ability to suppress antisocial behavior and spur individuals to act in ways that benefit their groups. Group-serving behaviors sometimes impose a terrible cost on outsiders (as in warfare). But in general, groupishness is focused on improving the welfare of the in-group, not on harming an out-group.

IN SUM

Darwin believed that morality was an adaptation that evolved by natural selection operating at the individual level *and* at the group level. Tribes with more virtuous members replaced tribes with more selfish members. But Darwin's idea was banished from the academic world when Williams and Dawkins argued that the free rider problem dooms group selection. The sciences then entered a three-decade period during which competition *between* groups was downplayed and everyone focused on competition among individuals *within* groups. Seemingly altruistic acts had to be explained as covert forms of selfishness.

But in recent years new scholarship has emerged that elevates the role of groups in evolutionary thinking. Natural selection works at multiple levels simultaneously, sometimes including groups of organisms. I can't say for sure that human nature was shaped by group selection—there are scientists whose views I respect on both sides of the debate. But as a psychologist studying morality, I can say that multilevel selection would go a long way toward explaining why people are simultaneously so selfish and so groupish.[91]

There is a great deal of new scholarship since the 1970s that compels us to think anew about group selection (as a part of multilevel selection). I organized that scholarship into four "exhibits" that collectively amount to a defense[92] of group selection.

> *Exhibit A: Major transitions produce superorganisms.*
> The history of life on Earth shows repeated examples
> of "major transitions." When the free rider problem is
> muted at one level of the biological hierarchy, larger and
> more powerful vehicles (superorganisms) arise at the

next level up in the hierarchy, with new properties such as a division of labor, cooperation, and altruism within the group.

Exhibit B: Shared intentionality generates moral matrices. The Rubicon crossing that let our ancestors function so well in their groups was the emergence of the uniquely human ability to share intentions and other mental representations. This ability enabled early humans to collaborate, divide labor, and develop shared norms for judging each other's behavior. These shared norms were the beginning of the moral matrices that govern our social lives today.

Exhibit C: Genes and cultures coevolve. Once our ancestors crossed the Rubicon and began to share intentions, our evolution became a two-stranded affair. People created new customs, norms, and institutions that altered the degree to which many groupish traits were adaptive. In particular, gene-culture coevolution gave us a set of tribal instincts: we love to mark group membership, and then we cooperate preferentially with members of our group.

Exhibit D: Evolution can be fast. Human evolution did not stop or slow down 50,000 years ago. It sped up. Gene-culture coevolution reached a fever pitch during the last 12,000 years. We can't just examine modern-day hunter-gatherers and assume that they represent universal human nature as it was locked into place 50,000 years ago. Periods of massive environmental change (as occurred between 70,000 and 140,000 years ago) and cultural change (as occurred during the Holocene era) should figure more prominently in our attempts to understand who we are, and how we got our righteous minds.

Most of human nature was shaped by natural selection operating at the level of the individual. Most, but not all. We have a few group-related adaptations too, as many Americans discovered in the days after 9/11. We humans have a dual nature—we are selfish primates who long to be a part of something larger and nobler than ourselves. We are 90 percent chimp and 10 percent bee.[93] If you take that claim metaphorically, then the groupish and hivish things that people do will make a lot more sense. It's almost as though there's a switch in our heads that activates our hivish potential when conditions are just right.

TEN

The Hive Switch

In September 1941, William McNeill was drafted into the U.S. Army. He spent several months in basic training, which consisted mostly of marching around the drill field in close formation with a few dozen other men. At first McNeill thought the marching was just a way to pass the time, because his base had no weapons with which to train. But after a few weeks, when his unit began to synchronize well, he began to experience an altered state of consciousness:

> Words are inadequate to describe the emotion aroused by the prolonged movement in unison that drilling involved. A sense of pervasive well-being is what I recall; more specifically, a strange sense of personal enlargement; a sort of swelling out, becoming bigger than life, thanks to participation in collective ritual.[1]

McNeill fought in World War II and later became a distinguished historian. His research led him to the conclusion that the key innovation of Greek, Roman, and later European armies was the sort of synchronous drilling and marching the army had forced him to do years before. He hypothesized that the process of "muscular bonding"—

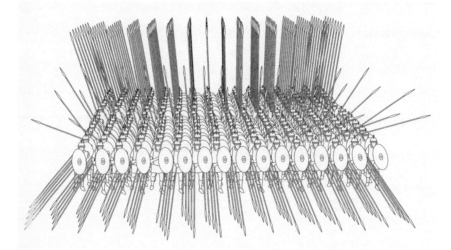

FIGURE 10.1. *The Macedonian phalanx.*

moving together in time—was a mechanism that evolved long before the beginning of recorded history for shutting down the self and creating a temporary superorganism. Muscular bonding enabled people to forget themselves, trust each other, function as a unit, and then crush less cohesive groups. Figure 10.1 shows the superorganism that Alexander the Great used to defeat much larger armies.

McNeill studied accounts of men in battle and found that men risk their lives not so much for their country or their ideals as for their comrades-in-arms. He quoted one veteran who gave this example of what happens when "I" becomes "we":

> Many veterans who are honest with themselves will admit, I believe, that the experience of communal effort in battle . . . has been the high point of their lives. . . . Their "I" passes insensibly into a "we," "my" becomes "our," and individual fate loses its central importance. . . . I believe that it is nothing less than the assurance of immortality that makes self sacrifice at these moments so relatively easy. . . . I may fall, but I do not die, for that which is real in me goes forward and lives on in the comrades for whom I gave up my life.[2]

THE HIVE HYPOTHESIS

In the last chapter, I suggested that human nature is 90 percent chimp and 10 percent bee. We are like chimps in being primates whose minds were shaped by the relentless competition of individuals with their neighbors. We are descended from a long string of winners in the game of social life. This is why we are Glauconians, usually more concerned about the appearance of virtue than the reality (as in Glaucon's story about the ring of Gyges).[3]

But human nature also has a more recent groupish overlay. We are like bees in being ultrasocial creatures whose minds were shaped by the relentless competition of groups with other groups. We are descended from earlier humans whose groupish minds helped them cohere, cooperate, and outcompete other groups. That doesn't mean that our ancestors were mindless or unconditional team players; it means they were selective. Under the right conditions, they were able to enter a mind-set of "one for all, all for one" in which they were truly working for the good of the group, and not just for their own advancement within the group.

My hypothesis in this chapter is that *human beings are conditional hive creatures*. We have the ability (under special conditions) to transcend self-interest and lose ourselves (temporarily and ecstatically) in something larger than ourselves. That ability is what I'm calling *the hive switch*. The hive switch, I propose, is a group-related adaptation that can only be explained "by a theory of between-group selection," as Williams said.[4] It cannot be explained by selection at the individual level. (How would this strange ability help a person to outcompete his neighbors in the same group?) The hive switch is an adaptation for making groups more cohesive, and therefore more successful in competition with other groups.[5]

If the hive hypothesis is true, then it has enormous implications for how we should design organizations, study religion, and search for meaning and joy in our lives.[6] Is it true? Is there really a hive switch?

COLLECTIVE EMOTIONS

When Europeans began to explore the world in the late fifteenth century, they brought back an extraordinary variety of plants and animals. Each continent had its own wonders; the diversity of the natural world was vast beyond imagination. But reports about the inhabitants of these far-flung lands were, in some ways, more uniform. European travelers to every continent witnessed people coming together to dance with wild abandon around a fire, synchronized to the beat of drums, often to the point of exhaustion. In *Dancing in the Streets: A History of Collective Joy*, Barbara Ehrenreich describes how European explorers reacted to these dances: with disgust. The masks, body paints, and guttural shrieks made the dancers seem like animals. The rhythmically undulating bodies and occasional sexual pantomimes were, to most Europeans, degrading, grotesque, and thoroughly "savage."

The Europeans were unprepared to understand what they were seeing. As Ehrenreich argues, collective and ecstatic dancing is a nearly universal "biotechnology" for binding groups together.[7] She agrees with McNeill that it is a form of muscular bonding. It fosters love, trust, and equality. It was common in ancient Greece (think of Dionysus and his cult) and in early Christianity (which she says was a "danced" religion until dancing in church was suppressed in the Middle Ages).

But if ecstatic dancing is so beneficial and so widespread, then why did Europeans give it up? Ehrenreich's historical explanation is too nuanced to summarize here, but the last part of the story is the rise of individualism and more refined notions of the self in Europe, beginning in the sixteenth century. These cultural changes accelerated during the Enlightenment and the Industrial Revolution. It is the same historical process that gave rise to WEIRD culture in the nineteenth century (that is, Western, educated, industrialized, rich, and democratic).[8] As I said in chapter 5, the WEIRDer you are, the more you perceive a world full of separate objects, rather than relationships. The WEIRDer you are, the harder it is to understand what those "savages" were doing.

Ehrenreich was surprised to discover how little help she could get from psychology in her quest to understand collective joy. Psychology has a rich language for describing relationships among pairs of people, from fleeting attractions to ego-dissolving love to pathological obsession. But what about the love that can exist among dozens of people? She notes that "if homosexual attraction is the love that 'dares not speak its name,' the love that binds people to the collective has no name at all to speak."[9]

Among the few useful scholars she found in her quest was Emile Durkheim. Durkheim insisted that there were "social facts" that were not reducible to facts about individuals. Social facts—such as the suicide rate or norms about patriotism—emerge as people interact. They are just as real and worthy of study (by sociology) as are people and their mental states (studied by psychology). Durkheim didn't know about multilevel selection and major transitions theory, but his sociology fits uncannily well with both ideas.

Durkheim frequently criticized his contemporaries, such as Freud, who tried to explain morality and religion using only the psychology of individuals and their pairwise relationships. (God is just a father figure, said Freud.) Durkheim argued, in contrast, that *Homo sapiens* was really *Homo duplex*, a creature who exists at two levels: as an individual and as part of the larger society. From his studies of religion he concluded that people have two distinct sets of "social sentiments," one for each level. The first set of sentiments "bind[s] each individual to the person of his fellow-citizens: these are manifest within the community, in the day-to-day relationships of life. These include the sentiments of honour, respect, affection and fear which we may feel towards one another."[10] These sentiments are easily explained by natural selection operating at the level of the individual: just as Darwin said, people avoid partners who lack these sentiments.[11]

But Durkheim noted that people also had the capacity to experience another set of emotions:

> The second are those which bind me to the social entity as a whole; these manifest themselves primarily in the relationships of the society with other societies, and could be called "inter-social." The first [set of emotions]

leave[s] my autonomy and personality almost intact. No
doubt they tie me to others, but without taking much
of my independence from me. When I act under the
influence of the second, by contrast, *I am simply a part
of a whole, whose actions I follow, and whose influence I am
subject to.*[12]

I find it stunning that Durkheim invokes the logic of multilevel
selection, proposing that a new set of social sentiments exists to help
groups (which are real things) with their "inter-social" relationships.
These second-level sentiments flip the hive switch, shut down the
self, activate the groupish overlay, and allow the person to become
"simply a part of a whole."

The most important of these Durkheimian higher-level sentiments is "collective effervescence," which describes the passion and
ecstasy that group rituals can generate. As Durkheim put it:

The very act of congregating is an exceptionally powerful
stimulant. Once the individuals are gathered together, a
sort of electricity is generated from their closeness and
quickly launches them to an extraordinary height of
exaltation.[13]

In such a state, "the vital energies become hyperexcited, the
passions more intense, the sensations more powerful."[14] Durkheim
believed that these collective emotions pull humans fully but temporarily into the higher of our two realms, the realm of the *sacred,* where
the self disappears and collective interests predominate. The realm of
the *profane,* in contrast, is the ordinary day-to-day world where we
live most of our lives, concerned about wealth, health, and reputation,
but nagged by the sense that there is, somewhere, something higher
and nobler.

Durkheim believed that our movements back and forth between
these two realms gave rise to our ideas about gods, spirits, heavens,
and the very notion of an objective moral order. These are social facts
that cannot be understood by psychologists studying individuals (or

pairs) any more than the structure of a beehive could be deduced by entomologists examining lone bees (or pairs).

SO MANY WAYS TO FLIP THE SWITCH

Collective effervescence sounds great, right? Too bad you need twenty-three friends and a bonfire to get it. Or do you? One of the most intriguing facts about the hive switch is that there are many ways to turn it on. Even if you doubt that the switch is a group-level adaptation, I hope you'll agree with me that the switch exists, and that it generally makes people less selfish and more loving. Here are three examples of switch flipping that you might have experienced yourself.

1. Awe in Nature

In the 1830s, Ralph Waldo Emerson delivered a set of lectures on nature that formed the foundation of American Transcendentalism, a movement that rejected the analytic hyperintellectualism of America's top universities. Emerson argued that the deepest truths must be known by intuition, not reason, and that experiences of awe in nature were among the best ways to trigger such intuitions. He described the rejuvenation and joy he gained from looking at the stars, or at a vista of rolling farmland, or from a simple walk in the woods:

> Standing on the bare ground,—my head bathed by the blithe air and uplifted into infinite space,—*all mean egotism vanishes*. I become a transparent eye-ball; I am nothing; I see all; the currents of the Universal Being circulate through me; I am part or particle of God.[15]

Darwin records a similar experience in his autobiography:

> In my journal I wrote that whilst standing in midst of the grandeur of a Brazilian forest, "it is not possible to

give an adequate idea of the higher feelings of wonder, admiration, and devotion which fill and elevate
the mind." I well remember my conviction that there is
more in man than the breath of his body.[16]

Emerson and Darwin each found in nature a portal between the
realm of the profane and the realm of the sacred. Even if the hive
switch was originally a group-related adaptation, it can be flipped
when you're alone by feelings of awe in nature, as mystics and ascetics
have known for millennia.

The emotion of awe is most often triggered when we face situations with two features: vastness (something overwhelms us and
makes us feel small) and a need for accommodation (that is, our experience is not easily assimilated into our existing mental structures; we
must "accommodate" the experience by changing those structures).[17]
Awe acts like a kind of reset button: it makes people forget themselves and their petty concerns. Awe opens people to new possibilities, values, and directions in life. Awe is one of the emotions most
closely linked to the hive switch, along with collective love and collective joy. People describe nature in spiritual terms—as both Emerson and Darwin did—precisely because nature can trigger the hive
switch and shut down the self, making you feel that you are *simply a
part of a whole*.

2. Durkheimogens

When Cortés captured Mexico in 1519, he found the Aztecs prac-
ticing a religion based on mushrooms containing the hallucinogen
psilocybin. The mushrooms were called *teonanacatl*—literally "God's
flesh" in the local language. The early Christian missionaries noted
the similarity of mushroom eating to the Christian Eucharist, but
the Aztec practice was more than a symbolic ritual. *Teonanacatl*
took people directly from the profane to the sacred realm in about
thirty minutes.[18] Figure 10.2 shows a god about to grab hold of a
mushroom eater, from a sixteenth-century Aztec scroll. Religious
practices north of the Aztecs focused on consumption of peyote, har-

vested from a cactus containing mescaline. Religious practices south of the Aztecs focused on consumption of *ayahuasca* (Quechua for "spirit vine"), a brew made from vines and leaves containing DMT (dimethyltriptamine).

These three drugs are classed together as hallucinogens (along with LSD and other synthetic compounds) because the class of chemically similar alkaloids in such drugs induces a range of visual and auditory hallucinations. But I think these drugs could just as well be called Durkheimogens, given their unique (though unreliable) ability to shut down the self and give people experiences they later describe as "religious" or "transformative."[19]

Most traditional societies have some sort of ritual for transforming boys into men and girls into women. It's usually far more grueling than a bar mitzvah; it frequently involves fear, pain, symbolism of death and rebirth, and a revelation of knowledge by gods or elders.[20] Many societies used hallucinogenic drugs to catalyze this transformation. The drugs flip the hive switch and help the selfish child disappear. The person who returns from the other world is then treated as a morally responsible adult. One anthropological review of

FIGURE 10.2. *An Aztec mushroom eater, about to be whisked away to the realm of the sacred.* Detail from the Codex Magliabechiano, CL.XIII.3, sixteenth century.

such rites concludes: "These states were induced to heighten learning and to create a bonding among members of the cohort group, when appropriate, so that individual psychic needs would be subsumed to the needs of the social group."[21]

When Westerners take these drugs, shorn of all rites and rituals, they don't usually commit to any group, but they often have experiences that are hard to distinguish from the "peak experiences" described by the humanistic psychologist Abe Maslow.[22] In one of the few controlled experiments, done before the drugs were made illegal in most Western countries, twenty divinity students were brought together in the basement chapel of a church in Boston.[23] All took a pill, but for the first twenty minutes, nobody knew who had taken psilocybin and who had taken niacin (a B vitamin that gives people a warm, flushed feeling). But by forty minutes into the experiment, it was clear to all. The ten who took niacin (and who had been the first to feel something happening) were stuck on Earth wishing the other ten well on their fantastic voyage.

The experimenters collected detailed reports from all participants before and after the study, as well as six months later. They found that psilocybin had produced statistically significant effects on nine kinds of experiences: (1) unity, including loss of sense of self, and a feeling of underlying oneness, (2) transcendence of time and space, (3) deeply felt positive mood, (4) a sense of sacredness, (5) a sense of gaining intuitive knowledge that felt deeply and authoritatively true, (6) paradoxicality, (7) difficulty describing what had happened, (8) transiency, with all returning to normal within a few hours, and (9) persisting positive changes in attitude and behavior.

Twenty-five years later, Rick Doblin tracked down nineteen of the twenty original subjects and interviewed them.[24] He concluded that "all psilocybin subjects participating in the long-term follow-up, but none of the controls, still considered their original experience to have had genuinely mystical elements and to have made a uniquely valuable contribution to their spiritual lives." One of the psilocybin subjects recalled his experience like this:

> All of a sudden I felt sort of drawn out into infinity, and all of a sudden I had lost touch with my mind. I felt that

I was caught up in the vastness of Creation. . . . Sometimes you would look up and see the light on the altar and it would just be a blinding sort of light and radiations. . . . We took such an infinitesimal amount of psilocybin, and yet it connected me to infinity.

3. Raves

Rock music has always been associated with wild abandon and sexuality. American parents in the 1950s often shared the horror of those seventeenth-century Europeans faced with the ecstatic dancing of the "savages." But in the 1980s, British youth mixed together new technologies to create a new kind of dancing that replaced the individualism and sexuality of rock with more communal feelings. Advances in electronics brought new and more hypnotic genres of music, such as techno, trance, house, and drum and bass. Advances in laser technology made it possible to bring spectacular visual effects into any party. And advances in pharmacology made a host of new drugs available to the dancing class, particularly MDMA, a variant of amphetamine that gives people long-lasting energy, along with heightened feelings of love and openness. (Revealingly, the colloquial name for MDMA is ecstasy.) When some or all of these ingredients were combined, the result was so deeply appealing that young people began converging by the thousands for all-night dance parties, first in the United Kingdom and then, in the 1990s, throughout the developed world.

There's a description of a rave experience in Tony Hsieh's autobiography *Delivering Happiness*. Hsieh (pronounced "Shay") is the CEO of the online retailer Zappos.com. He made a fortune at the age of twenty-four when he sold his start-up tech company to Microsoft. For the next few years Hsieh wondered what to do with his life. He had a small group of friends who hung out together in San Francisco. The first time Hsieh and his "tribe" (as they called themselves) attended a rave, it flipped his hive switch. Here is his description:

What I experienced next changed my perspective forever. . . . Yes, the decorations and lasers were pretty cool, and yes, this was the largest single room full of people dancing that I had ever seen. But neither of those things explained the feeling of awe that I was experiencing . . . As someone who is usually known as being the most logical and rational person in a group, I was surprised to find myself swept with an overwhelming sense of spirituality—not in the religious sense, but a sense of *deep connection with everyone who was there as well as the rest of the universe.* There was a feeling of no judgment. . . . Here there was *no sense of self-consciousness* or feeling that anyone was dancing to be seen dancing. . . . Everyone was facing the DJ, who was elevated up on a stage. . . . The entire room felt like *one massive, united tribe of thousands of people*, and the DJ was the tribal leader of the group. . . . The steady wordless electronic beats were the unifying heartbeats that synchronized the crowd. It was as if *the existence of individual consciousness had disappeared and been replaced by a single unifying group consciousness.*[25]

Hsieh had stumbled into a modern version of the muscular bonding that Ehrenreich and McNeill had described. The scene and the experience awed him, shut down his "I," and merged him into a giant "we." That night was a turning point in his life; it started him on the path to creating a new kind of business embodying some of the communalism and ego suppression he had felt at the rave.

There are many other ways to flip the hive switch. In the ten years during which I've been discussing these ideas with my students at UVA, I've heard reports of people getting "turned on" by singing in choruses, performing in marching bands, listening to sermons, attending political rallies, and meditating. Most of my students have experienced the switch at least once, although only a few had a life-changing experience. More commonly, the effects fade away within a few hours or days.

Now that I know what can happen when the hive switch gets

flipped in the right way at the right time, I look at my students differently. I still see them as individuals competing with each other for grades, honors, and romantic partners. But I have a new appreciation for the zeal with which they throw themselves into extracurricular activities, most of which turn them into team players. They put on plays, compete in sports, rally for political causes, and volunteer for dozens of projects to help the poor and the sick in Charlottesville and in faraway countries. I see them searching for a calling, which they can only find as part of a larger group. I now see them striving and searching on two levels simultaneously, for we are all *Homo duplex*.

THE BIOLOGY OF THE HIVE SWITCH

If the hive switch is real—if it's a group-level adaptation designed by group-level selection for group binding—then it must be made out of neurons, neurotransmitters, and hormones. It's not going to be a spot in the brain—a clump of neurons that humans have and chimpanzees lack. Rather, it will be a *functional* system cobbled together from preexisting circuits and substances reused in slightly novel ways to produce a radically novel ability. In the last ten years there's been an avalanche of research on the two[26] most likely building materials of this functional system.[27]

If evolution chanced upon a way to bind people together into large groups, the most obvious glue is oxytocin, a hormone and neurotransmitter produced by the hypothalamus. Oxytocin is widely used among vertebrates to prepare females for motherhood. In mammals it causes uterine contractions and milk letdown, as well as a powerful motivation to touch and care for one's children. Evolution has often reused oxytocin to forge other kinds of bonds. In species in which males stick by their mates or protect their own offspring, it's because male brains were slightly modified to be more responsive to oxytocin.[28]

In people, oxytocin reaches far beyond family life. If you squirt oxytocin spray into a person's nose, he or she will be more trusting in a game that involves transferring money temporarily to an anonymous partner.[29] Conversely, people who behave trustingly cause oxytocin levels to increase in the partner they trusted. Oxytocin levels also rise when people watch videos about other people suffering—at least among those who report feelings of empathy and a desire to help.[30] Your brain secretes more oxytocin when you have intimate contact with another person, even if that contact is just a back rub from a stranger.[31]

What a lovely hormone! It's no wonder the press has swooned in recent years, dubbing it the "love drug" and the "cuddle hormone." If we could put oxytocin into the world's drinking water, might there be an end to war and cruelty?

Unfortunately, no. If the hive switch is a product of group selection, then it should show the signature feature of group selection: parochial altruism.[32] Oxytocin should bond us to our partners and our groups, so that we can more effectively compete with other groups. It should not bond us to humanity in general.

Several recent studies have validated this prediction. In one set of studies, Dutch men played a variety of economic games while sitting alone in cubicles, linked via computers into small teams.[33] Half of the men had been given a nasal spray of oxytocin, and half got a placebo spray. The men who received oxytocin made less selfish decisions—they cared more about helping their group, but they showed no concern at all for improving the outcomes of men in the other groups. In one of these studies, oxytocin made men more willing to hurt other teams (in a prisoner's dilemma game) because doing so was the best way to protect their own group. In a set of follow-up studies, the authors found that oxytocin caused Dutch men to like Dutch names more and to value saving Dutch lives more (in trolley-type dilemmas). Over and over again the researchers looked for signs that this increased in-group love would be paired with increased out-group hate (toward Muslims), but they failed to find it.[34] Oxytocin simply makes people love their in-group more. It makes them parochial altruists. The authors conclude that their findings "provide evidence for the idea that neurobiological mechanisms in general, and oxytocinergic systems in particular, evolved to sustain and facilitate within-group coordination and cooperation."

The second candidate for sustaining within-group coordination is the mirror neuron system. Mirror neurons were discovered accidentally in the 1980s when a team of Italian scientists began inserting tiny electrodes into individual neurons in the brains of Macaque monkeys. The researchers were trying to find out what some individual cells were doing in a region of the cerebral cortex that they knew controls fine motor movements. They discovered that there were some neurons that fired rapidly only when the monkey made a very specific movement, such as grasping a nut between thumb and forefinger (versus, say, grabbing the nut with the entire hand). But once they had these electrodes implanted and hooked up to a speaker (so that they could hear the rate of firing), they began to hear firing noises at odd times, such as when a monkey was perfectly still and it was the *researcher* who had just picked up something with his thumb and forefinger. This made no sense because perception and action were supposed to occur in separate regions of the brain. Yet here were neurons that didn't care whether the monkey was doing something or watching someone else do it. The monkey seemed to *mirror* the actions of others in the same part of its brain that it would use to do those actions itself.[35]

Later work demonstrated that most mirror neurons fire not when they see a specific physical movement but when they see an action that indicates a more general goal or intention. For example, watching a video of a hand picking up a cup from a clean table, as if to bring it to the person's mouth, triggers a mirror neuron for eating. But the exact same hand movement and the exact same cup picked up from a *messy* table (where a meal seems to be finished) triggers a different mirror neuron for picking things up in general. The monkeys have neural systems that infer the *intentions* of others—which is clearly a prerequisite for Tomasello's shared intentionality[36]—but they aren't yet ready to share. Mirror neurons seem designed for the monkeys' own *private* use, either to help them learn from others or to help them predict what another monkey will do next.

In humans the mirror neuron system is found in brain regions that correspond directly to those studied in macaques. But in humans the mirror neurons have a much stronger connection to emotion-related areas of the brain—first to the insular cortex, and from there to the amygdala and other limbic areas.[37] People feel each other's pain and joy to a much greater degree than do any other primates. Just seeing someone else smile activates some of the same neurons as when you smile. The other person is effectively smiling in your brain, which makes you happy and likely to smile, which in turn passes the smile into someone else's brain.

Mirror neurons are perfectly suited for Durkheim's collective sentiments, particularly the emotional "electricity" of collective effervescence. But their Durkheimian nature comes out even more clearly in a study led by the neuroscientist Tania Singer.[38] Subjects first played an economic game with two strangers, one of whom played nicely while the other played selfishly. In the next part of the study, subjects' brains were scanned while mild electric shocks were delivered randomly to the hand of the subject, the hand of the nice player, or the hand of the selfish player. (The other players' hands were visible to the subject, near her own while she was in the scanner.) Results showed that subjects' brains responded in the same way when the "nice" player received a shock as when they themselves were shocked. The subjects used their mirror neurons, empathized, and felt the other's pain. But when the selfish player got a shock, people showed less empathy, and some even showed neural evidence of pleasure.[39] In other words, people don't just blindly empathize; they don't sync up with everyone they see. We are *conditional* hive creatures. We are more likely to mirror and then empathize with others when they have conformed to our moral matrix than when they have violated it.[40]

HIVES AT WORK

From cradle to grave we are surrounded by corporations and things made by corporations. What exactly are corporations, and how did they come to cover the Earth? The word itself comes from *corpus*, Latin for "body." A corporation is, quite literally, a superorganism. Here is an early definition, from Stewart Kyd's 1794 *Treatise on the Law of Corporations:*

> [A corporation is] a collection of many individuals
> *united into one body*, under a special denomination, hav-
> ing perpetual succession under an artificial form, and
> vested, by policy of the law, with the capacity of acting,
> in several respects, *as an individual*.[41]

This legal fiction, recognizing "a collection of many individuals" as a new kind of individual, turned out to be a winning formula. It let people place themselves into a new kind of boat within which they could divide labor, suppress free riding, and take on gigantic tasks with the potential for gigantic rewards.

Corporations and corporate law helped England pull out ahead of the rest of the world in the early days of the industrial revolution. As with the transition to beehives and city-states, it took a while for the new superorganisms to work out the kinks, perfect the form, and develop effective defenses against external attacks and internal subversion. But once those problems were addressed, there was explosive growth. During the twentieth century, small businesses got pushed to the margins or to extinction as corporations dominated the most lucrative markets. Corporations are now so powerful that only national governments can restrain the largest of them (and even then it's only some governments, and some of the time).

It is possible to build a corporation staffed entirely by *Homo economicus*. The gains from cooperation and division of labor are so vast that large companies can pay more than small businesses and then use a series of institutionalized carrots and sticks—including expensive monitoring and enforcement mechanisms—to motivate self-serving employees to act in ways the company desires. But this approach (sometimes called transactional leadership)[42] has its limits. Self-interested employees are Glauconians, far more interested in looking good and getting promoted than in helping the company.[43]

In contrast, an organization that takes advantage of our hivish nature can activate pride, loyalty, and enthusiasm among its employees and then monitor them less closely. This approach to leadership (sometimes called transformational leadership)[44] generates more social capital—the bonds of trust that help employees get more work done at a lower cost than employees at other firms. Hivish employees work harder, have more fun, and are less likely to quit or to sue the company. Unlike *Homo economicus*, they are truly team players.

What can leaders do to create more hivish organizations? The first step is to stop thinking so much about leadership. One group of scholars has used multilevel selection to think about what leadership really is. Robert Hogan, Robert Kaiser, and Mark van Vugt argue that leadership can only be understood as the complement of follower-ship.[45] Focusing on leadership alone is like trying to understand clapping by studying only the left hand. They point out that leadership is not even the more interesting hand; it's no puzzle to understand why people want to lead. The real puzzle is why people are willing to follow.

These scholars note that people evolved to live in groups of up to 150 that were relatively egalitarian and wary of alpha males (as Chris Boehm said).[46] But we also evolved the ability to rally around leaders when our group is under threat or is competing with other groups. Remember how the Rattlers and the Eagles instantly became more tribal and hierarchical the instant they discovered the presence of the other group?[47] Research also shows that strangers will spontaneously organize themselves into leaders and followers when natural disasters strike.[48] People are happy to follow when they see that their group needs to get something done, and when the person who emerges as the leader doesn't activate their hypersensitive oppression detectors. A leader must construct a moral matrix based in some way on the Authority foundation (to legitimize the authority of the leader), the Liberty foundation (to make sure that subordinates don't feel oppressed, and don't want to band together to oppose a bullying alpha male), and above all, the Loyalty foundation (which I defined in chapter 7 as a response to the challenge of forming cohesive coalitions).

Using this evolutionary framework, we can draw some direct lessons for anyone who wants to make a team, company, school, or other organization more hivish, happy, and productive. You don't need to slip ecstasy into the watercooler and then throw a rave party in the cafeteria. The hive switch may be more of a slider switch than an on-off switch, and with a few institutional changes you can create environments that will nudge everyone's sliders a bit closer to the hive position. For example:

- *Increase similarity, not diversity.* To make a human hive, you want to make everyone feel like a family. So don't call attention to racial and ethnic differences; make them less relevant by ramping up similarity and celebrating the group's shared values and common identity.[49] A great deal of research in social psychology shows that people are warmer and more trusting toward people who look like them, dress like them, talk like them, or even just share their first name or birthday.[50] There's nothing special about race. You can make people care less about race by drowning race differences in a sea of similarities, shared goals, and mutual interdependencies.[51]

- *Exploit synchrony.* People who move together are saying, "We are one, we are a team; just look how perfectly we are able to do that Tomasello shared-intention thing." Japanese corporations such as Toyota begin their days with synchronous companywide exercises. Groups prepare for battle—in war and sports—with group chants and ritualized movements. (If you want to see an impressive one in rugby, Google "All Blacks Haka.") If you ask people to sing a song together, or to march in step, or just to tap out some beats together on a table, it makes them trust each other more and be more willing to help each other out, in part because it makes people feel more similar to each other.[52] If it's too creepy to ask your employees or fellow group members to do synchronized calisthenics, perhaps you can just try to have more parties with dancing or karaoke. Synchrony builds trust.

- *Create healthy competition among teams, not individuals.* As McNeill said, soldiers don't risk their lives for their country or for the army; they do so for their buddies in the same squad or platoon. Studies show that intergroup competition increases love of the in-group far more than it increases dislike of the out-group.[53] Intergroup competitions, such as friendly rivalries between corporate divisions, or intramural sports competitions, should have a net positive effect on hivishness and social capital. But pitting individuals against each other in a competition for scarce resources (such as bonuses) will destroy hivishness, trust, and morale.

Much more could be said about leading a hivish organization.[54] Kaiser and Hogan offer this summary of the research literature:

> Transactional leadership appeals to followers' self-interest, but transformational leadership changes the way followers see themselves—*from isolated individuals to members of a larger group*. Transformational leaders do this by modeling collective commitment (e.g., through self-sacrifice and the use of "we" rather than "I"), emphasizing the similarity of group members, and reinforcing collective goals, shared values, and common interests.[55]

In other words, transformational leaders understand (at least implicitly) that human beings have a dual nature. They set up organizations that engage, to some degree, the higher level of that nature. Good leaders create good followers, but followership in a hivish organization is better described as membership.

POLITICAL HIVES

Great leaders understand Durkheim, even if they've never read his work. For Americans born before 1950, you can activate their Durkheimian higher nature by saying just two words: "Ask not." The full sentence they'll hear in their minds comes from John F. Kennedy's 1961 inaugural address. After calling on all Americans to "bear the burden of a long twilight struggle"—that is, to pay the costs and take the risks of fighting the cold war against the Soviet Union— Kennedy delivered one of the most famous lines in American history: "And so, my fellow Americans, ask not what your country can do for you; ask what you can do for your country."

The yearning to serve something larger than the self has been the basis of so many modern political movements. Here's another brilliantly Durkheimian appeal:

> [Our movement rejects the view of man] as an individual, standing by himself, self-centered, subject to natural law, which instinctively urges him toward a life of selfish momentary pleasure; it sees not only the individual but the nation and the country; individuals and generations bound together by a moral law, with common traditions and a mission which, suppressing the instinct for life closed in a brief circle of pleasure, builds up a higher life, founded on duty, a life free from the limitations of time and space, in which the individual, by self-sacrifice, the renunciation of self-interest . . . can achieve that purely spiritual existence in which his value as a man consists.

Inspiring stuff, until you learn that it's from *The Doctrine of Fascism*, by Benito Mussolini.[56] Fascism is hive psychology scaled up to grotesque heights. It's the doctrine of the nation as a superorganism, within which the individual loses all importance. So hive psychology is bad stuff, right? Any leader who tries to get people to forget themselves and merge into a team pursuing a common goal is flirting with fascism, no? Asking your employees to exercise together—isn't that the sort of thing Hitler did at his Nuremberg rallies?

Ehrenreich devotes a chapter of *Dancing in the Streets* to refuting this concern. She notes that ecstatic dancing is an evolved biotechnology for *dissolving* hierarchy and bonding people *to each other as a community*. Ecstatic dancing, festivals, and carnivals invariably erase or invert the hierarchies of everyday life. Men dress as women, peasants pretend to be nobles, and leaders can be safely mocked. When it's all over and people have returned to their normal social stations, those stations are a bit less rigid, and the connections among people in different stations are a bit warmer.[57]

Fascist rallies, Ehrenreich notes, were nothing like this. They were *spectacles*, not festivals. They used awe to *strengthen* hierarchy and to bond people to the *godlike figure of the leader*. People at fascist rallies didn't dance, and they surely didn't mock their leaders. They stood around passively for hours, applauding when groups of soldiers marched by, or cheering wildly when the dear leader arrived and spoke to them.[58]

Fascist dictators clearly exploited many aspects of humanity's groupish psychology, but is that a valid reason for us to shun or fear the hive switch? Hiving comes naturally, easily, and joyfully to us. Its normal function is to bond dozens or at most hundreds of people together into communities of trust, cooperation, and even love. Those bonded groups may care less about outsiders than they did before their bonding—the nature of group selection is to suppress selfishness within groups to make them more effective at competing with other groups. But is that really such a bad thing overall, given how shallow our care for strangers is in the first place? Might the world be a better place if we could greatly increase the care people get within their existing groups and nations while slightly decreasing the care they get from strangers in other groups and nations?

Let's imagine two nations, one full of small-scale hives, one devoid of them. In the hivish nation, let's suppose that most people participate in several cross-cutting hives—perhaps one at work, one at church, and one in a weekend sports league. At universities, most students join fraternities and sororities. In the workplace, most leaders structure their organizations to take advantage of our groupish overlay. Throughout their lives, citizens regularly enjoy muscular bonding, team building, and moments of self-transcendence with groups of fellow citizens who may be different from them racially, but with whom they feel deep similarity and interdependence. This bonding is often accompanied by the excitement of intergroup competition (as in sports and business), but sometimes not (as in church).

In the second nation, there's no hiving at all. Everyone cherishes their autonomy and respects the autonomy of their fellow citizens. Groups form only to the extent that they advance the interests of their members. Businesses are led by transactional leaders who align the material interests of employees as closely as possible with the interests of the company, so that if everyone pursues their self-interest, the business will thrive. In this non-hivish nation you'll find families and plenty of friendships; you'll find altruism (both kin and reciprocal). You'll find all the stuff described by evolutionary psychologists who doubt that group selection occurred, but you'll find no evidence of group-related adaptations such as the hive switch. You'll find no culturally approved or institutionalized ways to lose yourself in a larger group.

Which nation do you think would score higher on measures of social capital, mental health, and happiness? Which nation will produce more successful businesses and a higher standard of living?[59]

When a single hive is scaled up to the size of a nation and is led by a dictator with an army at his disposal, the results are invariably disastrous. But that is no argument for removing or suppressing hives at lower levels. In fact, a nation that is full of hives is a nation of happy and satisfied people. It's not a very promising target for takeover by a demagogue offering people meaning in exchange for their souls. Creating a nation of multiple competing groups and parties was, in fact, seen by America's founding fathers as a way of preventing tyranny.[60] More recently, research on social capital has demonstrated that bowling leagues, churches, and other kinds of groups, teams, and clubs are crucial for the health of individuals and of a nation. As political scientist Robert Putnam put it, the social capital that is generated by such local groups "makes us smarter, healthier, safer, richer, and better able to govern a just and stable democracy."[61]

A nation of individuals, in contrast, in which citizens spend all their time in Durkheim's lower level, is likely to be hungry for meaning. If people can't satisfy their need for deep connection in other ways, they'll be more receptive to a smooth-talking leader who urges them to renounce their lives of "selfish momentary pleasure" and follow him onward to "that purely spiritual existence" in which their value as human beings consists.

IN SUM

When I began writing *The Happiness Hypothesis*, I believed that happiness came from within, as Buddha and the Stoic philosophers said thousands of years ago. You'll never make the world conform to your wishes, so focus on changing yourself and your desires. But by the time I finished writing, I had changed my mind: Happiness comes from between. It comes from getting the right relationships between yourself and others, yourself and your work, and yourself and something larger than yourself.

Once you understand our dual nature, including our groupish overlay, you can see why happiness comes from between. We evolved to live in groups. Our minds were designed not only to help us win the competition within our groups, but also to help us unite with those in our group to win competitions across groups.

In this chapter I presented the hive hypothesis, which states that human beings are conditional hive creatures. We have the ability (under special circumstances) to transcend self-interest and lose ourselves (temporarily and ecstatically) in something larger than ourselves. I called this ability the hive switch. The hive switch is another way of stating Durkheim's idea that we are *Homo duplex;* we live most of our lives in the ordinary (profane) world, but we achieve our greatest joys in those brief moments of transit to the sacred world, in which we become "simply a part of a whole."

I described three common ways in which people flip the hive switch: awe in nature, Durkheimian drugs, and raves. I described recent findings about oxytocin and mirror neurons that suggest that they are the stuff of which the hive switch is made. Oxytocin bonds people to their groups, not to all of humanity. Mirror neurons help people empathize with others, but particularly those that share their moral matrix.

It would be nice to believe that we humans were designed to love everyone unconditionally. Nice, but rather unlikely from an evolutionary perspective. Parochial love—love within groups—amplified by similarity, a sense of shared fate, and the suppression of free riders, may be the most we can accomplish.

ELEVEN

Religion Is a Team Sport

Every Saturday in the fall, at colleges across the United States, millions of people pack themselves into stadiums to participate in a ritual that can only be described as tribal. At the University of Virginia, the ritual begins in the morning as students dress in special costumes. Men wear dress shirts with UVA neckties, and if the weather is warm, shorts. Women typically wear skirts or dresses, sometimes with pearl necklaces. Some students paint the logo of our sports teams, the Cavaliers (a *V* crossed by two swords), on their faces or other body parts.

The students attend pregame parties that serve brunch and alcoholic drinks. Then they stream over to the stadium, sometimes stopping to mingle with friends, relatives, or unknown alumni who have driven for hours to reach Charlottesville in time to set up tailgate parties in every parking lot within a half mile of the stadium. More food, more alcohol, more face painting.

By the time the game starts, many of the 50,000 fans are drunk, which makes it easier for them to overcome self-consciousness and participate fully in the synchronous chants, cheers, jeers, and songs that will fill the next three hours. Every time the Cavaliers score, the students sing the same song UVA students have sung together on such occasions for over a century. The first verse comes straight out of

Durkheim and Ehrenreich. The students literally lock arms and sway as a single mass while singing the praises of their community (to the tune of "Auld Lang Syne"):

> *That good old song of Wah-hoo-wah—we'll sing it o'er and o'er*
> *It cheers our hearts and warms our blood to hear them shout and roar*
> *We come from old Virgin-i-a, where all is bright and gay*
> *Let's all join hands and give a yell for dear old U-V-A.*

Next, the students illustrate McNeill's thesis that "muscular bonding" warms people up for coordinated military action.[1] The students let go of each other's arms and make aggressive fist-pumping motions in the air, in sync with a nonsensical battle chant:

> *Wah-hoo-wah! Wah-hoo-wah! Uni-v, Virgin-i-a!*
> *Hoo-rah-ray! Hoo-rah-ray! Ray, ray—U-V-A!*

It's a whole day of hiving and collective emotions. Collective effervescence is guaranteed, as are feelings of collective outrage at questionable calls by the referees, collective triumph if the team wins, and collective grief if the team loses, followed by more collective drinking at postgame parties.

Why do the students sing, chant, dance, sway, chop, and stomp so enthusiastically during the game? Showing support for their football team may help to motivate the players, but is that the *function* of these behaviors? Are they done *in order to* achieve victory? No. From a Durkheimian perspective these behaviors serve a very different function, and it is the same one that Durkheim saw at work in most religious rituals: *the creation of a community.*

A college football game is a superb analogy for religion.[2] From a naive perspective, focusing only on what is most visible (i.e., the game being played on the field), college football is an extravagant, costly, wasteful institution that impairs people's ability to think rationally while leaving a long trail of victims (including the players themselves, plus the many fans who suffer alcohol-related injuries). But from a sociologically informed perspective, it is a religious rite that does just what it is supposed to do: it pulls people up from Durkheim's lower level (the profane) to his higher level (the sacred). It flips the hive switch and makes people feel, for a few hours, that they are "simply a part of a whole." It augments the school spirit for which UVA is renowned, which in turn attracts better students and more alumni donations, which in turn improves the experience for the entire community, including professors like me who have no interest in sports.

Religions are social facts. Religion cannot be studied in lone individuals any more than hivishness can be studied in lone bees. Durkheim's definition of religion makes its binding function clear:

> A religion is a unified system of beliefs and practices relative to sacred things, that is to say, things set apart and forbidden—beliefs and practices which unite into one single moral community called a Church, all those who adhere to them.[3]

In this chapter I continue exploring the third principle of moral psychology: *Morality binds and blinds.* Many scientists misunderstand religion because they ignore this principle and examine only what is most visible. They focus on individuals and their supernatural beliefs, rather than on groups and their binding practices. They conclude that religion is an extravagant, costly, wasteful institution that impairs people's ability to think rationally while leaving a long trail of victims. I do not deny that religions do, at times, fit that description. But if we are to render a fair judgment about religion—and understand its relationship to morality and politics—we must first describe it accurately.

THE LONE BELIEVER

When nineteen Muslims hijacked four planes and used them to destroy the World Trade Center and a section of the Pentagon, they forced into the open a belief that many in the Western world had harbored since the 1980s: that there is a special connection between Islam and terrorism. Commentators on the right were quick to blame Islam. Commentators on the left were just as quick to say that Islam is a religion of peace and that the blame should be placed on fundamentalism.[4]

But an interesting rift opened up on the left. Some scientists whose politics were otherwise quite liberal began to attack not just Islam but all religions (other than Buddhism).[5] After decades of culture war in the United States over the teaching of evolution in public schools, some scientists saw little distinction between Islam and Christianity. All religions, they said, are delusions that prevent people from embracing science, secularism, and modernity. The horror of 9/11 motivated several of these scientists to write books, and between 2004 and 2007, so many such books were published that a movement was born: the New Atheism.

The titles were combative. The first one out was Sam Harris's *The End of Faith: Religion, Terror, and the Future of Reason,* followed by Richard Dawkins's *The God Delusion,* Daniel Dennett's *Breaking the Spell: Religion as a Natural Phenomenon,* and, with the most explicit title of all, Christopher Hitchens's *God Is Not Great: How Religion Poisons Everything.* These four authors are known as the four horsemen of New Atheism, but I'm going to set Hitchens aside because he is a journalist whose book made no pretense to be anything other than a polemical diatribe. The other three authors, however, are men of science: Harris was a graduate student in neuroscience at the time, Dawkins is a biologist, and Dennett is a philosopher who has written widely on evolution. These three authors claimed to speak for science and to exemplify the values of science—particularly its open-mindedness and its insistence that claims be grounded in reason and empirical evidence, not faith and emotion.

I also group these three authors together because they offer similar definitions of religion, all focusing on belief in supernatural agents. Here is Harris: "Throughout this book, I am criticizing faith in its ordinary, scriptural sense—as belief in, and life orientation toward, certain historical and metaphysical propositions."[6] Harris's own research examines what happens in the brain when people believe or disbelieve various propositions, and he justifies his focus on religious belief with this psychological claim: "A belief is a lever that, once pulled, moves almost everything else in a person's life."[7] For Harris, beliefs are the key to understanding the psychology of religion because in his view, believing a falsehood (e.g., martyrs will be rewarded with seventy-two virgins in heaven) makes religious people do harmful things (e.g., suicide bombing). I've illustrated Harris's psychological model in figure 11.1.

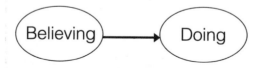

FIGURE 11.1. *The New Atheist model of religious psychology.*

Dawkins takes a similar approach. He defines the "God Hypothesis" as the proposition that "there exists a superhuman, supernatural intelligence who deliberately designed and created the universe and everything in it, including us."[8] The rest of the book is an argument that "God, in the sense defined, is a delusion; and, as later chapters will show, a pernicious delusion."[9] Once again, religion is studied as a set of beliefs about supernatural agents, and these beliefs are said to be the cause of a wide range of harmful actions. Dennett takes that approach too.[10]

Supernatural agents do of course play a central role in religion, just as the actual football is at the center of the whirl of activity on game day at UVA. But trying to understand the persistence and passion of religion by studying beliefs about God is like trying to understand the persistence and passion of college football by studying the movements of the ball. You've got to broaden the inquiry. You've got to look at the ways that religious beliefs work with religious practices to create a religious community.[11]

Believing, doing, and belonging are three complementary yet distinct aspects of religiosity, according to many scholars.[12] When you look at all three aspects at the same time, you get a view of the psychology of religion that's very different from the view of the New Atheists. I'll call this competing model the Durkheimian model, because it says that the function of those beliefs and practices is ultimately to create a community. Often our beliefs are post hoc constructions designed to justify what we've just done, or to support the groups we belong to.

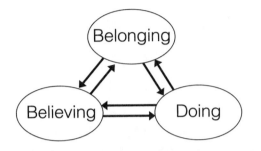

FIGURE 11.2. *The Durkheimian model of religious psychology.*

The New Atheist model is based on the Platonic rationalist view of the mind, which I introduced in chapter 2: Reason is (or at least could be) the charioteer guiding the passions (the horses). So as long as reason has the proper factual beliefs (and has control of the unruly passions), the chariot will go in the right direction. In chapters 2, 3, and 4, however, I reviewed a great deal of evidence against the Platonic view and in favor of a Humean view in which reason (the rider) is a servant of the intuitions (the elephant).

Let's continue the debate between rationalism and social intuitionism as we examine religion. To understand the psychology of religion, should we focus on the false beliefs and faulty reasoning of individual believers? Or should we focus on the automatic (intuitive) processes of people embedded in social groups that are striving to create a moral community? That depends on what we think religion is, and where we think it came from.

THE NEW ATHEIST STORY: BY-PRODUCTS, THEN PARASITES

To an evolutionist, religious behaviors "stand out like peacocks in a sunlit glade," as Dennett put it.[13] Evolution ruthlessly eliminates costly and wasteful behaviors from an animal's repertoire (over many generations), yet, to quote Dawkins, "no known culture lacks some version of the time-consuming, wealth-consuming, hostility-provoking rituals, the anti-factual, counterproductive fantasies of religion."[14] To resolve this puzzle, either you have to grant that religiosity is (or at least, used to be) beneficial or you have to construct a complicated, multistep explanation of how humans in all known cultures came to swim against the tide of adaptation and do so much self-destructive religious stuff. The New Atheists choose the latter course. Their accounts all begin with a discussion of multiple evolutionary "by-products" that explain the accidental origin of God beliefs, and some then continue on to an account of how these beliefs evolved as sets of parasitic memes.[15]

The first step in the New Atheist story—one that I won't challenge—is the hypersensitive agency detection device.[16] The idea makes a lot of sense: we see faces in the clouds, but never clouds in faces, because we have special cognitive modules for face detection.[17] The face detector is on a hair trigger, and it makes almost all of its mistakes in one direction—false positives (seeing a face when no real face is present, e.g., ☺), rather than false negatives (failing to see a face that is really present). Similarly, most animals confront the challenge of distinguishing events that are caused by the presence of another animal (an agent that can move under its own power) from those that are caused by the wind, or a pinecone falling, or anything else that lacks agency.

The solution to this challenge is an agency detection module, and like the face detector, it's on a hair trigger. It makes almost all of its mistakes in one direction—false positives (detecting an agent when none is present), rather than false negatives (failing to detect the presence of a real agent). If you want to see the hypersensitive agency detector in action, just slide your fist around under a blanket, within sight of a puppy or a kitten. If you want to know why it's on a hair trigger, just think about which kind of error would be more costly the next time you are walking alone at night in the deep forest or a dark alley. The hypersensitive agency detection device is finely tuned to maximize survival, not accuracy.

But now suppose that early humans, equipped with a hypersensitive agency detector, a new ability to engage in shared intentionality, and a love of stories, begin to talk about their many misperceptions. Suppose they begin attributing agency to the weather. (Thunder and lightning sure make it *seem* as though somebody up in the sky is angry at us.) Suppose a group of humans begins jointly creating a pantheon of invisible agents who cause the weather, and other assorted cases of good or bad fortune. Voilà—the birth of supernatural agents, not as an adaptation for anything but as a by-product of a cognitive module that is otherwise highly adaptive. (For a more mundane example of a by-product, think about the bridge of the nose as an anatomical feature useful for holding up eyeglasses. It evolved for other reasons, but we humans reuse it for an entirely new purpose.)

Now repeat this sort of analysis on five or ten more traits. Dawkins proposes a "gullible learning" module: "There will be a selective advantage to child brains that possess the rule of thumb: believe, without question, whatever your grown-ups tell you."[18] Dennett suggests that the circuitry for falling in love has gotten commandeered by some religions to make people fall in love with God.[19] The developmental psychologist Paul Bloom has shown that our minds were designed for dualism—we think that minds and bodies are different but equally real sorts of things—and so we readily believe that we have immortal souls housed in our temporary bodies.[20] In all cases the logic is the same: a bit of mental machinery evolved because it conferred a real benefit, but the machinery sometimes misfires, producing accidental cognitive effects that make people prone to believing in gods. *At no point* was religion itself beneficial to individuals or groups. *At no point* were genes selected because individuals or groups who were better at "godding" outcompeted those who failed to produce, fear, or love their gods. According to these theorists, the genes for constructing these various modules were all in place by the time modern humans left Africa, and *the genes did not change in response to selection pressures* either for or against religiosity during the 50,000 years since then.

The gods changed, however, and this brings us to the second step of the New Atheist story: cultural evolution. Once people began to believe in supernatural agents, and to talk about them and transmit them to their children, the race was on. But the race was not run by people or genes; it was a race among the various supernatural *concepts* that people generated. As Dennett put it:

> The memorable nymphs and fairies and goblins and demons that crowd the mythologies of every people are the imaginative offspring of a hyperactive habit of finding agency wherever anything puzzles or frightens us. This mindlessly generates a vast overpopulation of agent-ideas, most of which are too stupid to hold our attention for an instant; only a well-designed few make it through the rehearsal tournament, mutating and improving as they go. The ones that get shared and remembered are the souped-up winners of billions of competitions for rehearsal time in the brains of our ancestors.[21]

To Dennett and Dawkins, religions are sets of memes that have undergone Darwinian selection.[22] Like biological traits, religions are heritable, they mutate, and there is selection among these mutations. The selection occurs not on the basis of the benefits religions confer upon individuals or groups but on the basis of their ability to survive and reproduce themselves. Some religions are better than others at hijacking the human mind, burrowing in deeply, and then getting themselves transmitted to the next generation of host minds. Dennett opens *Breaking the Spell* with the story of a tiny parasite that commandeers the brains of ants, causing them to climb to the tops of blades of grass, where they can more easily be eaten by grazing animals. The behavior is suicide for the ant, but it's adaptive for the parasite, which requires the digestive system of a ruminant to reproduce itself. Dennett proposes that religions survive because, like those parasites, they make their hosts do things that are bad for themselves (e.g., suicide bombing) but good for the parasite (e.g., Islam). Dawkins similarly describes religions as viruses. Just as a cold virus makes its host sneeze to spread itself, successful religions make their hosts expend precious resources to spread the "infection."[23]

These analogies have clear implications for social change. If religion is a virus or a parasite that exploits a set of cognitive by-products for its benefit, not ours, then we ought to rid ourselves of it. Scientists, humanists, and the small number of others who have escaped infection and are still able to reason must work together to break the spell, lift the delusion, and bring about the end of faith.

A BETTER STORY: BY-PRODUCTS, THEN CULTURAL GROUP SELECTION

Scientists who are not on the New Atheist team have been far more willing to say that religion might be an adaptation (i.e., it might have evolved because it conferred benefits on individuals or groups). The anthropologists Scott Atran and Joe Henrich recently published a paper that tells a more nuanced story about the evolution of religiosity, one that is consistent with a broader set of empirical findings.[24]

Like the New Atheists, their story has two steps, and the first step is the same: a diverse set of cognitive modules and abilities (including the hypersensitive agency detector) evolved as adaptations to solve a variety of problems, but they often misfired, producing beliefs (such as in supernatural agents) that then contributed (as by-products) to the earliest quasi-religious behaviors. These modules were all in place by the time humans began leaving Africa more than 50,000 years ago. As with the New Atheists, this first step was followed by a second step involving cultural (not genetic) evolution. But instead of talking about religions as parasitic memes evolving for their own benefit, Atran and Henrich suggest that religions are sets of cultural innovations that spread to the extent that they make groups more cohesive and cooperative. Atran and Henrich argue that the cultural evolution of religion has been driven largely by competition among groups. Groups that were able to put their by-product gods to some good use had an advantage over groups that failed to do so, and so their ideas (not their genes) spread. Groups with less effective religions didn't necessarily get wiped out; often they just adopted the more effective variations. So it's really the *religions* that evolved, not the people or their genes.[25]

Among the best things to do with a by-product God, according to Atran and Henrich, is to create a moral community. The gods of hunter-gatherers are often capricious and malevolent. They some-times punish bad behavior, but they bring suffering to the virtuous as well. As groups take up agriculture and grow larger, however, their gods become far more moralistic.[26] The gods of larger societies are usually quite concerned about actions that foment conflict and divi-sion within the group, such as murder, adultery, false witness, and the breaking of oaths.

If the gods evolve (culturally) to condemn selfish and divisive behaviors, they can then be used to promote cooperation and trust within the group. You don't need a social scientist to tell you that people behave less ethically when they think nobody can see them. That was Glaucon's point about the ring of Gyges, and a great many social scientists have proven him right. For example, people cheat more on a test when the lights are dimmed.[27] They cheat less when there is a cartoonlike image of an eye nearby,[28] or when the concept of God is activated in memory merely by asking people to unscramble sentences that include words related to God.[29] Creating gods who can see everything, and who hate cheaters and oath breakers, turns out to be a good way to reduce cheating and oath breaking.

Another helpful cultural innovation, according to Atran and Henrich, are gods who administer collective punishment. When people believe that the gods might bring drought or pestilence on the whole village for the adultery of two people, you can bet that the vil-lagers will be much more vigilant for—and gossipy about—any hint of an extramarital liaison. Angry gods make shame more effective as a means of social control.

Atran and Henrich begin with the same claim about by-products as do the New Atheists. But because these anthropologists see groups as real entities that have long been in competition, they are able to see the role that religion plays in helping some groups to win that competition. There is now a great deal of evidence that religions do in fact help groups to cohere, solve free rider problems, and win the competition for group-level survival.

The clearest evidence comes from the anthropologist Richard Sosis, who examined the history of two hundred communes founded in the United States in the nineteenth century.[30] Communes are natural experiments in cooperation without kinship. Communes can survive only to the extent that they can bind a group together, suppress self-interest, and solve the free rider problem. Communes are usually founded by a group of committed believers who reject the moral matrix of the broader society and want to organize themselves along different principles. For many nineteenth-century communes, the principles were religious; for others they were secular, mostly socialist. Which kind of commune survived longer? Sosis found that the difference was stark: just 6 percent of the secular communes were still functioning twenty years after their founding, compared to 39 percent of the religious communes.

What was the secret ingredient that gave the religious communes a longer shelf life? Sosis quantified everything he could find about life in each commune. He then used those numbers to see if any of them could explain why some stood the test of time while others crumbled. He found one master variable: the number of costly sacrifices that each commune demanded from its members. It was things like giving up alcohol and tobacco, fasting for days at a time, conforming to a communal dress code or hairstyle, or cutting ties with outsiders. For religious communes, the effect was perfectly linear: the more sacrifice a commune demanded, the longer it lasted. But Sosis was surprised to discover that demands for sacrifice did not help secular communes. Most of them failed within eight years, and there was no correlation between sacrifice and longevity.[31]

Why doesn't sacrifice strengthen secular communes? Sosis argues that rituals, laws, and other constraints work best when they are sacralized. He quotes the anthropologist Roy Rappaport: "To invest social conventions with sanctity is to hide their arbitrariness in a cloak of seeming necessity."[32] But when secular organizations demand sacrifice, every member has a right to ask for a cost-benefit analysis, and many refuse to do things that don't make logical sense. In other words, *the very ritual practices that the New Atheists dismiss as costly, inefficient, and irrational turn out to be a solution to one of the hardest problems humans face: cooperation without kinship.* Irrational beliefs can sometimes help the group function more rationally, particularly when those beliefs rest upon the Sanctity foundation.[33] Sacredness binds people together, and then blinds them to the arbitrariness of the practice.

Sosis's findings support Atran and Henrich. Gods really do help groups cohere, succeed, and outcompete other groups. This is a form of group selection, but Atran and Henrich say it's purely *cultural* group selection. Religions that do a better job of binding people together and suppressing selfishness spread at the expense of other religions, but not necessarily by killing off the losers. Religions can spread far faster than genes, as in the case of Islam in the seventh and eighth centuries, or Mormonism in the nineteenth century. A successful religion can be adopted by neighboring people or by vanquished populations.

Atran and Henrich therefore doubt that there has been any *genetic* evolution for religiosity. Moralistic high gods are just too recent, they say, having emerged along with agriculture in the last 10,000 years.[34] Atran and Henrich believe that gene-culture coevolution happened slowly during the Pleistocene (when the modules were forged that later produced gods as by-products). By the time humans left Africa, the genes were set and the rest is all culture. Atran and Henrich join the New Atheists in claiming that our minds were not shaped, tuned, or adapted for religion.

But now that we know how quickly genetic evolution can occur, I find it hard to imagine that the genes stood still for more than 50,000 years.[35] How could the genetic partner in the "swirling waltz"[36] of gene-culture coevolution not take a single step as the cultural partner began dancing to religious music? Fifty thousand years may not be enough time to evolve a complex new module (such as the hypersensitive agency detector or the hive switch) from scratch. But how could there be no optimizing, no fine-tuning of modules to make people more prone to adaptive forms of hiving, sacralizing, or godding, and less prone to self-destructive or group-destructive forms?

THE DURKHEIMIAN STORY: BY-PRODUCTS, THEN MAYPOLES

David Sloan Wilson, a biologist at Binghamton University, was the most vigorous protester at the trial, conviction, and banishment of group selection in the 1970s. He then spent thirty years trying to prove that group selection was innocent. He produced mathematical demonstrations that genetic group selection could indeed occur, under special conditions that might well have been the conditions of earlier human societies.[37] And then he did the difficult cross-disciplinary work of exploring the history of many religions, to see if they truly provided those special conditions.[38]

Wilson's great achievement was to merge the ideas of the two most important thinkers in the history of the social sciences: Darwin and Durkheim. Wilson showed how they complete each other. He begins with Darwin's hypothesis about the evolution of morality by group selection, and he notes Darwin's concern about the free rider problem. He then gives Durkheim's definition of religion as a "unified system of beliefs and practices" that unites members into "one single moral community." If Durkheim is right that religions create cohesive groups that can function like organisms, then it supports Darwin's hypothesis: tribal morality can emerge by group selection. And if Darwin is right that we are products of multilevel selection, including group selection, then it supports Durkheim's hypothesis: we are *Homo duplex*, designed (by natural selection) to move back and forth between the lower (individual) and higher (collective) levels of existence.

In his book *Darwin's Cathedral*, Wilson catalogues the ways that religions have helped groups cohere, divide labor, work together, and prosper.[39] He shows how John Calvin developed a strict and demanding form of Christianity that suppressed free riding and facilitated trust and commerce in sixteenth-century Geneva. He shows how medieval Judaism created "cultural fortresses that kept outsiders out and insiders in."[40] But his most revealing example (based on research by the anthropologist Stephen Lansing)[41] is the case of water temples among Balinese rice farmers in the centuries before Dutch colonization.

Rice farming is unlike any other kind of agriculture. Rice farmers must create large irrigated paddies that they can drain and fill at precise times during the planting cycle. It takes a cast of hundreds. In one region of Bali, rainwater flows down the side of a high volcano through rivulets and rivers in the soft volcanic rock. Over several centuries the Balinese carved hundreds of terraced pools into the mountainside and irrigated them with an elaborate series of aqueducts and tunnels, some running underground for more than a kilometer. At the top of the whole system, near the crest of the volcano, they built an immense temple for the worship of the Goddess of the Waters. They staffed the temple with twenty-four full-time priests selected in childhood, and a high priest who was thought to be the earthly representative of the goddess herself.

The lowest level of social organization was the *subak,* a group of several extended families that made decisions democratically. Each *subak* had its own small temple, with its own deities, and each *subak* did the hard work of rice farming more or less collectively. But how did the *subak*s work together to build the system in the first place? And how did they maintain it and share its waters fairly and sustainably? These sorts of common dilemmas (where people must share a common resource without depleting it) are notoriously hard to solve.[42]

The ingenious religious solution to this problem of social engineering was to place a small temple at every fork in the irrigation system. The god in each such temple united all the *subak*s that were downstream from it into a community that worshipped that god, thereby helping the *subak*s to resolve their disputes more amicably. This arrangement minimized the cheating and deception that would otherwise flourish in a zero-sum division of water. The system made it possible for thousands of farmers, spread over hundreds of square kilometers, to cooperate without the need for central government, inspectors, and courts. The system worked so efficiently that the Dutch—who were expert hydrologists themselves—could find little to improve.

What are we to make of the hundreds of gods and temples woven into this system? Are they just by-products of mental systems that were designed for other purposes? Are they examples of what Dawkins called the "time-consuming, wealth-consuming ... counterproductive fantasies of religion?" No. I think the best way to understand these gods is as maypoles.

Suppose you observe a young woman with flowers in her hair,

dancing in a clockwise circle while holding one end of a ribbon. The other end is attached to the top of a tall pole. She circles the pole repeatedly, but not in a neat circle. Rather, she bobs and weaves a few steps closer to or further from the pole as she circles. Viewed in isolation, her behavior seems pointless, reminiscent of mad Ophelia on her way to suicide. But now add in five other young women doing exactly what she is doing, and add in six young men doing the same thing in

FIGURE 11.3. *The maypole dance.* From *The Illustrated London News,* August 14, 1858, p. 150.

a counterclockwise direction, and you've got a maypole dance. As the men and women pass each other and swerve in and out, their ribbons weave a kind of tubular cloth around the pole. The dance symbolically enacts the central miracle of social life: *e pluribus unum*.

Maypole dancing seems to have originated somewhere in the mists of pre-Christian northern Europe, and it is still done regularly in Germany, the United Kingdom, and Scandinavia, often as part of May Day festivities. Whatever its origins, it's a great metaphor for the role that gods play in Wilson's account of religion. Gods (like maypoles) are tools that let people bind themselves together as a community by circling around them. Once bound together by circling, these communities can function more effectively. As Wilson puts it: "Religions exist primarily for people to achieve together what they cannot achieve on their own."[43]

According to Wilson, this kind of circling and binding has been going on a lot longer than 10,000 years. You don't need moralistic high gods thundering against adultery to bring people together; even the morally capricious gods of hunter-gatherers can be used to create trust and cohesion. One group of !Kung, for example, believe in an omnipotent sky god named //Gauwa, and in spirits of the dead, called //gauwasi (! and // indicate click sounds). These supernatural beings offer no moral guidance, no rewards for good behavior, and no punishments for sin; they simply cause things to happen. One day your hunt goes well because the spirits helped you, and the next day a snake bites you because the spirits turned against you. These beings are perfect examples of the hypersensitive agency detector in action: people perceive agency where there is none.

Yet even these sometimes nasty spirits play a crucial role in the "healing dances" that are among the central religious rites of the !Kung. The anthropologist Lorna Marshall describes them like this:

> People bind together subjectively against external forces of evil.... The dance draws everyone together....
> Whatever their relationship, whatever the state of their feelings, whether they like or dislike each other, whether they are on good terms or bad terms with each other,

they become a unit, singing, clapping, moving together in an extraordinary unison of stamping feet and clapping hands, swept along by the music. No words divide them; they act in concert for their spiritual and physical good and do something together that enlivens them and gives them pleasure.[44]

I think the !Kung would have a great time at a UVA football game.

If human groups have been doing this sort of thing since before the exodus from Africa, and if doing it in some ways rather than others improved the survival of the group, then it's hard to believe that there was no gene-culture coevolution, no reciprocal fitting of mental modules to social practices, during the last 50,000 years. It's particularly hard to believe that the genes for all those by-product modules sat still even as the genes for everything else about us began changing more rapidly, reaching a crescendo of genetic change during the Holocene era,[45] which is precisely the time that gods were getting bigger and more moralistic. If religious behavior had consequences, for individuals and for groups, in a way that was stable over a few millennia, then there was almost certainly some degree of gene-culture coevolution for righteous minds that believed in gods and then used those gods to create moral communities.

In *The Faith Instinct* the science writer Nicholas Wade reviews what is known about prehistoric religious practices and strongly endorses Wilson's theory of religion. He notes that it's hard to tell an evolutionary story in which these ancient practices conferred an advantage on individuals as they competed with their less religious neighbors in the same group, but it's obvious that these practices helped groups to compete with other groups. He summarizes the logic of group selection lucidly:

> People belonging to such a [religiously cohesive] society are more likely to survive and reproduce than those in less cohesive groups, who may be vanquished by their enemies or dissolve in discord. In the population as a whole, *genes that promote religious behavior are likely to*

become more common in each generation as the less cohesive societies perish and the more united ones thrive.[46]

Gods and religions, in sum, are group-level adaptations for producing cohesiveness and trust. Like maypoles and beehives, they are
created by the members of the group, and they then organize the
activity of the group. Group-level adaptations, as Williams noted,
imply a selection process operating at the group level.[47] And group
selection can work very quickly (as in the case of those group-selected
hens that became more peaceful in just a few generations).[48] Ten
thousand years is plenty of time for gene-culture coevolution, including some genetic changes, to have occurred.[49] And 50,000 years is
more than plenty of time for genes, brains, groups, and religions to
have coevolved into a very tight embrace.

This account—Wilson's account—has implications profoundly
different from those of the pure by-product theories we considered
earlier. In Wilson's account, human minds and human religions have
been coevolving (just like bees and their physical hives) for tens or
hundreds of thousands of years. And if this is true, then we cannot
expect people to abandon religion so easily. Of course people can and
do forsake *organized* religions, which are extremely recent cultural
innovations. But even those who reject all religions cannot shake the
basic religious psychology of figure 11.2: doing linked to believing
linked to belonging. Asking people to give up all forms of sacralized
belonging and live in a world of purely "rational" beliefs might be
like asking people to give up the Earth and live in colonies orbiting
the moon. It can be done, but it would take a great deal of careful
engineering, and even after ten generations, the descendants of those
colonists might find themselves with inchoate longings for gravity
and greenery.

IS GOD A FORCE FOR GOOD OR EVIL?

Does religion make people good or bad? The New Atheists assert
that religion is the root of most evil. They say it is a primary cause

of war, genocide, terrorism, and the oppression of women.[50] Religious believers, for their part, often say that atheists are immoral, and that they can't be trusted. Even John Locke, one of the leading lights of the Enlightenment, wrote that "promises, covenants, and oaths, which are the bonds of human society, can have no hold upon an atheist. The taking away of God, though but even in thought, dissolves all." So who is right?

For several decades, the contest appeared to be a draw. On surveys, religious people routinely claimed to give more money to charity, and they expressed more altruistic values. But when social psychologists brought people into the lab and gave them the chance to actually help strangers, religious believers rarely acted any better than did nonbelievers.[51]

But should we really expect religion to turn people into *unconditional* altruists, ready to help strangers under any circumstances? Whatever Christ said about the good Samaritan who helped an injured Jew, if religion is a group-level adaptation, then it should produce *parochial* altruism. It should make people exceedingly generous and helpful toward members of their own moral communities, particularly when their reputations will be enhanced. And indeed, religion does exactly this. Studies of charitable giving in the United States show that people in the least religious fifth of the population give just 1.5 percent of their money to charity. People in the most religious fifth (based on church attendance, not belief) give a whopping 7 percent of their income to charity, and the majority of that giving is to religious organizations.[52] It's the same story for volunteer work: religious people do far more than secular folk, and the bulk of that work is done for, or at least through, their religious organizations.

There is also some evidence that religious people behave better in lab experiments—especially when they get to work with each other. A team of German economists asked subjects to play a game in which one person is the "truster," who is given some money on each round of the game.[53] The truster is then asked to decide how much money, if any, to pass on to an anonymous "trustee." Any money passed gets tripled by the experimenter, at which point the "trustee" can choose how much, if any, to return to the truster. Each person plays many rounds of the game, with different people each time, sometimes as the truster, sometimes as the trustee.

Behavioral economists use this game often, but the novel twist in this study was to reveal one piece of real, true personal information about the trustees to the trusters, before the trusters made their initial decision to trust. (The information was taken from questionnaires that all subjects had filled out weeks before.) In some cases, the truster learned the trustee's level of religiosity, on a scale of 1 to 5. When trusters learned that their trustee was religious, they transferred more money, which shows that these Germans held the same belief as did Locke (about religious believers being more trustworthy). More important, the religious trustees really did transfer back more money than did the nonreligious trustees, even though they never knew anything about their trusters. The highest levels of wealth, therefore, would be created when religious people get to play a trust game with other religious people. (Richard Sosis found this same outcome too, in a field experiment done at several Israeli kibbutzim.)[54]

Many scholars have talked about this interaction of God, trust, and trade. In the ancient world, temples often served an important commercial function: oaths were sworn and contracts signed before the deity, with explicit threats of supernatural punishment for abrogation.[55] In the medieval world, Jews and Muslims excelled in long-distance trade in part because their religions helped them create trustworthy relationships and enforceable contracts.[56] Even today, markets that require very high trust to function efficiently (such as a diamond market) are often dominated by religiously bound ethnic groups (such as ultra-Orthodox Jews), who have lower transaction and monitoring costs than their secular competitors.[57]

So religions do what they are supposed to do. As Wilson put it, they help people "to achieve together what they cannot achieve on their own." But that job description applies equally well to the Mafia. Do religions help their practitioners by binding them together into superorganisms that can prey on—or at least turn their backs on—everyone else? Is religious altruism a boon or a curse to outsiders?

In their book *American Grace: How Religion Divides and Unites Us*, political scientists Robert Putnam and David Campbell analyzed a variety of data sources to describe how religious and nonreligious

Americans differ. Common sense would tell you that the more time and money people give to their religious groups, the less they have left over for everything else. But common sense turns out to be wrong. Putnam and Campbell found that the more frequently people attend religious services, the more generous and charitable they become across the board.[58] Of course religious people give a lot to religious charities, but they also give as much as or more than secular folk to secular charities such as the American Cancer Society.[59] They spend a lot of time in service to their churches and synagogues, but they also spend more time than secular folk serving in neighborhood and civic associations of all sorts. Putnam and Campbell put their findings bluntly:

> By many different measures religiously observant Americans are better neighbors and better citizens than secular Americans—they are more generous with their time and money, especially in helping the needy, and they are more active in community life.[60]

Why are religious people better neighbors and citizens? To find out, Putnam and Campbell included on one of their surveys a long list of questions about religious beliefs (e.g., "Do you believe in hell? Do you agree that we will all be called before God to answer for our sins?") as well as questions about religious practices (e.g., "How often do you read holy scriptures? How often do you pray?"). These beliefs and practices turned out to matter very little. Whether you believe in hell, whether you pray daily, whether you are a Catholic, Protestant, Jew, or Mormon . . . none of these things correlated with generosity. The only thing that was reliably and powerfully associated with the moral benefits of religion was *how enmeshed people were in relationships with their co-religionists.* It's the friendships and group activities, carried out within a moral matrix that emphasizes selflessness. That's what brings out the best in people.

Putnam and Campbell reject the New Atheist emphasis on belief and reach a conclusion straight out of Durkheim: "It is religious belongingness that matters for neighborliness, not religious believing."[61]

CHIMPS AND BEES AND GODS

Putnam and Campbell's work shows that religion in the United States nowadays generates such vast surpluses of social capital that much of it spills over and benefits outsiders. But there is no reason to think that religion in most times and places has provided so much benefit beyond its borders. Religions, I'm claiming, are sets of cultural practices that coevolved with our religious minds by a process of multilevel selection. To the extent that some group-level selection occurred, we can expect religions and religious minds to be parochial—focused on helping the in-group—even when a religion preaches universal love and benevolence. Religiosity evolved because successful religions made groups more efficient at "turning resources into offspring," as Lesley Newson put it (in chapter 9).

Religion is therefore well suited to be the handmaiden of groupishness, tribalism, and nationalism. To take one example, religion does not seem to be the *cause* of suicide bombing. According to Robert Pape, who has created a database of every suicide terrorist attack in the last hundred years, suicide bombing is a nationalist response to military occupation by a culturally alien democratic power.[62] It's a response to boots and tanks on the ground—never to bombs dropped from the air. It's a response to contamination of the sacred homeland. (Imagine a fist punched into a beehive, and left in for a long time.)

Most military occupations don't lead to suicide bombings. There has to be an ideology in place that can rally young men to martyr themselves for a greater cause. The ideology can be secular (as was the case with the Marxist-Leninist Tamil Tigers of Sri Lanka) or it can be religious (as was the case with the Shiite Muslims who first demonstrated that suicide bombing works, driving the United States out of Lebanon in 1983). Anything that binds people together into a moral matrix that glorifies the in-group *while at the same time demonizing another group* can lead to moralistic killing, and many religions are well suited for that task. Religion is therefore often an *accessory* to atrocity, rather than the driving force of the atrocity.

But if you look at the long history of humanity and see our righteous minds as nearly miraculous freaks of evolution that cry out for explanation, then you might feel some appreciation for the role that religion played in getting us here. We are *Homo duplex;* we are 90 percent chimp and 10 percent bee. Successful religions work on both levels of our nature to suppress selfishness, or at least to channel it in ways that often pay dividends for the group. Gods were helpful in creating moral matrices within which Glauconian creatures have strong incentives to conform. And gods were an essential part of the evolution of our hivish overlay; sometimes we really do transcend self-interest and devote ourselves to helping others, or our groups.

Religions are moral exoskeletons. If you live in a religious community, you are enmeshed in a set of norms, relationships, and institutions that work primarily on the elephant to influence your behavior. But if you are an atheist living in a looser community with a less binding moral matrix, you might have to rely somewhat more on an internal moral compass, read by the rider. That might sound appealing to rationalists, but it is also a recipe for anomie—Durkheim's word for what happens to a society that no longer has a shared moral order.[63] (It means, literally, "normlessness.") We evolved to live, trade, and trust within shared moral matrices. When societies lose their grip on individuals, allowing all to do as they please, the result is often a decrease in happiness and an increase in suicide, as Durkheim showed more than a hundred years ago.[64]

Societies that forgo the exoskeleton of religion should reflect carefully on what will happen to them over several generations. We don't really know, because the first atheistic societies have only emerged in Europe in the last few decades. They are the least efficient societies ever known at turning resources (of which they have a lot) into offspring (of which they have few).

THE DEFINITION OF MORALITY (AT LAST)

You're nearly done reading a book on morality, and I have not yet given you a definition of morality. There's a reason for that. The definition I'm about to give you would have made little sense back in chapter 1. It would not have meshed with your intuitions about morality, so I thought it best to wait. Now, after eleven chapters in which I've challenged rationalism (in Part I), broadened the moral domain (in Part II), and said that groupishness was a key innovation that took us beyond selfishness and into civilization (Part III), I think we're ready.

Not surprisingly, my approach starts with Durkheim, who said: "What is moral is everything that is a source of solidarity, everything that forces man to . . . regulate his actions by something other than . . . his own egoism."[65] As a sociologist, Durkheim focused on social facts—things that exist outside of any individual mind—which constrain the egoism of individuals. Examples of such social facts include religions, families, laws, and the shared networks of meaning that I have called moral matrices. Because I'm a psychologist, I'm going to insist that we include inside-the-mind stuff too, such as the moral emotions, the inner lawyer (or press secretary), the six moral foundations, the hive switch, and all the other evolved psychological mechanisms I've described in this book.

My definition puts these two sets of puzzle pieces together to define moral *systems*:

> Moral systems are interlocking sets of values, virtues, norms, practices, identities, institutions, technologies, and evolved psychological mechanisms that work together to suppress or regulate self-interest and make co-operative societies possible.[66]

I'll just make two points about this definition now, and then we'll use it in the final chapter to examine some of the major political ideologies in Western society.

First, this is a functionalist definition. I define morality by what it *does*, rather than by specifying what content counts as moral. Turiel, in contrast, defined morality as being about "justice, rights, and welfare."[67] But any effort to define morality by designating a few issues as the truly moral ones and dismissing the rest as "social convention" is bound to be parochial. It's a moral community saying, "Here are our central values, and we define morality as being about our central values; to hell with the rest of you." As I showed in chapters 1 and 7, Turiel's definition doesn't even apply to all Americans; it's a definition by and for educated and politically liberal Westerners.

Of course, it is possible that one moral community actually *has* gotten it right in some sense, and the rest of the world is wrong, which brings us to the second point. Philosophers typically distinguish between *descriptive* definitions of morality (which simply describe what people happen to think is moral) and *normative* definitions (which specify what is really and truly right, regardless of what anyone thinks). So far in this book I have been entirely descriptive. I told you that some people (especially secular liberals such as Turiel, Kohlberg, and the New Atheists) think that morality refers to matters of harm and fairness. Other people (especially religious conservatives and people in non-WEIRD cultures) think that the moral domain is much broader, and they use most or all of the six moral foundations to construct their moral matrices. These are empirical, factual, verifiable propositions, and I offered evidence for them in chapters 1, 7, and 8.

But philosophers are rarely interested in what people happen to think. The field of normative ethics is concerned with figuring out which actions are *truly* right or wrong. The best-known systems of normative ethics are the one-receptor systems I described in chapter 6: utilitarianism (which tells us to maximize overall welfare) and deontology (which in its Kantian form tells us to make the rights and autonomy of others paramount). When you have a single clear principle, you can begin making judgments across cultures. Some cultures get a higher score than others, which means that they are morally superior.

My definition of morality was designed to be a descriptive definition; it cannot stand alone as a normative definition. (As a normative definition, it would give high marks to fascist and communist societies as well as to cults, so long as they achieved high levels of cooperation by creating a shared moral order.) But I think my definition works well as an adjunct to other normative theories, particularly those that have often had difficulty seeing groups and social facts. Utilitarians since Jeremy Bentham have focused intently on individuals. They try to improve the welfare of society by giving individuals what they want. But a Durkheimian version of utilitarianism would recognize that human flourishing requires social order and embeddedness. It would begin with the premise that social order is extraordinarily precious and difficult to achieve. A Durkheimian utilitarianism would be open to the possibility that the binding foundations—Loyalty, Authority, and Sanctity—have a crucial role to play in a good society.

I don't know what the best normative ethical theory is for individuals in their private lives.[68] But when we talk about making laws and implementing public policies in Western democracies that contain some degree of ethnic and moral diversity, then I think there is no compelling alternative to utilitarianism.[69] I think Jeremy Bentham was right that laws and public policies should aim, as a first approximation, to produce the greatest total good.[70] I just want Bentham to read Durkheim and recognize that we are *Homo duplex* before he tells any of us, or our legislators, how to go about maximizing that total good.[71]

IN SUM

If you think about religion as a set of beliefs about supernatural agents, you're bound to misunderstand it. You'll see those beliefs as foolish delusions, perhaps even as parasites that exploit our brains for their own benefit. But if you take a Durkheimian approach to religion (focusing on belonging) and a Darwinian approach to morality (involving multilevel selection), you get a very different picture. You see that religious practices have been binding our ancestors into groups for tens of thousands of years. That binding usually involves some blinding—once any person, book, or principle is declared sacred, then devotees can no longer question it or think clearly about it.

Our ability to believe in supernatural agents may well have begun as an accidental by-product of a hypersensitive agency detection device, but once early humans began believing in such agents, the groups that used them to construct moral communities were the ones that lasted and prospered. Like those nineteenth-century religious communes, they used their gods to elicit sacrifice and commitment from members. Like those subjects in the cheating studies and trust games, their gods helped them to suppress cheating and increase trustworthiness. Only groups that can elicit commitment and suppress free riding can grow.

This is why human civilization grew so rapidly after the first plants and animals were domesticated. Religions and righteous minds had been coevolving, culturally and genetically, for tens of thousands of years before the Holocene era, and both kinds of evolution sped up when agriculture presented new challenges and opportunities. Only groups whose gods promoted cooperation, and whose individual minds responded to those gods, were ready to rise to these challenges and reap the rewards.

We humans have an extraordinary ability to care about things beyond ourselves, to circle around those things with other people, and in the process to bind ourselves into teams that can pursue larger projects. That's what religion is all about. And with a few adjustments, it's what politics is about too. In the final chapter we'll take one last look at political psychology. We'll try to figure out why people choose to bind themselves into one political team or another. And we'll look especially at how team membership blinds people to the motives and morals of their opponents—and to the wisdom that is to be found scattered among diverse political ideologies.

TWELVE

Can't We All Disagree More Constructively?

"Politics ain't beanbag," said a Chicago humorist in 1895;[1] it's not a game for children. Ever since then the saying has been used to justify the rough-and-tumble nastiness of American politics. Rationalists might dream of a utopian state where policy is made by panels of unbiased experts, but in the real world there seems to be no alternative to a political process in which parties compete to win votes and money. That competition always involves trickery and demagoguery, as politicians play fast and loose with the truth, using their inner press secretaries to portray themselves in the best possible light and their opponents as fools who would lead the country to ruin.

And yet, does it have to be *this* nasty? A lot of Americans have noticed things getting worse. The country now seems polarized and embattled to the point of dysfunction. They are right. Up until a few years ago, there were some political scientists who claimed that the so-called culture war was limited to Washington, and that Americans had not in fact become more polarized in their attitudes toward most policy issues.[2] But in the last twelve years Americans have begun to move further apart. There's been a decline in the number of people calling themselves centrists or moderates (from 40 percent in 2000 down to 36 percent in 2011), a rise in the number of conservatives

FIGURE 12.1. *Civility now.* These posters were created by Jeff Gates, a graphic designer for the Chamomile Tea Party, drawing on American posters from the World War II era. (See www.chamomileteaparty.com. Used with permission.)

(from 38 percent to 41 percent), and a rise in the number of liberals (from 19 percent to 21 percent).[3]

But this slight spreading out of the electorate is nothing compared to what's happened in Washington, the media, and the political class more broadly. Things changed in the 1990s, beginning with new rules and new behaviors in Congress.[4] Friendships and social contacts across party lines were discouraged. Once the human connections were weakened, it became easier to treat members of the other party as the permanent enemy rather than as fellow members of an elite club. Candidates began to spend more time and money on "oppo" (opposition research), in which staff members or paid consultants dig up dirt on opponents (sometimes illegally) and then shovel it to the media. As one elder congressman recently put it, "This is not a collegial body any more. It is more like gang behavior. Members walk into the chamber full of hatred."[5]

This shift to a more righteous and tribal mentality was bad enough in the 1990s, a time of peace, prosperity, and balanced budgets. But nowadays, when the fiscal and political situations are so much worse, many Americans feel that they're on a ship that's sinking, and the crew is too busy fighting with each other to bother plugging the leaks.

In the summer of 2011, the stakes were raised. The failure of the two parties to agree on a routine bill to raise the debt ceiling, and their failure to agree on a "grand bargain" to reduce the long-term deficit, led a bond rating agency to downgrade America's credit rating. The downgrade sent stock markets plummeting around the globe and increased the prospects for a "double dip" recession at home—which would be a disaster for the many developing nations that export to America. America's hyperpartisanship is now a threat to the world.

What's going on here? In chapter 8, I portrayed the American culture war as a battle between a three-foundation morality and a six-foundation morality. But what leads people to adopt either of these moralities in the first place? Psychologists have discovered a lot about the psychological origins of partisanship. Morality binds and blinds, and to understand the mess we're in, we've got to understand why some people bind themselves to the liberal team, some to the conservative team, some to other teams or to no team at all.

A NOTE ABOUT POLITICAL DIVERSITY

I'm going to focus on what is known about the psychology of liberals and conservatives—the two end points of a one-dimensional scale. Many people resist and resent attempts to reduce ideology to a single dimension. Indeed, one of the great strengths of Moral Foundations Theory is that it gives you six dimensions, allowing for millions of possible combinations of settings. People don't come in just two types. Unfortunately, most research on political psychology has used the left-right dimension with American samples, so in many cases that's all we have to go on. But I should also note that this one dimension is still quite useful. Most people in the United States and in Europe can place themselves somewhere along it (even if most people are somewhat near the middle).[6] And it is the principal axis of the American culture war and of congressional voting,[7] so even if relatively few people fit perfectly into the extreme types I'm going to describe, understanding the psychology of liberalism and conservatism is vital for understanding a problem that threatens the entire world.

FROM GENES TO MORAL MATRICES

Here's a simple definition of ideology: "A set of beliefs about the proper order of society and how it can be achieved."[8] And here's the most basic of all ideological questions: Preserve the present order, or change it? At the French Assembly of 1789, the delegates who favored preservation sat on the right side of the chamber, while those who favored change sat on the left. The terms *right* and *left* have stood for conservatism and liberalism ever since.

Political theorists since Marx had long assumed that people chose ideologies to further their self-interest. The rich and powerful want to preserve and conserve; the peasants and workers want to change things (or at least they would if their consciousness could be raised and they could see their self-interest properly, said the Marxists). But even though social class may once have been a good predictor of ideology, that link has been largely broken in modern times, when the rich go both ways (industrialists mostly right, tech billionaires mostly left) and so do the poor (rural poor mostly right, urban poor mostly left). And when political scientists looked into it, they found that self-interest does a remarkably poor job of predicting political attitudes.[9]

So for most of the late twentieth century, political scientists embraced blank-slate theories in which people soaked up the ideology of their parents or the TV programs they watched.[10] Some political scientists even said that most people were so confused about political issues that they had no real ideology at all.[11]

But then came the studies of twins. In the 1980s, when scientists began analyzing large databases that allowed them to compare identical twins (who share *all* of their genes, plus, usually, their prenatal and childhood environments) to same-sex fraternal twins (who share *half* of their genes, plus their prenatal and childhood environments), they found that the identical twins were more similar on just about everything.[12] And what's more, identical twins reared in separate households (because of adoption) usually turn out to be very similar, whereas unrelated children reared together (because of adoption) rarely turn out similar to each other, or to their adoptive parents; they tend to be more similar to their genetic parents. Genes contribute, somehow, to just about every aspect of our personalities.[13]

We're not just talking about IQ, mental illness, and basic personality traits such as shyness. We're talking about the degree to which you like jazz, spicy foods, and abstract art; your likelihood of getting a divorce or dying in a car crash; your degree of religiosity, and your political orientation as an adult. Whether you end up on the right or the left of the political spectrum turns out to be just as heritable as most other traits: genetics explains between a third and a half of the variability among people on their political attitudes.[14] Being raised in a liberal or conservative household accounts for much less.

How can that be? How can there be a genetic basis for attitudes about nuclear power, progressive taxation, and foreign aid when these issues only emerged in the last century or two? And how can there be a genetic basis for ideology when people sometimes change their political parties as adults?

To answer these questions it helps to return to the definition of *innate* that I gave in chapter 7. Innate does not mean unmalleable; it means organized in advance of experience. The genes guide the construction of the brain in the uterus, but that's only the first draft, so to speak. The draft gets revised by childhood experiences. To understand the origins of ideology you have to take a developmental perspective, starting with the genes and ending with an adult voting for a particular candidate or joining a political protest. There are three major steps in the process.

Step 1: Genes Make Brains

After analyzing the DNA of 13,000 Australians, scientists recently found several genes that differed between liberals and conservatives.[15] Most of them related to neurotransmitter functioning, particularly glutamate and serotonin, both of which are involved in the brain's response to threat and fear. This finding fits well with many studies showing that conservatives react more strongly than liberals to signs of danger, including the threat of germs and contamination, and even low-level threats such as sudden blasts of white noise.[16] Other studies have implicated genes related to receptors for the neurotransmitter dopamine, which has long been tied to sensation-seeking and openness to experience, which are among the best-established correlates of liberalism.[17] As the Renaissance writer Michel de Montaigne said: "The only things I find rewarding . . . are variety and the enjoyment of diversity."[18]

Even though the effects of any single gene are tiny, these findings are important because they illustrate one *sort* of pathway from genes to politics: the genes (collectively) give some people brains that are more (or less) reactive to threats, and that produce less (or more) pleasure when exposed to novelty, change, and new experiences.[19] These are two of the main personality factors that have consistently been found to distinguish liberals and conservatives. A major review paper by political psychologist John Jost found a few other traits, but nearly all of them are conceptually related to threat sensitivity (e.g., conservatives react more strongly to reminders of death) or openness to experience (e.g., liberals have less need for order, structure, and closure).[20]

Step 2: Traits Guide Children Along Different Paths

Where do our personalities come from? To answer that question, we need to distinguish among three different levels of personality, according to a useful theory from psychologist Dan McAdams.[21] The lowest level of our personalities, which he calls "dispositional traits," are the sorts of broad dimensions of personality that show themselves in many different situations and are fairly consistent from childhood through old age. These are traits such as threat sensitivity, novelty seeking, extraversion, and conscientiousness. These traits are not mental modules that some people have and others lack; they're more like adjustments to dials on brain systems that everyone has.

Let's imagine a pair of fraternal twins, a brother and sister raised together in the same home. During their nine months together in their mother's womb, the brother's genes were busy constructing a brain that was a bit higher than average in its sensitivity to threats, a bit lower than average in its tendency to feel pleasure when exposed to radically new experiences. The sister's genes were busy making a brain with the opposite settings.

The two siblings grow up in the same house and attend the same schools, but they gradually create different worlds for themselves. Even in nursery school, their behavior causes adults to treat them differently. One study found that women who called themselves liberals as adults had been rated by their nursery school teachers as having traits consistent with threat insensitivity and novelty-seeking.[22] Future liberals were described as being more curious, verbal, and self-reliant, but also more assertive and aggressive, less obedient and neat. So if we could observe our fraternal twins in their first years of schooling, we'd find teachers responding differently to them. Some teachers might be drawn to the creative but rebellious little girl; others would crack down on her as an unruly brat, while praising her brother as a model student.

But dispositional traits are just the lowest of the three levels, according to McAdams. The second level is our "characteristic adaptations." These are traits that emerge as we grow. They are called adaptations because people develop them in response to the specific environments and challenges that they happen to face. For example, let's follow our twins into adolescence, and let's suppose they attend a fairly strict and well-ordered school. The brother fits in well, but the sister engages in constant battles with the teachers. She becomes angry and socially disengaged. These are now parts of her personality—her characteristic adaptations—but they would not have developed had she gone to a more progressive and less structured school.

By the time they reach high school and begin to take an interest in politics, the two siblings have chosen different activities (the sister joins the debate team in part for the opportunity to travel; the brother gets more involved with his family's church) and amassed different friends (the sister joins the goths; the brother joins the jocks). The sister chooses to go to college in New York City, where she majors in Latin American studies and finds her calling as an advocate for the children of illegal immigrants. Because her social circle is entirely composed of liberals, she is enmeshed in a moral matrix based primarily on the Care/harm foundation. In 2008, she is electrified by Barack Obama's concern for the poor and his promise of change.

The brother, in contrast, has no interest in moving far away to a big, dirty, and threatening city. He chooses to stay close to family and friends by attending the local branch of the state university. He earns a degree in business and then works for a local bank, gradually rising to a high position. He becomes a pillar of his church and his community, the sort of person that Putnam and Campbell praised for generating large amounts of social capital.[23] The moral matrices that surround him are based on all six foundations. There is occasional talk in church sermons of helping victims of oppression, but the most common moral themes in his life are personal responsibility (based on the Fairness foundation—not being a free rider or a burden on others) and loyalty to the many groups and teams to which he belongs. He resonates to John McCain's campaign slogan, "Country First."

Things didn't have to work out this way. On the day they were born, the sister was not predestined to vote for Obama; the brother was not guaranteed to become a Republican. But their different sets of genes gave them different first drafts of their minds, which led them down different paths, through different life experiences, and into different moral subcultures. By the time they reach adulthood they have become very different people whose one point of political agreement is that they must not talk about politics when the sister comes home for the holidays.

Step 3: People Construct Life Narratives

The human mind is a story processor, not a logic processor. Everyone loves a good story; every culture bathes its children in stories.

Among the most important stories we know are stories about ourselves, and these "life narratives" are McAdams's third level of personality. McAdams's greatest contribution to psychology has been his insistence that psychologists connect their quantitative data (about the two lower levels, which we assess with questionnaires and reaction-time measures) to a more qualitative understanding of the narratives people create to make sense of their lives. These narratives are not necessarily *true* stories—they are simplified and selective reconstructions of the past, often connected to an idealized vision of the future. But even though life narratives are to some degree post hoc fabrications, they still influence people's behavior, relationships, and mental health.[24]

Life narratives are saturated with morality. In one study, McAdams used Moral Foundations Theory to analyze narratives he collected from liberal and conservative Christians. He found the same patterns in these stories that my colleagues and I had found using questionnaires at YourMorals.org:

> When asked to account for the development of their own religious faith and moral beliefs, conservatives underscored deep feelings about respect for authority, allegiance to one's group, and purity of the self, whereas liberals emphasized their deep feelings regarding human suffering and social fairness.[25]

Life narratives provide a bridge between a developing adolescent self and an adult political identity. Here, for example, is how Keith Richards describes a turning point in his life in his recent autobiography. Richards, the famously sensation-seeking and nonconforming lead guitarist of the Rolling Stones, was once a marginally well-behaved member of his school choir. The choir won competitions with other schools, so the choir master got Richards and his friends excused from many classes so that they could travel to ever larger choral events. But when the boys reached puberty and their voices changed, the choir master dumped them. They were then informed that they would have to repeat a full year in school to make up for their missed classes, and the choir master didn't lift a finger to defend them.

It was a "kick in the guts," Richards says. It transformed him in ways with obvious political ramifications:

> The moment that happened, Spike, Terry and I, we became terrorists. I was so mad, I had a burning desire for revenge. I had reason then to bring down this country and everything it stood for. I spent the next three years trying to fuck them up. If you want to breed a rebel, that's the way to do it. . . . It still hasn't gone out, the fire. That's when I started to look at the world in a different way, not their way anymore. That's when I realized that there's bigger bullies than just bullies. There's them, the authorities. And a slow-burning fuse was lit.[26]

Richards may have been predisposed by his personality to become a liberal, but his politics were not predestined. Had his teachers treated him differently—or had he simply interpreted events differently when creating early drafts of his narrative—he could have ended up in a more conventional job surrounded by conservative colleagues and sharing their moral matrix. But once Richards came to understand himself as a crusader against abusive authority, there was no way he was ever going to vote for the British Conservative Party. His own life narrative just fit too well with the stories that all parties on the left tell in one form or another.

THE GRAND NARRATIVES OF LIBERALISM AND CONSERVATISM

In the book *Moral, Believing Animals,* the sociologist Christian Smith writes about the moral matrices within which human life takes place.[27] He agrees with Durkheim that every social order has at its core something sacred, and he shows how stories, particularly "grand narratives," identify and reinforce the sacred core of each matrix. Smith is a master at extracting these grand narratives and condensing them into single paragraphs. Each narrative, he says, identifies a beginning ("once upon a time"), a middle (in which a threat or challenge arises), and an end (in which a resolution is achieved). Each narrative is designed to orient listeners morally—to draw their attention to a set of virtues and vices, or good and evil forces—and to impart lessons about what must be done now to protect, recover, or attain the sacred core of the vision.

One such narrative, which Smith calls the "liberal progress narrative," organizes much of the moral matrix of the American academic left. It goes like this:

> Once upon a time, the vast majority of human persons suffered in societies and social institutions that were unjust, unhealthy, repressive, and oppressive. These traditional societies were reprehensible because of their deep-rooted inequality, exploitation, and irrational traditionalism. . . . But the noble human aspiration for autonomy, equality, and prosperity struggled mightily against the forces of misery and oppression, and eventually succeeded in establishing modern, liberal, democratic, capitalist, welfare societies. While modern social conditions hold the potential to maximize the individual freedom and pleasure of all, there is much work to be done to dismantle the powerful vestiges of inequality, exploitation, and repression. This struggle for the good society in which individuals are equal and free to pursue their self-defined happiness is the one mission truly worth dedicating one's life to achieving.[28]

This narrative may not mesh perfectly with the moral matrices of the left in European countries (where, for example, there is more distrust of capitalism). Nonetheless, its general plotline should be recognizable to leftists everywhere. It's a heroic liberation narrative. Authority, hierarchy, power, and tradition are the chains that must be broken to free the "noble aspirations" of the victims.

Smith wrote this narrative before Moral Foundations Theory existed, but you can see that the narrative derives its moral force primarily from the Care/harm foundation (concern for the suffering of victims) and the Liberty/oppression foundation (a celebration of liberty as freedom *from* oppression, as well as freedom *to* pursue self-defined happiness). In this narrative, Fairness is political equality (which is part of opposing oppression); there are only oblique hints of Fairness as proportionality.[29] Authority is mentioned only as an evil, and there is no mention of Loyalty or Sanctity.

Contrast that narrative to one for modern conservatism. The clinical psychologist Drew Westen is another master of narrative analysis, and in his book *The Political Brain* he extracts the master narrative that was implicit, and sometimes explicit, in the major speeches of Ronald Reagan.

Reagan defeated Democrat Jimmy Carter in 1980, a time when Americans were being held hostage in Iran, the inflation rate was over 10 percent, and America's cities, industries, and self-confidence were declining. The Reagan narrative goes like this:

> Once upon a time, America was a shining beacon. Then liberals came along and erected an enormous federal bureaucracy that handcuffed the invisible hand of the free market. They subverted our traditional American values and opposed God and faith at every step of the way. . . . Instead of requiring that people work for a living, they siphoned money from hardworking Americans and gave it to Cadillac-driving drug addicts and welfare queens. Instead of punishing criminals, they tried to "understand" them. Instead of worrying about the victims of crime, they worried about the rights of criminals. . . . Instead of adhering to traditional American values of family, fidelity, and personal responsibility, they preached promiscuity, premarital sex, and the gay lifestyle . . . and they encouraged a feminist agenda that undermined traditional family roles. . . . Instead of projecting strength to those who would do evil around the world, they cut military budgets, disrespected our soldiers in uniform, burned our flag, and chose negotiation and multilateralism. . . . Then Americans decided to take their country back from those who sought to undermine it.[30]

This narrative would have to be edited for use in other countries and eras, where what is being "conserved" differs from the American case. Nonetheless, its general plotline and moral breadth should be recognizable to conservatives everywhere. This too is a heroic narrative, but it's a heroism of *defense*. It's less suited to being turned into a major motion picture. Rather than the visually striking image of crowds storming the Bastille and freeing the prisoners, this narrative looks more like a family reclaiming its home from termites and then repairing the joists.

The Reagan narrative is also visibly conservative in that it relies for its moral force on at least five of the six moral foundations. There's only a hint of Care (for the victims of crime), but there are very clear references to Liberty (as freedom *from* government constraint), Fairness (as proportionality: taking money from those who work hard and giving it to welfare queens), Loyalty (soldiers and the flag), Authority (subversion of the family and of traditions), and Sanctity (replacing God with the celebration of promiscuity).

The two narratives are as opposed as could be. Can partisans even *understand* the story told by the other side? The obstacles to empathy are not symmetrical. If the left builds its moral matrices on a smaller number of moral foundations, then there is no foundation used by the left that is not also used by the right. Even though conservatives score slightly lower on measures of empathy[31] and may therefore be less moved by a story about suffering and oppression, they can still recognize that it is awful to be kept in chains. And even though many conservatives opposed some of the great liberations of the twentieth century—of women, sweatshop workers, African Americans, and gay people—they have applauded others, such as the liberation of Eastern Europe from communist oppression.

But when liberals try to understand the Reagan narrative, they have a harder time. When I speak to liberal audiences about the three "binding" foundations—Loyalty, Authority, and Sanctity—I find that many in the audience don't just fail to resonate; they actively reject these concerns as immoral. Loyalty to a group shrinks the moral circle; it is the basis of racism and exclusion, they say. Authority is oppression. Sanctity is religious mumbo-jumbo whose only function is to suppress female sexuality and justify homophobia.

In a study I did with Jesse Graham and Brian Nosek, we tested how well liberals and conservatives could understand each other. We asked more than two thousand American visitors to fill out the Moral Foundations Questionnaire. One-third of the time they were asked to fill it out normally, answering as themselves. One-third of the time they were asked to fill it out as they think a "typical liberal" would respond. One-third of the time they were asked to fill it out as a "typical conservative" would respond. This design allowed us to examine the stereotypes that each side held about the other. More important, it allowed us to assess how accurate they were by comparing people's expectations about "typical" partisans to the actual responses from partisans on the left and the right.[32] Who was best able to pretend to be the other?

The results were clear and consistent. Moderates and conservatives were most accurate in their predictions, whether they were pretending to be liberals or conservatives. Liberals were the least accurate, especially those who described themselves as "very liberal." The biggest errors in the whole study came when liberals answered the Care and Fairness questions while pretending to be conservatives. When faced with questions such as "One of the worst things a person could do is hurt a defenseless animal" or "Justice is the most important requirement for a society," liberals assumed that conservatives would disagree. If you have a moral matrix built primarily on intuitions about care and fairness (as equality), and you listen to the Reagan narrative, what else could you think? Reagan seems completely unconcerned about the welfare of drug addicts, poor people, and gay people. He's more interested in fighting wars and telling people how to run their sex lives.

If you don't see that Reagan is pursuing positive values of Loyalty, Authority, and Sanctity, you almost have to conclude that Republicans see no positive value in Care and Fairness. You might even go as far as Michael Feingold, a theater critic for the liberal newspaper the *Village Voice*, when he wrote:

> Republicans don't believe in the imagination, partly because so few of them have one, but mostly because it gets in the way of their chosen work, which is to destroy

the human race and the planet. Human beings, who have imaginations, can see a recipe for disaster in the making; Republicans, whose goal in life is to profit from disaster and who don't give a hoot about human beings, either can't or won't. Which is why I personally think they should be exterminated before they cause any more harm.[33]

One of the many ironies in this quotation is that it shows the inability of a theater critic—who skillfully enters fantastical imaginary worlds for a living—to imagine that Republicans act within a moral matrix that differs from his own. Morality binds and blinds.

THE LEFT'S BLIND SPOT: MORAL CAPITAL

My own intellectual life narrative has had two turning points. In chapter 5 I recounted the first one, in India, in which my mind opened to the existence of the broader moralities described by Richard Shweder (i.e., the ethics of community and divinity). But from that turning point in 1993 through the election of Barack Obama in 2008, I was still a partisan liberal. I wanted my team (the Democrats) to beat the other team (the Republicans). In fact, I first began to study politics precisely because I was so frustrated by John Kerry's ineffectual campaign for the presidency. I was convinced that American liberals simply did not "get" the morals and motives of their conservative countrymen, and I wanted to use my research on moral psychology to help liberals win.

To learn about political psychology, I decided to teach a graduate seminar on the topic in the spring of 2005. Knowing that I'd be teaching this new class, I was on the lookout for good readings. So when I was visiting friends in New York a month after the Kerry defeat, I went to a used-book store to browse its political science section. As I scanned the shelves, one book jumped out at me— a thick brown book with one word on its spine: *Conservatism*. It was a volume of readings edited by the historian Jerry Muller. I started reading Muller's introduction while standing in the aisle, but by the third page I had to sit down on the floor. I didn't realize it until years later, but Muller's essay was my second turning point.

Muller began by distinguishing conservatism from orthodoxy. Orthodoxy is the view that there exists a "transcendent moral order, to which we ought to try to conform the ways of society."[34] Christians who look to the Bible as a guide for legislation, like Muslims who want to live under sharia, are examples of orthodoxy. They want their society to match an externally ordained moral order, so they advocate change, sometimes radical change. This can put them at odds with true conservatives, who see radical change as dangerous.

Muller next distinguished conservatism from the counter-Enlightenment. It is true that most resistance to the Enlightenment can be said to have been conservative, by definition (i.e., clerics and aristocrats were trying to conserve the old order). But modern conservatism, Muller asserts, finds its origins *within* the main currents of Enlightenment thinking, when men such as David Hume and Edmund Burke tried to develop a reasoned, pragmatic, and essentially utilitarian critique of the Enlightenment project. Here's the line that quite literally floored me:

> What makes social and political arguments *conservative* as opposed to *orthodox* is that the critique of liberal or progressive arguments takes place on the enlightened grounds of the search for human happiness based on the use of reason.[35]

As a lifelong liberal, I had assumed that conservatism = orthodoxy = religion = faith = rejection of science. It followed, therefore, that as an atheist and a scientist, I was obligated to be a liberal. But Muller asserted that modern conservatism is really about creating the best possible society, the one that brings about the greatest happiness given local circumstances. Could it be? Was there a kind of conservatism that could compete against liberalism in the court of social science? Might conservatives have a better formula for how to create a healthy, happy society?

I kept reading. Muller went through a series of claims about human nature and institutions, which he said are the core beliefs of conservatism. Conservatives believe that people are inherently imperfect and are prone to act badly when all constraints and accountability are removed (yes, I thought; see Glaucon, Tetlock, and Ariely in chapter 4). Our reasoning is flawed and prone to overconfidence, so it's dangerous to construct theories based on pure reason, unconstrained by intuition and historical experience (yes; see Hume in chapter 2 and Baron-Cohen on systemizing in chapter 6). Institutions emerge gradually as social facts, which we then respect and even sacralize, but if we strip these institutions of authority and treat them as arbitrary contrivances that exist only for our benefit, we render them less effective. We then expose ourselves to increased anomie and social disorder (yes; see Durkheim in chapters 8 and 11).

Based on my own research, I had no choice but to agree with these conservative claims. As I continued to read the writings of conservative intellectuals, from Edmund Burke in the eighteenth century through Friedrich Hayek and Thomas Sowell in the twentieth, I began to see that they had attained a crucial insight into the sociology of morality that I had never encountered before. They understood the importance of what I'll call *moral capital*. (Please note that I am praising conservative intellectuals, not the Republican Party.)[36]

The term *social capital* swept through the social sciences in the 1990s, jumping into the broader public vocabulary after Robert Putnam's 2000 book *Bowling Alone*.[37] Capital, in economics, refers to the resources that allow a person or firm to produce goods or services. There's financial capital (money in the bank), physical capital (such as a wrench or a factory), and human capital (such as a well-trained sales force). When everything else is equal, a firm with more of any kind of capital will outcompete a firm with less.

Social capital refers to a kind of capital that economists had largely overlooked: the social ties among individuals and the norms of reciprocity and trustworthiness that arise from those ties.[38] When everything else is equal, a firm with more social capital will outcompete its less cohesive and less internally trusting competitors (which makes sense given that human beings were shaped by multilevel selection to be contingent cooperators). In fact, discussions of social capital sometimes use the example of ultra-Orthodox Jewish diamond merchants, which I mentioned in the previous chapter.[39] This tightly knit ethnic group has been able to create the most efficient market because their transaction and monitoring costs are so low—there's less overhead on every deal. And their costs are so low because they trust each other. If a rival market were to open up across town composed of ethnically and religiously diverse merchants, they'd have to spend a lot more money on lawyers and security guards, given how easy it is to commit fraud or theft when sending diamonds out for inspection by other merchants. Like the nonreligious communes studied by Richard Sosis, they'd have a much harder time getting individuals to follow the moral norms of the community.[40]

Everyone loves social capital. Whether you're left, right, or center, who could fail to see the value of being able to trust and rely upon others? But now let's broaden our focus beyond firms trying to produce goods and let's think about a school, a commune, a corporation, or even a whole nation that wants to improve moral behavior. Let's set aside problems of moral diversity and just specify the goal as increasing the "output" of prosocial behaviors and decreasing the "output" of antisocial behaviors, however the group defines those terms. To achieve almost any moral vision, you'd probably want high levels of social capital. (It's hard to imagine how anomie and distrust could be beneficial.) But will linking people together into healthy, trusting relationships be enough to improve the ethical profile of the group?

If you believe that people are inherently good, and that they flourish when constraints and divisions are removed, then yes, that may be sufficient. But conservatives generally take a very different view of human nature. They believe that people need external structures or constraints in order to behave well, cooperate, and thrive. These external constraints include laws, institutions, customs, traditions, nations, and religions. People who hold this "constrained"[41] view are therefore very concerned about the health and integrity of these "outside-the-mind" coordination devices. Without them, they believe, people will begin to cheat and behave selfishly. Without them, social capital will rapidly decay.

If you are a member of a WEIRD society, your eyes tend to fall on individual objects such as people, and you don't automatically see the relationships among them. Having a concept such as social capital is helpful because it forces you to see the relationships within which those people are embedded, and which make those people more productive. I propose that we take this approach one step further. To understand the miracle of moral communities that grow beyond the bounds of kinship we must look not just at people, and not just at the relationships among people, but at the *complete environment* within which those relationships are embedded, and which makes those people more virtuous (however they themselves define that term). It takes a great deal of outside-the-mind stuff to support a moral community.

For example, on a small island or in a small town, you typically don't need to lock your bicycle, but in a big city in the same country, if you only lock the bike frame, your wheels may get stolen. Being small, isolated, or morally homogeneous are examples of environmental conditions that increase the moral capital of a community. That doesn't mean that small islands and small towns are better places to live overall—the diversity and crowding of big cities makes them more creative and interesting places for many people—but that's the trade-off. (Whether you'd trade away some moral capital to gain some diversity and creativity will depend in part on your brain's settings on traits such as openness to experience and threat sensitivity, and this is part of the reason why cities are usually so much more liberal than the countryside.)

Looking at a bunch of outside-the-mind factors and at how well they mesh with inside-the-mind moral psychology brings us right back to the definition of moral systems that I gave in the last chapter. In fact, we can define moral capital as *the resources that sustain a moral community*.[42] More specifically, moral capital refers to

> the degree to which a community possesses interlocking sets of values, virtues, norms, practices, identities, institutions, and technologies that mesh well with evolved psychological mechanisms and thereby enable the community to suppress or regulate selfishness and make cooperation possible.

To see moral capital in action, let's do a thought experiment using the nineteenth-century communes studied by Richard Sosis. Let's assume that every commune was started by a group of twenty-five adults who knew, liked, and trusted one another. In other words, let's assume that every commune started with a high and equal quantity of social capital on day one. What factors enabled some communes to maintain their social capital and generate high levels of prosocial behavior for decades while others degenerated into discord and distrust within the first year?

In the last chapter, I said that belief in gods and costly religious rituals turned out to be crucial ingredients of success. But let's put religion aside and look at other kinds of outside-the-mind stuff. Let's assume that each commune started off with a clear list of values and virtues that it printed on posters and displayed throughout the commune. A commune that valued self-expression over conformity and that prized the virtue of tolerance over the virtue of loyalty might be more attractive to outsiders, and this could indeed be an advantage in recruiting new members, but it would have lower moral capital than a commune that valued conformity and loyalty. The stricter commune would be better able to suppress or regulate selfishness, and would therefore be more likely to endure.

Moral communities are fragile things, hard to build and easy to destroy. When we think about very large communities such as nations, the challenge is extraordinary and the threat of moral entropy is intense. There is not a big margin for error; many nations are failures as moral communities, particularly corrupt nations where dictators and elites run the country for their own benefit. If you don't value moral capital, then you won't foster values, virtues, norms, practices, identities, institutions, and technologies that increase it.

Let me state clearly that moral capital is not always an unalloyed good. Moral capital leads automatically to the suppression of free riders, but it does not lead automatically to other forms of fairness such as equality of opportunity. And while high moral capital helps a community to function efficiently, the community can use that efficiency to inflict harm on other communities. High moral capital can be obtained within a cult or a fascist nation, as long as most people truly accept the prevailing moral matrix.

Nonetheless, if you are trying to change an organization or a society and you do not consider the effects of your changes on moral capital, you're asking for trouble. This, I believe, is *the fundamental blind spot of the left*. It explains why liberal reforms so often backfire,[43] and why communist revolutions usually end up in despotism. It is the reason I believe that liberalism—which has done so much to bring about freedom and equal opportunity—is not sufficient as a governing philosophy. It tends to overreach, change too many things too quickly, and reduce the stock of moral capital inadvertently. Conversely, while conservatives do a better job of preserving moral capital, they often fail to notice certain classes of victims, fail to limit the predations of certain powerful interests, and fail to see the need to change or update institutions as times change.

A YIN AND TWO YANGS

In Chinese philosophy, yin and yang refer to any pair of contrasting or seemingly opposed forces that are in fact complementary and interdependent. Night and day are not enemies, nor are hot and cold, summer and winter, male and female. We need both, often in a shifting or alternating balance. John Stuart Mill said that liberals and conservatives are like this: "A party of order or stability, and a party of progress or reform, are both necessary elements of a healthy state of political life."[44]

The philosopher Bertrand Russell saw this same dynamic at work throughout Western intellectual history: "From 600 BC to the present day, philosophers have been divided into those who wished to tighten social bonds and those who wished to relax them."[45] Russell then explained why both sides are partially right, using terms that are about as close a match to *moral capital* as I could ever hope to find:

> It is clear that each party to this dispute—as to all that persist through long periods of time—is partly right and partly wrong. Social cohesion is a necessity, and mankind has never yet succeeded in enforcing cohe-

sion by merely rational arguments. Every community is exposed to two opposite dangers: ossification through too much discipline and reverence for tradition, on the one hand; on the other hand, dissolution, or subjection to foreign conquest, through the growth of an individualism and personal independence that makes cooperation impossible.[46]

I'm going to take a risk and apply Mill's and Russell's insights to some current debates in American society. It's a risk because partisan readers may be able to accept my claims about yin and yang in the abstract, but not when I start saying that the "other side" has something useful to say about specific controversial issues. I'm willing to run this risk, however, because I want to show that public policy might really be improved by drawing on insights from all sides. I'll use the framework of Durkheimian utilitarianism that I developed at the end of chapter 11. That is, I'm going to evaluate each issue based on how well the ideology in question can advance the overall good of a society (that's the utilitarian part), but I'm going to adopt a view of humankind as being *Homo duplex* (or 90 percent chimp, 10 percent bee), which means that we humans need access to healthy hives in order to flourish (that's the Durkheimian part).

Rather than just contrasting the left and the right, I'm going to divide the opponents of the left into two groups—the social conservatives (such as the religious right) and the libertarians (sometimes called "classical liberals" because of their love of free markets). These are two groups we've studied a lot at YourMorals.org, and we find that they have very different personalities and moralities. In what follows I'll say briefly why I think that liberals are justified on two major points. I'll then say where I think libertarians and social conservatives are justified, on two counterpoints.

YIN: LIBERAL WISDOM

The left builds its moral matrix on three of the six foundations, but it rests most firmly and consistently on the Care foundation.[47] We might illustrate it as in figure 12.2, where the thickness of each line corresponds to the importance of each foundation.

Liberals are often suspicious of appeals to loyalty, authority, and sanctity, although they don't reject these intuitions in all cases (think of the sanctification of nature), so I drew those lines as thin, but still existing. Liberals have many specific values, but I think it's helpful, for each group, to identify its most sacred value—the "third rail" that will get you electrocuted if you touch it. For American liberals since the 1960s, I believe that the most sacred value is caring for victims of oppression. Anyone who blames such victims for their own problems or who displays or merely excuses prejudice against sacralized victim groups can expect a vehement tribal response.[48]

Our findings at YourMorals.org match up with philosophical and popular definitions of liberalism that emphasize care for the vulnerable, opposition to hierarchy and oppression, and an interest in changing laws, traditions, and institutions to solve social problems.[49] The liberal radio host Garrison Keillor captured the spirit and self-image of the modern American left when he wrote:

> I am a liberal, and liberalism is the politics of kindness.
> Liberals stand for tolerance, magnanimity, community
> spirit, the defense of the weak against the powerful, love
> of learning, freedom of belief, art and poetry, city life,
> the very things that make America worth dying for.[50]

I'm not sure how many Americans have sacrificed their lives for kindness and poetry, but I believe this moral matrix leads liberals to make two points consistently, points that I believe are essential for the health of a society.

Point #1: Governments Can and Should Restrain Corporate Superorganisms

I loved the movie *Avatar*, but it contained the most foolish evolutionary thinking I've ever seen. I found it easier to believe that islands could float in the sky than to believe that all creatures could live in

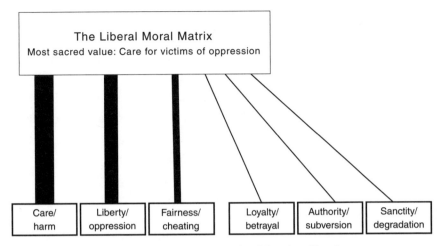

FIGURE 12.2. *The moral matrix of American liberals.*

harmony, willingly lying down to let others eat them. There was one futuristic element that I found quite believable, however. The movie depicts Earth a few centuries from now as a planet run by corporations that have turned national governments into their lackeys.

In chapter 9 I talked about major transitions in the evolution of life. I described the process by which superorganisms emerge, dominate their preferred niches, change their ecosystems, and push their competitors to the margins or to extinction. In chapter 10 I showed that corporations are superorganisms. They're not *like* superorganisms; they are actual superorganisms. So, if the past is any guide, corporations will grow ever more powerful as they evolve, and as they change the legal and political systems of their host countries to become ever more hospitable. The only force left on Earth that can stand up to the largest corporations are national governments, some of which still maintain the power to tax, regulate, and divide corporations into smaller pieces when they get too powerful.

Economists speak of "externalities"—the costs (or benefits) incurred by third parties who did not agree to the transaction causing the cost (or benefit). For example, if a farmer begins using a new kind of fertilizer that increases his yield but causes more damaging runoff into nearby rivers, he keeps the profit but the costs of his decision are borne by others. If a factory farm finds a faster way to fatten up cattle but thereby causes the animals to suffer more digestive problems and broken bones, it keeps the profit and the animals pay the cost. Corporations are obligated to maximize profit for shareholders, and that means looking for any and all opportunities to lower costs, including passing costs on to others (when legal) in the form of externalities.

I am not anticorporate, I am simply a Glauconian. When corporations operate in full view of the public, with a free press that is willing and able to report on the externalities being foisted on the public, they are likely to behave well, as most corporations do. But many corporations operate with a high degree of secrecy and public invisibility (for example, America's giant food processors and factory farms).[51] And many corporations have the ability to "capture" or otherwise influence the politicians and federal agencies whose job it is to regulate them (especially now that the U.S. Supreme Court has given corporations and unions the "right" to make unlimited donations to political causes).[52] When corporations are given the ring of Gyges, we can expect catastrophic results (for the ecosystem, the banking system, public health, etc.).

I think liberals are right that a major function of government is to stand up for the public interest against corporations and their tendency to distort markets and impose externalities on others, particularly on those least able to stand up for themselves in court (such as the poor, or immigrants, or farm animals). Efficient markets require government regulation. Liberals go too far sometimes—indeed, they are often reflexively antibusiness,[53] which is a huge mistake from a utilitarian point of view. But it is healthy for a nation to have a constant tug-of-war, a constant debate between yin and yang over how and when to limit and regulate corporate behavior.

Point #2: Some Problems Really Can Be Solved by Regulation

As automobile ownership skyrocketed in the 1950s and 1960s, so did the tonnage of lead being blown out of American tailpipes and into the atmosphere—200,000 *tons* of lead a year by 1973.[54] (Gasoline refiners had been adding lead since the 1930s to increase the efficiency of the refining process.) Despite evidence that the rising tonnage of lead was making its way into the lungs, bloodstreams, and brains of Americans and was retarding the neural development of millions of children, the chemical industry had been able to block all efforts to ban lead additives from gasoline for decades. It was a classic case of corporate superorganisms using all methods of leverage to preserve their ability to pass a deadly externality on to the public.

The Carter administration began a partial phaseout of leaded gasoline, but it was nearly reversed when Ronald Reagan crippled the Environmental Protection Agency's ability to draft new regulations or enforce old ones. A bipartisan group of congressmen stood up for children and against the chemical industry, and by the 1990s lead had been completely removed from gasoline.[55] This simple public health intervention worked miracles: lead levels in children's blood dropped in lockstep with declining levels of lead in gasoline, and the decline has been credited with some of the rise in IQ that has been measured in recent decades.[56]

Even more amazingly, several studies have demonstrated that the phaseout, which began in the late 1970s, may have been responsible for up to *half* of the extraordinary and otherwise unexplained drop in crime that occurred in the 1990s.[57] Tens of millions of children, particularly poor children in big cities, had grown up with high levels of lead, which interfered with their neural development from the 1950s until the late 1970s. The boys in this group went on to cause the giant surge of criminality that terrified America—and drove it to the right—from the 1960s until the early 1990s. These young men were eventually replaced by a new generation of young men with unleaded brains (and therefore better impulse control), which seems to be part of the reason the crime rate plummeted.

From a Durkheimian utilitarian perspective, it is hard to imagine a better case for government intervention to solve a national health problem. This one regulation saved vast quantities of lives, IQ points, money, and moral capital all at the same time.[58] And lead is far from the only environmental hazard that disrupts neural development. When young children are exposed to PCBs (polychlorinated biphenyls), organophosphates (used in some pesticides), and methyl mercury (a by-product of burning coal), it lowers their IQ and raises their risk of ADHD (attention deficit hyperactivity disorder).[59] Given these brain disruptions, future studies are likely to find a link to violence and crime as well. Rather than building more prisons, the cheapest (and most humane) way to fight crime may be to give more money and authority to the Environmental Protection Agency.

When conservatives object that liberal efforts to intervene in markets or engage in "social engineering" always have unintended consequences, they should note that sometimes those consequences are positive. When conservatives say that markets offer better solutions than do regulations, let them step forward and explain their plan to eliminate the dangerous and unfair externalities generated by many markets.[60]

YANG #1: LIBERTARIAN WISDOM

Libertarians are sometimes said to be socially liberal (favoring individual freedom in private matters such as sex and drug use) and economically conservative (favoring free markets), but those labels reveal how confused these terms have become in the United States.

Libertarians are the direct descendants of the eighteenth- and nineteenth-century Enlightenment reformers who fought to free people and markets from the control of kings and clergy. Libertarians love liberty; that is their sacred value. Many libertarians wish they could simply be known as liberals,[61] but they lost that term in the United States (though not in Europe) when liberalism split into two camps in the late nineteenth century. Some liberals began to see powerful corporations and wealthy industrialists as the chief threats to liberty. These "new liberals" (also known as "left liberals" or "progressives") looked to government as the only force capable of protecting the public and rescuing the many victims of the brutal practices of early industrial capitalism. Liberals who continued to fear government as the chief threat to liberty became known as "classical liberals," "right liberals" (in some countries), or libertarians (in the United States).

Those who took the progressive path began to use government

not just to safeguard liberty but to advance the general welfare of the people, particularly those who could not fend for themselves. Progressive Republicans (such as Theodore Roosevelt) and Democrats (such as Woodrow Wilson) took steps to limit the growing power of corporations, such as breaking up monopolies and creating new government agencies to regulate labor practices and to ensure the quality of foods and medicines. Some progressive reforms intruded far more deeply into private life and personal liberty, such as forcing parents to send their children to school and banning the sale of alcohol.

You can see this fork in the road by looking at the liberal moral matrix (figure 12.2). It rests on two foundations primarily: Care and Liberty (plus some Fairness, because everybody values proportionality to some extent). Liberals in 1900 who relied most heavily on the Care foundation—those who felt the pain of others most keenly—were predisposed to take the left-hand (progressive) fork. But liberals in 1900 who relied more heavily on the Liberty foundation—those who felt the bite of restrictions on their liberty most keenly—refused to follow (see Figure 12.3). In fact, the libertarian writer Will Wilkinson has recently suggested that libertarians are basically liberals who love markets and lack bleeding hearts.[62]

At YourMorals.org, we've found that Wilkinson is correct. In a project led by Ravi Iyer and Sena Koleva, we analyzed dozens of surveys completed by 12,000 libertarians and we compared their responses to those of tens of thousands of liberals and conservatives. We found that libertarians look more like liberals than like conservatives on most measures of personality (for example, both groups score higher than conservatives on openness to experience, and lower than conservatives on disgust sensitivity and conscientiousness). On the Moral Foundations Questionnaire, libertarians join liberals in scoring very low on the Loyalty, Authority, and Sanctity foundations. Where they diverge from liberals most sharply is on two measures: the Care foundation, where they score very low (even lower than conservatives), and on some new questions we added about *economic* liberty, where they score extremely high (a little higher than conservatives, a lot higher than liberals).

For example, do you agree that "the government should do more

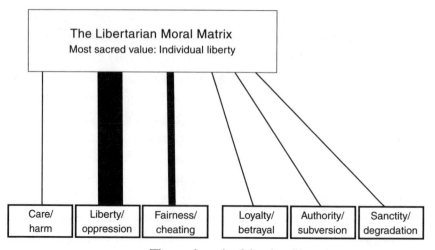

FIGURE 12.3. *The moral matrix of American libertarians.*

to advance the common good, even if that means limiting the freedom and choices of individuals"? If so, then you are probably a liberal.
If not, then you could be either a libertarian or a conservative. The
split between liberals (progressives) and libertarians (classical liberals) occurred over exactly this question more than a hundred years
ago, and it shows up clearly in our data today. People with libertarian
ideals have generally supported the Republican Party since the 1930s
because libertarians and Republicans have a common enemy: the liberal welfare society that they believe is destroying America's liberty
(for libertarians) and moral fiber (for social conservatives).

I believe that libertarians are right on many points,[63] but I'll focus
on just one counterpoint to liberalism here.

Counterpoint #1: Markets Are Miraculous

In 2007, David Goldhill's father was killed by an infection he caught
while in the hospital. In trying to make sense of this unnecessary
death, Goldhill began to read about the American health care system,
which kills about 100,000 people annually by such accidental infec-
tions. He learned that the death rate can be cut by two-thirds when
hospitals follow a simple checklist of sanitary procedures, but most
hospitals don't adopt the checklist.

Goldhill, a businessman (and Democrat), wondered how it was possible for any organization to pass up a simple measure that yielded such massive payoffs. In the business world, such inefficiency would soon lead to bankruptcy. As he learned more and more about the health care system, he discovered just how bad things get when goods and services are provided without a properly functioning market.

In 2009, Goldhill published a provocative essay in *The Atlantic* titled "How American Health Care Killed My Father":[64] One of his main points was the absurdity of using insurance to pay for routine purchases. Normally we buy insurance to cover the risk of a catastrophic loss. We enter an insurance pool with other people to spread the risk around, and we hope never to collect a penny. We handle routine expenses ourselves, seeking out the highest quality for the lowest price. We would never file a claim on our car insurance to pay for an oil change.

The next time you go to the supermarket, look closely at a can of peas. Think about all the work that went into it—the farmers, truckers, and supermarket employees, the miners and metalworkers who made the can—and think how miraculous it is that you can buy this can for under a dollar. At every step of the way, competition among suppliers rewarded those whose innovations shaved a penny off the cost of getting that can to you. If God is commonly thought to have created the world and then arranged it for our benefit, then the free market (and its invisible hand) is a pretty good candidate for being a god. You can begin to understand why libertarians sometimes have a quasi-religious faith in free markets.

Now let's do the devil's work and spread chaos throughout the marketplace. Suppose that one day all prices are removed from all products in the supermarket. All labels too, beyond a simple description of the contents, so you can't compare products from different companies. You just take whatever you want, as much as you want, and you bring it up to the register. The checkout clerk scans in your food insurance card and helps you fill out your itemized claim. You pay a flat fee of $10 and go home with your groceries. A month later you get a bill informing you that your food insurance company will pay the supermarket for most of the remaining cost, but you'll have to send in a check for an additional $15. It might sound like a bargain to get a cartload of food for $25, but you're really paying your grocery bill every month when you fork over $2,000 for your food insurance premium.

Under such a system, there is little incentive for anyone to find innovative ways to reduce the cost of food or increase its quality. The supermarkets get paid by the insurers, and the insurers get their premiums from you. The cost of food insurance begins to rise as supermarkets stock only the foods that net them the highest insurance payments, not the foods that deliver value to you.

As the cost of food insurance rises, many people can no longer afford it. Liberals (motivated by Care) push for a new government program to buy food insurance for the poor and the elderly. But once the government becomes the major purchaser of food, then success in the supermarket and food insurance industries depends primarily on maximizing yield from government payouts. Before you know it, that can of peas costs the government $30, and all of us are paying 25 percent of our paychecks in taxes just to cover the cost of buying groceries for each other at hugely inflated costs.

That, says Goldhill, is what we've done to ourselves. As long as consumers are spared from taking price into account—that is, as long as someone else is always paying for your choices—things will get worse. We can't fix the problem by convening panels of experts to set the maximum allowable price for a can of peas. Only a working market[65] can bring supply, demand, and ingenuity together to provide health care at the lowest possible price. For example, there is an open market for LASIK surgery (a kind of laser eye surgery that removes the need to wear contact lenses). Doctors compete with one another to attract customers, and because the procedure is rarely covered by insurance, patients take price into account. Competition and innovation have driven down the price of the surgery by nearly 80 percent since it was first introduced. (Other developed nations have had more success controlling costs, but they too face rapidly rising costs that may become fiscally ruinous.[66] Like America, they often lack the political will to raise taxes or cut services.)

When libertarians talk about the miracle of "spontaneous order" that emerges when people are allowed to make their own choices (and take on the costs and benefits of those choices), the rest of us should listen.[67] Care and compassion sometimes motivate liberals to interfere in the workings of markets, but the result can be extraordinary harm on a vast scale. (Of course, as I said above, governments often need to intervene to correct market *distortions*, thereby making markets work properly.) Liberals want to use government for so many purposes, but health care expenses are crowding out all other possibilities. If you think your local, state, and federal governments are broke now, just wait until the baby boom generation is fully retired.

I find it ironic that liberals generally embrace Darwin and reject "intelligent design" as the explanation for design and adaptation in the natural world, but they don't embrace Adam Smith as the explanation for design and adaptation in the economic world. They sometimes prefer the "intelligent design" of socialist economies, which often ends in disaster from a utilitarian point of view.[68]

YANG #2: SOCIAL CONSERVATIVE WISDOM

Conservatives are the "party of order and stability," in Mill's formulation. They generally resist the changes implemented by the "party of progress or reform." But to put things in those terms makes conservatives sound like fearful obstructionists, trying to hold back the hands of time and the "noble human aspirations" of the liberal progress narrative.

A more positive way to describe conservatives is to say that their broader moral matrix allows them to detect threats to moral capital that liberals cannot perceive. They do not oppose change of all kinds (such as the Internet), but they fight back ferociously when they believe that change will damage the institutions and traditions that provide our moral exoskeletons (such as the family). Preserving those institutions and traditions is their most sacred value.

For example, the historian Samuel Huntington noted that conservatism can't be defined by the particular institutions it sacralizes (which could be monarchy in eighteenth-century France, or the Con-

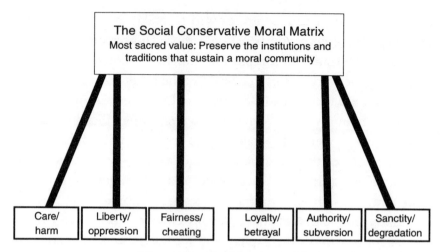

FIGURE 12.4. *The moral matrix of American social conservatives.*

stitution in twenty-first-century America). Rather, he said, "when the foundations of society are threatened, the conservative ideology reminds men of the necessity of some institutions and the desirability of the existing ones."[69]

At YourMorals.org, we have found that social conservatives have the broadest set of moral concerns, valuing all six foundations relatively equally (figure 12.4). This breadth—and particularly their relatively high settings on the Loyalty, Authority, and Sanctity foundations—give them insights that I think are valuable, from a Durkheimian utilitarian perspective.

Counterpoint #2: You Can't Help the Bees by Destroying the Hive

Liberals hate the idea of exclusion. At a talk I attended a few years ago, a philosophy professor bashed the legitimacy of nation-states. "They're just arbitrary lines on the map," he said. "Some people draw a line and say, 'Everything on this side is ours. The rest of you keep out.'" Others in the room laughed along with him. At a talk that I gave recently, I found the same dislike of exclusion applied to religions. A graduate student was surprised by my claim that religions are often good for the rest of society, and she said, "But religions are all exclusive!" I asked her what she meant, and she replied: "Well, the Catholic Church won't accept anyone who doesn't believe its teachings." I couldn't believe she was serious. I pointed out that our graduate program at UVA was more exclusive than the church—we rejected almost all applicants. In the course of our discussion it became clear that her overriding concern was for victims of discrimination, particularly gay people who are told that they don't belong in many religious communities.

Comments such as these convince me that John Lennon captured a common liberal dream in his haunting song "Imagine." Imagine if there were no countries, and no religion too. If we could just erase the borders and boundaries that divide us, then the world would "be as one." It's a vision of heaven for liberals, but conservatives believe it would quickly descend into hell. I think conservatives are on to something.

Throughout this book I've argued that large-scale human societies are nearly miraculous achievements. I've tried to show how our complicated moral psychology coevolved with our religions and our other cultural inventions (such as tribes and agriculture) to get us where we are today. I have argued that we are products of multilevel selection, including group selection, and that our "parochial altruism" is part of what makes us such great team players. We need groups, we love groups, and we develop our virtues in groups, even though those groups necessarily exclude nonmembers. If you destroy all groups and dissolve all internal structure, you destroy your moral capital.

Conservatives understand this point. Edmund Burke said it in 1790:

> To be attached to the subdivision, to love the little platoon we belong to in society, is the first principle (the germ as it were) of public affections. It is the first link in the series by which we proceed towards a love to our country, and to mankind.[70]

Adam Smith argued similarly that patriotism and parochialism are good things because they lead people to exert themselves to improve the things they can improve:

> That wisdom which contrived the system of human affections ... seems to have judged that the interest of the great society of mankind would be best promoted by directing the principal attention of each individual to that particular portion of it, which was most within the sphere both of his abilities and of his understanding.[71]

Now that's Durkheimian utilitarianism. It's utilitarianism done by somebody who understands human groupishness.

Robert Putnam has provided a wealth of evidence that Burke and Smith were right. In the previous chapter I told you about his finding that religions make Americans into "better neighbors and better citizens." I told you his conclusion that the active ingredient that made people more virtuous was enmeshing them into relationships with their co-religionists. Anything that binds people together into dense networks of trust makes people less selfish.

In an earlier study, Putnam found that ethnic diversity had the opposite effect. In a paper revealingly titled "E Pluribus Unum," Putnam examined the level of social capital in hundreds of American communities and discovered that high levels of immigration and ethnic diversity seem to cause a reduction in social capital. That may not surprise you; people are racist, you might think, and so they don't trust people who don't look like themselves. But that's not quite right. Putnam's survey was able to distinguish two different kinds of social capital: *bridging capital* refers to trust between groups, between people who have different values and identities, while *bonding capital* refers to trust within groups. Putnam found that diversity reduced *both* kinds of social capital. Here's his conclusion:

> Diversity seems to trigger not in-group/out-group division, but anomie or social isolation. In colloquial language, people living in ethnically diverse settings appear to "hunker down"—that is, to pull in like a turtle.

Putnam uses Durkheim's ideas (such as anomie) to explain why diversity makes people turn inward and become more selfish, less interested in contributing to their communities. What Putnam calls turtling is the exact opposite of what I have called hiving.

Liberals stand up for victims of oppression and exclusion. They fight to break down arbitrary barriers (such as those based on race, and more recently on sexual orientation). But their zeal to help victims, combined with their low scores on the Loyalty, Authority, and Sanctity foundations, often lead them to push for changes that weaken groups, traditions, institutions, and moral capital. For example, the urge to help the inner-city poor led to welfare programs in the 1960s that reduced the value of marriage, increased out-of-wedlock births, and weakened African American families.[72] The urge to empower students by giving them the right to sue their teachers and schools in the 1970s has eroded authority and moral capital in schools, creating disorderly environments that harm the poor above all.[73] The urge to help Hispanic immigrants in the 1980s led to multicultural education programs that emphasized the differences among Americans rather than their shared values and identity. Emphasizing differences makes many people more racist, not less.[74]

On issue after issue, it's as though liberals are trying to help a subset of bees (which really does need help) even if doing so damages the hive. Such "reforms" may lower the overall welfare of a society, and sometimes they even hurt the very victims liberals were trying to help.

TOWARD MORE CIVIL POLITICS

The idea of opposites as yin and yang comes from ancient China, a culture that valued group harmony. But in the ancient Middle East, where monotheism first took root, the metaphor of war was more common than the metaphor of balance. The third-century Persian prophet Mani preached that the visible world is the battleground between the forces of light (absolute goodness) and the forces of darkness (absolute evil). Human beings are the frontline in the battle; we contain both good and evil, and we each must pick one side and fight for it.

Mani's preaching developed into Manichaeism, a religion that spread throughout the Middle East and influenced Western thinking. If you think about politics in a Manichaean way, then compromise is a sin. God and the devil don't issue many bipartisan proclamations, and neither should you.

America's political class has become far more Manichaean since the early 1990s, first in Washington and then in many state capitals. The result is an increase in acrimony and gridlock, a decrease in the ability to find bipartisan solutions. What can be done? Many groups and organizations have urged legislators and citizens alike to take "civility pledges," promising to be "more civil" and to "view everyone in positive terms." I don't believe such pledges will work. Riders can sign as many of them as they please, but the pledges are not binding for elephants.

To escape from this mess, I believe that psychologists must work with political scientists to identify changes that will indirectly undermine Manichaeism. I ran a conference that tried to do this in 2007, at Princeton University. We learned that much of the increase in polarization was unavoidable. It was the natural result of the political realignment that took place after President Lyndon Johnson signed the Civil Rights Act in 1964. The conservative southern states, which had been solidly Democratic since the Civil War (because Lincoln was a Republican) then began to leave the Democratic Party, and by the 1990s the South was solidly Republican. Before this realignment there had been liberals and conservatives in both parties, which made it easy to form bipartisan teams who could work together on legislative projects. But after the realignment, there was no longer any overlap, either in the Senate or in the House of Representatives. Nowadays the most liberal Republican is typically more conservative than the most conservative Democrat. And once the two parties became ideologically pure—a liberal party and a conservative party—there was bound to be a rise in Manichaeism.[75]

But we also learned about factors that might possibly be reversed. The most poignant moment of the conference came when Jim Leach, a former Republican congressman from Iowa, described the changes that began in 1995. Newt Gingrich, the new speaker of the House of

Representatives, encouraged the large group of incoming Republican congressmen to leave their families in their home districts rather than moving their spouses and children to Washington. Before 1995, congressmen from both parties attended many of the same social events on weekends; their spouses became friends; their children played on the same sports teams. But nowadays most congressmen fly to Washington on Monday night, huddle with their teammates and do battle for three days, and then fly home on Thursday night. Cross-party friendships are disappearing; Manichaeism and scorched Earth politics are increasing.

I don't know how Americans can convince their legislators to move their families to Washington, and I don't know if even that change would revive cross-party friendships in today's poisoned atmosphere, but this is an example of the kind of indirect change that might change elephants.[76] Intuitions come first, so anything we can do to cultivate more positive social connections will alter intuitions and, thus, downstream reasoning and behavior. Other structural changes that might reduce Manichaeism include changing the ways that primary elections are run, the ways that electoral districts are drawn, and the ways that candidates raise money for their campaigns. (See a full list of potential remedies at www.CivilPolitics.org.)

The problem is not just limited to politicians. Technology and changing residential patterns have allowed each of us to isolate ourselves within cocoons of like-minded individuals. In 1976, only 27 percent of Americans lived in "landslide counties"—counties that voted either Democratic or Republican by a margin of 20 percent or more. But the number has risen steadily; in 2008, 48 percent of Americans lived in a landslide county.[77] Our counties and towns are becoming increasingly segregated into "lifestyle enclaves," in which ways of voting, eating, working, and worshipping are increasingly aligned. If you find yourself in a Whole Foods store, there's an 89 percent chance that the county surrounding you voted for Barack Obama. If you want to find Republicans, go to a county that contains a Cracker Barrel restaurant (62 percent of these counties went for McCain).[78]

Morality binds and blinds. This is not just something that happens to people on the other side. We all get sucked into tribal moral communities. We circle around sacred values and then share post hoc arguments about why we are so right and they are so wrong. We think the other side is blind to truth, reason, science, and common sense, but in fact everyone goes blind when talking about their sacred objects.

If you want to understand another group, *follow the sacredness*. As a first step, think about the six moral foundations, and try to figure out which one or two are carrying the most weight in a particular controversy. And if you really want to open your mind, open your heart first. If you can have at least one friendly interaction with a member of the "other" group, you'll find it far easier to listen to what they're saying, and maybe even see a controversial issue in a new light. You may not agree, but you'll probably shift from Manichaean disagreement to a more respectful and constructive yin-yang disagreement.

IN SUM

People don't adopt their ideologies at random, or by soaking up whatever ideas are around them. People whose genes gave them brains that get a special pleasure from novelty, variety, and diversity, while simultaneously being less sensitive to signs of threat, are predisposed (but not predestined) to become liberals. They tend to develop certain "characteristic adaptations" and "life narratives" that make them resonate—unconsciously and intuitively—with the grand narratives told by political movements on the left (such as the liberal progress narrative). People whose genes give them brains with the opposite settings are predisposed, for the same reasons, to resonate with the grand narratives of the right (such as the Reagan narrative).

Once people join a political team, they get ensnared in its moral matrix. They see confirmation of their grand narrative everywhere, and it's difficult—perhaps impossible—to convince them that they are wrong if you argue with them from outside of their matrix. I suggested that liberals might have even more difficulty understanding conservatives than the other way around, because liberals often have difficulty understanding how the Loyalty, Authority, and Sanctity foundations have anything to do with morality. In particular, liberals often have difficulty seeing moral capital, which I defined as the resources that sustain a moral community.

I suggested that liberals and conservatives are like yin and yang—both are "necessary elements of a healthy state of political life," as John Stuart Mill put it. Liberals are experts in care; they are better able to see the victims of existing social arrangements, and they continually push us to update those arrangements and invent new ones. As Robert F. Kennedy said: "There are those that look at things the way they are, and ask why? I dream of things that never were, and ask why not?" I showed how this moral matrix leads liberals to make two points that are (in my opinion) profoundly important for the health of a society: (1) governments can and should restrain corporate superorganisms, and (2) some big problems really can be solved by regulation.

I explained how libertarians (who sacralize liberty) and social conservatives (who sacralize certain institutions and traditions) provide a crucial counterweight to the liberal reform movements that have been so influential in America and Europe since the early twentieth century. I said that libertarians are right that markets are miraculous (at least when their externalities and other failures can be addressed), and I said that social conservatives are right that you don't usually help the bees by destroying the hive.

Finally, I said that the increasing Manichaeism of American political life is not something we can address by signing pledges and resolving to be nicer. Our politics will become more civil when we find ways to change the procedures for electing politicians and the institutions and environments within which they interact.

Morality binds and blinds. It binds us into ideological teams that fight each other as though the fate of the world depended on our side winning each battle. It blinds us to the fact that each team is composed of good people who have something important to say.

Conclusion

In this book I took you on a tour of human nature and human history. I tried to show that my beloved topic of inquiry—moral psychology— is the key to understanding politics, religion, and our spectacular rise to planetary dominance. I fear that I crammed too many sights into the tour, so let me close by highlighting the most important ones.

In Part I, I presented the first principle of moral psychology: *Intuitions come first, strategic reasoning second.* I explained how I came to develop the social intuitionist model, and I used the model to challenge the "rationalist delusion." The heroes of this part were David Hume (for helping us escape from rationalism and into intuitionism) and Glaucon (for showing us the overriding importance of reputation and other external constraints for creating moral order).

If you bring one thing home from this part of the trip, may I suggest that it be the image of yourself—and everyone else around you—as being a small rider on a very large elephant. Thinking in this way can make you more patient with other people. When you catch yourself making up ridiculous post hoc arguments, you might be slower to dismiss other people just because you can so easily refute their arguments. The action in moral psychology is not really in the pronouncements of the rider.

The second part of our tour explored the second principle of moral psychology: *There's more to morality than harm and fairness.* I recounted my time in India, and how it helped me to step out of my moral matrix and perceive additional moral concerns. I offered the metaphor that the righteous mind is like a tongue with six taste receptors. I presented Moral Foundations Theory and the research that my colleagues and I have conducted at YourMorals.org on the psychology of liberals and conservatives. The heroes of this part were

Richard Shweder (for broadening our understanding of the moral domain) and Emile Durkheim (for showing us why many people, particularly social conservatives, value the binding foundations of loyalty, authority, and sanctity).

If you take home one souvenir from this part of the tour, may I suggest that it be a suspicion of moral monists. Beware of anyone who insists that there is one true morality for all people, times, and places—particularly if that morality is founded upon a single moral foundation. Human societies are complex; their needs and challenges are variable. Our minds contain a toolbox of psychological systems, including the six moral foundations, which can be used to meet those challenges and construct effective moral communities. You don't need to use all six, and there may be certain organizations or subcultures that can thrive with just one. But anyone who tells you that all societies, in all eras, should be using one particular moral matrix, resting on one particular configuration of moral foundations, is a fundamentalist of one sort or another.

The philosopher Isaiah Berlin wrestled throughout his career with the problem of the world's moral diversity and what to make of it. He firmly rejected moral relativism:

> I am not a relativist; I do not say "I like my coffee with milk and you like it without; I am in favor of kindness and you prefer concentration camps"—each of us with his own values, which cannot be overcome or integrated. This I believe to be false.[1]

He endorsed pluralism instead, and justified it in this way:

> I came to the conclusion that there is a plurality of ideals, as there is a plurality of cultures and of temperaments. . . . There is not an infinity of [values]: the number of human values, of values which I can pursue while maintaining my human semblance, my human character, is finite—let us say 74, or perhaps 122, or 27, but finite, whatever it may be. And the difference this

makes is that if a man pursues one of these values, *I,
who do not, am able to understand why he pursues it* or
what it would be like, in his circumstances, for me to
be induced to pursue it. Hence the possibility of human
understanding.[2]

In the third part of our tour I presented the principle that *morality binds and blinds*. We are products of multilevel selection, which turned us into *Homo duplex*. We are selfish and we are groupish. We are 90 percent chimp and 10 percent bee. I suggested that religion played a crucial role in our evolutionary history—our religious minds coevolved with our religious practices to create ever-larger moral communities, particularly after the advent of agriculture. I described how political teams form, and why some people gravitate to the left, others to the right. The heroes of this part were Charles Darwin (for his theory of evolution, including multilevel selection) and Emile Durkheim (for showing us that we are *Homo duplex*, with part of our nature forged, perhaps, by group-level selection).

If you bring one thing home from this last part of the trip, may I suggest that it be the image of a small bump on the back of our heads—the hive switch, just under the skin, waiting to be turned on. We've been told for fifty years now that human beings are fundamentally selfish. We're assaulted by reality TV programs showing people at their worst. Some people actually believe that a woman should shout "fire" if she's being raped, on the grounds that everyone is so selfish that they won't even come out to investigate unless they fear for their own lives.[3]

It's not true. We may spend most of our waking hours advancing our own interests, but we all have the capacity to transcend self-interest and become simply a part of a whole. It's not just a capacity; it's the portal to many of life's most cherished experiences.

This book explained why people are divided by politics and religion. The answer is not, as Manichaeans would have it, because some people are good and others are evil. Instead, the explanation is that

*"Your mother and I are separating because I want what's
best for the country and your mother doesn't."*

FIGURE 13.1. *Why Manichaeans think they are divided by politics.*

our minds were designed for groupish righteousness. We are deeply intuitive creatures whose gut feelings drive our strategic reasoning. This makes it difficult—but not impossible—to connect with those who live in other matrices, which are often built on different configurations of the available moral foundations.

So the next time you find yourself seated beside someone from another matrix, give it a try. Don't just jump right in. Don't bring up morality until you've found a few points of commonality or in some other way established a bit of trust. And when you do bring up issues of morality, try to start with some praise, or with a sincere expression of interest.

We're all stuck here for a while, so let's try to work it out.

Acknowledgments

I learned from my former graduate student Sara Algoe that we don't express gratitude in order to repay debts or balance ledgers but rather to strengthen relationships. Furthermore, feelings of gratitude make us want to praise the other person publicly, to bring him or her honor. There are so many relationships I want to strengthen, so many people I want to honor for their help in creating this book.

First, I thank the five advisors who taught me how to think about morality. John Martin Fischer and Jonathan Baron drew me into the field with their enthusiasm and support. Paul Rozin led me to study disgust, food, and the psychology of purity, and he showed me how much fun it is to be a general psychologist. Alan Fiske taught me to look at culture, cognition, and evolution simultaneously, and showed me how to think like a social scientist. Richard Shweder taught me to see that every culture has expertise in some aspects of human potential and not in others; he pried my mind open and made me a pluralist but not a relativist. Moral Foundations Theory draws heavily on his "three ethics," as well as on Fiske's Relational Models Theory.

Next, I thank my gang, the team at YourMorals.org: Pete Ditto, Jesse Graham, Ravi Iyer, Sena Koleva, Matt Motyl, and Sean Wojcik. Together we've become 90 percent bee, 10 percent chimp. It has been a joyous collaboration that has taken us far beyond our initial hopes. I also thank the extended YourMorals family: Craig Joseph, who developed Moral Foundations Theory with me; Brian Nosek, who got our research going, gave us statistical rigor, and shares ideas and expertise with us at every turn; and Gary Sherman, the "data whisperer," who can find the most astonishing relationships in our data set, which is now so large that it has nearly attained consciousness.

I am fortunate to have found a home at University of Virginia in one of the most collegial psychology departments in America. I have an extraordinary network of collaborators, including Jerry Clore, Jim Coan, Ben Converse, Judy DeLoache, Jamie Morris, Brian Nosek, Shige Oishi, Bobbie Spellman, Sophie Trawalter, and Tim Wilson. I have also been fortunate to work with many excellent graduate students who helped me develop these ideas and who discussed and debated every chapter with me: Sara Algoe, Becca Frazier, Jesse Graham, Carlee Hawkins, Selin Kesebir, Jesse Kluver, Calvin Lai, Nicole Lindner, Matt Motyl, Patrick Seder, Gary Sherman, and Thomas Talhelm. I thank undergraduates Scott Murphy, Chris Oveis, and Jen Silvers for their contributions to my thinking.

I thank my colleagues at New York University's Stern School of Business—Dean Peter Henry, Ingo Walter, and Bruce Buchanan—for welcoming me in July 2011 as a visiting professor. Stern gave me time to finish the book and has surrounded me with great colleagues, from whom I'm now learning about business ethics (which is where I hope to apply moral psychology next).

Many friends and colleagues gave me detailed comments on the whole manuscript. In addition to the YourMorals team, I thank Paul Bloom, Ted Cadsby, Michael Dowd, Wayne Eastman, Everett Frank, Christian Galgano, Frieda Haidt, Sterling Haidt, James Hutchinson, Craig Joseph, Suzanne King, Sarah Carlson Menon, Jayne Riew, Arthur Schwartz, Barry Schwartz, Eric Schwitzgebel, Mark Shulman, Walter Sinnott-Armstrong, Ed Sketch, Bobbie Spellman, and Andy Thomson. Stephen Clarke organized a reading group of philosophers at Oxford that offered constructive critiques of every chapter; it included Katrien Devolder, Tom Douglas, Michelle Hutchinson, Guy Kahane, Neil Levy, Francesca Minerva, Trung Nguyen, Pedro Perez, Russell Powell, Julian Savulescu, Paul Troop, Michael Webb, and Graham Wood. I want particularly to recognize three conservative readers who each wrote to me years ago with mixed reviews of my work: Bo Ledbetter, Stephen Messenger, and William Modahl. We have since developed email friendships that testify to the value of sustained civil interaction across moral divides. I benefited immensely from their generosity with advice, criticism, and suggested readings on conservatism.

Many friends and colleagues gave me advice on one or several chapters. I thank them all: Gerard Alexander, Scott Atran, Simon Baron-Cohen, Paul Bloomfield, Chris Boehm, Rob Boyd, Arthur Brooks, Teddy Downey, Dan Fessler, Mike Gazzaniga, Sarah Estes Graham, Josh Greene, Rebecca Haidt, Henry Haslam, Robert Hogan, Tony Hsieh, Darrell Icenogle, Brad Jones, Rob Kaiser, Doug Kenrick, Judd King, Rob Kurzban, Brian Lowe, Jonathan Moreno, Lesley Newson, Richard Nisbett, Ara Norenzayan, Steve Pinker, David Pizarro, Robert Posacki, N. Sriram, Don Reed, Pete Richerson, Robert Sapolsky, Azim Shariff, Mark Shepp, Richard Shweder, Richard Sosis, Phil Tetlock, Richard Thaler, Mike Tomasello, Steve Vaisey, Nicholas Wade, Will Wilkinson, David Sloan Wilson, Dave Winsborough, Keith Winsten, and Paul Zak.

Many others contributed in a variety of ways: Rolf Degen found me dozens of relevant readings; Bo Ledbetter did background research for me on public policy issues; Thomas Talhelm improved my writing in the early chapters; Surojit Sen and his father, the late Sukumar Sen of Orissa, India, were my generous hosts and teachers in Bhubaneswar.

I am particularly grateful to the team of professionals who turned my original idea into the book you are now holding. My agent, John Brockman, has done so much to create an audience for science trade books, and he opened up so many opportunities for me. My editor at Pantheon, Dan Frank, applied his great wisdom and light touch to make this book better focused and much shorter. Jill Verrillo at Pantheon made the last hectic months of manuscript preparation so much easier. Stefan Sagmeister designed the jacket, which serves so effectively as an opening statement for the book. Don't we all want to fix the rip?

Finally, I have been blessed and supported by my family. My wife, Jayne Riew, nurtured our growing family while I worked long hours over the last three years. She also edits and improves everything I write. My parents, Harold and Elaine Haidt, inducted me and my sisters, Rebecca and Samantha, into the Jewish American moral matrix of hard work, love of learning, and pleasure in debate. My father passed away in March 2010, at the age of eighty-three, having done all he could to help his children succeed.

Notes

INTRODUCTION

1. A sure sign that King's appeal has become a catchphrase is that it has been altered. A Google search on "can't we all get along" (which King never said) turns up three times as many hits as "can we all get along."

2. See Pinker 2011 for an explanation of how civilization brought about a spectacular drop in violence and cruelty, even when the wars and genocides of the twentieth century are included. See also Keeley 1996 on the very high prevalence of intergroup violence before civilization.

3. *Oxford English Dictionary*.

4. *Webster's Third New International Dictionary*. This is definition #3 of *righteous;* the first definition is "doing that which is right: acting rightly or justly: conforming to the standard of the divine or the moral law."

5. *Webster's Third New International Dictionary*.

6. Evolution *is* a design process; it's just not an intelligent design process. See Tooby and Cosmides 1992.

7. In my academic writings, I describe *four* principles of moral psychology, not three. For simplicity and ease of memory, I have merged the first two together in this book because they are both about aspects of the social intuitionist model (Haidt 2001). When separated, the two principles are: *Intuitive primacy but not dictatorship*, and *moral thinking is for social doing*. See extensive discussion of all four principles in Haidt and Kesebir 2010.

8. See T. D. Wilson 2002 on the "adaptive unconscious."

9. To quote the title of Rob Kurzban's (2010) excellent recent book.

10. As Nick Clegg, leader of the UK Liberal Democrats put it, "But we are not on the left and we are not on the right. We have our own label: Liberal" (speech to the Liberal Democrat Spring Conference, Sheffield, UK, March 13, 2011). European liberals rarely go as far as American libertarians in their devotion to free markets and small government. See Iyer, Koleva, Graham, Ditto, and Haidt 2011 for a literature review and new findings on libertarians.

11. Sen-ts'an, *Hsin hsin ming*. In Conze 1954.

1. WHERE DOES MORALITY COME FROM?

1. My conclusion at graduation was that psychology and literature would have been better fields to help a young person on an existential quest. But philosophy has gotten better since then—see Wolf 2010.

2. See for example Jeremiah 31:33–34: "I will put my law within them, and I will write it on their hearts." See also Darwin 1998/1871.

3. *Empiricism* has two different meanings. I'm using it here as psychologists typically do, to mean the belief, in contrast to nativism, that the mind is more or less a "blank slate" at birth, and that nearly all of its content is learned from experience. I believe this view is wrong. Empiricism is also used by philosophers of science to refer to the devotion to empirical methods—methods of observing, measuring, and manipulating the world in order to derive reliable conclusions about it. As a scientist, I fully endorse empiricism in this sense.

4. Locke 1979/1690.

5. Piaget 1932/1965.

6. Although now we know that knowledge of physics is, to some extent, innate (Baillargeon 2008), and so is much moral knowledge (Hamlin, Wynn, and Bloom 2007). More on this in chapter 3.

7. Piaget seems to have been wrong about this. It now appears that when you use more sensitive measures that don't require kids to respond verbally, they begin reacting to violations of fairness by the age of three (LoBue et al. 2011), and perhaps even by the age of fifteen months (Schmidt and Sommerville 2011). In other words, there is increasing support for nativist theories such as Moral Foundations Theory (see chapter 6).

8. My definition of rationalism is not far from philosophical definitions, e.g., rationalists believe in "the power of a priori reason to grasp substantial truths about the world" (B. Williams 1967, p. 69). But my approach avoids eighteenth-century debates about innate ideas and connects with twentieth-century concerns about whether reasoning, particularly the reasoning of an independent individual, is a reliable (versus dangerous) way to choose laws and public policies. See Oakeshott 1997/1947. Hayek 1988 argued that "constructivism" was the more accurate term for the kind of rationalism that believes it can construct a social or moral order on the basis of rational reflection. I note that Kohlberg did not actually call himself a rationalist; he called himself a constructivist. But I will refer to Kohlberg, Piaget, and Turiel as rationalists to highlight their contrast with intuitionism, as I develop it in the rest of this book.

9. Kohlberg 1969, 1971.

10. Kohlberg 1968.

11. See, for example, Killen and Smetana 2006.

12. Turiel 1983, p. 3, defined social conventions as "behavioral uniformities that serve to coordinate social interactions and are tied to the contexts of specific social systems."

13. Turiel 1983, p. 3.

14. Hollos, Leis, and Turiel 1986; Nucci, Turiel, and Encarnacion-Gawrych 1983.

15. Most of the experimental work was motivated by Kohlberg and Turiel, but I should also mention two other very influential figures: Carol Gilligan (1982) argued that Kohlberg had neglected the "ethic of care," which she said was more common in women than in men. Also, Martin Hoffman (1982) did important work on the development of empathy, highlighting a moral emotion at a time when most of the research was on moral reasoning. Tragically, Kohlberg committed suicide in January 1987. He had been suffering from depression, and from chronic pain due to a parasitic infection.

16. A. P. Fiske 1991.

17. Evans-Pritchard 1976.

18. I'll develop this idea in chapter 11, drawing heavily on the ideas of Emile Durkheim.

19. Rosaldo 1980.

20. Meigs 1984.

21. See Leviticus 11.

22. See Deuteronomy 22:9–11. Mary Douglas (1966) argues that the need to keep categories pure is the most important principle behind the kosher laws. I disagree, and think that disgust plays a much more powerful role; see Rozin, Haidt, and McCauley 2008.

23. The earliest record of this phrase is a sermon by John Wesley in 1778, but it clearly harks back to the book of Leviticus.

24. Shweder, Mahapatra, and Miller 1987.

25. Geertz 1984, p. 126.

26. Shweder and Bourne 1984. Shweder used the word *egocentric* rather than *individualistic*, but I fear that *egocentric* has too many negative connotations, and is too closely related to selfishness.

27. Shweder, Mahapatra, and Miller 1987. Each person responded to thirteen of the thirty-nine cases.

28. Turiel, Killen, and Helwig 1987.

29. I thank Dan Wegner, my colleague and mentor at UVA, for coining the term *moral dumbfounding*.

30. Hume 1969/1739–40, p. 462. Hume meant that reason finds the means to achieve whatever ends are chosen by the passions. He did not focus on post hoc justification as the function of reasoning. But as I'll show in later chapters,

justifying the self's actions and judgments is one of the principal ends that we are all passionate about.

31. Haidt, Koller, and Dias 1993.

2. THE INTUITIVE DOG AND ITS RATIONAL TAIL

1. This is the foundational truth of *The Happiness Hypothesis,* described in chapter 1 of that book.

2. Medea, in *Metamorphosis* (Ovid 2004), Book VII.

3. Plato 1997. Quote is from *Timaeus* 69d. Note that Timaeus seems to be speaking for Plato. He is not used as a foil, about to be refuted by Socrates.

4. Solomon 1993.

5. Hume used the word *slave,* but I'll switch to the less offensive and more accurate term *servant.* Hume was building on the ideas of other English and Scottish sentimentalists, such as Francis Hutcheson and the Earl of Shaftesbury. Other noted sentimentalists, or antirationalists, include Rousseau, Nietzsche, and Freud.

6. Ellis 1996.

7. Jefferson 1975/1786 p. 406.

8. Ibid., pp. 408–9.

9. Plato's model in the *Timaeus,* as in the *Phaedrus,* was actually that there are three parts to the soul: reason (in the head), spirit (including the desire for honor, in the chest), and appetite (the love of pleasure and money, in the stomach). But in this chapter I'll simplify it as a dual-process model, pitting reason (above the neck) against the two sets of passions (below).

10. This famous phrase was coined by Herbert Spencer, but Darwin used it too.

11. Darwin 1998/1871, part I, chapter 5. More on this in chapter 9.

12. The idea was developed by Herbert Spencer in the late nineteenth century, but it goes back to Thomas Malthus in the eighteenth century. Darwin did believe that tribes competed with tribes (see chapter 9), but he was no social Darwinist, according to Desmond and Moore 2009.

13. Hitler was a vegetarian too, but nobody would argue that endorsing vegetarianism makes one a Nazi.

14. Pinker 2002, p. 106.

15. Rawls remains one of the most cited political philosophers. He is famous for his thought experiment in Rawls 1971 asking people to imagine the society they would design if they had to do so from behind a "veil of ignorance" so that they would not know what position they would eventually occupy in that society. Rationalists tend to love Rawls.

16. Wilson's exact words bear repeating, for they were prophetic: "Ethical philosophers intuit the deontological canons of morality by consulting the emo-

tive centers of their own hypothalamic-limbic system. This is also true of the developmentalists [such as Kohlberg], even when they are being their most severely objective. Only by interpreting the activity of the emotive centers as a biological adaptation can the meaning of the canons be deciphered." E. O. Wilson 1975, p. 563.

17. E. O. Wilson 1998.

18. Leading biologists such as Stephen Jay Gould and Richard Lewontin wrote diatribes against sociobiology that explicitly linked science to the political agenda of social justice. See, for example, Allen et al. 1975.

19. See Pinker 2002, chapter 6.

20. The exception to this statement was work on empathy by Martin Hoffman, e.g., Hoffman 1982.

21. De Waal 1996. I read this one after graduate school, but I had gotten interested in de Waal's work during grad school.

22. Damasio 1994.

23. Three very influential works that brought emotions into morality were *Passions Within Reason* by the economist Robert Frank, *Wise Choices, Apt Feelings* by the philosopher Allan Gibbard, and *Varieties of Moral Personality* by the philosopher Owen Flanagan. Also, work by the social psychologist John Bargh was a crucial element of the revival of automatic processes—i.e., intuition, and the little flashes of affect that will feature prominently in chapter 3. See Bargh and Chartrand 1999.

24. I date the rebirth to 1992 because that is when an influential volume appeared with the provocative title *The Adapted Mind: Evolutionary Psychology and the Generation of Culture*. The book was edited by Jerome Barkow, Leda Cosmides, and John Tooby. Other leading figures in the field included David Buss, Doug Kenrick, and Steven Pinker. Morality (particularly cooperation and cheating) has been an important area of research in evolutionary psychology since the beginning.

25. I call this model "Jeffersonian" because it allows the "head" and the "heart" to reach independent and conflicting moral judgments, as happened in his letter to Cosway. But I note that Jefferson thought that the head was poorly suited to making moral judgments, and that it should confine itself to issues that can be determined by calculation. Jefferson himself was a sentimentalist about morality.

26. I conducted these studies with Stephen Stose and Fredrik Bjorklund. I never turned these data into a manuscript because at the time I thought these null findings would be unpublishable.

27. The idea for this task came from Dan Wegner, who got it from an episode of *The Simpsons* in which Bart sells his soul to his friend Milhouse.

28. We did not let anyone actually drink the juice; Scott stopped them just before the glass touched their lips.

29. The transcript is verbatim and is unedited, except that a few asides by the subject have been removed. This is the first half of the transcript for this subject on this story. We used a hidden video camera to record all interviews, and we obtained permission from all but one subject afterward to analyze the videos.

30. For example, in the harmless-taboo interviews, people were almost twice as likely to say "I don't know" compared to the Heinz interview. They were more than twice as likely to simply declare something without support ("That's just wrong!" or "You just don't do that!"); they were ten times as likely to say they couldn't explain themselves (as in the last round of the transcript above); and they were 70 percent more likely to reason themselves into what we called a dead end—an argument that the subject starts to make, but then drops after realizing that it won't work. This is what happened when the person described above started to argue that the brother and sister were too young to be having sex with anyone. Some of these dead ends were accompanied by what we called the self-doubt face, with people furrowing their brows and scowling while they talked, just as you might do when listening to someone *else* make a ridiculous argument. I never published this study, but you can read the report of it on my webpage, www.jonathanhaidt.com, under Publications, then Working Papers, then see Haidt and Murphy.

31. Wason 1969.

32. Johnson-Laird and Wason 1977, p. 155.

33. Margolis 1987, p. 21. See Gazzaniga 1985 for a similar argument.

34. Margolis 1987, p. 76. Some forms of reasoning can be done by creatures without language, but they cannot do "reasoning-why" because that kind of reasoning is done specifically to prepare to convince others.

35. In one of his last major works, Kohlberg stated that a pillar of his approach was the assumption that "moral reasoning is the process of using ordinary moral language" (Kohlberg, Levine, and Hewer 1983, p. 69). He was not interested in unconscious or nonverbal inferences (i.e., in intuition).

36. Several philosophers have developed this idea that moral reasoning should be understood as playing social and justificatory functions. See Gibbard 1990 and Stevenson 1960; in psychology, see Mercier and Sperber 2011.

37. See Neisser 1967. Greene (2008) is careful to define cognition in a more narrow way that can be contrasted with emotion, but he is the rare exception.

38. Ekman 1992; Ellsworth and Smith 1985; Scherer 1984.

39. Lazarus 1991.

40. Emotions are not entirely subcategories of intuition: emotions are often said to include all the bodily changes that prepare one for adaptive behavior, including hormonal changes in the rest of the body. Hormonal responses are not intu-

itions. But the cognitive elements of emotions—such as appraisals of events and alterations of attention and vigilance—are subtypes of intuition. They happen automatically and with conscious awareness of the outputs, but not of the processes.

41. Daniel Kahneman has long called these two kinds of cognition "system 1" (the elephant) and "system 2" (the rider). See Kahneman 2011 for a highly readable account of thinking and decision making from a two-system perspective.

42. The neuroscientist Michael Gazzaniga calls this "the interpreter module."

43. This is called the confirmation bias; see a review of this literature in chapter 4.

44. One of the most common criticisms of the social intuitionist model from philosophers is that links 5 and 6, which I show as dotted lines, might in fact be much more frequent in daily life than I assert. See, for example, Greene, forthcoming. These critics present no evidence, but, in fairness, I have no evidence either as to the actual frequency in daily life with which people reason their way to counterintuitive conclusions (link 5) or change their minds during private reflection about moral matters (link 6). Of course people change their minds on moral issues, but I suspect that in most cases the cause of change was a new intuitively compelling experience (link 1), such as seeing a sonogram of a fetus, or an intuitively compelling argument made by another person (link 3). I also suspect that philosophers are able to override their initial intuitions more easily than can ordinary folk, based on findings by Kuhn (1991).

45. Zimbardo 2007.

46. Latane and Darley, 1970.

47. Haidt 2001.

48. See especially Hauser 2006; Huebner, Dwyer, and Hauser 2009; Saltzstein and Kasachkoff 2004.

49. Hume 1960/1777, Part I, the opening paragraph.

50. Carnegie 1981/1936, p. 37.

3. ELEPHANTS RULE

1. The article I was writing is Haidt 2007. In that article, and in all of my academic writings, I describe *four* principles of moral psychology, the first two of which are *Intuitive primacy but not dictatorship* and *Moral thinking is for social doing*. In this book I am combining these two principles into a single principle—*Intuitions come first, strategic reasoning second*—because I think it will be easier to remember and apply.

2. It's a six-word summary of what happens in the first few seconds of judgment, according to the social intuitionist model. It doesn't capture the mutual influence that happens over time as two people give each other reasons and sometimes change each other's judgement.

3. Wheatley and Haidt 2005.

4. We used only highly hypnotizable subjects, selected from my Psych 101 lecture class on the day I lectured about hypnosis. There was a period in the 1980s when scientists thought that hypnosis was not a real phenomenon, it was just subjects adopting a role or playacting. But a string of studies has demonstrated effects that cannot be faked; for example, if you give people the posthypnotic suggestion that they can only see in black and white, and then you put them in an fMRI scanner, you find greatly reduced activity in color vision circuits of the brain when subjects are viewing images in color (Kosslyn et al. 2000).

5. *Dhammapada* verse 252 (Mascaro 1973). See chapter 4 of *The Happiness Hypothesis* for more on the psychology of this great truth.

6. This sentence is a reasonable approximation of the central claim of behaviorism; see Pavlov 1927 on the two basic orienting reflexes. With a slight change it applies to Freud as well—the various parts of the unconscious are constantly scanning the environment and triggering rapid automatic reactions, although sometimes they are at odds with each other. See also Osgood 1962, on the three fundamental dimensions of categorization, the first of which is valence good versus bad.

7. Wundt 1907/1896.

8. See LeDoux 1996 on how the amygdala can trigger an emotional reaction to something well before the cerebral cortex has had a chance to process the event.

9. The effect did not depend on whether people could remember having seen a particular stimulus. In one study, Zajonc flashed images up on a screen for a mere thousandth of a second, too fast for anyone to be able to identify consciously, yet when tested later, people preferred the images they had "seen" five times to the images they had previously been exposed to just once, or not at all (Zajonc 1968).

10. Zajonc 1980. I drew heavily on Zajonc when I formulated the metaphor of the elephant and rider.

11. Ibid., p. 171.

12. Fazio et al. 1986; Greenwald, McGhee, and Schwartz 1998.

13. Morris et al. 2003.

14. Greenwald, Nosek, and Banaji 2003.

15. Morris et al. 2003. The difference was found in the N400 component, which is larger when the brain encounters incongruity, i.e., when Morris paired words that had different emotional meanings. A more recent Dutch study (Van Berkum et al. 2009) asked partisans to read statements endorsing or opposing issues such as euthanasia. They found the same N400 effect, as well as a bigger and slower LPP (late positive potential) effect, linked to emotional responding in general, indicating that partisans began to feel different things within the first half-second of reading key words.

16. Dion, Berscheid, and Walster 1972.

17. For an experiment with mock jurors, see Efran 1974; for a field study showing that attractive defendants get off more lightly, see Stewart 1980. For a meta-analysis, see Mazzella and Feingold 1994. Being attractive is an advantage for defendants for most crimes, but not for those where attractiveness helped the criminal pull off the crime, such as swindling (Sigall and Ostrove 1975).

18. Todorov et al. 2005. He discarded the few cases in which participants could identify either candidate.

19. The original study found no decline of accuracy with a one-second exposure. The tenth-of-a-second finding is from a follow-up study, Ballew and Todorov 2007. This study also addressed the possibility that incumbency is a third variable that makes politicians look competent and also, coincidentally, win. It is not. Prediction by facial competence was just as accurate in races where there was no incumbent, or where the incumbent lost, as it was when the incumbent won.

20. For additional reviews on the role of intuition and automatic "moral heuristics," see Gigerenzer 2007 and Sunstein 2005.

21. See reviews in Damasio 2003; Greene, 2009a. For fairness and the insula, see Hsu, Anen, and Quartz 2008; Rilling et al. 2008; Sanfey et al. 2003.

22. Schnall et al. 2008, Study 1. All four judgments went in the predicted direction, although not every comparison was statistically significant. When the four stories were combined, which is the normal way such data are analyzed, the effect of the fart spray was highly significant, $p < .001$. There was also a third experimental condition, in which just one spray of fart spray was applied, but this condition did not differ from the two-spray condition.

23. Eskine, Kacinic, and Prinz 2011. See also Liljenquist, Zhong, and Galinsky 2010 on how good smells promote good behavior.

24. Clore, Schwarz, and Conway 1994. When people are made aware that some external factor caused their unpleasant feelings, the effect usually diminishes or disappears. Our affective reactions are usually good guides to whether we like something or not, but when psychologists "trick" subjects by triggering extraneous emotions, the "affect as information" heuristic makes mistakes.

25. Zhong, Strejcek, and Sivanathan 2010.

26. Zhong and Liljenquist 2006.

27. Helzer and Pizarro 2011. The first study in this paper, using the hand sanitizer, only asked for subjects' overall self-descriptions, and found that subjects called themselves more conservative when standing near the sanitizer. In the second study the authors replicated the effect and showed that reminders of cleanliness and washing made people more judgmental primarily on questions related to sexual purity.

28. Hare 1993.
29. Ibid., p. 54.
30. Ibid., p. 91.
31. Beaver et al. 2011; Blonigen et al. 2005; Viding et al. 2005.
32. Brain scanning studies confirm that many emotional areas, including the amygdala and the vmPFC, are much less reactive in psychopaths than in normal people; see Blair 2007; Kiehl 2006. If you hook them up to a skin conductance meter, as in a lie detector test, psychopaths show a normal response to a photograph of a shark with open jaws. But show them a picture of mutilated bodies or suffering children, and the meter doesn't budge (Blair 1999). For the best clinical portraits of psychopaths and their indifference to others, including their parents, see Cleckley 1955.
33. James 1950/1890, I:488.
34. Baillargeon 1987.
35. The first work demonstrating that infants have innate abilities to understand the social world, including abilities to infer intentions and react to harm, was done by David and Ann Premack; see Premack and Premack 1994 for a review summarizing the origins of moral cognition.
36. Hamlin, Wynn, and Bloom 2007. This looking-time difference was found only for the ten-month-old children, not the six-month-olds. But the reaching-out difference was found for both age groups. The puppets were not traditional puppets; they were different colors and shapes of wood blocks. You can view the puppet shows from links at www.yale.edu/infantlab/In_the_Media.html. This technique of measuring infants' attributions was first developed by Kuhlmeier, Wynn, and Bloom 2003.
37. Hamlin, Wynn, and Bloom 2007, p. 559.
38. For early writings on this idea, see Hoffman 1982; Kagan 1984.
39. The trolley dilemma was first discussed by philosophers Philippa Foot and Judith Jarvis Thompson.
40. Some philosophers note the difference that in the bridge story you are using the victim as a means to an end, whereas in the switch story the victim is not a means to an end; his death is just an unfortunate side effect. Greene and others have therefore tested alternative versions, such as the case where the switch only saves lives because it diverts the trolley onto a side loop where one man is standing. In that case the victim is still being used as a means to an end; if he were to step off the track, the trolley would continue on the loop, back onto the main track, and would kill the five people. In these cases, subjects tend to give responses in between the original switch and footbridge versions.
41. Greene et al. 2001. This study also reported that it took longer for subjects who did make the utilitarian choice to give their answer, as though reasoning was

struggling to overcome emotion, although that finding was later shown to be an artifact of the particular stories chosen, not a general principle (McGuire et al. 2009). But see Greene 2009b for a response.

42. Rilling et al. 2008; Sanfey et al. 2003.

43. For reviews see Greene 2009a and Greene forthcoming. The areas most frequently reported include the vmPFC, insula, and amygdala. For an exception, see Knoch, Pascual-Leone, Meyer, Treyer, and Fehr 2006.

44. Greene 2008; the quote is on p. 63. I asked Greene if he had known about the Wilson quote from p. 563 of *Sociobiology*, and he said no.

45. See my review of these works in Haidt and Kesebir 2010.

46. See Sinnott-Armstrong 2008 for a three-volume set of papers by this interdisciplinary community.

47. Paxton, Ungar, and Greene, forthcoming.

48. I should note that people vary in the degree to which they feel strong intuitions, in their ability to construct reasons, and in their openness to the reasons of others. See Bartels 2008 for a discussion of these individual differences.

4. VOTE FOR ME (HERE'S WHY)

1. *Republic,* 360c., trans. G. M. A. Grube and C. D. C. Reeve. In Plato 1997.

2. It is Glaucon's brother Adeimantus who states the challenge in this way, at 360e–361d, but he's just elaborating upon Glaucon's argument. Glaucon and Adeimantus want Socrates to succeed and refute their arguments. Nonetheless, I will use Glaucon for the rest of this book as a spokesman for the view that reputation matters more than reality.

3. *Republic,* 443–45.

4. Ibid., 473ff.

5. At least Plato stated his assumptions about human nature at great length. Many other moral philosophers, such as Kant and Rawls, simply make assertions about how minds work, what people want, or what seems "reasonable." These assertions seem to be based on little more than introspection about their own rather unusual personalities or value systems. For example, when some of Rawls's (1971) assumptions were tested—e.g., that most people would care more about raising the worst-off than about raising the average if they had to design a society from behind a "veil of ignorance," so that they don't know what position they'd occupy in the society—they were found to be false (Frohlich, Oppenheimer, and Eavey 1987).

6. His exact words were: "My thinking is first and last and always for the sake of my doing" (James 1950/1890, p. 333). Susan Fiske (1993) applied James's functionalism to social cognition, abbreviating his dictum as "thinking is for doing." For more on functionalism in the social sciences, see Merton 1968.

7. A rationalist can still believe that reasoning is easily corrupted, or that most people don't reason properly. But ought implies can, and rationalists are committed to the belief that reason *can* work this way, perhaps (as in Plato's case) because perfect rationality is the soul's true nature.

8. Lerner and Tetlock 2003, p. 434.

9. Gopnik, Meltzoff, and Kuhl 2000.

10. I could perhaps use the term *Machiavellian* instead of *Glauconian* throughout this book. But the word *Machiavellian* is too dark, too suggestive of leaders tricking people in order to dominate them. I think moral life is really about cooperation and alliance, rather than about power and domination. The dishonesty and hypocrisy of our moral reasoning is done to get people to like us and cooperate with us, so I prefer the term *Glauconian*.

11. See review in Lerner and Tetlock 2003. Tetlock 2002 presents three metaphors: intuitive politicians, intuitive prosecutors, and intuitive theologians. I focus on the intuitive politician here, and I present the intuitive prosecutor below, as being related to the needs of the intuitive politician. I cover the subject matter of the intuitive theologian when I discuss religion and the need to bind people together with shared beliefs about sacredness, in chapter 11.

12. For reviews see Ariely 2008; Baron 2007.

13. Lerner and Tetlock 2003, p. 438.

14. Ibid., p. 433; emphasis added.

15. Leary 2004.

16. Leary 2005, p. 85. There surely are differences among people in how obsessed they are with the opinions of others. But Leary's findings indicate that we are not particularly accurate at assessing our own levels of obsession.

17. Millon et al. 1998. Psychopaths often care what others think, but only as part of a plan to manipulate or exploit others. They don't have emotions such as shame and guilt that make it painful for them when others see through their lies and come to hate them. They don't have an automatic unconscious sociometer.

18. Wason 1960.

19. Shaw 1996. The confirmation bias is found widely in social, clinical, and cognitive psychology. It appears early in childhood and it lasts for life. See reviews in Kunda 1990; Mercier & Sperber 2010; Nickerson 1998; Pyszczynski and Greenberg 1987.

20. Kuhn 1989, p. 681.

21. Perkins, Farady, and Bushey 1991.

22. Ibid., p. 95. They did find a bit of overall improvement between the first and fourth year of high school, but this might have been simple maturation, rather than an effect of education. They didn't find it in college.

23. The *Daily Telegraph* got a leaked copy of the full expense report, which had

been prepared by the House of Commons in response to a Freedom of Information request that it had resisted for years.

24. Bersoff 1999. See also Dan Batson's research on "moral hypocrisy," e.g., Batson et al. 1999.

25. Perugini and Leone 2009.

26. Ariely 2008, p. 201; emphasis added.

27. This is the term I used in *The Happiness Hypothesis*.

28. Gilovich 1991, p. 84.

29. Ditto, Pizarro, and Tannenbaum 2009; Kunda 1990.

30. Frey and Stahlberg 1986.

31. Kunda 1987.

32. Ditto and Lopez 1992. See also Ditto et al. 2003, which finds that when we want to believe something, we often don't even bother to search for a single piece of supporting evidence. We just accept things uncritically.

33. Balcetis and Dunning 2006.

34. See Brockman 2009.

35. See review in Kinder 1998. The exception to this rule is that when the material benefits of a policy are "substantial, imminent, and well-publicized," those who would benefit from it are more likely to support it than those who would be harmed. See also D. T. Miller 1999 on the "norm of self-interest."

36. Kinder 1998, p. 808.

37. The term is from Smith, Bruner, and White, as quoted by Kinder 1998.

38. See the classic study by Hastorf and Cantril (1954) in which students at Dartmouth and Princeton came to very different conclusions about what had happened on the football field after watching the same film showing several disputed penalty calls.

39. Lord, Ross, and Lepper 1979; Munro et al. 2002; Taber and Lodge 2006. Polarization effects are not found in all studies, but as Taber and Lodge argue, the studies that failed to find the effect generally used cooler, less emotional stimuli that did not fully engage partisan motivations.

40. Westen et al. 2006.

41. The activated areas included insula, medial PFC, ventral ACC, ventromedial PFC, and posterior cingulate cortex. The areas associated with negative emotion are particularly the left insula, lateral orbital frontal cortex, and ventromedial PFC. The amygdala, closely related to fear and threat, did show greater activity in the early trials but had "habituated" in the later trials. Note that all of these findings come from subtracting reactions to hypocrisy by the neutral target (e.g., Tom Hanks) from reactions to hypocrisy by one's own candidate.

42. Greene (2008) refers to this area as "Mill" in the brain, because it tends to be

more active when subjects make the cool, utilitarian choice, rather than the more emotion-based deontological choice.

43. The dlPFC did not show an increase in activity until *after* the exculpatory information was given and the partisan was freed from the handcuffs. It was as if confirmatory reasoning could not even begin until subjects had a clear and emotionally acceptable explanation to confirm.

44. Olds and Milner 1954.

45. *Webster's Third New International Dictionary.* Related definitions include "false belief or a persistent error of perception occasioned by a false belief or mental derangement."

46. Dawkins 2006; Dennett 2006; Harris 2006. I'll discuss their arguments in detail in chapter 11.

47. Plato gives his childrearing advice in Book 3 of *The Republic;* Dawkins gives it in chapter 9 of *The God Delusion.*

48. Schwitzgebel and Rust 2009, 2011; Schwitzgebel et al. 2011.

49. Schwitzgebel 2009.

50. Mercier and Sperber 2011, p. 57.

51. See Lilienfeld, Ammirati, and Landfield 2009 for a report on how hard it has been to develop methods of "debiasing" human thinking. What little success there is in the "critical thinking" literature almost never finds (or even looks for) transfer of skills beyond the classroom.

52. Wilson 2002; Wilson and Schooler 1991.

53. Baron 1998.

54. Heath and Heath 2010.

55. See www.EthicalSystems.org for my attempt to bring together research on these "path changes," many of which are simple to do. One good example is Dan Ariely's finding that if you ask people to sign an expense report at the beginning, promising to be honest, rather than at the end, affirming that they were honest, you get a big drop in overclaiming of expenses. See Ariely 2008.

5. BEYOND WEIRD MORALITY

1. Mill 2003/1859, p. 80.

2. Henrich, Heine, and Norenzayan 2010.

3. Markus and Kitayama 1991.

4. For a review of these sorts of cultural differences, see Kitayama et al. 2009.

5. Nisbett et al. 2001.

6. In Analects 15:24, Confucius is asked whether there is a single word that could guide one's life. He responds: "Should it not be reciprocity? What you do not wish for yourself, do not do to others" (Lays 1997). But there is no way to reduce the moral teachings of the Analects to the golden rule. As I read them,

the Analects rely upon all six of the moral foundations I'll present in chapters 7 and 8.

7. See, for example, the books of Sam Harris, such as *The End of Faith* and *The Moral Landscape*.

8. Not entirely new. As Shweder 1990a explains, it has arisen several times in psychology. But if someone today calls herself a cultural psychologist, she probably orients herself to the field as it was reborn in the ten years after the publication of Shweder and LeVine 1984.

9. Shweder 1990a.

10. The first published mention of the three ethics was Shweder 1990b. The major statement of the theory is Shweder et al. 1997.

11. Peter Singer is the most prominent utilitarian philosopher of our time. See P. Singer 1979.

12. It need not be a soul in anything like the Christian sense. As Paul Bloom (2004) has shown, we are "natural born dualists." Despite wide religious variations, most people (including many atheists) believe that the mind, spirit, or soul is something separable from the body, something that inhabits the body.

13. This, for example, was the conclusion drawn by Sayyid Qutb, an Egyptian who spent two years studying in America in the 1940s. He was repulsed, and this moral repulsion influenced his later work as an Islamist philosopher and theorist, one of the main inspirations for Osama bin Laden and Al-Qaeda.

14. These text analyses are reported in Haidt et al. 1993. See also work by Lene Arnett Jensen (1997, 1998), which reached similar findings applying Shweder's three ethics to differences between progressive and orthodox participants, in India and in the United States.

15. I am forever grateful to the late Sukumar Sen and his son Surojit Sen, of Cuttack and Bhubaneswar, for their generosity and kindness.

16. In the Koran, see 2:222, 4:43, 24:30. In the Hebrew Bible, see the book of Leviticus in particular. For Christianity, see Thomas 1983, chapter 1. Also see New Testament passages on the purifications of Jesus and his followers, e.g., John 3:25, 11:55; Acts 15:9, 20:26, 21:26, 24:18.

17. We also wanted to explain why so many languages extend their word for "disgust" to apply not just to physically repulsive things like excrement but also to some moral violations—but not all violations, and not always the same ones across cultures (Haidt et al. 1997).

18. People intuitively associate up with good and down with bad, even when up and down are just relative positions on a computer monitor (Meier and Robinson 2004). For overviews of research on this psychological dimension, see Brandt and Reyna 2011; Rozin, Haidt, and McCauley 2008; and chapter 9 of *The Happiness Hypothesis*.

19. I describe my research on moral elevation and disgust in detail in chapter 9 of *The Happiness Hypothesis*. See also www.ElevationResearch.org.

20. Moral violations have often been shown to activate the frontal insula, a brain area important for disgust (Rilling et al. 2008; Sanfey et al. 2003), although so far the moral violations used have mostly involved cheating, not what Rozin, McCauley, and I would call moral disgust. See Rozin, Haidt, and Fincher 2009.

21. Andres Serrano's *Piss Christ* is a particularly difficult case because the resulting image is visually stunning. Strong light shining through the yellow urine gives the photo a quasi-divine glow. See also Chris Ofili's painting *The Holy Virgin Mary*, and the controversy over its exhibition in New York City in 1999. The painting portrayed the Virgin Mary as a black woman surrounded by images of vulvas cut out from pornographic magazines and smeared with actual elephant dung.

22. After I wrote this hypothetical example, Bruce Buchanan pointed out to me that something very much like it happened in Chicago in 1988. See the Wikipedia entry for *Mirth & Girth*, a painting that satirized the revered and recently deceased African American mayor of Chicago, Harold Washington.

23. Martha Nussbaum (2004) has made this case powerfully, in an extended argument with Leon Kass, beginning with Kass 1997.

24. Popes Benedict XVI and John Paul II have been particularly eloquent on these points. See also Bellah et al. 1985.

25. For example, the Hindu veil of Maya; the Platonic world of Forms and the escape from Plato's cave.

26. According to data from the American National Election Survey. Jews are second only to African Americans in their support for the Democratic Party. Between 1992 and 2008, 82 percent of Jews identified with or leaned toward the Democratic Party.

27. As I'll say in chapter 8, it is only recently that I've come to realize that conservatives care at least as much about fairness as do liberals; they just care more about proportionality than about equality.

28. I am not saying that all moral visions and ideologies are equally good, or equally effective at creating humane and morally ordered societies. I am not a relativist. I will address the issue of how well ideologies fit with human nature in chapter 12. But for now I want to insist on the point that long-standing ideological struggles almost invariably involve people who are pursuing a moral vision in which they believe passionately and sincerely. We often have the urge to attribute ulterior motives to our opponents, such as monetary gain. This is usually an error.

29. Shweder 1991, p. 5.

30. I have been involved in a dispute about this claim. I have collected materials relevant to the controversy at www.JonathanHaidt.com/postpartisan.html.

6. TASTE BUDS OF THE RIGHTEOUS MIND

1. Examples in philosophy include Jeremy Bentham, R. M. Hare, and Peter Singer. In psychology, morality is often operationalized as altruism or "pro-social behavior." It's about getting more people to help more people, ideally strangers. Even the Dalai Lama defines an ethical act as "one where we refrain from causing harm to others' experience or expectation of happiness" (Dalai Lama XIV 1999, p. 49).

2. Examples in philosophy include Immanuel Kant and John Rawls; in psychology, Lawrence Kohlberg. Elliot Turiel allows welfare and justice to be competing concerns.

3. See Berlin 2001 on the dangers of monism.

4. Chan 1963, p. 54.

5. As well as pleasing noses with a much more complex olfactory system, which I'll ignore to keep the analogy simple.

6. The word I want to use here is *empiricism*, but that word has two meanings, and I've already used it in chapter 1 as a contrast to nativism. I reject empiricism in that sense, which suggests a blank slate, but embrace it in its other meaning as the method by which scientists gain knowledge through empirical (observational, experience-based) methods.

7. E. O. Wilson pointed this out in chapter 11 of *Consilience*. Like Hume, he embraced naturalism/empiricism, rather than transcendentalism. I do too.

8. Hume noted that some passions and sentiments are so calm that they are sometimes mistaken for reason (*Treatise of Human Nature*, Book 2). This is why I think the word *intuition* is the best modern rendering of Hume's word *sentiments*.

9. Hume is here building on an argument from an earlier "moral sense" theorist, Frances Hutcheson. This text was in the first two editions of the *Enquiry Concerning Human Understanding*. It was removed from the last edition, but I have not found any indication that Hume changed his mind about the taste analogy. For example, in the final edition of the *Enquiry*, sec. xii, pt. 3, he says: "Morals and criticism are not so properly objects of the understanding as of taste and sentiment. Beauty, whether moral or natural, is felt, more properly than perceived."

10. Especially Adam Smith and Edmund Burke. See Frazier 2010.

11. Chapter 3 is my review of this research. See also my more academic review paper, Haidt and Kesebir 2010.

12. Baron-Cohen 1995.

13. Baron-Cohen 2002, p. 248.

14. Ibid.

15. Baron-Cohen 2009. One prenatal factor seems to be testosterone, which has many effects on the brain of a developing fetus. We all start off as girls in the first two months after conception. If the Y chromosome is present, it triggers the production of testosterone beginning in the eighth week; this converts both brain and body over to the male pattern. Autism is several times more common in boys than in girls.

16. Bentham 1996/1789, chapter I, section 2.

17. Lucas and Sheeran 2006.

18. Ibid., p. 5, quoting William Hazlitt.

19. Ibid., quoting Mill.

20. Lucas and Sheeran 2006, p. 1. Of course, postmortem psychiatric diagnosis is a difficult game. Whether or not Bentham had Asperger's, my main point here is that his thinking was unusual and his understanding of human nature was poor.

21. Denis 2008.

22. Kant 1993/1785, p. 30.

23. Fitzgerald 2005. Another possibility is that Kant developed a brain tumor at the age of forty-seven. He began complaining of headaches, and soon after that he lost vision in his left eye. His writing style and his philosophy changed after that too, and some have speculated that he developed a tumor that interfered with emotional processing in the left prefrontal cortex, leaving his high systemizing unchecked by normal empathizing. See Gazzaniga 1998, p. 121.

24. Scruton 1982.

25. I don't mean this statement to apply to all scientific inquiry. Chemists need no empathy. But to observe the inner lives of people, it helps to have empathy, as great novelists and playwrights do.

26. The authors of the WEIRD people article (Henrich et al. 2010; see chapter 5) do not comment on when Western thinking became WEIRD. But their thesis directly implies that during the nineteenth century, as the industrial revolution progressed and levels of wealth, education, and individualism increased (at least for the elite class), WEIRD thinking became increasingly common.

27. Moral philosophy has gotten better in the last twenty years, in my view, because it has returned somewhat to its ancient interest in the natural world, including psychology. Many philosophers nowadays are very well read in neuroscience, social psychology, and evolution. There has been a growing interest in "psychological realism" since the 1990s, e.g., Flanagan 1991 and Gibbard 1990. For the state of the art, see Appiah 2008 and the three-volume set of essays edited by Walter Sinnott-Armstrong 2008.

28. Only Buddha, for example, preached compassion for all sentient beings, including animals. For a review of culture and virtue theory, see Haidt and Joseph 2007.

29. Granted, there are olfactory receptors at work here too, but I'm ignoring those for simplicity's sake. And granted, many fruit drinks also trigger the sour receptor, but that works quite well with this analogy: many moral violations trigger one foundation primarily, and one or more other foundations weakly.

30. Sperber and Hirschfeld 2004. Modules are not usually specific spots in the brain; rather, they are defined by what they *do*. Craig and I reject the very demanding list of requirements for modularity proposed by Fodor 1983. Instead we embrace the "massive modularity" of Sperber 2005, which includes innate "learning modules" that generate many more specific modules during the course of childhood development. See Haidt and Joseph 2007, 2011.

31. In primates it's a bit more complicated. Primates are born not so much with an innate fear of snakes as with an innate "preparedness" to *learn* to fear snakes, after just one bad experience with a snake, or after merely seeing one other member of its species reacting with fear to a snake (Mineka and Cook 2008). They don't learn to fear flowers, or other objects to which another animal reacts with fear. The learning module is specific to snakes.

32. Sperber and Hirchfeld used the terms *proper domain* and *actual domain*, but many people (including me) find it hard to remember these terms, so I have swapped in *original triggers* and *current triggers*. The term *original trigger* is not meant to imply that there was once a time, long ago, when the module didn't make mistakes. I would use the term *intended trigger* except that evolutionary design has no intentions.

33. Natural selection is a design process; it is the cause of the design that abounds in the biological world. It is just not an intelligent or conscious designer. See Tooby and Cosmides 1992.

34. For more on the origins and details of the theory, see Haidt and Graham 2007; Haidt and Joseph 2004, 2007. The theory was strongly influenced by the work of Richard Shweder and Alan Fiske. Our choice of the five foundations is close to Shweder's three ethics. Our general approach of identifying evolved cognitive modules that get filled out in culturally variable ways was inspired by Alan Fiske's Relational Models Theory. See Rai and Fiske 2011 for the application of this theory to moral psychology.

35. For a recent list, see Neuberg, Kenrick, and Schaller 2010.

36. In our original article (Haidt and Joseph 2004), we described only four foundations, which we labeled Suffering, Hierarchy, Reciprocity, and Purity. We noted that there were probably many more, and we specifically noted "group-loyalty" in a footnote as a good candidate for a fifth. I am grateful to Jennifer Wright,

who had argued with me by email while I was working on that paper, that group loyalty is distinct from hierarchy, which is where Craig and I had put it originally. Beginning in 2005, we changed the names of the five foundations to use two related words for each one, in order to reduce the misunderstandings we were encountering. We used these names from 2005 to 2009: Harm/care, Fairness/reciprocity, In-group/loyalty, Authority/respect, and Purity/sanctity. In 2010 we reformulated the theory to expand it and fix shortcomings that I will describe in chapter 8. To avoid the confusion of talking about multiple names for the same foundations, I adopt the 2010 names here, when I describe the origins of the theory. For Authority, I have focused here on the psychology of the subordinate—the psychology of respect for authority. In the next chapter I'll explore the psychology of the superior leader as well.

37. See, for example, the "suite" of moral emotions that Trivers 1971 proposed as the mechanism behind reciprocal altruism (e.g., gratitude for favors received, indignation for favors not returned by the other person, guilt for favors not returned by the self.) For the Care foundation, for example, there might be one module that detects suffering, another for intentional infliction of harm, a third that detects kinship, and a fourth that detects efforts to care or comfort. The important point is that there is a set of innate "if-then" programs that work together to help people meet the adaptive challenge. Some of these innate modules may be innate as "learning modules," which generate more specific modules during childhood development, as described by Sperber. See Haidt and Joseph 2007 for a detailed discussion of moral modularity.

7. THE MORAL FOUNDATIONS OF POLITICS

1. E.g., Luce and Raiffa 1957.

2. Marcus 2004, p. 12.

3. Marcus 2004. I stitched this definition together from two pages. The first sentence is on p. 34, the second is on p. 40. But it's all part of a unified discussion in chapter 3.

4. It has recently been discovered that genetic kinship in hunter-gatherer groups is not nearly as high as anthropologists had long assumed (Hill et al. 2011). I assume, however, that this drop in relatedness came in the last few hundred thousand years, as our cultural complexity increased. I assume that the Care foundation had already been modified and intensified in the few million years before that, as our brain size and length of childhood increased.

5. Such as for tracking degree of kinship, or for distinguishing intentional from accidental harm so that you know when to get angry at someone who causes your child to cry. I repeat my note from the last chapter that these are not mod-

ules as Fodor 1983 originally defined them. Fodor's criteria were so stringent that pretty much nothing in higher cognition could qualify. For a discussion of how higher cognition can be partially modularized, see Haidt and Joseph 2007, and see Barrett and Kurzban 2006 on modules as functional systems rather than as spots in the brain.

6. Bowlby 1969.

7. See Sherman and Haidt 2011 for a review.

8. For a recent account of the evolution and neurology of empathy, see Decety 2011.

9. See Pinker 2011 on the long and steady rise of repugnance toward violence. For example, jokes about wife beating were common and acceptable in American movies and television programs up through the 1960s.

10. Sometimes a political bumper sticker will appeal to fear or monetary self-interest (e.g., "Drill here, drill now, pay less" for Republicans in 2008) but this is rare compared to moralistic appeals.

11. For non-American readers, I note again that by *liberal* I mean the political left. The data I'll show in the next chapter indicate that people on the left, in every country we have examined, score higher on the Care/harm foundation than do people on the political right.

12. Conservative Christians do send a great deal of money abroad, and do provide a great deal of help and relief to the poor, but it is generally done through missionary groups that strive to add converts to the group. It is still a form of parochial caring, not universalist caring.

13. It was a major concern for Darwin, in *Origin of Species* and in *Descent of Man*. I'll return to Darwin's puzzlement and his solutions in chapter 9.

14. Trivers 1971.

15. This point was demonstrated elegantly in Robert Axelrod's famous 1984 tournament in which strategies competed in an evolutionary simulation on a computer. No strategy was able to beat tit for tat. (But see Nowak 2010 for a discussion of his "Win Stay, Lose Shift" strategy, which is superior when you take account of errors and misperceptions.)

16. Rozin et al. 1999; Sanfey et al. 2003.

17. I visited just as this book was going to press. I published a photo essay in which I applied Moral Foundations Theory to the signs at Occupy Wall Street at http://reason.com/archives/2011/10/20/the-moral-foundations-of-occup.

18. I have argued that the moral motive of the Tea Partiers is primarily fairness as proportionality and karma. I do not believe it is liberty, as some libertarian groups have claimed. See Haidt 2010.

19. Sherif et al. 1961/1954, p. 94.

20. For example, boys spontaneously organize themselves for team competitions

far more often than do girls (Maccoby 1998), and male college students get more cooperative when a task is framed as an intergroup competition; female students are unaffected by the manipulation (Van Vugt, De Cremer, and Janssen 2007).

21. Baumeister and Sommer 1997; Maccoby 1998.

22. Boehm 2012; Goodall 1986.

23. Keeley 1996.

24. Glover 2000.

25. This verse is from Koran 4:56, translated by Arberry 1955. For more on killing apostates, see Koran 4:89, as well as many Hadith verses, e.g., Bukhari 52:260, Bukhari 84:58.

26. Scholars of liberalism often point this out (e.g., Gray 1995), and we find it in many studies on www.YourMorals.org; see Iyer et al. 2011.

27. Coulter 2003.

28. A point made forcefully by the sociologist Robert Nisbet 1993/1966 in his chapters 1 and 4.

29. Boehm 1999; de Waal 1996.

30. De Waal 1996, p. 92.

31. From a translation by L. W. King, retrieved from www.holyebooks.org/babylonia/the_code_of_hammurabi/hamo4.html.

32. This quote is from an overview of the theory on Fiske's website: www.sscnet.ucla.edu/anthro/faculty/fiske/relmodov.htm. For the full presentation of the theory, see Fiske 1991.

33. The evolutionary story is actually more complicated, and I'll address the important fact that humans went through a long period of egalitarianism in the next chapter. For now, I hope you'll simply entertain the possibility that we have some cognitive modules that make most people good at detecting and caring about hierarchy and respect.

34. De Waal 1996; Fiske 1991.

35. This is my explanation of why people low down in a hierarchy generally support the hierarchy. For more detail, see Haidt and Graham, 2009. For an alternative view see work on "system justification theory," e.g., Jost and Hunyady 2002.

36. Due to public outrage at the manslaughter sentence, the prosecutor's office appealed the sentence, won a retrial, and ultimately won a conviction for murder and a sentence of imprisonment for life. For a full account of this case, see Stampf 2008.

37. Rozin 1976 introduced this term; Michael Pollan then borrowed it as the title of his best-selling book.

38. McCrae 1996.

39. Rozin and Fallon 1987. We don't know when disgust arose, but we know that it

does not exist in any other animal. Other mammals reject foods based on their taste or smell, but only humans reject them based on what they have touched, or who handled them.

40. Schaller and Park 2011.

41. Thornhill, Fincher, and Aran 2009. Schaller's team has even demonstrated that they can increase Canadian students' fears of unfamiliar immigrants just by showing them images of disease and infection; students who saw images of other threats, such as electrocution, were less fearful (Faulkner et al. 2004).

42. I will address the evolutionary origins of sacralization and religion in chapters 9 and 11.

43. One might object that their actions were sure to disgust and offend people who learned about them. But that argument would commit you to prohibiting gay or interracial sex, or eating foods such as chicken feet and fish eyes, in the privacy of one's home, within communities that would be disgusted by such actions.

44. Libertarians, on average, experience less empathy and weaker disgust (Iyer et al., 2011), and they are more willing to allow people to violate taboos (Tetlock et al. 2000).

45. By the German-born painter Hans Memling, 1475. In the Musée Jacquemart-André, Paris. For information on this painting see http://www.ghc.edu/faculty/sandgren/sample2.pdf.

46. NRSV.

47. See D. Jensen 2008 as an example.

48. Kass 1997.

8. THE CONSERVATIVE ADVANTAGE

1. See Lakoff 2008 and Westen 2007 for a similar argument.

2. I equate Democrat with liberal and the left; I equate Republican with conservative and the right. That equation was not true before 1970, when both parties were broad coalitions, but since the 1980s, when the South changed its party allegiance from Democratic to Republican, the two parties have become sorted almost perfectly on the left-right axis. Data from the American National Election Survey shows this realignment clearly; the correlation of liberal-conservative self-identification with Democratic-Republican party identification has increased steadily since 1972, accelerating sharply in the 1990s (Abramowitz and Saunders 2008). Of course, not everyone fits neatly on this one-dimensional spectrum, and of those who do, most are somewhere in the middle, not near the extremes. But politics and policy are driven mostly by those who have strong partisan identities, and I focus in this chapter and in chapter 12 on understanding this kind of righteous mind.

3. Subjects in this study placed themselves on a scale from "strongly liberal" to

"strongly conservative," but I have changed "strongly" to "very" to match the wording used in Figure 8.2.

4. The longer and more accurate expansion of the shorthand is this: everyone can use any of the five foundations in some circumstances, but liberals like Care and Fairness best, and build their moral matrices mostly on those two foundations.

5. See report in Graham et al. 2011, Table 11, for data on the United States, United Kingdom, Canada, and Australia, plus the rest of the world aggregated into regions: Western Europe, Eastern Europe, Latin America, Africa, Middle East, South Asia, East Asia, and Southeast Asia. The basic pattern I've reported here holds in all of these countries and regions.

6. Four years later, in January 2011, I gave a talk at this conference urging the field to recognize the binding and blinding effects of shared ideology. The talk, and reactions to it, are collected at www.JonathanHaidt.com/postpartisan.html.

7. Wade 2007.

8. For people who say they are "very conservative" the lines actually cross, meaning that they value Loyalty, Authority, and Sanctity slightly more than Care and Fairness, at least if we go by the questions on the MFQ. The questions on this version of the MFQ are mostly different from those on the original version, shown in Figure 8.1, so it is difficult to compare the exact means across the two forms. What matters is that the slopes of the lines are similar across the various versions of the questionnaire, and in this one, with a much larger number of subjects, the lines become quite straight, indicating a simple linear effect of political ideology on each of the five foundations.

9. Linguistic Inquiry Word Count; Pennebaker, Francis, and Booth 2003.

10. Graham, Haidt, and Nosek 2009. I note that the first pass of simple word counts produced the predicted results for all foundations except for Loyalty. When we did a second pass, in which we had our research assistants read the words in context and then code whether a moral foundation was being supported or rejected, the differences between the two denominations got larger, and the predicted differences were found for all five foundations, including Loyalty.

11. We examined the N400 and the LPP components. See Graham 2010.

12. Speech of June 15, 2008, delivered at the Apostolic Church of God, Chicago, Illinois.

13. Speech of June 30, 2008, in Independence, Missouri.

14. Speech of July 14, 2008, to the NAACP, Cincinnati, Ohio.

15. Speech of July 24, 2008. He introduced himself as "a proud citizen of the United States, and a fellow citizen of the world." But conservative publications in the United States latched on to the "citizen of the world" part and did not quote the "proud citizen" part.

16. You can find the article here: www.edge.org/3rd_culture/haidt08/haidt08 _index.html. Brockman had recently become my literary agent.

17. See, for example, Adorno et al. 1950, and Jost et al. 2003. Lakoff 1996 offers a compatible analysis, although he does not present the conservative "strict father" morality as a pathology.

18. I learned to see the Durkheimian vision not just from reading Durkheim but from working with Richard Shweder and from living in India, as I described in chapter 5. I later discovered that much of the Durkheimian vision could be credited to the Irish philosopher Edmund Burke as well.

19. I want to emphasize that this analysis applies only to *social* conservatives. It does not apply to libertarians or to "laissez-faire" conservatives, also known as classical liberals. See chapter 12.

20. Of course, it's a lot easier in ethnically homogeneous nations with long histories and one language, such as the Nordic countries. This may be one reason those nations are far more liberal and secular than the United States. See further discussion in chapter 12.

21. It's interesting to note that Democrats have done much better in the U.S. Congress. Senators and congressmen are not priests. Legislation is a grubby and corrupt business in which the ability to bring money and jobs to one's district may count for more than one's ability to respect sacred symbols.

22. Bellah 1967.

23. Westen 2007, chapter 15, offered similar advice, also drawing on Durkheim's distinction between sacred and profane. I benefited from his analysis.

24. I present this and subsequent email messages verbatim, edited only for length and to protect the anonymity of the writer.

25. We had long gotten complaints from libertarians that the initial five foundations could not account for the morality of libertarians. After we completed a major study comparing libertarians to liberals and conservatives, we concluded that they were right (Iyer et al. 2011). Our decision to modify the list of moral foundations was also influenced by a "challenge" that we posted at www.MoralFoundations.org, asking people to criticize Moral Foundations Theory and propose additional foundations. Strong arguments came in for liberty. Additional candidates that we are still investigating include honesty, Property/ownership, and Waste/inefficiency. The sixth foundation, Liberty/ oppression, is provisional in that we are now in the process of developing multiple ways to measure concerns about liberty, and so we have not yet carried out the rigorous testing that went into our research on the original five foundations and the original MFQ. I describe the Liberty/oppression foundation here because I believe that the theoretical rationale for it is strong, and because we have already found that concerns about liberty are indeed the focal concerns of libertarians (Iyer et al. 2011), a substantial group that is largely overlooked

by political psychologists. But the empirical facts may prove otherwise. See www.MoralFoundations.org for updates on our research.

26. Boehm 1999.

27. Ibid. But see also the work of archaeologist Brian Hayden (2001), who finds that evidence of hierarchy and inequality often *precedes* the transition to agriculture by several thousand years as other technological innovations make it possible for "aggrandizers" to dominate production and also make it possible for groups to begin undertaking agriculture.

28. De Waal, 1996.

29. As described in de Waal 1982. Boehm 2012 tries to reconstruct a portrait of the last common ancestor of humans, chimpanzees, and bonobos. He concludes that the last common ancestor was more like the aggressive and territorial chimpanzee than like the more peaceful bonobo. Wrangham 2001 (and Wrangham and Pilbeam 2001) agrees, and suggests that bonobos and humans share many features because they might have both gone through a similar process of "self-domestication," which made both species more peaceful and playful by making both retain more childlike features into adulthood. But nobody knows for sure, and de Waal and Lanting 1997 suggests that the last common ancestor might have been more similar to the bonobo than to the chimp, although this paper too notes that bonobos are more neotonous (childlike) than chimps.

30. In chapter 9 I'll explain why the best candidate for this shift is *Homo heidelbergensis,* which first appears around seven or eight hundred thousand years ago, and then begins to master important new technologies such as fire and spear making.

31. Dunbar 1996.

32. De Waal 1996 argues that chimpanzees have a rudimentary ability to learn behavioral norms and then react to norm violators. As with so much else about comparisons between humans and chimps, there are hints of many advanced human abilities, yet norms don't seem to grow and build on one another and envelop everyone. De Waal says clearly that he does not believe chimpanzees have morality. I think we can't really speak about true "moral communities" until after *Homo heidelbergensis*, as I'll explain in the next chapter.

33. Lee 1979, quoted in Boehm 1999, p. 180.

34. The term may have first been used in an 1852 *New York Times* article about Marx, but Marx and Marxists soon embraced the term, and it shows up in Marx's 1875 *Critique of the Gotha Program.*

35. Brehm and Brehm 1981.

36. The question of free riders naturally arises; see Dawkins 1976. Wouldn't the best strategy be to hang back and let others risk their lives standing up to dangerous bullies? The free rider problem is quite pressing for species that

lack language, norms, and moralistic punishment. But as I'll show in the next chapter, its importance has been greatly overstated for humans. *Morality is, in large part, an evolved solution to the free rider problem.* Hunter-gatherer groups and also larger tribes can compel members to work and sacrifice for the group by punishing free riders; see Mathew and Boyd 2011.

37. Leaders often emerge in the struggle against tyranny, only to become tyrants themselves. As the rock band The Who famously put it: "Meet the new boss. Same as the old boss."

38. I thank Melody Dickson for permission to reprint from her email. All other quotations longer than one sentence from emails and blog posts in this chapter are used with permission of the authors, who chose to remain anonymous.

39. This was a reference to the Boston Tea Party of 1773, one of the first major acts of rebellion by the American colonists against Great Britain.

40. Hammerstein 2003.

41. I'm guilty of spreading this myth, in *The Happiness Hypothesis.* I was referring to work by Wilkinson 1984. But it turns out that Wilkinson's bats were probably close kin. See Hammerstein 2003.

42. See a review in S. F. Brosnan 2006. In the main experimental study documenting fairness concerns in capuchins (S. F. Brosnan and de Waal 2003), the monkeys failed the main control condition: they got upset whenever they saw a grape that they did not have, whether the grape was given to the other monkey or not. My own view is that Brosnan and de Waal are probably right; chimps and capuchins do keep track of favors and slights, and do have a primitive sense of fairness. But they don't live in moral matrices. In the absence of clear norms and gossip, they don't show this sense of fairness consistently in lab situations.

43. Trivers did discuss "moralistic reciprocity," but this is a very different process from reciprocal altruism. See Richerson and Boyd 2005, chapter 6.

44. Mathew and Boyd 2011.

45. Fehr and Gächter 2002.

46. Fehr and Gächter also ran a version of this study that was identical except that punishment was available in the first six rounds and taken away in the seventh round. The results were the same: high and rising levels of cooperation in the first six rounds, which plummeted at round 7 and declined from then on.

47. A PET study by de Quervain et al. 2004 found that reward areas of the brain were more active when people had a chance to inflict altruistic punishment. I should note that Carlsmith, Wilson, and Gilbert 2008 found that the pleasure of revenge is sometimes an "affective forecasting" error; revenge is often not as sweet as we expect. But whether they feel better or not afterward, the important point is that people *want* to punish when they are cheated.

48. This is Boehm's thesis, and I see confirmation of it in the fact that the left has

not been able to get the rest of the country upset by the extraordinary rise in American inequality since 1980. Finally, in 2011, the Occupy Wall Street protests have begun to move beyond simply pointing to the inequality, and have begun to make claims based on the Fairness/cheating foundation (about how the "1 percent" cheated to get to the top, and about how they "owe" us for the bailout we gave them), and also on the Liberty/oppression foundation (about how the 1 percent has seized control of the government and abuses its power to harm or enslave the 99 percent). But simply pointing to inequality, without also showing cheating or oppression, does not seem to trigger much outrage.

49. In factor and cluster analyses of our data at YourMorals.org, we repeatedly find that questions about equality go with questions about care, harm, and compassion (the Care foundation), not with questions about proportionality.

50. See the large body of research in social psychology called "equity theory," whose central axiom is that the ratio of net gains (outcome minus inputs) to inputs must be equal for all participants (Walster, Walster, and Berscheid 1978). That's a definition of proportionality.

51. Children generally like equality, until they near puberty, but as their social intelligence matures they stop being rigid egalitarians and start becoming proportionalists; see Almas et al. 2010.

52. Cosmides and Tooby 2005.

53. Our goal with Moral Foundations Theory and YourMorals.org has been to find the *best* bridges between anthropology and evolutionary psychology, not the complete set of bridges. We think the six we have identified are the most important ones, and we find that we can explain most moral and political controversies using these six. But there are surely additional innate modules that give rise to additional moral intuitions. Other candidates we are investigating include intuitions about honesty, ownership, self-control, and waste. See MoralFoundations.org to learn about our research on additional moral foundations.

54. If you see a child in pain, you feel compassion. It's like a drop of lemon juice on the tongue. I am arguing that witnessing inequality is not like this. It rankles us only when we perceive that the person is suffering (Care/harm), being oppressed by a bully (Liberty/oppression), or being cheated (Fairness/cheating). For an argument against me and in favor of equality as a basic foundation, see Rai and Fiske 2011.

55. You can see this finding across multiple surveys in Iyer et al. 2011.

56. Berlin 1997/1958 referred to this kind of liberty as "negative liberty"—the right to be left alone. He pointed out that the left had developed a new concept of "positive liberty" during the twentieth century—a conception of the rights and resources that people needed in order to enjoy liberty.

57. In a poll released October 26, 2004, the Pew Research Center found that small business owners favored Bush (56 percent) over Kerry (37 percent). A slight shift leftward in 2008 ended by 2010. See summary on HuffingtonPost.com by searching for "Small business polls: Dems get pummeled."

58. This was our empirical finding in Iyer et al. 2011, which can be printed from www.MoralFoundations.org.

59. Unpublished data, YourMorals.org. You can take this survey by going to Your Morals.org and then taking the MFQ version B. Also, see our discussions of our data on fairness on the YourMorals blog.

60. Bar and Zussman 2011.

61. Frank 2004.

9. WHY ARE WE SO GROUPISH?

1. In the social sciences and humanities, conservatives went from being merely underrepresented in the decades after World War II to being nearly extinct by the 1990s except in economics. One of the main causes of this change was that professors from the "greatest generation," which fought WWII and was not so highly polarized, were gradually replaced by more politically polarized baby boomers beginning in the 1980s (Rothman, Lichter, and Nevitte 2005).

2. This is a reference to Glaucon in Plato's *Republic*, who asks whether a man would behave well if he owned the ring of Gyges, which makes its wearer invisible and therefore free from concerns about reputation. See chapter 4.

3. As Dawkins 1976 so memorably put it. Genes can only code for traits that end up making more copies of those genes. Dawkins did not mean that selfish genes make thoroughly selfish people.

4. Of course we are groupish in the minimal sense that we like groups, we are drawn to groups. Every animal that lives in herds, flocks, or schools is groupish in that sense. I mean to say far more than this. We care about our groups and want to promote our group's interests, even at some cost to ourselves. This is not usually true about animals that live in herds and flocks (Williams 1966).

5. I don't doubt that there is a fair bit of Glauconianism going on when people put on displays of patriotism and other forms of group loyalty. I am simply asserting that our team spirit is not purely Glauconian. We sometimes do treat our groups as sacred, and would not betray them even if we could be assured of a large material reward and perfect secrecy for our betrayal.

6. See Dawkins 1999/1982, and also see Dawkins's use of the word *heresy* in Dicks 2000.

7. This is called *mutualism*—when two or more animals cooperate and all of them get some benefit from the interaction. It is not a form of altruism; it is not a puzzle for evolutionary theory. Mutualism may have been extremely

important in the early phases of the evolution of humanity's ultrasociality; see Baumard, André, and Sperber, unpublished; Tomasello et al., forthcoming.

8. I will focus on cooperation in this chapter, rather than altruism. But I am most interested in cooperation in these sorts of cases, in which a truly self-interested Glauconian would not cooperate. We might therefore call these focal cases "altruistic cooperation" to distinguish them from the sort of strategic cooperation that is so easy to explain by natural selection acting at the individual level.

9. Part I, chapter 4, p. 134; emphasis added. Dawkins 2006 does not consider this to be a case of true group selection because Darwin did not imagine the tribe growing and then splitting into "daughter tribes" the way a beehive splits into daughter hives. But if we add that detail (which is typically true in hunter-gatherer societies that tend to split when they grow larger than around 150 adults), then this would, by all accounts, be an example of group selection. Okasha 2005 calls this kind MLS-2, in contrast to the less demanding MLS-1, which he thinks is more common early in the process of a major transition. More on this below.

10. *Descent of Man,* chapter 5, p. 135; emphasis added. The free rider problem is the *only* objection that Dawkins raises against group selection in *The God Delusion,* chapter 5.

11. Price 1972.

12. I note that the old idea that there were genes "for" traits has fared poorly in the genomic age. There are not single genes, or even groups of dozens of genes, that can explain much of the variance in any psychological trait. Yet somehow, nearly every psychological trait is heritable. I will sometimes speak of a gene "for" a trait, but this is just a convenience. What I really mean is that the genome as a whole codes for certain traits, and natural selection alters the genome so that it codes for different traits.

13. I emphasize that group selection or colony-level selection as I have described it here is perfectly compatible with inclusive fitness theory (Hamilton 1964) and with Dawkins's "selfish gene" perspective. But people who work with bees, ants, and other highly social creatures sometimes say that multilevel selection helps them see phenomena that are less visible when they take the gene's-eye view; see Seeley 1997.

14. I'm oversimplifying here; species of bees, ants, wasps, and termites vary in the degree to which they have achieved the status of superorganisms. Self-interest is rarely reduced to absolute zero, particularly in bees and wasps, which retain the ability to breed under some circumstances. See Hölldobler and Wilson 2009.

15. I thank Steven Pinker for pointing this out to me, in a critique of an early version of this chapter. Pinker noted that war in pre-state societies is nothing

like our modern image of men marching off to die for a cause. There's a lot of posturing, a lot of Glauconian behavior going on as warriors strive to burnish their reputations. Suicide terrorism occurs only rarely in human history; see Pape 2005, who notes that such incidents occur almost exclusively in situations where a group is defending its sacred homeland from culturally alien invaders. See also Atran 2010 on the role of sacred values in suicide terrorism.

16. *Descent of Man*, chapter 5, p. 135.

17. See in particular Miller 2007, on how sexual selection contributed to the evolution of morality. People go to great lengths to advertise their virtues to potential mates.

18. *Descent of Man*, Part I, chapter 5, p.137. See Richerson and Boyd 2004, who make the case that Darwin basically got it right.

19. Wynne-Edwards 1962.

20. Williams 1966, p. 4.

21. Williams (ibid., pp. 8–9) defined an adaptation as a biological mechanism that produces at least one effect that can properly be called its goal.

22. Williams wrote about a "fleet herd of deer," but I have substituted the word *fast* for the less common word *fleet*.

23. Williams 1966, pp. 92–93.

24. Ibid., p. 93.

25. Walster, Walster, and Berscheid 1978, p. 6.

26. I agree that genes are always "selfish," and all parties to these debates agree that selfish genes can make strategically generous people. The debate is over whether human nature includes *any* mental mechanisms that make people put the good of the group ahead of their own interests, and if so, whether such mechanisms count as group-level adaptations.

27. This turns out not to be true. In a survey of thirty-two hunter-gatherer societies, Hill et al. 2011 found that for any target individual, only about 10 percent of his or her fellow group mates were close kin. The majority had no blood relationship. Hamilton's coefficient of genetic relatedness among the Ache was a mere 0.054. This is a problem for theories that try to explain human cooperation by kin selection.

28. Williams 1988, p. 438.

29. Dawkins 1976, p. 3. In his introduction to the thirtieth-anniversary edition, Dawkins regrets his choice of words, because selfish genes can and do cooperate with each other, and they can and do make vehicles such as people who can cooperate with each other. But his current views still seem incompatible with the sort of groupishness and team-spiritedness that I describe in this chapter and the next.

30. Primatologists have long reported acts that appear to be altruistic during their

observations of unconstrained interactions in several primate species, but until recently nobody was able to show altruism in a controlled lab setting in the chimpanzee. There is now one study (Horner et al. 2011) showing that chimps will choose the option that brings greater benefit to a partner at no cost to themselves. Chimps are aware that they can produce a benefit, and they choose to do so. But because this choice imposes no cost on the chooser, it fails to meet many definitions of altruism. I believe the anecdotes about chimp altruism, but I stand by my claim that humans are the "giraffes" of altruism. Even if chimps and other primates can do it a little bit, we do it vastly more.

31. I did not like George W. Bush at any point during his presidency, but I did trust that his vigorous response to the attacks, including the U.S. invasion of Afghanistan, was the right one. Of course, leaders can easily exploit the rally-round-the-flag response for their own ends, as many believe happened with the subsequent invasion of Iraq. See Clarke 2004.

32. The reflex doesn't require a flag; it refers to the reflex to come together and show signs of group solidarity in response to an external threat. For reviews of the literature on this effect, see Dion 1979; Kesebir, forthcoming.

33. The leading spokesmen for this view are David Sloan Wilson, Elliot Sober, Edward O. Wilson, and Michael Wade. For technical reviews, see Sober and D. S. Wilson 1998; D. S. Wilson and E. O. Wilson 2007. For an accessible introduction, see D. S. Wilson and E. O. Wilson 2008.

34. Racism, genocide, and suicide bombing are all manifestations of groupishness. They are not things that people do in order to outcompete their local peers; they are things people do to help their groups outcompete other groups. For evidence that rates of violence are vastly lower in civilized societies than among hunter-gatherers, see Pinker 2011. Pinker explains how increasingly strong states plus the spread of capitalism have led to ever decreasing levels of violence, even when you include the wars and genocides of the twentieth century. (The trend is not perfectly linear—individual nations can experience some regressions. But the overall trend of violence is steadily downward.)

35. Margulis 1970. In plant cells, chloroplasts also have their own DNA.

36. Maynard Smith and Szathmary 1997; Bourke 2011.

37. There is an important flaw in my "boat race" analogy: the new vehicles don't really "win" the race. Prokaryotes are still quite successful; they still represent most of the life on earth by weight and by number. But still, new vehicles seem to come out of nowhere and then claim a substantial portion of the earth's available bio-energy.

38. Maynard Smith and Szathmáry attribute the human transition to language, and suggest that the transition occurred around 40,000 years ago. Bourke 2011 offers an up-to-date discussion. He identifies six major *kinds* of transitions,

and notes that several of them have occurred dozens of times independently, e.g., the transition to eusociality.

39. Hölldobler and Wilson 2009. Many theorists prefer terms other than *super-organism*. Bourke 2011, for example, calls them simply "individuals."

40. Okasha 2006 calls this MLS-2. I'll call it *selection among stable groups* in contrast to MLS-1, which I'll call *selection among shifting groups*. This is a subtle distinction that is crucial in discussions among specialists who debate whether group selection has actually occurred. It is too subtle to explain in the main text, but the general idea is this: For selection among stable groups, we focus on the group as an entity, and we track its fitness as it competes with other groups. For this kind of selection to matter, groups must maintain strong boundaries with a high degree of genetic relatedness inside each group over many generations. Hunter-gatherer groups as we know them today do not do this; individuals come and go, through marriage or for other reasons. (Although, as I point out below, the ways of current hunter-gatherers cannot be taken to be the ways that our ancestors lived 100,000 years ago, or even 30,000 years ago.) In contrast, for selection among shifting groups to affect gene frequencies, all that is needed is that the social environment be composed of multiple kinds of groups which compete with each other, perhaps just for a few days or months. We focus not on the fitness of the groups, but on the fitness of individuals who either have, or lack, group-related adaptations. Individuals whose minds contain effective group-related adaptations end up playing on the winning team more often—at least if the population structure is somewhat lumpy or uneven, such that groupish individuals have a better than chance likelihood of finding themselves on the same team. Some critics say that this is not "real" group selection, or that it ends up being the same thing as individual-level selection, but Okasha disagrees. He points out that selection among shifting groups happens early in the process of a major transition, and it leads to adaptations that increase cohesiveness and suppress free riding, which then pave the way for selection among stable groups to operate in the later stages of a major transition. Some have argued that human beings are "stalled" midway through the major transition process (Stearns 2007). I think that's another way of saying that we are 90 percent chimp and 10 percent bee. For a full explanation of MLS-1 and MLS-2, see Okasha 2006 chapters 2 and 6.

41. I do not mean to imply that there is an overall or inevitable progression of life toward ever greater complexity and cooperation. Multilevel selection means that there are always antagonistic selection forces operating at different levels. Sometimes species revert from superorganisms to more solitary forms. But a world with bees, ants, wasps, termites, and humans in it has many more tons of cooperative individuals than did the world of 200 million years ago.

42. Bourke 2011; Hölldobler and Wilson 2009.

43. Hölldobler and Wilson 2009; E. O. Wilson 1990. I note that the new super-organisms don't shoot up to dominance right away after the free rider problem is addressed. Superorganisms go through a period of refinement until they begin to take maximum advantage of their new cooperation, which gets improved by group-level selection as they compete with other superorganisms. The eusocial hymenoptera first emerged more than 100 million years ago, but they didn't reach a state of world domination until closer to 50 million years ago. Same story, perhaps, for humans, who probably developed fully groupish minds in the late Pleistocene, but didn't achieve world dominance until the late Holocene.

44. Richerson and Boyd 1998.

45. The term *eusociality* arose for work with insects, and it is defined in a way that cannot apply to humans—i.e., it requires that members divide reproduction so that nearly all group members are effectively sterile. I therefore use the more general term *ultrasocial*, which encompasses the behavior of eusocial insects as well as of human beings.

46. Hölldobler and Wilson 2009, p. 30; emphasis added. The text I replaced with the bracketed text was "clades whose extant species."

47. Wilson and Hölldobler 2005, p. 13370.

48. Humans are just as closely related to the more peaceful bonobo as to the more violent chimpanzee. But I follow Boehm (2012) and Wrangham (2001; Wrangham and Pilbeam, 2001) in assuming that the last common ancestor of the three species was more chimplike, and that the features humans share with bonobos such as greater peacefulness and adult playfulness are the result of convergent evolution—both species changed in a similar direction long after the split with the common ancestor. Both changed to become more childlike as adults. See Wobber, Wrangham, and Hare 2010.

49. I am not saying that human brains or genes changed radically at this time. I follow Richerson and Boyd 2005 and Tooby and Cosmides 1992 in assuming that most of the genes that made life in city-states possible were shaped during hundreds of thousands of years of hunter-gatherer life. But as I'll say below, I think it's likely that there was *some* additional genetic evolution during the Holocene.

50. We're not literally a majority of the world's mammalian weight, but that's only because we raise so many cows, pigs, sheep, and dogs. If you include us together with our domesticated servants, our civilizations now account for an astonishing 98 percent of all mammalian life, by weight, according to a statement by Donald Johanson, made at a conference on "Origins" at Arizona State University in April 2009.

51. Critics of group selection add the criterion that the groups must reproduce

themselves, including "budding off" to form multiple new groups that closely resemble the original group. This is true for MLS-2 (selection among stable groups), but is not necessary for MLS-1 (selection among shifting groups); see Okasha 2006, and see note 40 above.

52. Tomasello gave three major lectures at UVA in October 2010. His basic argument, including a quote like this one, can be found in Tomasello et al. 2005. Chimpanzees can recruit a collaborator to help them get food in a task that requires two chimps to get any food (Melis, Hare, and Tomasello 2006) but they don't seem to be sharing intentions or truly coordinating with that collaborator.

53. Herrmann et al. 2007. The full descriptions of the tasks, including videos, can be downloaded at http://www.sciencemag.org/content/317/5843/1360/suppl/ DC1, but note that the videos always show chimps solving the tasks, even though they rarely did so on the social tasks. Note also that the experiment included a third group—orangutans, who fared worse than the chimps at both kinds of tasks.

54. Tomasello et al. 2005. Tomasello cites earlier work by autism researcher Simon Baron-Cohen (1995), who described a "shared attention mechanism" that develops in normal children, but not in children with autism, which leaves them "mind-blind."

55. Boesch 1994.

56. Tomasello et al., forthcoming. It is clear that chimps form political coalitions— two males will team up to oppose the current alpha male, as documented by de Waal 1982. But the *coordination* here is weak at best.

57. De Waal 1996 argues that chimpanzee communities develop norms and administer punishment to norm violators. However, examples of such norms among chimps are rare, and chimps certainly don't build up increasingly elabo- rate networks of norms over time. As with so much else about chimps, such as their cultural abilities, they seem to have many of the "building blocks" of human morality, but they don't seem to put them together to build moral systems.

58. A major topic of debate in evolutionary circles is why any individual would pay the costs of punishing another, which might include a violent reaction from the individual being punished. But if the punishment is very low cost—e.g., gossiping, or simply not choosing the transgressor for joint ventures (Bau- mard, André, and Sperber, unpublished)—then the cost becomes quite small, and computer models show various ways in which a tendency to punish could emerge; see Panchanathan and Boyd 2004. As the cost of free riding increases and it becomes increasingly rare, group-level selection on many other traits becomes increasingly powerful, compared to individual-level selection.

59. For more on cumulative culture and gene-culture coevolution, see Richerson

and Boyd's masterpiece *Not by Genes Alone*. I am heavily indebted to them for many ideas in this chapter.

60. It is likely that these creatures made some tools. Even chimpanzees make some tools. But there's not much evidence of tool use in the fossil record until the end of this period, nearing the emergence of the genus *Homo*.

61. Lepre et al. 2011.

62. Richerson and Boyd 2005 makes this point. Cultural artifacts almost never show such stability across time and space. Think, for example, about swords and teapots, which fill museum cases because cultures are so inventive in the ways they create objects that fulfill the same basic functions.

63. My account of *Homo heidelbergensis* is drawn from Potts and Sloan 2010 and from Richerson and Boyd 2005, chapter 4.

64. My account is speculative; it's always hazardous to guess when a specific event occurred or a specific ability emerged. Tomasello, who is more cautious than I am, has never identified a time or a species in which shared intentionality first emerged. But when I asked him if *Homo heidelbergensis* was the best candidate, he said yes.

65. There are two major differences: (1) cultural innovations spread laterally, as people see and then copy an innovation; genetic innovations can only spread vertically, from parent to child, and (2) cultural innovations can be driven by intelligent designers—people who are trying to solve a problem; genetic innovation happens only by random mutation. See Richerson and Boyd 2005. Dawkins 1976 first popularized the notion of cultural evolution being like genetic evolution with his notion of "memes," but Richerson and Boyd developed the coevolutionary implications more fully.

66. Tishkoff et al. 2007. Interestingly, it's a different gene in African populations than in Europeans. The genome is so flexible and adaptive that it often finds multiple ways to respond to a single adaptive pressure.

67. One might argue that modern industrial societies are cosmopolitan and not tribal. But our tendency to form groups within such societies has been linked to the basic social nature of tribalism; see Dunbar 1996. At the other extreme, hunter-gatherers are not just small bands of close kin, as many people suppose. People move in and out of co-residing groups for marriage and for other reasons. Bands maintain close ties of trade and exchange with other bands that are not based on kinship directly, although they may be facilitated by the fact that children of one band so often marry out, joining neighboring bands, while maintaining ties with parents and siblings. Marital exchanges bind *groups* together, well beyond the individual families involved in the marriage. See Hill et al. 2011.

68. Colored powders and pigments have been found at human campsites dating

back as far as 160,000 years ago, and they are thought to have been used for symbolic and ceremonial purposes; see Marean et al. 2007.

69. Kinzler, Dupoux, and Spelke 2007; see Kesebir, forthcoming, for a review.

70. Richerson and Boyd 2005, p. 214. See also Fessler 2007 on how shame evolved from an emotion of submission to authority into an emotion of conformity to norms.

71. Hare, Wobber, and Wrangham, unpublished; Wrangham 2001. Self-domestication (sometimes called autodomestication) is a form of the more general process known as social selection, in which selection results from the choices made by members of one's own species.

72. Hare, Wobber, and Wrangham, unpublished.

73. By saying that our older primate nature is more selfish, I do not mean to contradict Frans de Waal's work showing the presence of empathy and other building blocks of the human moral sense in chimpanzees and bonobos. I mean only that these building blocks are all easily explained as mechanisms that helped individuals prosper within groups. I don't think you need group selection to explain chimpanzee nature, but I think you need it to explain human nature. De Waal (2006) criticizes "veneer theorists" who think that morality is a thin veneer covering our true nature, which is selfish. I am not a veneer theorist in that sense. However, I am a veneer theorist in suggesting that we humans have some recent adaptations, shaped by group-level selection, that evolved out of our older primate nature but that makes us very different from other primates.

74. See Bourke 2011, pp. 3–4.

75. Other than two species of African mole rats, which are the only mammals that qualify as eusocial. The mole rats achieve their eusociality in the same way as bees and ants—by suppressing breeding in all except for a single breeding couple, such that all members of the colony are very close kin. Also, because they dig extensive underground tunnels, they have a shared defensible nest.

76. Some *Homo sapiens* had left Africa by 70,000 years ago, and were living in and around Israel. During this time there seems to have been some interbreeding with Neanderthals (Green et al. 2010). Some humans may have left Africa between 70,000 and 60,000 years ago and traveled through Yemen and South Asia to become the ancestors of people in New Guinea and Australia. But the group that left Africa and Israel around 50,000 years ago is the group that is believed to have populated Eurasia and the Americas. I therefore use 50,000 years ago as the date for the great dispersion, even though some people had already left in the 20,000 years before that. See Potts and Sloan 2010.

77. Gould in an interview in *Leader to Leader Journal* 15 (Winter 2000). Available at http://www.pfdf.org/knowledgecenter/journal.aspx?ArticleID=64. Emphasis added.

78. This is known as Lamarckism. Darwin believed it too, erroneously. Lamarckism was helpful to a dictatorship bent on producing a new breed of human being, Soviet Man. Trofim Lysenko was the preferred biologist, rather than Mendel.

79. Trut 1999.

80. Muir 1996.

81. See Hawks et al. 2007; Williamson et al. 2007. The short explanation is that you examine the degree to which each gene tends to pull neighboring DNA along with it as it goes through the chromosomal shuffle of meiosis. If it's just random drift, then neighboring nucleotides don't get dragged along.

82. Richerson and Boyd 2005 note that when environments change rapidly, such as every few millennia, the genes don't respond; all adaptation is done by cultural innovation. But they formulated their theory back when everyone thought genetic evolution required tens or hundreds of thousands of years. Now that we know that genes can respond within a single millennium, I think my statement here is accurate.

83. Yi et al. 2010.

84. Pickrell et al. 2009.

85. See e.g., Clark 2007.

86. Some readers may fear, as perhaps Gould did, that if genetic evolution continued during the last 50,000 years, then there could be genetic differences among the races. I think such concerns are valid but overstated. There were few selection pressures that ever applied to all Europeans, or all Africans, or all Asians. Continent-wide races are not the relevant units of analysis for the evolution of morality. Rather, there were many selection pressures facing each group that moved into a new ecological niche, or that took up a new way of making a living, or that developed a particular way of regulating marriages. Furthermore, when gene-culture coevolution favored certain traits, these traits were usually adaptations to some challenge or other, so differences among groups do not imply defects. And finally, even if there do turn out to be ethnic differences in moral behavior that are related to genetic differences, the genetic contribution to such behavioral differences would likely be tiny compared to the effects of culture. Anyone could have made up a just-so story in 1945 to explain how Germans evolved to be so well suited to militaristic conquest while Ashkenazi Jews evolved to be meek and pacifistic. But fifty years later, comparing Israel to Germany, they'd have to explain the opposite behavioral pattern. (I thank Steven Pinker for this example.)

87. Potts and Sloan 2010. See also Richerson and Boyd 2005 for a theory about how an earlier period of climatic instability may have driven the first jump in humanity's transformation into cultural creatures, around 500,000 years ago.

88. Ambrose 1998. Whether or not this specific volcanic eruption changed the course of human evolution, I'm trying to make the larger point that evolution is not a smooth and gradual process, as is assumed in most computer simulations. There were probably many "black swan" events, the highly improbable events described by Taleb (2007) that disrupt our efforts to model processes with just a few variables and some assumptions based on "normal" conditions.

89. Potts and Sloan 2010.

90. The latter part of this period is when the archaeological record begins to show clear signs of decorated objects, beads, symbolic and quasi-religious activities, and tribal behavior more generally. See Henshilwood et al. 2004 on findings from Blombos Cave in South Africa, circa 75,000 years ago. See also Kelly 1995; Tomasello et al., forthcoming; Wade 2009. Something really interesting was going on in Africa between 70,000 and 80,000 years ago.

91. For an attempt to explain human groupishness without invoking group selection, see Tooby and Cosmides 2010. See also Henrich and Henrich 2007; they allow for cultural group selection, but with no genetic effects. I think these approaches can explain much of our groupishness, but I don't think they can explain things like the hive switch, which I describe in the next chapter.

92. These issues are all complicated, and as a social psychologist I am not an expert in any of the four areas I have reviewed. So it may be more accurate to describe my presentation not as a defense in a legal trial, but as an appellate brief to the high court of science explaining why I think the case should be reopened and retried by the experts, in light of the new evidence.

93. The numbers 90 percent and 10 percent should not be taken literally. I am just trying to say that most of human nature was forged by the same sorts of individual-level processes that forged chimpanzee nature, while a substantially smaller portion of human nature was forged by group-level selection, which is a process more commonly associated with bees, ants, and other eusocial creatures. Of course the psychology of bees has nothing in common with human psychology—they achieve their extraordinary cooperation without anything like morality or the moral emotions. I'm merely using bees as an illustration of how group-level selection creates team players.

10. THE HIVE SWITCH

1. McNeill 1995, p. 2.

2. J. G. Gray 1970/1959, pp. 44–47. The quotes are from Gray himself, speaking as a veteran across several pages. The quotes were assembled in this way by McNeill 1995, p. 10.

3. See chapter 4. I repeat that Glaucon himself was not a Glauconian; he was Plato's brother, and in *The Republic* he wants Socrates to succeed. But he for-

mulated the argument so clearly—that people freed from all reputational consequences tend to behave abominably—that I use him as a spokesman for this view, which I believe is correct.

4. G. C. Williams 1966, pp. 92–93; see discussion of Williams in the previous chapter.

5. I first developed this argument in Haidt, Seder, and Kesebir 2008, where I explored the implications of hive psychology for positive psychology and public policy.

6. My use of the word *should* in this sentence is purely pragmatic, not normative. I'm saying that if you want to achieve X, then you should know about this hive stuff when you make your plan for achieving X. I'm not trying to tell people what X is.

7. This idea was developed earlier by Freeman 1995 and by McNeill 1995.

8. The acronym and the concept come from Henrich, Heine, and Norenzayan 2010.

9. Ehrenreich 2006, p. 14.

10. Durkheim 1992/1887, p. 220.

11. As described in chapter 9; on "social selection," see Boehm 2012.

12. Durkheim 1992/1887, pp. 219–20; emphasis added.

13. Durkheim 1995/1915, p. 217.

14. Durkheim 1995/1915, p. 424.

15. Emerson 1960/1838, p. 24.

16. From Darwin's autobiography, quoted in Wright 1994, p. 364.

17. Keltner and Haidt 2003.

18. For a cautious and often critical review of the wild claims sometimes made about mushrooms and human history, see Lechter 2007. Lechter says that the evidence for mushroom use among the Aztecs is extremely strong.

19. See the extensive library of drug experiences at www.Erowid.org. For each of the hallucinogens there are many accounts of mystical experiences and many of bad or terrifying trips.

20. For an example and analysis of initiation rites, see Herdt 1981.

21. Grob and de Rios 1994.

22. See in particular Appendix B in Maslow 1964. Maslow lists twenty-five features, including: "The whole universe is perceived as an integrated and unified whole"; "The world . . . is seen only as beautiful"; "The peak-experiencer becomes more loving and more accepting."

23. Pahnke 1966.

24. Doblin 1991. Only one of the control subjects said that the experiment had resulted in beneficial growth, and that, ironically, was because it convinced the subject to try psychedelic drugs as soon as possible. Doblin's study adds

an important note that was not reported in Pahnke's original study: most of the psilocybin subjects experienced some fear and negativity along the way, although all said that the experience overall was highly positive.

25. Hsieh 2010, p. 79; emphasis added.

26. There are two other candidates that I won't cover because there is far less research on them. V. S. Ramachandran has identified a spot in the left temporal lobe that, when stimulated electrically, sometimes gives people religious experiences; see Ramachandran and Blakeslee 1998. And Newberg, D'Aquili, and Rause 2001 studied the brains of people who achieve altered states of consciousness via meditation. The researchers found a reduction in activity in two areas of the parietal cortex that the brain uses to maintain a mental map of the body in space. When those areas are quieter, the person experiences a pleasurable loss of self.

27. My goal is not to present a full account of the neurobiology of the hive switch. It is simply to point out that there is a great deal of convergence between my functional description of the hive switch and two of the hottest areas of social neuroscience—oxytocin and mirror neurons. I hope that experts in neuroscience will look more closely at how the brain and body respond to the kind of groupish and synchronous activities I'm describing. For more on the neurobiology of ritual and synchrony, see Thomson 2011.

28. Carter 1998.

29. Kosfeld et al. 2005.

30. Zak 2011 describes the biology of the system in some detail. Of particular note, oxytocin causes group bonding and altruism in part by working through two additional neurotransmitters: dopamine, which motivates action and makes it rewarding, and serotonin, which reduces anxiety and makes people more sociable—common effects of Prozac-like drugs that raise serotonin levels.

31. Morhenn et al. 2008, although back rubs in this study only increased oxytocin levels when the back rub was paired with a sign of trust. Physical touch has a variety of bonding effects; see Keltner 2009.

32. *Parochial* means local or restricted, as if within the borders of a church parish. The concept of parochial altruism has been developed by Sam Bowles and others, e.g., Choi and Bowles 2007.

33. De Dreu et al. 2010.

34. De Dreu et al. 2011; quote is from p. 1264.

35. The initial report of this work was Iacoboni et al. 1999. For a recent overview, see Iacoboni 2008.

36. Tomasello et al. 2005; see chapter 9.

37. Iacoboni 2008, p. 119.

38. T. Singer et al. 2006. The game was a repeated prisoner's dilemma.

39. The findings were that men showed a big drop in empathy, and on average they showed activation in neural circuits associated with reward as well. They liked seeing the selfish player get shocked. Women showed only a small drop in empathic responding. This drop was not statistically significant, but I think it is very likely that women are able to cut off their empathy under *some* circumstances. With a larger sample size, or a more serious offense, I would bet that women would show a statistically significant drop in empathy as well.

40. Of course in this case the "bad" player directly cheated the subject, so some subjects felt anger. The key test, which has not yet been done, will be to see if empathic responding drops toward a "bad" player whom the subject merely observed cheating another person, not the subject. I predict that empathy will drop there too.

41. Kyd 1794, p. 13; emphasis added.

42. Burns 1978.

43. Kaiser, Hogan, and Craig 2008.

44. Burns 1978.

45. Kaiser, Hogan, and Craig 2008; Van Vugt, Hogan, and Kaiser 2008.

46. The number 150 is sometimes called "Dunbar's number" after Robin Dunbar noted that this very roughly seems to be the upper limit on the size of a group in which everyone can know each other, and know the relationships among the others; see Dunbar 1996.

47. Sherif et al. 1961/1954, as described in chapter 7.

48. Baumeister, Chesner, Senders, and Tice 1989; Hamblin 1958.

49. See work on common in-group identity (Gaertner and Dovidio 2000; Motyl et al. 2011) for a demonstration that increasing perceptions of similarity reduces implicit and explicit prejudice. See Haidt, Rosenberg, and Hom 2003 on the problem of moral diversity.

50. See Batson 1998 for a review of the ways that similarity increases altruism.

51. See Kurzban, Tooby, and Cosmides 2001 for an experiment showing that you can "erase race"—that is, you can get people to fail to notice and remember the race of other people when race is not a useful cue to "coalitional membership."

52. Wiltermuth and Heath 2008; Valdesolo, Ouyang, and DeSteno 2010. See also Cohen et al. 2009 for a demonstration that synchronous rowing increases pain tolerance (compared to equally vigorous rowing alone) because it increases endorphin release.

53. Brewer and Campbell 1976.

54. I'll say more at www.RighteousMind.com, and at www.EthicalSystems.org.

55. Kaiser, Hogan, and Craig 2008, p. 104; emphasis added.

56. Mussolini 1932. The phrase removed on the second to last line is "by death itself." Mussolini may not have written these lines; the essay was written

mostly or entirely by the philosopher Giovanni Gentile, but it was published with Mussolini's name as the author.

57. See in particular V. Turner 1969.

58. Compare the effects of fascist rallies, where people are awed by displays of military synchrony and devote themselves to the leader, to the effects that McNeill reported of marching with a small group of men in formation. Basic training bonds soldiers to each other, not to the drill sergeant.

59. If you think this statement comes close to making a value judgment, you are right. This is an example of Durkheimian utilitarianism, the normative theory I'll develop in the next chapter. I do believe that hiving contributes to the well-being and decency of a modern democratic society, which is in no danger of binding individuals too tightly; see Haidt, Seder, and Kesebir 2008. For recent empirical support, see Putnam and Campbell 2010.

60. See James Madison's notes for June 6 in *The Records of the Federal Convention of 1787*: "The only remedy [for the risk of oppression by a majority] is to enlarge the sphere, and thereby divide the community into so great a number of interests and parties, that, in the first place, a majority will not be likely, at the same moment, to have a common interest separate from that of the whole, or of the minority; and in the second place, that in case they should have such an interest, they may not be so apt to unite in the pursuit of it." The Founders were talking about political factions which rarely rise to the cohesion of hives. Nonetheless, they envisioned a nation whose strength came from people's commitment to local groups and institutions, in line with Putnam's (2000) analysis of social capital.

61. Putnam 2000, p. 209.

11. RELIGION IS A TEAM SPORT

1. McNeill 1995, see Chapter 10. The link to aggression is more obvious at some other universities where the motion used during their chant is the swinging of a tomahawk (e.g., Florida State University) or the snapping of an alligator's jaws (University of Florida) toward the fans of the opposing team, on the other side of the stadium.

2. I developed this analogy, and many of the ideas in this chapter, with Jesse Graham in Graham and Haidt 2010.

3. Durkheim 1965/1915, p. 62.

4. Or, for some on the far left, blame was placed on America itself. See, for example, Ward Churchill's 2003 claim that the people in the Twin Towers deserved to die. I note that there is a long history of left-wing hostility to religion, going back to Marx, and to the French *philosophes* in the eighteenth century. I believe that the current left-wing defense of Islam in Western nations is not a defense

of religion in any way; it is the result of the growing tendency on the left of seeing Muslims as victims of oppression in Europe and Palestine. I also note that in the days after the 9/11 attacks, President Bush placed himself firmly on the side of those who said that Islam is a religion of peace.

5. Buddhism is usually spared from critique, and sometimes even embraced— e.g., by Sam Harris—perhaps because it can easily be secularized and taken as a philosophical and ethical system resting firmly on the Care/harm foundation. The Dalai Lama does precisely this in his 1999 book *Ethics for the New Millennium*.

6. Harris 2004, p. 65.

7. Ibid., p. 12. Harris elevates belief to be the quintessence of humanity: "The very humanness of any brain consists largely in its capacity to evaluate new statements of propositional truth in light of innumerable others that it already accepts" (ibid., p. 51). That's a fine definition for a rationalist, but as a social intuitionist I think the humanness of any brain consists in its ability to share intentions and enter into the consensual hallucinations (i.e., moral matrices) that create cooperative moral communities. See my discussion of Tomasello's work in chapter 9. See also Harris et al. 2009.

8. Dawkins 2006, p. 31.

9. Ibid.

10. Dennett 2006, p. 9, says that religions are "social systems whose participants avow belief in a supernatural agent or agents whose approval is to be sought." Dennett does at least acknowledge that religions are "social systems," but most of the rest of his book focuses on the causes and consequences of false beliefs held by individuals, and in the footnote to his definition he explicitly contrasts his definition with Durkheim's.

11. See, for example, Ault 2005; Eliade 1957/1959. I note that the greatest scholar of religion in psychology, William James (1961/1902), took a lone-believer perspective too. He defined religion as "the feelings, acts, and experiences of individual men in their solitude, so far as they apprehend themselves to stand in relation to whatever they may consider the divine." The focus on belief is not unique to the New Atheists. It is common to psychologists, biologists, and other natural scientists, as contrasted to sociologists, anthropologists, and scholars in religious studies departments, all of whom are more skilled at thinking about what Durkheim called "social facts."

12. See, e.g., Froese and Bader 2007; Woodberry and Smith 1998.

13. Dennett 2006, p. 141.

14. Dawkins 2006, p. 166.

15. A meme is a bit of cultural information that can evolve in some of the same ways that a gene evolves. See Dawkins 1976.

16. Barrett 2000; Boyer 2001.

17. This idea was popularized by Guthrie 1993.

18. Dawkins 2006, p. 174. But religious commitment and religious conversion experiences begin in earnest in the teen years, which are precisely the years when children seem *least* likely to believe whatever grown-ups tell them.

19. Dennett 2006, chapter 9. I believe Dennett is correct.

20. Bloom 2004; 2012. Bloom is not a New Atheist. I think his suggestion here is correct—this is one of the most important psychological precursors of supernatural beliefs.

21. Dennett 2006, p. 123.

22. See also Blackmore 1999. Blackmore is a meme theorist who originally shared Dawkins's view that religions were memes that spread like viruses. But after seeing the evidence that religious people are happier, more generous, and more fertile, she recanted. See Blackmore 2010.

23. Dawkins 2006, p. 188.

24. Atran and Henrich 2010.

25. For detailed accounts of how gods and religions have evolved, see Wade 2009; Wright 2009.

26. Roes and Raymond 2003; Norenzayan and Shariff 2008.

27. Zhong, Bohns, and Gino 2010.

28. Haley and Fessler 2005.

29. Shariff and Norenzayan 2007.

30. Sosis 2000; Sosis and Alcorta 2003.

31. Sosis and Bressler 2003.

32. Rappaport 1971, p. 36.

33. By "rational" here I mean that the group can act in ways that further its long-term interests, rather than dissipating because individuals pursue their own private interests. See Frank 1988 for a similar analysis of how the moral emotions can make people "strategically irrational" in a way that helps them to solve "commitment problems."

34. Or maybe a few thousand years before agriculture, if the mysterious site at Göbekli Tepe, in Turkey, was devoted to high or moralistic gods. See Scham 2008.

35. See Hawks et al. 2007, and chapter 9, for reviews of the speed of genetic evolution. See Powell and Clark, forthcoming, for a critique of by-product models that also makes this point—that by-product theories do not preclude subsequent biological adaptation.

36. Richerson and Boyd 2005, p. 192, as I described in chapter 9.

37. Along with Eliot Sober, e.g., Sober and Wilson 1998.

38. Dawkins 2006, p. 171, grants that religion might provide those special con-

ditions. He then offers no argument against the possibility that religion facilitated group selection, even though if this possibility is true, it refutes his argument that religion is a parasite, rather than an adaptation. I urge readers to examine pp. 170–72 of *The God Delusion* carefully.

39. If I seem at times to be overenthusiastic about group selection, it's because I read *Darwin's Cathedral* in 2005, just as I was writing the last chapter of *The Happiness Hypothesis*. By the time I finished Wilson's book, I felt I had found the missing link in my understanding not only of happiness and why it comes from "between" but also of morality and why it binds and blinds.

40. D. S. Wilson 2002, p. 136.

41. Lansing 1991.

42. Hardin 1968.

43. D. S. Wilson 2002, p. 159.

44. Marshall 1999, quoted in Wade 2009, p. 106.

45. Hawks et al. 2007, described in chapter 9; Roes and Raymond 2003.

46. Wade 2009, p. 107; emphasis added.

47. G. C. Williams 1966.

48. Muir 1996; see chapter 9. I repeat that selection pressures on humans were probably never as strong and consistent as those applied in breeding experiments, so I would not talk about genetic evolution occurring in five or ten generations. But thirty or forty generations would be consistent with many of the genetic changes found in human populations and described in Cochran and Harpending 2009.

49. See Bowles 2009.

50. This statement is most true for Harris and Hitchens, least true for Dennett.

51. For a concise review of these two literatures, see Norenzayan and Shariff 2008.

52. Putnam and Campbell 2010.

53. Tan and Vogel 2008.

54. Ruffle and Sosis 2006 had members of secular and religious kibbutzim in Israel play a one-shot cooperation game, in pairs. Religious males who pray together frequently were best able to restrain their own selfishness and maximize the pot of money that they divided at the end of the game.

55. Larue 1991.

56. See discussion in Norenzayan and Shariff 2008.

57. Coleman 1988.

58. Putnam and Campbell are careful about drawing causal inferences from their correlational data. But because they have data collected over several years, they were able to see whether increases or decreases in religious participation predicted changes in behavior the following year, within individuals. They conclude that the data is most consistent with a causal explanation, rather than resulting from a spurious third variable.

59. Arthur Brooks reached this same conclusion in his 2006 book *Who Really Cares*.

60. Putnam and Campbell 2010, p. 461.

61. Ibid., p. 473.

62. Pape 2005. The reason it's mostly democracies that are the targets of suicide terrorism is that democracies are more responsive to public opinion. Suicide bombing campaigns against dictatorships are unlikely to provoke a withdrawal from the terrorists' homeland.

63. I acknowledge that such looser societies are a boon to those who are excluded from a religious moral order, such as gay people living in areas dominated by conservative Christians or Muslims.

64. Durkheim 1951/1897. For evidence that Durkheim's observations about suicide rates still hold true today, see Eckersley and Dear 2002, and see the sharp spike in suicide rates among young people that began in the United States in the 1960s, as anomie increased. (See www.suicide.org/suicide-statistics.html.)

65. Durkheim 1984/1893, p. 331.

66. I have given and justified this definition in earlier publications, including Haidt and Kesebir 2010.

67. Turiel 1983, p. 3, and see chapter 1.

68. I personally think that virtue ethics is the normative framework that fits human nature most closely. See Haidt and Joseph 2007 for a review.

69. I agree with Harris 2010 in his choice of utilitarianism, but with two big differences: (1) I endorse it only for public policy, as I do not think individuals are obligated to produce the greatest total benefit, and (2) Harris claims to be a monist. He says that what is right is whatever maximizes the happiness of conscious creatures, and he believes that happiness can be measured with objective techniques, such as an fMRI scanner. I disagree. I am a pluralist, not a monist. I follow Shweder (1991; Shweder and Haidt 1993) and Berlin 2001 in believing that there are multiple and sometimes conflicting goods and values, and there is no simple arithmeticical way of ranking societies along a single dimension. There is no way to eliminate the need for philosophical reflection about what makes a good society.

70. I am endorsing here a version of utilitarianism known as "rule utilitarianism," which says that we should aim to create the system and rules that will, in the long run, produce the greatest total good. This is in contrast to "act utilitarianism," which says that we should aim to maximize utility in each case, with each act.

71. I grant that utilitarianism, defined abstractly, already includes Durkheim. If it could be proven that Durkheim was correct about how to make people flourish, then many utilitarians would agree that we should implement Durkheimian policies. But in practice, utilitarians tend to be high systemizers who focus on

individuals and have difficulty seeing groups. They also tend to be politically liberal, and are therefore likely to resist drawing on the Loyalty, Authority, or Sanctity foundations. I therefore think the term *Durkheimian utilitarianism* is useful as a constant reminder that humans are *Homo duplex*, and that both levels of human nature must be included in utilitarian thinking.

12. CAN'T WE ALL DISAGREE MORE CONSTRUCTIVELY?

1. Finley Peter Dunne; first printed in the *Chicago Evening Post* in 1895. The full quote, in an 1898 version in Irish brogue, is: "Politics ain't beanbag. 'Tis a man's game; an' women, childher, an' pro-hybitionists 'd do well to keep out iv it."

2. Fiorina, Abrams, and Pope 2005.

3. Go to Gallup.com and search for "U.S. Political Ideology" for the latest findings. Those reported here are from the "2011 Half-Year Update."

4. The causes of the decline in civility are complex, including changes in the media, the replacement of the "greatest generation" by the baby boomers, and the increasing role of money in politics. See analysis and references at CivilPolitics.org. Several former congressmen I have met or listened to at conferences, from both parties, point to procedural and cultural changes implemented by Newt Gingrich when he became Speaker of the House in 1995.

5. Democratic congressman Jim Cooper of Tennessee, quoted in Nocera 2011.

6. Jost 2006.

7. Poole and Rosenthal 2000.

8. Erikson and Tedin 2003, p. 64, cited in Jost, Federico, and Napier 2009, p. 309.

9. Kinder 1998. See further discussion in chapter 4.

10. Zaller 1992, for example, focused on exposure to the opinions of political elites.

11. Converse 1964.

12. Bouchard 1994.

13. Turkheimer 2000, although Turkheimer showed that environment is always a contributor as well.

14. Alford, Funk, and Hibbing 2005, 2008.

15. Hatemi et al. 2011.

16. Helzer and Pizarro 2011; Inbar, Pizarro, and Bloom 2009; Oxley et al. 2008; Thórisdóttir and Jost 2011.

17. McCrae 1996; Settle et al. 2010.

18. Montaigne 1991/1588, Book III, section 9, on vanity.

19. The effects of these *single* genes are all tiny, and some only show up when certain environmental conditions are also present. One great puzzle of the genomic age is that while the genes collectively explain more than a third of the variability on most traits, there's almost never a single gene, or even a handful of genes, that are found to account for more than a few percentage

points of the variance, even for seemingly simple traits like physical height. See, e.g., Weedon et al. 2008.

20. Jost et al. 2003.

21. McAdams and Pals 2006.

22. Block and Block 2006. This study is widely misdescribed as showing that future conservatives had much less attractive personalities as young children. This seems to be true for the boys, but the list of traits for future liberal girls is quite mixed.

23. Putnam and Campbell 2010, as described in chapter 11.

24. People who are able to construct a good narrative, particularly one that connects early setbacks and suffering to later triumph, are happier and more productive than those who lack such a "redemption" narrative; see McAdams 2006; McAdams and Pals 2006. Of course, the simple correlation does not show that writing a good narrative *causes* good outcomes. But experiments done by Pennebaker show that giving people the opportunity to make sense of a trauma by writing about it causes better mental and even physical health. See Pennebaker 1997.

25. McAdams et al. 2008, p. 987.

26. Richards 2010, p. 53.

27. C. Smith 2003. Smith uses the term "moral order," but he means what I mean by the term "moral matrix."

28. Ibid., p. 82.

29. I don't mean to minimize the importance of equality as a moral good; I am simply arguing as I did in chapter 8 that political equality is a passion that grows out of the Liberty foundation and its emotional reaction to bullying and oppression, along with the Care foundation and its concern for victims. I do not think the love of political equality is derived from the Fairness foundation and its concerns for reciprocity and proportionality.

30. Westen 2007, pp. 157–58.

31. Iyer et al. 2011.

32. Graham, Nosek, and Haidt 2011. We used several baselines to measure the reality. One was our own data collected in this study, using all self-described liberals and conservatives. Another was this same data set but limited to those who called themselves "very liberal" or "very conservative." A third baseline was obtained from a nationally representative dataset using the MFQ. In all analyses, conservatives were more accurate than liberals.

33. M. Feingold, "Foreman's Wake-Up Call," 2004, retrieved March 28, 2011, from http://www.villagevoice.com/2004–01–13/theater/foreman-s-wake-up-call/. I assume the last line is not serious, but I could find no sign in the essay that Feingold was engaging in parody or was speaking as someone else.

34. Muller 1997, p. 4, citing Russell Kirk. See also Hunter 1991 for a similar definition of orthodoxy, which he then contrasts with progressivism.

35. Muller 1997, p. 5.

36. Political parties are messy things that must please many constituencies and donors, and so they never instantiate an ideology perfectly. Both major parties have serious problems, in my opinion. I wish the Democrats would become more Durkheimian, and I wish the Republicans would become more utilitarian. But right now I have less hope that the Republicans will change because they are so caught up in the binding (and blinding) passions of the Tea Partiers. Since 2009, and in particular in 2011, the Republicans have shown themselves to be less willing to compromise than the Democrats. And the issue they have sacralized is, unfortunately, taxes. Sacredness means no tradeoffs, and they are willing to sacrifice all the good things government can do to preserve low tax rates for the wealthiest Americans. This commitment exacerbates the rapidly growing income inequality that is poisonous to social trust, and therefore to moral capital (Wilkinson and Pickett 2009). As a Durkheimian utilitarian, I see much to like in conservatism, but much less to like in the Republican Party.

37. Putnam 2000.

38. That's Putnam's definition.

39. Coleman 1988.

40. Sosis and Bressler 2003; see chapter 11.

41. Sowell 2002.

42. The term *moral capital* has been used before, but it has usually been said to be a property of an *individual*, akin to integrity, which makes others trust and respect the person. See Kane 2001. I'm using the term in a different way. I'm defining it as a property of a *community* or social system. Rosenberg 1990 used it in this sense, attributing the idea but not the term to Adam Smith.

43. McWhorter 2005; Rieder 1985; Voegeli 2010.

44. Mill 2003/1859, p. 113. The quote continues: "Each of these modes of thinking derives its utility from the deficiencies of the other; but it is in a great measure the opposition of the other that keeps each within the limits of reason and sanity."

45. Russell 2004/1946, p. 9.

46. Ibid.

47. In the United States, and in every other nation and region we have examined on YourMorals.org. See Graham et al. 2011.

48. See, for example, the response to Daniel Patrick Moynihan's 1965 report on the black family, and the attacks and ostracism he had to endure; Patterson 2010.

49. Definitions of morality from liberal philosophers tend to focus on care, harm, or harm-reduction (The Utilitarian Grill), or on rights and the autonomy of

the individual (The Deontological Diner), as I described in chapter 6. See also definitions of morality in Gewirth 1975; P. Singer 1979.

50. Keillor 2004, p. 20.

51. See Pollan 2006 for a horrific description of the American industrial food system as a tangle of market distortions, particularly externalities imposed on America's farm animals, ecosystems, taxpayers, and waistlines.

52. *Citizens United v. Federal Election Commission*, 558 U.S. 08–205.

53. Kahan 2010. Only capitalism and an energetic private sector can generate the massive wealth that lifts the great majority of people out of poverty.

54. According to an EPA calculation done around that time; see Needleman 2000.

55. Needleman 2000.

56. Nevin 2000.

57. See Carpenter and Nevin 2010; Nevin 2000; Reyes 2007. The phaseout occurred in different states at different times, which allowed researchers to look at the lag between declines in lead exposure and declines in criminality.

58. It is true that producing gasoline without lead raises its cost. But Reyes 2007 calculated that the cost of removing lead from gasoline is "approximately twenty times smaller than the full value including quality of life of the crime reductions." That calculation does not include lives saved and other direct health benefits of lead reductions.

59. Carpenter and Nevin 2010.

60. Along with the other major causes of market failures and inefficiencies, such as monopoly power and the depletion of public goods, all of which frequently require government intervention to achieve market efficiency.

61. Murray, 1997, p. xii, says, "The correct word for my view of the world is '*liberal*.'"

62. Wilkinson, personal communication, 2010.

63. My short list of additional points: (1) power corrupts, so we should beware of concentrating power in any hands, including those of the government; (2) ordered liberty is the best recipe for flourishing in Western democracies; (3) nanny states and "cradle-to-grave" care infantilize people and make them behave less responsibly, thereby requiring even more government protection. See Boaz 1997.

64. Goldhill 2009.

65. Goldhill acknowledges that government has many roles to play in a market-based health system, as there are certain things that only the government can do. He specifically mentions enforcing safety standards, ensuring competition among providers, running an insurance pool for truly catastrophic cases, and subsidizing the poor, who could not afford to purchase their own health care even if prices dropped by 50 percent.

66. See *The Future of Healthcare in Europe*, a report prepared by *The Economist* magazine. Available at http://www.businessresearch.eiu.com/future-healthcare -europe.html-0.

67. Hayek 1988 referred to this belief that order comes from rational planning as "the fatal conceit."

68. See Cosmides and Tooby 2006 on how organizing labor along Marxist or socialist principles, which assume that people will cooperate in large groups, usually runs afoul of moral psychology. People do not cooperate well in large groups when they perceive that many others are free riding. Therefore, communist or heavily socialist nations often resort to the increasing application of threats and force to compel cooperation. Five-year plans rarely work as well as the invisible hand.

69. From "Conservatism as an ideology," as quoted by Muller 1997, p.3.

70. Burke 2003/1790, p. 40. I don't think Burke was right that the love of one's platoon leads, in general, to a love of humanity. But it does seem as though increasing the love of one's in-group usually doesn't lead to an increase in hate for out-groups (see Brewer and Campbell 1976; de Dreu et al. 2011), so I'd be content to live in a world with vastly more parochial love and little or no decrease in love of humanity.

71. Smith 1976/1759, Part VI, section ii, chapter 2.

72. McWhorter 2005; Rosenzweig 2009.

73. Arum 2003.

74. Stenner 2005, p. 330, concludes from her studies of authoritarians: "Ultimately, nothing inspires greater tolerance from the intolerant than an abundance of common and unifying beliefs, practices, rituals, institutions and processes. And regrettably, nothing is more certain to provoke increased expression of their latent predispositions than the likes of 'multicultural education.' "

75. See Pildes 2011 for an up-to-date review of the many factors that have contributed to our "hyperpolarized" state. Pildes argues that the political realignment, along with other historical trends, fully explains the rise in polarization. He therefore asserts that nothing can be done to reverse it. I disagree. Even if historical changes could explain 100 percent of the increase, that does not mean that institutional changes would have no effect. I prefer to follow Herbst 2010, who points out that civility and incivility are strategies that are used when they achieve desired results. There are many things we can do to reduce the payoff for incivility. See www.CivilPolitics.org.

76. No pun intended. Manichaean thinking is a problem for donkeys as well as elephants.

77. Bishop 2008.

78. Based on research by David Wasserman of *The Cook Political Report*, reported by Stolberg 2011.

CONCLUSION

1. Berlin 2001, pp. 11–12.
2. Ibid., p. 12; emphasis added. See also Shweder 1991; Shweder and Haidt 1993.
3. This is incredibly bad advice; it will just confuse people, and ambiguity leads to inaction (Latane and Darley 1970). It would be far better to define the situation clearly and identify the right course of action. For example, yell, "Help, I'm being raped. Call 911, then come here."

References

Abramowitz, A. I., and K. L. Saunders. 2008. "Is Polarization a Myth?" *Journal of Politics* 70:542–55.

Adorno, T. W., E. Frenkel-Brunswik, D. J. Levinson, and R. N. Sanford. 1950. *The Authoritarian Personality*. New York: Harper and Row.

Alford, J. R., C. L. Funk, and J. R. Hibbing. 2005. "Are Political Orientations Genetically Transmitted?" *American Political Science Review* 99:153–67.

———. 2008. "Beyond Liberals and Conservatives to Political Genotypes and Phenotypes." *Perspectives on Politics* 6:321–28.

Allen, E., et al. 1975. "Against 'Sociobiology.'" *New York Review of Books* 22:43–44.

Almas, I., A. W. Cappelen, E. O. Sorensen, and B. Tungodden. 2010. "Fairness and the Development of Inequality Acceptance." *Science* 328:1176–8.

Ambrose, S. H. 1998. "Late Pleistocene Human Population Bottlenecks, Volcanic-Winter, and the Differentiation of Modern Humans." *Journal of Human Evolution* 34:623–51.

Appiah, K. A. 2008. *Experiments in Ethics*. Cambridge, MA: Harvard University Press.

Arberry, A. J. 1955. *The Koran Interpreted*. New York: Simon and Schuster.

Ariely, D. 2008. *Predictably Irrational: The Hidden Forces That Shape Our Decisions*. New York: HarperCollins.

Arum, R. 2003. *Judging School Discipline: The Crisis of Moral Authority*. Cambridge, MA: Harvard University Press.

Atran, S. 2010. *Talking to the Enemy: Faith, Brotherhood, and the (Un)making of Terrorists*. New York: HarperCollins.

Atran, S., and J. Henrich. 2010. "The Evolution of Religion: How Cognitive By-products, Adaptive Learning Heuristics, Ritual Displays, and Group Competition Generate Deep Commitments to Prosocial Religions." *Biological Theory* 5:18–30.

Ault, J. M. J. 2005. *Spirit and Flesh: Life in a Fundamentalist Baptist Church*. New York: Knopf.

Axelrod, R. 1984. *The Evolution of Cooperation*. New York: Basic Books.

Baillargeon, R. 1987. "Object Permanence in 3 1/2- and 4 1/2-Month-Old Infants." *Developmental Psychology* 23:655–64.

———. 2008. "Innate Ideas Revisited: For a Principle of Persistence in Infants' Physical Reasoning." *Perspectives on Psychological Science* 3:2–13.

Balcetis, E., and D. Dunning. 2006. "See What You Want to See: Motivational Influences on Visual Perception." *Journal of Personality and Social Psychology* 91:612–25.

Ballew, C. C., and A. Todorov. 2007. "Predicting Political Elections from Rapid and Unreflective Face Judgments." *Proceedings of the National Academy of Sciences* 104:17948–53.

Bar, T., and A. Zussman. 2011. "Partisan Grading." *American Economic Journal: Applied Economics*. Forthcoming.

Bargh, J. A., and T. L. Chartrand. 1999. "The Unbearable Automaticity of Being." *American Psychologist* 54:462–79.

Barkow, J. H., L. Cosmides, and J. Tooby, eds. 1992. *The Adapted Mind: Evolutionary Psychology and the Generation of Culture*. New York: Oxford University Press.

Baron, J. 1998. *Judgment Misguided: Intuition and Error in Public Decision Making*. New York: Oxford.

———. 2007. *Thinking and Deciding*. 4th ed. Cambridge, UK: Cambridge University Press.

Baron-Cohen, S. 1995. *Mindblindness: An Essay on Autism and Theory of Mind*. Cambridge, MA: MIT Press.

———. 2002. "The Extreme Male Brain Theory of Autism." *Trends in Cognitive Sciences* 6:248–54.

———. 2009. "Autism: The Empathizing-Systemizing (E-S) Theory." In "The Year in Cognitive Neuroscience," special issue of *Annals of the New York Academy of Science* 1156:68–80.

Barrett, H. C., and Kurzban, R. 2006. "Modularity in Cognition: Framing the Debate." *Psychological Review* 113:628–47.

Barrett, J. L. 2000. "Exploring the Natural Foundations of Religion." *Trends in Cognitive Sciences* 4:29.

Bartels, D. M. 2008. "Principled Moral Sentiment and the Flexibility of Moral Judgment and Decision Making." *Cognition* 108:381–417.

Batson, C. D. 1991. *The Altruism Question: Toward a Social-Psychological Answer*. Hillsdale, NJ: Lawrence Erlbaum.

———. 1998. "Altruism and Prosocial Behavior." In *The Handbook of Social Psychology*, ed. D. T. Gilbert and S. T. Fiske, 4th ed., 2:262–316. Boston: McGraw-Hill.

Batson, C. D., E. R. Thompson, G. Seuferling, H. Whitney, and J. A. Strongman. 1999. "Moral Hypocrisy: Appearing Moral to Oneself Without Being So." *Journal of Personality and Social Psychology* 77:525–37.

Baumard, N., J.-B. André, and D. Sperber. Unpublished. "A Mutualistic Approach to Morality." Institute of Cognitive and Evolutionary Anthropology, University of Oxford.

Baumeister, R. F., S. P. Chesner, P. S. Senders, and D. M. Tice. 1989. "Who's in Charge Here? Group Leaders Do Lend Help in Emergencies." *Personality and Social Psychology Bulletin* 14:17–22.

Baumeister, R. F., and K. L. Sommer. 1997. "What Do Men Want? Gender Differences and Two Spheres of Belongingness: Comment on Cross and Madson (1997)." *Psychological Bulletin* 122:38–44.

Beaver, K. M., M. W. Rowland, J. A. Schwartz, and J. L. Nedelec. 2011. "The Genetic Origins of Psychopathic Personality Traits in Adult Males and Females: Results from an Adoption-Based Study." *Journal of Criminal Justice* 39:426–32.

Bellah, R. N. 1967. "Civil Religion in America." *Daedalus* 96:1–21.

Bellah, R. N., R. Madsen, W. M. Sullivan, A. Swidler, and S. Tipton. 1985. *Habits of the Heart.* New York: Harper and Row.

Bentham, J. 1996/1789. *An Introduction to the Principles of Morals and Legislation.* Oxford: Clarendon.

Berlin, I. 1997/1958. "Two Concepts of Liberty." In *The Proper Study of Mankind*, ed. H. Hardy and R. Hausheer, 191–242. New York: Farrar, Straus and Giroux.

———. 2001. "My Intellectual Path." In Isaiah Berlin, *The Power of Ideas*, ed. H. Hardy, 1–23. Princeton, NJ: Princeton University Press.

Bersoff, D. 1999. "Why Good People Sometimes Do Bad Things: Motivated Reasoning and Unethical Behavior." *Personality and Social Psychology Bulletin* 25:28–39.

Bishop, B. 2008. *The Big Sort: Why the Clustering of Like-Minded Americans Is Tearing Us Apart.* Boston: Houghton Mifflin Harcourt.

Blackmore, S. 1999. *The Meme Machine.* New York: Oxford University Press.

Blackmore, S. 2010. "Why I No Longer Believe Religion Is a Virus of the Mind." *The Guardian* (UK), Sept. 16; http://www.guardian.co.uk/commentisfree/belief/2010/sep/16/why-no-longer-believe-religion-virus-mind.

Blair, R. J. R. 1999. "Responsiveness to Distress Cues in the Child with Psychopathic Tendencies." *Personality and Individual Differences* 27:135–45.

———. 2007. "The Amygdala and Ventromedial Prefrontal Cortex in Morality and Psychopathy." *Trends in Cognitive Sciences* 11:387–92.

Block, J., and J. H. Block. 2006. "Nursery School Personality and Political Orientation Two Decades Later." *Journal of Research in Personality* 40:734–49.

Blonigen, D. M., B. M. Hicks, R. F. Krueger, W. G. Iacono, and C. J. Patrick. 2005. "Psychopathic Personality Traits: Heritability and Genetic Overlap with Internalizing and Externalizing Psychopathology." *Psychological Medicine* 35:637–48.

Bloom, P. 2004. *Descartes' Baby: How the Science of Child Development Explains What Makes Us Human.* New York: Basic Books.

———. 2009. "Religious Belief as an Evolutionary Accident." In *The Believing Primate: Scientific, Philosophical, and Theological Reflections on the Origin of Religion*, ed. J. Schloss and M. J. Murray, 118–27. Oxford: Oxford University Press.

_____. 2012. "Religion, Morality, Evolution." *Annual Review of Psychology* 63.

Boaz, D. 1997. *Libertarianism: A Primer*. New York: Free Press.

Boehm, C. 1999. *Hierarchy in the Forest: The Evolution of Egalitarian Behavior*. Cambridge, MA: Harvard University Press.

_____. 2012. *Moral Origins: The Evolution of Virtue, Altruism, and Shame*. New York: Basic Books.

Boesch, C. 1994. "Cooperative Hunting in Wild Chimpanzees." *Animal Behavior* 48:653–67.

Bouchard, T. J. J. 1994. "Genes, Environment, and Personality." *Science* 264:1700–1701.

Bourke, A. F. G. 2011. *Principles of Social Evolution*. New York: Oxford University Press.

Bowlby, J. 1969. *Attachment and Loss*, vol. 1: *Attachment*. New York: Basic Books.

Bowles, S. 2009. "Did Warfare Among Ancestral Hunter-Gatherers Affect the Evolution of Human Social Behaviors?" *Science* 324:1293–98.

Boyer, P. 2001. *Religion Explained: The Evolutionary Origins of Religious Thought*. New York: Basic Books.

Brandt, M. J., and C. Reyna. 2011. "The Chain of Being." *Perspectives on Psychological Science* 6:428–46.

Brehm, S. S., and Brehm, J. W. 1981. *Psychological Reactance: A Theory of Freedom and Control*. New York: Academic Press.

Brewer, M. B., and D. T. Campbell. 1976. *Ethnocentrism and Intergroup Attitudes: East African Evidence*. Beverly Hills, CA: Sage.

Brockman, J., ed. 2009. *What Have You Changed Your Mind About?* New York: HarperCollins.

Brooks, A. C. 2006. *Who Really Cares: The Surprising Truth About Compassionate Conservatism*. New York: Basic Books.

Brosnan, S. F. 2006. "Nonhuman Species' Reactions to Inequity and Their Implications for Fairness." *Social Justice Research* 19:153–85.

Brosnan, S. F., and F. de Waal. 2003. "Monkeys Reject Unequal Pay." *Nature* 425:297–99.

Buckholtz, J. W., C. L. Asplund, P. E. Dux, D. H. Zald, J. C. Gore, O. D. Jones, et al. 2008. "The Neural Correlates of Third-Party Punishment." *Neuron* 60:930–40.

Burke, E. 2003/1790. *Reflections on the Revolution in France*. New Haven, CT: Yale University Press.

Burns, J. M. 1978. *Leadership*. New York: Harper and Row.

Carlsmith, K. M., T. D. Wilson, and D. T. Gilbert. 2008. "The Paradoxical Consequences of Revenge." *Journal of Personality and Social Psychology* 95:1316–24.

Carnegie, D. 1981/1936. *How to Win Friends and Influence People*. Rev. ed. New York: Pocket Books.

Carney, D. R., J. T. Jost, S. D. Gosling, and K. Kiederhoffer. 2008. "The Secret Lives of Liberals and Conservatives: Personality Profiles, Interaction Styles, and the Things They Leave Behind." *Political Psychology* 29:807–40.

Carpenter, D. O., and R. Nevin. 2010. "Environmental Causes of Violence." *Physiology and Behavior* 99:260–68.

Carter, C. S. 1998. "Neuroendocrine Perspectives on Social Attachment and Love." *Psychoneuroendocrinology* 23:779–818.

Chan, W. T. 1963. *A Source Book in Chinese Philosophy.* Princeton, NJ: Princeton University Press.

Choi, J.-K., and S. Bowles. 2007. "The Coevolution of Parochial Altruism and War." *Science* 318:636–40.

Churchill, W. 2003. *On the Justice of Roosting Chickens: Reflections on the Consequences of U.S. Imperial Arrogance and Criminality.* Oakland, CA: AK Press.

Clark, G. 2007. *A Farewell to Alms: A Brief Economic History of the World.* Princeton: Princeton University Press.

Clarke, R. A. 2004. *Against All Enemies: Inside America's War on Terror.* New York: Free Press.

Cleckley, H. 1955. *The Mask of Sanity.* St. Louis, MO: Mosby.

Clore, G. L., N. Schwarz, and M. Conway. 1994. "Affective Causes and Consequences of Social Information Processing." In *Handbook of Social Cognition,* ed. R. S. Wyer and T. K. Srull, 1:323–417. Hillsdale, NJ: Lawrence Erlbaum.

Cochran, G., and H. Harpending. 2009. *The 10,000 Year Explosion: How Civilization Accelerated Human Evolution.* New York: Basic Books.

Cohen, E. E. A., R. Ejsmond-Frey, N. Knight, and R. I. M. Dunbar. 2009. "Rowers' High: Behavioral Synchrony Is Correlated With Elevated Pain Thresholds." *Biology Letters* 6:106–8.

Coleman, J. S. 1988. "Social Capital in the Creation of Human Capital." *American Journal of Sociology* 94:S95–S120.

Converse, P. E. 1964. "The Nature of Belief Systems in Mass Publics." In *Ideology and Discontent,* ed. D. E. Apter, 206–61. New York: Free Press.

Conze, E. 1954. *Buddhist Texts Through the Ages.* New York: Philosophical Library.

Cosmides, L., and J. Tooby. 2005. "Neurocognitive Adaptations Designed for Social Exchange." In *The Handbook of Evolutionary Psychology,* ed. D. M. Buss, 584–627. Hoboken, NJ: John Wiley and Sons.

———. 2006. "Evolutionary Psychology, Moral Heuristics, and the Law." In *Heuristics and the Law,* ed. G. Gigerenzer and C. Engel, 175–205. Cambridge, MA: MIT Press.

Coulter, A. 2003. *Treason: Liberal Treachery from the Cold War to the War on Terrorism.* New York: Crown.

Dalai Lama XIV. 1999. *Ethics for the New Millennium.* New York: Riverhead Books.

Damasio, A. 1994. *Descartes' Error: Emotion, Reason, and the Human Brain*. New York: Putnam.

———. 2003. *Looking for Spinoza*. Orlando, FL: Harcourt.

Darwin, C. 1998/1871. *The Descent of Man and Selection in Relation to Sex*. Amherst, NY: Prometheus Books.

Dawkins, R. 1976. *The Selfish Gene*. New York: Oxford University Press.

———. 1999/1982. *The Extended Phenotype: The Long Reach of the Gene*. New York: Oxford University Press.

———. 2006. *The God Delusion*. Boston: Houghton Mifflin.

Decety, J. 2011. "The Neuroevolution of Empathy." *Annals of the New York Academy of Sciences* 1231:35–45.

De Dreu, C. K., L. L. Greer, M. J. Handgraaf, S. Shalvi, G. A. Van Kleef, M. Baas, et al. 2010. "The Neuropeptide Oxytocin Regulates Parochial Altruism in Intergroup Conflict Among Humans." *Science* 328:1408–11.

De Dreu, C. K., L. L. Greer, G. A. Van Kleef, S. Shalvi, and M. J. Handgraaf. 2011. "Oxytocin Promotes Human Ethnocentrism." *Proceedings of the National Academy of Sciences of the United States of America* 108:1262–66.

Denis, L. 2008. "Kant and Hume on Morality." *Stanford Encyclopedia of Philosophy*. Stanford, CA: The Metaphysics Research Lab.

Dennett, D. C. 2006. *Breaking the Spell: Religion as a Natural Phenomenon*. New York: Penguin.

de Quervain, D. J. F., U. Fischbacher, V. Treyer, M. Schellhammer, U. Schnyder, A. Buck, et al. 2004. "The Neural Basis of Altruistic Punishment." *Science* 305:1254–58.

Desmond, A., and J. Moore. 2009. *Darwin's Sacred Cause: How a Hatred of Slavery Shaped Darwin's Views on Human Evolution*. Boston: Houghton Mifflin.

de Waal, F. B. M. 1982. *Chimpanzee Politics*. New York: Harper and Row.

———. 1996. *Good Natured: The Origins of Right and Wrong in Humans and Other Animals*. Cambridge, MA: Harvard University Press.

———. 2006. *How Morality Evolved*. Princeton, NJ: Princeton University Press.

de Waal, F. B. M., and F. Lanting. 1997. *Bonobo: The Forgotten Ape*. Berkeley: University of California Press.

Dicks, L. 2000. "All for One!" *New Scientist* 167:30.

Dion, K. 1979. "Intergroup Conflict and Intragroup Cohesiveness." In *The Social Psychology of Intergroup Relations*, ed. W. G. Austin and S. Worchel, 211–24. Monterey, CA: Brooks/Cole.

Dion, K., E. Berscheid, and E. Walster. 1972. "What Is Beautiful Is Good." *Journal of Personality and Social Psychology* 24:285–90.

Ditto, P. H., and D. F. Lopez. 1992. "Motivated Skepticism: Use of Differential Decision Criteria for Preferred and Nonpreferred Conclusions." *Journal of Personality and Social Psychology* 63:568–84.

Ditto, P. H., G. D. Munro, A. M. Apanovitch, J. A. Scepansky, and L. K. Lockhart. 2003. "Spontaneous Skepticism: The Interplay of Motivation and Expectation in Responses to Favorable and Unfavorable Medical Diagnoses." *Personality and Social Psychology Bulletin* 29:1120–32.

Ditto, P. H., D. A. Pizarro, and D. Tannenbaum. 2009. "Motivated Moral Reasoning." In *The Psychology of Learning and Motivation,* ed. D. M. Bartels, C. W. Bauman, L. J. Skitka, and D. L. Medin, 50:307–38. Burlington, VT: Academic Press.

Doblin, R. 1991. "Pahnke's 'Good Friday Experiment': A Long-Term Follow-up and Methodological Critique." *Journal of Transpersonal Psychology* 23:1–28.

Douglas, M. 1966. *Purity and Danger.* London: Routledge and Kegan Paul.

Dunbar, R. 1996. *Grooming, Gossip, and the Evolution of Language.* Cambridge, MA: Harvard University Press.

Durkheim, E. 1951/1897. *Suicide.* Trans. J. A. Spalding and G. Simpson. New York: Free Press.

———. 1984/1893. *The Division of Labor in Society.* Trans. W. D. Halls. New York: Free Press.

———. 1992/1887. "Review of Guyau's *L'irreligion de l'avenir.*" Trans. A. Giddens. In *Emile Durkheim: Selected Writings,* ed. A. Giddens. New York: Cambridge University Press.

———. 1995/1915. *The Elementary Forms of Religious Life.* Trans. K. E. Fields. New York: Free Press.

Eckersley, R., and K. Dear. 2002. "Cultural Correlates of Youth Suicide." *Social Science and Medicine* 55:1891–904.

Efran, M. G. 1974. "The Effect of Physical Appearance on the Judgment of Guilt, Interpersonal Attraction, and Severity of Recommended Punishment in a Simulated Jury Task." *Journal of Research in Personality* 8:45–54.

Ehrenreich, B. 2006. *Dancing in the Streets: A History of Collective Joy.* New York: Metropolitan Books.

Ekman, P. 1992. "Are There Basic Emotions?" *Psychological Review* 99:550–53.

Elgar, F. J., and N. Aitken. 2010. "Income Inequality, Trust and Homicide in 33 Countries." *European Journal of Public Health* 21:241–46.

Eliade, M. 1957/1959. *The Sacred and the Profane: The Nature of Religion.* Trans. W. R. Task. San Diego, CA: Harcourt Brace.

Ellis, J. J. 1996. *American Sphinx: The Character of Thomas Jefferson.* New York: Vintage.

Ellsworth, P. C., and C. A. Smith. 1985. "Patterns of Cognitive Appraisal in Emotion." *Journal of Personality and Social Psychology* 48:813–38.

Emerson, R. W. 1960/1838. "Nature." In *Selections from Ralph Waldo Emerson,* ed. S. Whicher, 21–56. Boston: Houghton Mifflin.

Eskine, K. J., N. A. Kacinic, and J. J. Prinz. 2011. "A Bad Taste in the Mouth: Gustatory Influences on Moral Judgment." *Psychological Science* 22:295–99.

Evans-Pritchard, E. E. 1976. *Witchcraft, Oracles, and Magic Among the Azande.* Oxford: Clarendon Press.

Faulkner, J., M. Schaller, J. H. Park, and L. A. Duncan. 2004. "Evolved Disease-Avoidance Mechanisms and Contemporary Xenophobic Attitudes." *Group Processes and Intergroup Relations* 7:333–53.

Fazio, R. H., D. M. Sanbonmatsu, M. C. Powell, and F. R. Kardes. 1986. "On the Automatic Evaluation of Attitudes." *Journal of Personality and Social Psychology* 50:229–38.

Fehr, E., and S. Gachter. 2002. "Altruistic Punishment in Humans." *Nature* 415:137–40.

Fessler, D. M. T. 2007. "From Appeasement to Conformity: Evolutionary and Cultural Perspectives on Shame, Competition, and Cooperation." In *The Self-Conscious Emotions: Theory and Research*, ed. J. L. Tracy, R. W. Robins, and J. P. Tangney, 174–93. New York: Guilford.

Fiorina, M., S. J Abrams, and J. C. Pope. 2005. *Culture War? The Myth of a Polarized America.* New York: Pearson Longman.

Fiske, A. P. 1991. *Structures of Social Life.* New York: Free Press.

Fiske, S. T. 1993. "Social Cognition and Social Perception." *Annual Review of Psychology* 44:155–94.

Fitzgerald, M. 2005. *The Genesis of Artistic Creativity.* London: Jessica Kingsley.

Flanagan, O. 1991. *Varieties of Moral Personality: Ethics and Psychological Realism.* Cambridge, MA: Harvard University Press.

Fodor, J. 1983. *Modularity of Mind.* Cambridge, MA: MIT Press.

Frank, R. 1988. *Passions Within Reason: The Strategic Role of the Emotions.* New York: Norton.

Frank, T. 2004. *What's the Matter with Kansas?* New York: Henry Holt.

Frazier, M. L. 2010. *The Enlightenment of Sympathy: Justice and the Moral Sentiments in the Eighteenth Century and Today.* New York: Oxford University Press.

Freeman, W. J. 1995. *Societies of Brains: A Study in the Neurobiology of Love and Hate.* Mahwah, NJ: Lawrence Erlbaum.

Frey, D., and D. Stahlberg. 1986. "Selection of Information After Receiving More or Less Reliable Self-Threatening Information." *Personality and Social Psychology Bulletin* 12:434–41.

Froese, P., and C. D. Bader. 2007. "God in America: Why Theology Is Not Simply the Concern of Philosophers." *Journal for the Scientific Study of Religion* 46:465–81.

Frohlich, N., J. A. Oppenheimer, and C. L. Eavey. 1987. "Choices of Principles of Distributive Justice in Experimental Groups." *American Journal of Political Science* 31:606–36.

Gaertner, S. L., and J. F. Dovidio. 2000. *Reducing Intergroup Bias: The Common Ingroup Identity Model.* Philadelphia: Psychology Press.

Gazzaniga, M. S. 1985. *The Social Brain.* New York: Basic Books.

———. 1998. *The Mind's Past.* Berkeley: University of California Press.

Geertz, C. 1984. "From the Native's Point of View: On the Nature of Anthropological Understanding." In *Culture Theory,* ed. R. Shweder and R. LeVine, 123–36. Cambridge, UK: Cambridge University Press.

Gewirth, A. 1975. "Ethics." In *Encyclopaedia Britannica,* 15th ed., 6:976–98. Chicago: Encyclopaedia Britannica.

Gibbard, A. 1990. *Wise Choices, Apt Feelings.* Cambridge, MA: Harvard University Press.

Gigerenzer, G. 2007. *Gut Feelings: The Intelligence of the Unconscious.* New York: Penguin.

Gilligan, C. 1982. *In a Different Voice: Psychological Theory and Women's Development.* Cambridge, MA: Harvard University Press.

Gilovich, T. 1991. *How We Know What Isn't So.* New York: Free Press.

Glover, J. 2000. *Humanity: A Moral History of the Twentieth Century.* New Haven: Yale University Press.

Goldhill, D. 2009. "How American Health Care Killed My Father." *The Atlantic,* September.

Goodall, J. 1986. *The Chimpanzees of Gombe: Patterns of Behavior.* Cambridge, MA: Belknap Press.

Gopnik, A., A. M. Meltzoff, and P. K. Kuhl. 2000. *The Scientist in the Crib: What Early Learning Tells Us About the Mind.* New York: Harper.

Graham, J., 2010. "Left Gut, Right Gut." Ph.D. diss., Department of Psychology, University of Virginia.

Graham, J., and J. Haidt. 2010. "Beyond Beliefs: Religions Bind Individuals into Moral Communities." *Personality and Social Psychology Review* 14:140–50.

Graham, J., J. Haidt, and B. Nosek. 2009. "Liberals and Conservatives Rely on Different Sets of Moral Foundations." *Journal of Personality and Social Psychology* 96:1029–46.

Graham, J., B. A. Nosek, and J. Haidt. 2011. "The Moral Stereotypes of Liberals and Conservatives." Unpublished ms., Department of Psychology, University of Virginia. Available at www.MoralFoundations.org.

Graham, J., B. A. Nosek, J. Haidt, R. Iyer, S. Koleva, and P. H. Ditto. 2011. "Mapping the Moral Domain." *Journal of Personality and Social Psychology* 101:366–85.

Gray, J. 1995. *Liberalism.* 2nd ed. Minneapolis: University of Minnesota Press.

Gray, J. G. 1970/1959. *The Warriors: Reflections of Men in Battle.* New York: Harper and Row.

Green, R. E., J. Krause, A. W. Briggs, T. Maricic, U. Stenzel, M. Kircher, et al. 2010. "A Draft Sequence of the Neandertal Genome." *Science* 328:710–22.

Greene, J. D. 2008. "The Secret Joke of Kant's Soul." In *Moral Psychology,* vol. 3: *The*

Neuroscience of Morality, ed. W. Sinnott-Armstrong, 35–79. Cambridge, MA: MIT Press.

———. 2009a. "The Cognitive Neuroscience of Moral Judgment." In *The Cognitive Neurosciences,* ed. M. Gazzaniga, 4th ed., 987–1002. Cambridge, MA: MIT Press.

———. 2009b. "Dual-Process Morality and the Personal/Impersonal Distinction: A Reply to McGuire, Langdon, Coltheart, and Mackenzie." *Journal of Experimental Social Psychology* 45:581–84.

———. Forthcoming. *The Moral Brain, and How to Use It.* New York: Penguin.

Greene, J. D., R. B. Sommerville, L. E. Nystrom, J. M. Darley, and J. D. Cohen. 2001. "An fMRI Study of Emotional Engagement in Moral Judgment." *Science* 293:2105–8.

Greenwald, A. G., D. E. McGhee, and J. L. Schwartz. 1998. "Measuring Individual Differences in Implicit Cognition: The Implicit Association Test." *Journal of Personality and Social Psychology* 74:1464–80.

Greenwald, A. G., B. A. Nosek, and M. R. Banaji. 2003. "Understanding and Using the Implicit Association Test." *Journal of Personality and Social Psychology* 85:197–216.

Grob, C. S., and M. D. de Rios. 1994. "Hallucinogens, Managed States of Consciousness, and Adolescents: Cross-Cultural Perspectives." In *Psychological Anthropology,* ed. P. K. Bock, 315–29. Westport, CT: Praeger.

Guthrie, S. E. 1993. *Faces in the Clouds.* New York: Oxford University Press.

Haidt, J. 2001. "The Emotional Dog and Its Rational Tail: A Social Intuitionist Approach to Moral Judgment." *Psychological Review* 108:814–34.

———. 2006. *The Happiness Hypothesis: Finding Modern Truth in Ancient Wisdom.* New York: Basic Books.

———. 2007. "The New Synthesis in Moral Psychology." *Science* 316:998–1002.

———. 2010. "What the Tea Partiers Really Want." *Wall Street Journal,* October 16.

Haidt, J., and F. Bjorklund. 2008. "Social Intuitionists Answer Six Questions About Morality." In *Moral Psychology,* vol. 2: *The Cognitive Science of Morality,* ed. W. Sinnott-Armstrong, 181–217. Cambridge, MA: MIT Press.

Haidt, J., and J. Graham. 2007. "When Morality Opposes Justice: Conservatives Have Moral Intuitions That Liberals May Not Recognize." *Social Justice Research* 20:98–116.

———. 2009. "Planet of the Durkheimians, Where Community, Authority, and Sacredness Are Foundations of Morality." In *Social and Psychological Bases of Ideology and System Justification,* ed. J. Jost, A. C. Kay, and H. Thórisdóttir, 371–401. New York: Oxford University Press.

Haidt, J., and C. Joseph. 2004. "Intuitive Ethics: How Innately Prepared Intuitions Generate Culturally Variable Virtues." *Daedalus,* fall, 55–66.

———. 2007. "The Moral Mind: How 5 Sets of Innate Intuitions Guide the Development of Many Culture-Specific Virtues, and Perhaps Even Modules." In *The Innate Mind*, ed. P. Carruthers, S. Laurence, and S. Stich, 3:367–91. New York: Oxford University Press.

———. 2011. "How Moral Foundations Theory Succeeded in Building on Sand: A Response to Suhler and Churchland." *Journal of Cognitive Neuroscience* 23:2117–22.

Haidt, J., and S. Kesebir. 2010. "Morality." In *Handbook of Social Psychology*, ed. S. T. Fiske, D. Gilbert, and G. Lindzey, 5th ed., 797–832. Hoboken, NJ: Wiley.

Haidt, J., S. Koller, and M. Dias. 1993. "Affect, Culture, and Morality, or Is It Wrong to Eat Your Dog?" *Journal of Personality and Social Psychology* 65:613–28.

Haidt, J., E. Rosenberg, and H. Hom. 2003. "Differentiating Diversities: Moral Diversity Is Not Like Other Kinds." *Journal of Applied Social Psychology* 33:1–36.

Haidt, J., P. Rozin, C. R. McCauley, and S. Imada. 1997. "Body, Psyche, and Culture: The Relationship Between Disgust and Morality." *Psychology and Developing Societies* 9:107–31.

Haidt, J., J. P. Seder, and S. Kesebir. 2008. "Hive Psychology, Happiness, and Public Policy." *Journal of Legal Studies* 37:S133–S16.

Haley, K. J., and D. M. T. Fessler. 2005. "Nobody's Watching? Subtle Cues Affect Generosity in an Anonymous Economic Game." *Evolution and Human Behavior* 26:245–56.

Hamblin, R. L. 1958. "Leadership and Crises." *Sociometry* 21:322–35.

Hamilton, W. D. 1964. "The Genetical Evolution of Social Behavior, Parts 1 and 2." *Journal of Theoretical Biology* 7:1–52.

Hamlin, J. K., K. Wynn, and P. Bloom. 2007. "Social Evaluation by Preverbal Infants." *Nature* 450:557–60.

Hammerstein, P. 2003. "Why Is Reciprocity So Rare in Social Animals?" In *Genetic and Cultural Evolution of Cooperation*, ed. P. Hammerstein, 55–82. Cambridge, MA: MIT Press.

Hardin, G. 1968. "Tragedy of the Commons." *Science* 162:1243–8.

Hare, B., V. Wobber, and R. Wrangham. Unpublished. "The Self-Domestication Hypothesis: Bonobo Psychology Evolved Due to Selection Against Male Aggression." Unpublished ms., Department of Evolutionary Anthropology, Duke University.

Hare, R. D. 1993. *Without Conscience*. New York: Pocket Books.

Harris, S. 2004. *The End of Faith: Religion, Terror, and the Future of Reason*. New York: Norton.

———. 2006. *Letter to a Christian Nation*. New York: Knopf.

———. 2010. *The Moral Landscape: How Science Can Determine Human Values*. New York: Free Press.

Harris, S., J. T. Kaplan, A. Curiel, S. Y. Bookheimer, M. Iacoboni, and M. S. Cohen. 2009. "The Neural Correlates of Religious and Nonreligious Belief." *PLoS ONE* 4 (10); doi:10.1371/journal.pone.0007272.

Hastorf, A. H., and H. Cantril. 1954. "They Saw a Game: A Case Study." *Journal of Abnormal and Social Psychology* 49:129–34.

Hatemi, P. K., N. A. Gillespie, L. J. Eaves, B. S. Maher, B. T. Webb, A. C. Heath, et al. 2011. "A Genome-Wide Analysis of Liberal and Conservative Political Attitudes." *Journal of Politics* 73:271–85.

Hauser, M. 2006. *Moral Minds: How Nature Designed Our Universal Sense of Right and Wrong.* New York: HarperCollins.

Hawks, J., E. T. Wang, G. M. Cochran, H. C. Harpending, and R. K. Moyzis. 2007. "Recent Acceleration of Human Adaptive Evolution." *Proceedings of the National Academy of Sciences of the United States of America* 104:20753–58.

Hayden, B. 2001. "Richman, Poorman, Beggarman, Chief: The Dynamics of Social Inequality." In *Archaeology at the Millennium: A Sourcebook,* ed. G. M. Feinman and T. D. Price, 231–72. New York: Kluwer/Plenum.

Hayek, F. 1988. *The Fatal Conceit: The Errors of Socialism.* Chicago: University of Chicago Press.

———. 1997/1970. "The Errors of Constructivism." In *Conservatism,* ed. J. Z. Muller, 318–25. Princeton, NJ: Princeton University Press.

Heath, C., and D. Heath. 2010. *Switch: How to Change Things When Change Is Hard.* New York: Broadway.

Helzer, E. G., and D. A. Pizarro. 2011. "Dirty Liberals! Reminders of Physical Cleanliness Influence Moral and Political Attitudes." *Psychological Science* 22:517–22.

Henrich, J., S. Heine, and A. Norenzayan. 2010. "The Weirdest People in the World?" *Behavioral and Brain Sciences* 33:61–83.

Henrich, N., and Henrich, J. 2007. *Why Humans Cooperate: A Cultural and Evolutionary Explanation.* New York: Oxford University Press.

Henshilwood, C., F. d'Errico, M. Vanhaeren, K. van Niekerk, and Z. Jacobs. 2004. "Middle Stone Age Shell Beads from South Africa." *Science* 304:404.

Herbst, S. 2010. *Rude Democracy: Civility and Incivility in American Politics.* Philadelphia: Temple University Press.

Herdt, G. H. 1981. *Guardians of the Flutes.* New York: Columbia University Press.

Herrmann, E., J. Call, M. V. Hernandez-Lloreda, B. Hare, and M. Tomasello. 2007. "Humans Have Evolved Specialized Skills of Social Cognition: The Cultural Intelligence Hypothesis." *Science* 317:1360–66.

Hill, K. R., R. S. Walker, M. Bozicevic, J. Eder, T. Headland, B. Hewlett, et al. 2011. "Co-Residence Patterns in Hunter-Gatherer Societies Show Unique Human Social Structure." *Science* 331:1286–89.

Hoffman, M. L. 1982. "Affect and Moral Development." In *New Directions for Child*

Development, vol. 16: *Emotional Development,* ed. D. Ciccetti and P. Hesse, 83–103. San Francisco: Jossey-Bass.

Hölldobler, B., and E. O. Wilson. 2009. *The Superorganism: The Beauty, Elegance, and Strangeness of Insect Societies.* New York: Norton.

Hollos, M., P. Leis, and E. Turiel. 1986. "Social Reasoning in Ijo Children and Adolescents in Nigerian Communities." *Journal of Cross-Cultural Psychology* 17:352–74.

Horner, V., J. D. Carter, M. Suchak, and F. de Waal. 2011. "Spontaneous Prosocial Choice by Chimpanzees." *Procedings of the National Academy of Sciences,* early edition, doc: 10.1073/pnas.1111088108.

Hsieh, T. 2010. *Delivering Happiness: A Path to Profits, Passion, and Purpose.* New York: Grand Central.

Hsu, M., C. Anen, and S. R. Quartz. 2008. "The Right and the Good: Distributive Justice and Neural Encoding of Equity and Efficiency." *Science* 320:1092–95.

Huebner, B., S. Dwyer, and Hauser, M. 2009. "The Role of Emotion in Moral Psychology." *Trends in Cognitive Sciences* 13:1–6.

Hume, D. 1960/1777. *An Enquiry Concerning the Principles of Morals.* La Salle, IL: Open Court.

———. 1969/1739–40. *A Treatise of Human Nature.* London: Penguin.

Hunter, J. D. 1991. *Culture Wars: The Struggle to Define America.* New York: Basic Books.

Iacoboni, M. 2008. *Mirroring People: The New Science of How We Connect with Others.* New York: Farrar, Straus and Giroux.

Iacoboni, M., R. P. Woods, M. Brass, H. Bekkering, J. C. Mazziotta, and G. Rizzolatti. 1999. "Cortical Mechanisms of Imitation." *Science* 286:2526–28.

Inbar, Y., D. A. Pizarro, and P. Bloom. 2009. "Conservatives Are More Easily Disgusted than Liberals." *Cognition and Emotion* 23:714–25.

Iyer, R., S. P. Koleva, J. Graham, P. H. Ditto, and J. Haidt. 2011. "Understanding Libertarian Morality: The Psychological Roots of an Individualist Ideology." Unpublished ms., Department of Psychology, University of Southern California. Available at www.MoralFoundations.org.

James, W. 1950/1890. *The Principles of Psychology.* New York: Dover.

———. 1961/1902. *The Varieties of Religious Experience.* New York: Macmillan.

Jefferson, T. 1975/1786. *Letter to Maria Cosway.* New York: Penguin.

Jensen, D. 2008. *How Shall I Live My Life? On Liberating the Earth from Civilization.* Oakland, CA: PM Press.

Jensen, L. A. 1997. "Culture Wars: American Moral Divisions Across the Adult Lifespan." *Journal of Adult Development* 4:107–21.

———. 1998. "Moral Divisions Within Countries Between Orthodoxy and Progressivism: India and the United States." *Journal for the Scientific Study of Religion* 37:90–107.

Johnson-Laird, P. N., and P. C. Wason. 1977. *Thinking: Readings in Cognitive Science.* Cambridge, UK: Cambridge University Press.

Jost, J. T. 2006. "The End of the End of Ideology." *American Psychologist* 61:651–70.

Jost, J. T., C. M. Federico, and J. L. Napier. 2009. "Political Ideology: Its Structure, Functions, and Elective Affinities." *Annual Review of Psychology* 60:307–37.

Jost, J. T., J. Glaser, A. W. Kruglanski, and F. J. Sulloway. 2003. "Political Conservatism as Motivated Social Cognition." *Psychological Bulletin* 129:339–75.

Jost, J. T., and O. Hunyady. 2002. "The Psychology of System Justification and the Palliative Function of Ideology." *European Review of Social Psychology* 13:111–53.

Kagan, J. 1984. *The Nature of the Child.* New York: Basic Books.

Kahan, A. S. 2010. *Mind vs. Money: The War Between Intellectuals and Capitalism.* New Brunswick, NJ: Transaction.

Kahneman, D. 2011. *Thinking Fast and Slow.* New York: Farrar, Straus and Giroux.

Kaiser, R. B., R. Hogan, and S. B. Craig. 2008. "Leadership and the Fate of Organizations." *American Psychologist* 63:96–110.

Kane, J. 2001. *The Politics of Moral Capital.* New York: Cambridge University Press.

Kant, I. 1993/1785. *Grounding for the Metaphysics of Morals,* 3rd ed. Trans. J. W. Ellington. Indianapolis: Hackett.

Kass, L. R. 1997. "The Wisdom of Repugnance." *New Republic,* June 2, 17–26.

Keeley, L. H. 1996. *War Before Civilization.* New York: Oxford University Press.

Keillor, G. 2004. *Homegrown Democrat: A Few Plain Thoughts from the Heart of America.* New York: Viking.

Kelly, R. L. 1995. *The Foraging Spectrum: Diversity in Hunter-Gatherer Lifeways.* Washington, DC: Smithsonian Institution Press.

Keltner, D. 2009. *Born to Be Good: The Science of a Meaningful Life.* New York: Norton.

Keltner, D., and J. Haidt. 2003. "Approaching Awe, a Moral, Spiritual, and Aesthetic Emotion." *Cognition and Emotion* 17:297–314.

Kesebir, S. Forthcoming. "The Superorganism Account of Human Sociality: How and When Human Groups Are Like Beehives." *Personality and Social Psychology Review.*

Kiehl, K. A. 2006. "A Cognitive Neuroscience Perspective on Psychopathy: Evidence for Paralimbic System Dysfunction." *Psychiatry Research* 142:107–28.

Killen, M., and J. G. Smetana. 2006. *Handbook of Moral Development.* Mahwah, NJ: Lawrence Erlbaum.

Kinder, D. E. 1998. "Opinion and Action in the Realm of Politics." In *Handbook of Social Psychology,* 4th ed., ed. D. Gilbert, S. Fiske, and G. Lindzey, 778–867. New York: McGraw-Hill.

Kinzler, K. D., E. Dupoux, and E. S. Spelke. 2007. "The Native Language of Social Cognition." *Proceedings of the National Academy of Sciences of the United States of America* 104:12577–80.

Kitayama, S., H. Park, A. T. Sevincer, M. Karasawa, and A. K. Uskul. 2009. "A Cultural Task Analysis of Implicit Independence: Comparing North America, Western Europe, and East Asia." *Journal of Personality and Social Psychology* 97:236–55.

Knoch, D., A. Pascual-Leone, K. Meyer, V. Treyer, and E. Fehr. 2006. "Diminishing Reciprocal Fairness by Disrupting the Right Prefrontal Cortex." *Science* 314:829–32.

Kohlberg, L. 1968. "The Child as a Moral Philosopher." *Psychology Today*, September, 25–30.

———. 1969. "Stage and Sequence: The Cognitive-Developmental Approach to Socialization." In *Handbook of Socialization Theory and Research*, ed. D. A. Goslin, 347–480. Chicago: Rand McNally.

———. 1971. "From Is to Ought: How to Commit the Naturalistic Fallacy and Get Away with It in the Study of Moral Development." In *Psychology and Genetic Epistemology*, ed. T. Mischel, 151–235. New York: Academic Press.

Kohlberg, L., C. Levine, and A. Hewer. 1983. *Moral Stages: A Current Formulation and a Response to Critics*. Basel: Karger.

Kosfeld, M., M. Heinrichs, P. J. Zak, U. Fischbacher, and E. Fehr. 2005. "Oxytocin Increases Trust in Humans." *Nature* 435:673–76.

Kosslyn, S. M., W. L. Thompson, M. F. Costantini-Ferrando, N. M. Alpert, and D. Spiegel. 2000. "Hypnotic Visual Illusion Alters Color Processing in the Brain." *American Journal of Psychiatry* 157:1279–84.

Kuhlmeier, V., K. Wynn, and P. Bloom. 2003. "Attribution of Dispositional States by 12-Month-Olds." *Psychological Science* 14:402–8.

Kuhn, D. 1989. "Children and Adults as Intuitive Scientists." *Psychological Review* 96:674–89.

———. 1991. *The Skills of Argument*. Cambridge, UK: Cambridge University Press.

Kunda, Z. 1987. "Motivated Inference: Self-Serving Generation and Evaluation of Causal Theories." *Journal of Personality and Social Psychology* 53:636–47.

———. 1990. "The Case for Motivated Reasoning." *Psychological Bulletin* 108:480–98.

Kurzban, R. 2010. *Why Everyone (Else) Is a Hypocrite*. Princeton, NJ: Princeton University Press.

Kurzban, R., J. Tooby, and L. Cosmides. 2001. "Can Race Be Erased? Coalitional Computation and Social Categorization." *Proceedings of the National Academy of Sciences* 98:15387–92.

Kyd, S. 1794. *A Treatise on the Law of Corporations*, vol. 1. London: J. Butterworth.

Lakoff, G. 1996. *Moral Politics: What Conservatives Know That Liberals Don't*. Chicago: University of Chicago Press.

———. 2008. *The Political Mind: Why You Can't Understand 21st-Century American Politics with an 18th-Century Brain.* New York: Viking, 2008.

Lansing, J. S. 1991. *Priests and Programmers: Technologies of Power in the Engineered Landscape of Bali.* Princeton, NJ: Princeton University Press.

Larue, G. A. 1991. "Ancient Ethics." In *A Companion to Ethics,* ed. P. Singer, 29–40. Malden, MA: Blackwell.

Latane, B., and J. M. Darley. 1970. *The Unresponsive Bystander.* Englewood Cliffs, NJ: Prentice Hall.

Lazarus, R. S. 1991. *Emotion and Adaptation.* New York: Oxford University Press.

Leary, M. R. 2004. *The Curse of the Self: Self-Awareness, Egotism, and the Quality of Human Life.* Oxford: Oxford University Press.

———. 2005. "Sociometer Theory and the Pursuit of Relational Value: Getting to the Root of Self-Esteem." *European Review of Social Psychology* 16:75–111.

Lechter. A. 2007. *Shroom: A Cultural History of the Magic Mushroom.* New York: HarperCollins.

LeDoux, J. 1996. *The Emotional Brain.* New York: Simon and Schuster.

Lee, R. B. 1979. *The !Kung San: Men, Women, and Work in a Foraging Society.* Cambridge, UK: Cambridge University Press.

Lepre, C. J., H. Roche, D. V. Kent, S. Harmand, R. L. Quinn, J. P. Brugal, P. J. Texier, A. Lenoble, and C. S. Feibel. 2011. "An Earlier Origin for the Acheulian." *Nature* 477:82–85.

Lerner, J. S., and P. E. Tetlock. 2003. "Bridging Individual, Interpersonal, and Institutional Approaches to Judgment and Decision Making: The Impact of Accountability on Cognitive Bias." In *Emerging Perspectives on Judgment and Decision Research,* ed. S. L. Schneider and J. Shanteau, 431–57. New York: Cambridge University Press.

Lilienfeld, S. O., R. Ammirati, and K. Landfield. 2009. "Giving Debiasing Away: Can Psychological Research on Correcting Cognitive Errors Promote Human Welfare?" *Perspectives on Psychological Science* 4:390–98.

Liljenquist, K., C. B. Zhong, and A. D. Galinsky. 2010. "The Smell of Virtue: Clean Scents Promote Reciprocity and Charity." *Psychological Science,* 21:381–83.

LoBue, V., C. Chong, T. Nishida, J. DeLoache, and J. Haidt. 2011. "When Getting Something Good Is Bad: Even Three-Year-Olds React to Inequality." *Social Development* 20:154–70.

Locke, J. 1979/1690. *An Essay Concerning Human Understanding.* New York: Oxford University Press.

Lord, C. G., L. Ross, and M. R. Lepper. 1979. "Biased Assimilation and Attitude Polarization: The Effects of Prior Theories on Subsequently Considered Evidence." *Journal of Personality and Social Psychology* 37:2098–109.

Lucas, P., and A. Sheeran. 2006. "Asperger's Syndrome and the Eccentricity and Genius of Jeremy Bentham." *Journal of Bentham Studies* 8:1–20.

Luce, R. D., and H. Raiffa. 1957. *Games and Decisions: Introduction and Critical Survey.* New York: Wiley.

Luo, Q., M. Nakic, T. Wheatley, R. Richell, A. Martin, and R. J. R. Blair. 2006. "The Neural Basis of Implicit Moral Attitude—An IAT Study Using Event-Related fMRI." *Neuroimage* 30:1449–57.

Maccoby, E. E. 1998. *The Two Sexes: Growing Up Apart, Coming Together.* Cambridge, MA: Harvard University Press.

Marcus, G. 2004. *The Birth of the Mind.* New York: Basic Books.

Marean, C. W., M. Bar-Matthews, J. Bernatchez, E. Fisher, P. Goldberg, A. I. R. Herries, et al. 2007. "Early Human Use of Marine Resources and Pigment in South Africa During the Middle Pleistocene." *Nature* 449:905–8.

Margolis, H. 1987. *Patterns, Thinking, and Cognition.* Chicago: University of Chicago Press.

Margulis, L. 1970. *Origin of Eukaryotic Cells.* New Haven, CT: Yale University Press.

Markus, H. R., and S. Kitayama. 1991. "Culture and the Self: Implications for Cognition, Emotion, and Motivation." *Psychological Review* 98:224–53.

Marshall, L. 1999. "Nyae Nyae !Kung Beliefs and Rites." *Peabody Museum Monographs* 8:63–90.

Mascaro, J., ed. 1973. *The Dhammapada.* Harmondsworth, UK: Penguin.

Maslow, A. H. 1964. *Religions, Values, and Peak-Experiences.* Columbus: Ohio State University Press.

Mathew, S., and R. Boyd. 2011. "Punishment Sustains Large-Scale Cooperation in Prestate Warfare." *Proceedings of the National Academy of Sciences,* early edition, doi: 10.1073/pnas.1105604108.

Maynard Smith, J., and E. Szathmary. 1997. *The Major Transitions in Evolution.* Oxford: Oxford University Press.

Mazzella, R., and A. Feingold. 1994. "The Effects of Physical Attractiveness, Race, Socioeconomic Status, and Gender of Defendants and Victims on Judgments of Mock Jurors: A Meta-analysis." *Journal of Applied Social Psychology* 24:1315–44.

McAdams, D. P. 2006. *The Redemptive Self: Stories Americans Live By.* New York: Oxford University Press.

McAdams, D. P., M. Albaugh, E. Farber, J. Daniels, R. L. Logan, and B. Olson. 2008. "Family Metaphors and Moral Intuitions: How Conservatives and Liberals Narrate Their Lives." *Journal of Personality and Social Psychology* 95:978–90.

McAdams, D. P., and J. L. Pals. 2006. "A New Big Five: Fundamental Principles for an Integrative Science of Personality." *American Psychologist* 61:204–17.

McCrae, R. R. 1996. "Social Consequences of Experiential Openness." *Psychological Bulletin* 120:323–37.

McGuire, J., R. Langdon, M. Coltheart, and C. Mackenzie. 2009. "A Reanalysis of the Personal/Impersonal Distinction in Moral Psychology Research." *Journal of Experimental Social Psychology* 45:577–80.

McNeill, W. H. 1995. *Keeping Together in Time: Dance and Drill in Human History.* Cambridge, MA: Harvard University Press.

McWhorter, J. 2005. *Winning the Race: Beyond the Crisis in Black America.* New York: Gotham Books.

Meier, B. P., and M. D. Robinson. 2004. "Why the Sunny Side Is Up: Automatic Inferences About Stimulus Valence Based on Vertical Position." *Psychological Science* 15:243–47.

Meigs, A. 1984. *Food, Sex, and Pollution: A New Guinea Religion.* New Brunswick, NJ: Rutgers University Press.

Melis, A. P., B. Hare, and M. Tomasello. 2006. "Chimpanzees Recruit the Best Collaborators." *Science* 311:1297–300.

Mercier, H., and D. Sperber. 2011. "Why Do Humans Reason? Arguments for an Argumentative Theory." *Behavioral and Brain Sciences* 34:57–74.

Merton, R. K. 1968. *Social Theory and Social Structure.* New York: Free Press.

Mill, J. S. 2003/1859. *On Liberty.* New Haven, CT: Yale University Press.

Miller, D. T. 1999. "The Norm of Self-Interest." *American Psychologist* 54:1053–60.

Miller, G. F. 2007. "Sexual Selection for Moral Virtues." *Quarterly Review of Biology* 82:97–125.

Millon, T., E. Simonsen, M. Birket-Smith, and R. D. Davis. 1998. *Psychopathy: Antisocial, Criminal, and Violent Behavior.* New York: Guilford Press.

Mineka, S., and M. Cook. 1988. "Social Learning and the Acquisition of Snake Fear in Monkeys." In *Social Learning: Psychological and Biological Perspectives,* ed. T. R. Zentall and J. B. G. Galef, 51–74. Hillsdale, NJ: Lawrence Erlbaum.

Moll, J., F. Krueger, R. Zahn, M. Pardini, R. de Oliveira-Souza, and J. Grafman. 2006. "Human Fronto-Mesolimbic Networks Guide Decisions About Charitable Donation." *Proceedings of the National Academy of Sciences of the United States of America* 103:15623–28.

Montaigne, M. de. 1991/1588. *The Complete Essays.* Trans. M. A. Screech. London: Penguin.

Morhenn, V. B., J. W. Park, E. Piper, and P. J. Zak. 2008. "Monetary Sacrifice Among Strangers Is Mediated by Endogenous Oxytocin Release After Physical Contact." *Evolution and Human Behavior* 29:375–83.

Morris, J. P., N. K. Squires, C. S. Taber, and M. Lodge. 2003. "Activation of Political Attitudes: A Psychophysiological Examination of the Hot Cognition Hypothesis." *Political Psychology* 24:727–45.

Motyl, M., J. Hart, T. Pyszczynski, D. Weise, M. Maxfield, and A. Siedel. 2011. "Subtle Priming of Shared Human Experiences Eliminates Threat-Induced Negativity Toward Arabs, Immigrants, and Peace-making." *Journal of Experimental Social Psychology* 47:1179–84.

Muir, W. M. 1996. "Group Selection for Adaptation to Multiple-Hen Cages: Selection Program and Direct Responses." *Poultry Science* 75:447–58.

Muller, J. Z. 1997. "What Is Conservative Social and Political Thought?" In *Conservatism: An Anthology of Social and Political Thought from David Hume to the Present*, ed. J. Z. Muller, 3–31. Princeton, NJ: Princeton University Press.

Munro, G. D., P. H. Ditto, L. K. Lockhart, A. Fagerlin, M. Gready, and E. Peterson. 2002. "Biased Assimilation of Sociopolitical Arguments: Evaluating the 1996 U.S. Presidential Debate." *Basic and Applied Social Psychology* 24:15–26.

Murray, C. 1997. *What It Means to Be a Libertarian: A Personal Interpretation*. New York: Broadway.

Mussolini, B. 1932. "The Doctrine of Fascism." *Enciclopedia Italiana*, vol 14. In *Princeton Readings in Political Thought*, ed. M. Cohen and N. Fermon. Princeton, NJ: Princeton University Press.

Needleman, H. L. 2000. "The Removal of Lead from Gasoline: Historical and Personal Reflections." *Environmental Research* 84:20–35.

Neisser, U. 1967. *Cognitive Psychology*. New York: Appleton-Century-Crofts.

Neuberg, S. L., D. T. Kenrick, and M. Schaller. 2010." Evolutionary Social Psychology." In *Handbook of Social Psychology*, ed. S. T. Fiske, D. T. Gilbert, and G. Lindzey, 5th ed., 2:761–96. Hoboken, NJ: John Wiley and Sons.

Nevin, R. 2000. "How Lead Exposure Relates to Temporal Change in IQ, Violent Crime, and Unwed Pregnancy." *Enviromental Research* 83:1–22.

Newberg, A., E. D'Aquili, and V. Rause. 2001. *Why God Won't Go Away: Brain Science and the Biology of Belief*. New York: Ballantine.

Nickerson, R. S. 1998. "Confirmation Bias: A Ubiquitous Phenomenon in Many Guises." *Review of General Psychology* 2:175–220.

Nisbet, R. A. 1993/1966. *The Sociological Tradition*, 2nd ed. New Brunswick, NJ: Transaction.

Nisbett, R. E., G. T. Fong, D. R. Lehman, and P. W. Cheng. 1987. "Teaching Reasoning." *Science* 238:625–31.

Nisbett, R. E., K. Peng, I. Choi, and A. Norenzayan. 2001. "Culture and Systems of Thought: Holistic Versus Analytical Cognition." *Psychological Review* 108:291–310.

Nocera, J. 2011. "The Last Moderate." *New York Times*, September 6, A27.

Norenzayan, A., and A. F. Shariff. 2008. "The Origin and Evolution of Religious Prosociality." *Science* 322:58–62.

Nowak, M. A., and R. Highfield. 2011. *SuperCooperators: Altruism, Evolution, and Why We Need Each Other to Succeed*. New York: Free Press.

Nucci, L., E. Turiel, and G. Encarnacion-Gawrych. 1983. "Children's Social Interactions and Social Concepts: Analyses of Morality and Convention in the Virgin Islands." *Journal of Cross-Cultural Psychology* 14:469–87.

Nussbaum, M. C. 2004. *Hiding from Humanity*. Princeton, NJ: Princeton University Press.

Oakeshott, M. 1997/1947. "Rationalism in Politics." In *Conservatism,* ed. J. Z. Muller, 292–311. Princeton, NJ: Princeton University Press.

Okasha, S. 2006. *Evolution and the Levels of Selection.* Oxford: Oxford University Press.

Olds, J., and P. Milner. 1954. "Positive Reinforcement Produced by Electrical Stimulation of Septal Areas and Other Regions of Rat Brains." *Journal of Comparative and Physiological Psychology* 47:419–27.

Osgood, C. E. 1962. "Studies on the Generality of Affective Meaning Systems." *American Psychologist* 17:10–28.

Ovid. 2004. *Metamorphoses.* Trans. David Raeburn. London: Penguin.

Oxley, D. R., K. B. Smith, J. R. Alford, M. V. Hibbing, J. L. Miller, M. Scalora, et al. 2008. "Political Attitudes Vary with Physiological Traits." *Science* 321:1667–70.

Pahnke, W. N. 1966. "Drugs and Mysticism." *International Journal of Parapsychology* 8:295–313.

Panchanathan, K., and R. Boyd. 2004. "Indirect Reciprocity Can Stabilize Cooperation Without the Second-Order Free Rider Problem." *Nature* 432:499–502.

Pape, R. A. 2005. *Dying to Win: The Strategic Logic of Suicide Terrorism.* New York: Random House.

Patterson, J. T. 2010. *Freedom Is Not Enough. The Moynihan Report and America's Struggle over Black Family Life—from LBJ to Obama.* New York: Basic Books.

Pavlov, I. 1927. *Conditioned Reflexes: An Investigation into the Physiological Activity of the Cortex.* Trans. G. Anrep. New York: Dover.

Paxton, J. M., L. Ungar, and J. Greene. Forthcoming. "Reflection and Reasoning in Moral Judgment." *Cognitive Science.*

Pennebaker, J. 1997. *Opening UP: The Healing Power of Expressing Emotions.* Rev. ed. New York: Guilford.

Pennebaker, J. W., M. E. Francis, and R. J. Booth. 2003. *Linguistic Inquiry and Word Count: LIWC2001 Manual.* Mahwah, NJ: Lawrence Erlbaum.

Perkins, D. N., M. Farady, and B. Bushey. 1991. "Everyday Reasoning and the Roots of Intelligence." In *Informal Reasoning and Education,* ed. J. F. Voss, D. N. Perkins, and J. W. Segal, 83–105. Hillsdale, NJ: Lawrence Erlbaum.

Perugini, M., and L. Leone. 2009. "Implicit Self-Concept and Moral Action." *Journal of Research in Personality* 43:747–54.

Piaget, J. 1932/1965. *The Moral Judgement of the Child.* Trans. M. Gabain. New York: Free Press.

Pickrell, J. K., G. Coop, J. Novembre, S. Kudaravalli, J. Z. Li, D. Absher, et al. 2009. "Signals of Recent Positive Selection in a Worldwide Sample of Human Populations." *Genome Research* 19:826–37.

Pildes, R. H. 2011. "Why the Center Does Not Hold: The Causes of Hyperpolarized Democracy in America." *California Law Review* 99:273–334.

Pinker, S. 2002. *The Blank Slate: The Modern Denial of Human Nature.* New York: Viking.

———. 2011. *The Better Angels of Our Nature: Why Violence Has Declined.* New York: Viking.

Plato. 1997. *Timaeus.* Trans. D. J. Zeyl. In *Plato: Complete Works,* ed. J. M. Cooper. Indianapolis: Hackett.

Pollan, M. 2006. *The Omnivore's Dilemma: A Natural History of Four Meals.* New York: Penguin.

Poole, K. T., and H. Rosenthal. 2000. *Congress: A Political-Economic History of Roll Call Voting.* New York: Oxford University Press.

Potts, R., and C. Sloan. 2010. *What Does It Mean to Be Human?* Washington, DC: National Geographic.

Powell, R., and S. Clarke. Forthcoming. "Religion as an Evolutionary Byproduct: A Critique of the Standard Model." *British Journal for the Philosophy of Science.*

Premack, D., and A. J. Premack. 2004. "Moral Belief: Form Versus Content." In *Mapping the Mind: Domain Specificity in Cognition and Culture,* ed. L. A. Hirschfeld and S. A. Gelman, 149–68. Cambridge, UK: Cambridge University Press.

Price, G. 1972. "Extensions of Covariance Selection Mathematics." *Annals of Human Genetics* 35:485–90.

Putnam, R. D. 2000. *Bowling Alone: The Collapse and Revival of American Community.* New York: Simon and Schuster.

Putnam, R. D., and D. E. Campbell. 2010. *American Grace: How Religion Divides and Unites Us.* New York: Simon and Schuster.

Pyszczynski, T., and J. Greenberg. 1987. "Toward an Integration of Cognitive and Motivational Perspectives on Social Inference: A Biased Hypothesis-Testing Model." *Advances in Experimental Social Psychology* 20:297–340.

Rai, T. S., and A. P. Fiske. 2011. "Moral Psychology Is Relationship Regulation: Moral Motives for Unity, Hierarchy, Equality, and Proportionality." *Psychological Review* 118:57–75.

Ramachandran, V. S., and S. Blakeslee. 1998. *Phantoms in the Brain: Probing the Mysteries of the Human Mind.* New York: William Morrow.

Rappaport, R. 1971. "The Sacred in Human Evolution." *Annual Review of Ecology and Systematics* 2:23–44.

Rawls, J. 1971. *A Theory of Justice.* Cambridge, MA: Harvard University Press.

Reyes, J. W. 2007. "Environmental Policy as Social Policy? The Impact of Childhood Lead Exposure on Crime." Working Paper No. 13097, National Bureau of Economic Research, Washington, DC.

Richards, K. 2010. *Life.* New York: Little, Brown.

Richerson, P. J., and R. Boyd. 1998. "The Evolution of Human Ultra-Sociality."

In *Indoctrinability, Ideology, and Warfare: Evolutionary Perspectives,* ed. I. Eibl-Eibesfeldt and F. K. Salter, 71–95. New York: Berghahn.

———. 2004. "Darwinian Evolutionary Ethics: Between Patriotism and Sympathy." In *Evolution and Ethics: Human Morality in Biological and Religious Perspective,* ed. P. Clayton and J. Schloss, 50–77. Grand Rapids, MI: Eerdmans.

———. 2005. *Not by Genes Alone: How Culture Transformed Human Evolution.* Chicago: University of Chicago Press.

Rieder, J. 1985. *Canarsie: The Jews and Italians of Brooklyn Against Liberalism.* Cambridge, MA: Harvard University Press.

Rilling, J. K., D. R. Goldsmith, A. L. Glenn, M. R. Jairam, H. A. Elfenbein, J. E. Dagenais, et al. 2008. "The Neural Correlates of the Affective Response to Unreciprocated Cooperation." *Neuropsychologia* 46:1256–66.

Roes, F. L., and M. Raymond. 2003. "Belief in Moralizing Gods." *Evolution and Human Behavior* 24:126–35.

Rosaldo, M. 1980. *Knowledge and Passion: Ilongot Notions of Self and Social Life.* Cambridge, UK: Cambridge University Press.

Rosenberg, N. 1990. "Adam Smith and the Stock of Moral Capital." *History of Political Economy* 22:1–17.

Rosenzweig, M. R. 1999. "Welfare, Marital Prospects, and Nonmarital Childbearing." *Journal of Political Economy* 107:S3–S32.

Rothman, S., S. R. Lichter, and N. Nevitte. 2005. "Politics and Professional Advancement Among College Faculty." *The Forum* (electronic journal), vol. 3, iss. 1, article 2.

Rozin, P. 1976. "The Selection of Food by Rats, Humans, and Other Animals." In *Advances in the Study of Behavior,* ed. J. Rosenblatt, R. A. Hinde, C. Beer, and E. Shaw, 6:21–76. New York: Academic Press.

Rozin, P., and A. Fallon. 1987. "A Perspective on Disgust." *Psychological Review* 94:3–41.

Rozin, P., J. Haidt, and K. Fincher. 2009. "From Oral to Moral." *Science* 323:1179–80.

Rozin, P., J. Haidt, and C. R. McCauley. 2008. "Disgust." In *Handbook of Emotions,* ed. M. Lewis, J. M. Haviland-Jones, and L. F. Barrett, 3rd ed., 757–76. New York: Guilford Press.

Rozin, P., L. Lowery, S. Imada, and J. Haidt. 1999. "The CAD Triad Hypothesis: A Mapping Between Three Moral Emotions (Contempt, Anger, Disgust) and Three Moral Codes (Community, Autonomy, Divinity)." *Journal of Personality and Social Psychology* 76:574–86.

Ruffle, B. J., and R. Sosis. 2006. "Cooperation and the In-Group-Out-Group Bias: A Field Test on Israeli Kibbutz Members and City Residents." *Journal of Economic Behavior and Organization* 60:147–63.

Russell, B. 2004/1946. *History of Western Philosophy.* London: Routledge.

Saltzstein, H. D., and T. Kasachkoff. 2004. "Haidt's Moral Intuitionist Theory." *Review of General Psychology* 8:273–82.

Sanfey, A. G., J. K. Rilling, J. A. Aronson, L. E. Nystrom, and J. D. Cohen. 2003. "The Neural Basis of Economic Decision-Making in the Ultimatum Game." *Science* 300:1755–58.

Schaller, M., and J. H. Park. 2011. "The Behavioral Immune System (and Why It Matters)." *Current Directions in Psychological Science* 20:99–103.

Scham, S. 2008. "The World's First Temple." *Archaeology* 61, November/December, online article.

Scherer, K. R. 1984. "On the Nature and Function of Emotion: A Component Process Approach." In *Approaches to Emotion*, ed. K. R. Scherer and P. Ekman, 293–317. Hillsdale, NJ: Lawrence Erlbaum.

Schmidt, M. F. H., and J. A. Sommerville. 2011. "Fairness Expectations and Altruistic Sharing in 15-Month-Old Human Infants." *PLoS ONE* 6:e23223.

Schnall, S., J. Haidt, G. L. Clore, and A. H. Jordan. 2008. "Disgust as Embodied Moral Judgment." *Personality and Social Psychology Bulletin* 34:1096–109.

Schwitzgebel, E. 2009. "Do Ethicists Steal More Books?" *Philosophical Psychology* 22:711–25.

Schwitzgebel, E., and J. Rust. 2009. "Do Ethicists and Political Philosophers Vote More Often than Other Professors?" *Review of Philosophy and Psychology* 1:189–99.

———. 2011. "The Self-Reported Moral Behavior of Ethics Professors." Unpublished ms., University of California at Riverside.

Schwitzgebel, E., J. Rust, L. T.-L. Huang, A. Moore, and J. Coates. 2011. "Ethicists' Courtesy at Philosophy Conferences." Unpublished ms., University of California at Riverside.

Scruton, R. 1982. *Kant.* Oxford: Oxford University Press.

Secher, R. 2003/1986. *A French Genocide: The Vendée.* Trans. G. Holoch. South Bend, IN: Notre Dame University Press.

Seeley, T. D. 1997. "Honey Bee Colonies Are Group-Level Adaptive Units." *American Naturalist* 150:S22–S41.

Settle, J. E., C. T. Dawes, N. A. Christakis, and J. H. Fowler. 2010. "Friendships Moderate an Association Between a Dopamine Gene Variant and Political Ideology." *Journal of Politics* 72:1189–98.

Shariff, A. F., and A. Norenzayan. 2007. "God Is Watching You: Priming God Concepts Increases Prosocial Behavior in an Anonymous Economic Game." *Psychological Science* 18:803–9.

Shaw, V. F. 1996. "The Cognitive Processes in Informal Reasoning." *Thinking and Reasoning* 2:51–80.

Sherif, M., O. J. Harvey, B. J. White, W. Hood, and C. Sherif. 1961/1954. *Intergroup*

Conflict and Cooperation: The Robbers Cave Experiment. Norman: University of Oklahoma Institute of Group Relations.

Sherman, G. D., and J. Haidt. 2011. "Cuteness and Disgust: The Humanizing and Dehumanizing Effects of Emotion." Emotion Review 3:245–51.

Shweder, R. A. 1990a. "Cultural Psychology: What Is It?" In *Cultural Psychology: Essays on Comparative Human Development,* ed. J. W. Stigler, R. A. Shweder, and G. Herdt, 1–43. New York: Cambridge University Press.

———. 1990b. "In Defense of Moral Realism: Reply to Gabennesch." *Child Development* 61:2060–67.

———. 1991. *Thinking Through Cultures: Expeditions in Cultural Psychology.* Cambridge, MA: Harvard University Press.

Shweder, R. A., and E. Bourne. 1984. "Does the Concept of the Person Vary Cross-Culturally?" In *Cultural Theory,* ed. R. Shweder and R. LeVine, 158–99. Cambridge, UK: Cambridge University Press.

Shweder, R. A., and J. Haidt. 1993. "The Future of Moral Psychology: Truth, Intuition, and the Pluralist Way." *Psychological Science* 4:360–65.

Shweder, R. A., and R. A. LeVine, eds. 1984. *Culture Theory: Essays on Mind, Self, Emotion.* Cambridge, UK: Cambridge University Press.

Shweder, R. A., M. Mahapatra, and J. Miller. 1987. "Culture and Moral Development." In *The Emergence of Morality in Young Children,* ed. J. Kagan and S. Lamb, 1–83. Chicago: University of Chicago Press.

Shweder, R. A., N. C. Much, M. Mahapatra, and L. Park. 1997. "The 'Big Three' of Morality (Autonomy, Community, and Divinity), and the 'Big Three' Explanations of Suffering." In *Morality and Health,* ed. A. Brandt and P. Rozin, 119–69. New York: Routledge.

Sigall, H., and N. Ostrove. 1975. "Beautiful but Dangerous: Effects of Offender Attractiveness and Nature of the Crime on Juridic Judgment." *Journal of Personality and Social Psychology* 31:410–14.

Singer, P. 1979. *Practical Ethics.* Cambridge, UK: Cambridge University Press.

Singer, T., B. Seymour, J. P. O'Doherty, K. E. Stephan, R. J. Dolan, and C. D. Frith. 2006. "Empathic Neural Responses Are Modulated by the Perceived Fairness of Others." *Nature* 439:466–69.

Sinnott-Armstrong, W., ed. 2008. *Moral Psychology.* 3 vols. Cambridge, MA: MIT Press.

Smith, A. 1976/1759. *The Theory of Moral Sentiments.* Oxford: Oxford University Press.

Smith, C. 2003. *Moral, Believing Animals: Human Personhood and Culture.* Oxford: Oxford University Press.

Sober, E., and D. S. Wilson. 1998. *Unto Others: The Evolution and Psychology of Unselfish Behavior.* Cambridge, MA: Harvard University Press.

Solomon, R. C. 1993. "The Philosophy of Emotions." In *Handbook of Emotions,* ed. M. Lewis and J. Haviland, 3–15. New York: Guilford Press.

Sosis, R. 2000. "Religion and Intragroup Cooperation: Preliminary Results of a Comparative Analysis of Utopian Communities." *Cross-Cultural Research* 34:70–87.

Sosis, R., and C. S. Alcorta. 2003. "Signaling, Solidarity, and the Sacred: The Evolution of Religious Behavior." *Evolutionary Anthropology* 12:264–74.

Sosis, R., and E. R. Bressler. 2003. "Cooperation and Commune Longevity: A Test of the Costly Signaling Theory of Religion." *Cross-Cultural Research: The Journal of Comparative Social Science* 37:211–39.

Sowell, T. 2002. *A Conflict of Visions: The Ideological Origins of Political Struggles.* New York: Basic Books.

Sperber, D. 2005. "Modularity and Relevance: How Can a Massively Modular Mind Be Flexible and Context-Sensitive?" In *The Innate Mind: Structure and Contents,* ed. P. Carruthers, S. Laurence, and S. Stich, 53–68. New York: Oxford University Press.

Sperber, D., and L. A. Hirschfeld. 2004. "The Cognitive Foundations of Cultural Stability and Diversity." *Trends in Cognitive Sciences* 8:40–46.

Stampf, G. 2008. *Interview with a Cannibal: The Secret Life of the Monster of Rotenburg.* Beverly Hills, CA: Phoenix Books.

Stearns, S. C. 2007. "Are We Stalled Part Way Through a Major Evolutionary Transition from Individual to Group?" *Evolution: International Journal of Organic Evolution* 61:2275–80.

Stenner, K. 2005. *The Authoritarian Dynamic.* New York: Cambridge University Press.

Stevenson, C. L. 1960. *Ethics and Language.* New Haven: Yale University Press.

Stewart, J. E. 1980. "Defendant's Attractiveness as a Factor in the Outcome of Criminal Trials: An Observational Study." *Journal of Applied Social Psychology* 10:348–61.

Stolberg, S. G. 2011. "You Want Compromise. Sure You Do." *New York Times,* Sunday Review, August 14.

Sunstein, C. R. 2005. "Moral Heuristics." *Brain and Behavioral Science* 28:531–73.

Taber, C. S., and M. Lodge. 2006. "Motivated Skepticism in the Evaluation of Political Beliefs." *American Journal of Political Science* 50:755–69.

Taleb, N. 2007. *The Black Swan: The Impact of the Highly Improbable.* New York: Random House.

Tan, J. H. W., and C. Vogel. 2008. "Religion and Trust: An Experimental Study." *Journal of Economic Psychology* 29:832–48.

Tattersall, I. 2009. *The Fossil Trail: How We Know What We Think We Know About Human Evolution.* 2nd ed. New York: Oxford University Press.

Tetlock, P. E. 2002. "Social Functionalist Frameworks for Judgment and Choice:

Intuitive Politicians, Theologians, and Prosecutors." *Psychological Review* 109:451–57.

Tetlock, P. E., O. V. Kristel, B. Elson, M. Green, and J. Lerner. 2000. "The Psychology of the Unthinkable: Taboo Trade-offs, Forbidden Base Rates, and Heretical Counterfactuals." *Journal of Personality and Social Psychology* 78:853–70.

Thomas, K. 1983. *Man and the Natural World*. New York: Pantheon.

Thomson, J. A., and C. Aukofer. 2011. *Why We Believe in God(s): A Concise Guide to the Science of Faith*. Charlottesville, VA: Pitchstone Publishing.

Thórisdóttir, H., and J. T. Jost. 2011. "Motivated Closed-Mindedness Mediates the Effect of Threat on Political Conservatism." *Political Psychology* 32:785–811.

Thornhill, R., C. L. Fincher, and D. Aran. 2009. "Parasites, Democratization, and the Liberalization of Values Across Contemporary Countries." *Biological Reviews of the Cambridge Philosophical Society* 84:113–31.

Tishkoff, S. A., F. A. Reed, A. Ranciaro, et al. 2007. "Convergent Adaptation of Human Lactase Persistence in Africa and Europe." *Nature Genetics* 39:31–40.

Todorov, A., A. N. Mandisodza, A. Goren, and C. C. Hall. 2005. "Inferences of Competence from Faces Predict Election Outcomes." *Science* 308:1623–26.

Tomasello, M., M. Carpenter, J. Call, T. Behne, and H. Moll. 2005. "Understanding and Sharing Intentions: The Origins of Cultural Cognition." *Behavioral and Brain Sciences* 28:675–91.

Tomasello, M., A. Melis, C. Tennie, E. Wyman, E. Herrmann, and A. Schneider. Forthcoming. "Two Key Steps in the Evolution of Human Cooperation: The Mutualism Hypothesis." *Current Anthropology*.

Tooby, J., and L. Cosmides. 1992. "The Psychological Foundations of Culture." In *The Adapted Mind: Evolutionary Psychology and the Generation of Culture*, ed. J. H. Barkow, L. Cosmides, and J. Tooby, 19–136. New York: Oxford University Press.

———. 2010. "Groups in Mind: The Coalitional Roots of War and Morality." In *Human Morality and Sociality: Evolutionary and Comparative Perspectives*, ed. H. Høgh-Olesen. New York: Palgrave Macmillan.

Trivers, R. L. 1971. "The Evolution of Reciprocal Altruism." *Quarterly Review of Biology* 46:35–57.

Trut, L. N. 1999. "Early Canid Domestication: The Farm Fox Experiment." *American Scientist* 87:160–69.

Turiel, E. 1983. *The Development of Social Knowledge: Morality and Convention*. Cambridge, UK: Cambridge University Press.

Turiel, E., M. Killen, and C. C. Helwig. 1987. "Morality: Its Structure, Function, and Vagaries." In *The Emergence of Morality in Young Children*, ed. J. Kagan and S. Lamb, 155–243. Chicago: University of Chicago Press.

Turkheimer, E. 2000. "Three Laws of Behavior Genetics and What They Mean." *Current Directions in Psychological Science* 9:160–64.

Turner, V. W. 1969. *The Ritual Process: Structure and Anti-Structure.* Chicago: Aldine.

Valdesolo, P., J. Ouyang, and D. DeSteno. 2010. "The Rhythm of Joint Action: Synchrony Promotes Cooperative Ability." *Journal of Experimental Social Psychology* 46:693–95.

Van Berkum, J. J. A., B. Holleman, M. Nieuwland, M. Otten, and J. Murre. 2009. "Right or Wrong? The Brain's Fast Response to Morally Objectionable Statements." *Psychological Science* 20:1092–99.

Van Vugt, M., D. De Cremer, and D. P. Janssen. 2007. "Gender Differences in Cooperation and Competition: The Male-Warrior Hypothesis." *Psychological Science* 18:19–23.

Van Vugt, M., R. Hogan, and R. B. Kaiser. 2008. "Leadership, Followership, and Evolution: Some Lessons from the Past." *American Psychologist* 63:182–96.

Viding, E., R. J. R. Blair, T. E. Moffitt, and R. Plomin. 2005. "Evidence for Substantial Genetic Risk for Psychopathy in 7-Year-Olds." *Journal of Child Psychology and Psychiatry* 46:592–97.

Voegeli, W. 2010. *Never Enough: America's Limitless Welfare State.* New York: Encounter Books.

Wade, N. 2007. "Is 'Do Unto Others' Written Into Our Genes?" *New York Times.* September 18, p. 1 of Science Times.

———. 2009. *The Faith Instinct: How Religion Evolved and Why It Endures.* New York: Penguin.

Walster, E., G. W. Walster, and E. Berscheid. 1978. *Equity: Theory and Research.* Boston: Allyn and Bacon.

Wason, P. C. 1960. "On the Failure to Eliminate Hypotheses in a Conceptual Task." *Quarterly Journal of Experimental Psychology* 12:129–40.

———. 1969. "Regression in Reasoning?" *British Journal of Psychology* 60:471–80.

Weedon, M. N., H. Lango, C. M. Lindgren, C. Wallace, D. M. Evans, M. Mangino, et al. 2008. "Genome-Wide Association Analysis Identifies 20 Loci That Influence Adult Height." *Nature Genetics* 40:575–83.

Westen, D. 2007. *The Political Brain: The Role of Emotion in Deciding the Fate of the Nation.* New York: Public Affairs.

Westen, D., P. S. Blagov, K. Harenski, S. Hamann, and C. Kilts. 2006. "Neural Bases of Motivated Reasoning: An fMRI Study of Emotional Constraints on Partisan Political Judgment in the 2004 U.S. Presidential Election." *Journal of Cognitive Neuroscience* 18:1947–58.

Wheatley, T., and J. Haidt. 2005. "Hypnotic Disgust Makes Moral Judgments More Severe." *Psychological Science* 16:780–84.

Wilkinson, G. S. 1984. "Reciprocal Food Sharing in the Vampire Bat." *Nature* 308:181–84.

Wilkinson, R., and K. Pickett. 2009. *The Spirit Level: Why Greater Equality Makes Societies Stronger.* New York: Bloomsbury.

Williams, B. 1967. "Rationalism." In *The Encyclopedia of Philosophy*, ed. P. Edwards, 7–8:69–75. New York: Macmillan.

Williams, G. C. 1966. *Adaptation and Natural Selection: A Critique of Some Current Evolutionary Thought*. Princeton, NJ: Princeton University Press.

Williams, G. C. 1988. Reply to comments on "Huxley's Evolution and Ethics in Sociobiological Perspective." *Zygon* 23:437–38.

Williamson, S. H., M. J. Hubisz, A. G. Clark, B. A. Payseur, C. D. Bustamante, and R. Nielsen. 2007. "Localizing Recent Adaptive Evolution in the Human Genome." *PLoS Genetics* 3:e90.

Wilson, D. S. 2002. *Darwin's Cathedral: Evolution, Religion, and the Nature of Society*. Chicago: University of Chicago Press.

Wilson, D. S., and E. O. Wilson. 2007. "Rethinking the Theoretical Foundation of Sociobiology." *Quarterly Review of Biology* 82:327–48.

———. 2008. "Evolution 'for the Good of the Group.'" *American Scientist* 96:380–89.

Wilson, E. O. 1975. *Sociobiology*. Cambridge, MA: Harvard University Press.

———. 1990. *Success and Dominance in Ecosystems: The Case of the Social Insects*. Oldendorf, Germany: Ecology Institute.

———. 1998. *Consilience: The Unity of Knowledge*. New York: Knopf.

Wilson, E. O., and B. Hölldobler. 2005. "Eusociality: Origin and Consequences." *Proceedings of the National Academy of Sciences of the United States of America* 102:13367–71.

Wilson, T. D. 2002. *Strangers to Ourselves: Discovering the Adaptive Unconscious*. Cambridge, MA: Belknap Press.

Wilson, T. D., and J. W. Schooler. 1991. "Thinking Too Much: Introspection Can Reduce the Quality of Preferences and Decisions." *Journal of Personality and Social Psychology* 60:181–92.

Wiltermuth, S., and C. Heath. 2008. "Synchrony and Cooperation." *Psychological Science* 20:1–5.

Wobber, V., R. Wrangham, and B. Hare. 2010. "Application of the Heterochrony Framework to the Study of Behavior and Cognition." *Communicative and Integrative Biology* 3:337–39.

Wolf, S. 2010. *Meaning in Life and Why It Matters*. Princeton, NJ: Princeton University Press.

Woodberry, R. D., and C. Smith. 1998. *Fundamentalism et al.: Conservative Protestants in America*. Palo Alto, CA: Annual Reviews.

Wrangham, R. W. 2001. "The Evolution of Cooking." Conversation with John Brockman on Edge.org.

Wrangham, R. W., and D. Pilbeam. 2001. "African Apes as Time Machines." In *All Apes Great and Small*, ed. B. M. F. Galdikas, N. E. Briggs, L. K. Sheeran, G. L. Shapiro, and J. Goodall, 1:5–18. New York: Kluwer.

Wright, R. 1994. *The Moral Animal.* New York: Pantheon.

———. 2009. *The Evolution of God.* New York: Little, Brown.

Wundt, W. 1907/1896. *Outlines of Psychology.* Leipzig: Wilhelm Englemann.

Wynne-Edwards, V. C. 1962. *Animal Dispersion in Relation to Social Behaviour.* Edinburgh: Oliver and Boyd.

Yi, X., Y. Liang, E. Huerta-Sanchez, X. Jin, Z. X. P. Cuo, J. E. Pool, et al. 2010. "Sequencing of 50 Human Exomes Reveals Adaptation to High Altitude." *Science* 329:75–78.

Zajonc, R. B. 1968. "Attitudinal Effects of Mere Exposure." *Journal of Personality and Social Psychology* 9:1–27.

———. 1980. "Feeling and Thinking: Preferences Need No Inferences." *American Psychologist* 35:151–75.

Zak, P. J. 2011. "The Physiology of Moral Sentiments." *Journal of Economic Behavior and Organization* 77:53–65.

Zaller, J. R. 1992. *The Nature and Origins of Mass Opinion.* New York: Cambridge University Press.

Zhong, C. B., V. K. Bohns, and F. Gino. 2010. "Good Lamps Are the Best Police: Darkness Increases Dishonesty and Self-Interested Behavior." *Psychological Science* 21:311–14.

Zhong, C. B., and K. Liljenquist. 2006. "Washing Away Your Sins: Threatened Morality and Physical Cleansing." *Science* 313:1451–52.

Zhong, C. B., B. Strejcek, and N. Sivanathan. 2010. "A Clean Self Can Render Harsh Moral Judgment." *Journal of Experimental Social Psychology* 46:859–62.

Zimbardo, P. G. 2007. *The Lucifer Effect: Understanding How Good People Turn Evil.* New York: Random House.

Index

Page numbers in *italics* refer to illustrations. Page numbers beginning with 323 refer to notes.

ILLUSTRATION CREDITS

All photographs and figures not listed below were taken or created by Jonathan Haidt.

133 Mirrorpix
137 Emily Ekins
145 (*top*) This originally appeared as an advertisement in *The Nation* and is used here with permission.
(*bottom*) Photo by Sarah Estes Graham
209 © Robert Harding Picture Library Ltd/Alamy
214 Photo courtesy of Lyudmila Trut, used with permission
222 St. Martin's Press
229 Codex Magliabechiano, facsimile edition, Adeva, Graz 1970
261 Original sheet of newsprint scanned by Jonathan Haidt
275 Permission obtained from Jeff Gates
318 © Frank Cotham/*The New Yorker* Collection/www.cartoonbank.com

A NOTE ON THE TYPE

This book was set in a modern adaptation of a type designed by the first William Caslon (1692–1766). The Caslon face, an artistic, easily read type, has enjoyed more than two centuries of popularity. It is of interest to note that the first copies of the American Declaration of Independence and the first paper currency distributed to the citizens of the newborn nation were printed in this typeface.

Composed by North Market Street Graphics
Lancaster, Pennsylvania

Printed and bound by Berryville Graphics,
Berryville, Virginia